THE CAMBRIDGE COMPANION TO
SHAKESPEARE AND POPULAR CULTURI

This *Companion* explores the remarkable variety of forms that Shakespeare's life and works have taken over the course of four centuries, ranging from the early modern theatrical marketplace to the age of mass media, and including stage and screen performance, music and the visual arts, the television serial, and popular prose fiction. The book asks what happens when Shakespeare is popularized, and when the popular is Shakespeareanized; it queries the factors that determine the definitions of and boundaries between the legitimate and illegitimate, the canonical and the authorized, and the subversive, the oppositional, the scandalous, and the inane. Leading scholars discuss the ways in which the plays and poems of Shakespeare, as well as Shakespeare himself, have been interpreted and reinvented, adapted and parodied, transposed into other media, and act as a source of inspiration for writers, performers, artists, and film-makers worldwide.

A complete list of books in the series is at the back of this book

THE CAMBRIDGE COMPANION TO
SHAKESPEARE AND POPULAR CULTURE

EDITED BY
ROBERT SHAUGHNESSY
University of Kent

CAMBRIDGE
UNIVERSITY PRESS

CAMBRIDGE UNIVERSITY PRESS
Cambridge, New York, Melbourne, Madrid, Cape Town, Singapore, São Paulo

Cambridge University Press
The Edinburgh Building, Cambridge CB2 8RU, UK

Published in the United States of America by Cambridge University Press, New York

www.cambridge.org
Information on this title: www.cambridge.org/9780521605809

First published 2007

Printed in the United Kingdom at the University Press, Cambridge

A catalogue record for this publication is available from the British Library

ISBN 978-0-521-84429-1 hardback
ISBN 978-0-521-60580-9 paperback

CONTENTS

ILLUSTRATIONS

CONTRIBUTORS

STEPHEN M. BUHLER, University of Nebraska

SUSANNE GREENHALGH, Roehampton University, London

DIANA E. HENDERSON, Massachusetts Institute of Technology

BARBARA HODGDON, University of Michigan

PETER HOLLAND, University of Notre Dame, Indiana

DOUGLAS LANIER, University of New Hampshire

STEPHEN ORGEL, Stanford University, California

LAURIE OSBORNE, Colby College, Maine

CAROL CHILLINGTON RUTTER, University of Warwick

ROBERT SHAUGHNESSY, University of Kent

EMMA SMITH, University of Oxford

NICOLA J. WATSON, Open University

W. B. WORTHEN, University of Michigan

ROBERT SHAUGHNESSY

Introduction

In recent years, the study of the past and present relationships between Shakespeare and popular culture has been transformed: from an occasional, ephemeral, and anecdotal field of research, which, if it registered at all, was generally considered peripheral to the core concerns of scholarship and pedagogy, to one which is making an increasingly significant contribution to our understanding of how Shakespeare's works came into being, and of how and why they continue to exercise the imaginations of readers, theatergoers, viewers, and scholars worldwide. A range of factors have prompted this shift, among them the increased priority afforded to theatrical performance; the growth of interest in Shakespeare on film and television; the theoretical debates and methodological innovations of the 1980s and 1990s, which have encouraged new kinds of interdisciplinarity in the field of Shakespeare studies, as well as turning attention to the larger forces that have shaped Shakespearean production and reproduction in material culture; the condition of postmodernity itself, in which traditional distinctions between high and low culture have been eroded; and, not least, the changing patterns of educational participation and provision that have characterized the end of the twentieth century and the beginning of the twenty-first. Contemporary research and pedagogy in the field of Shakespeare and popular culture is concerned with the Shakespearean theatre and drama's immersion within the festivities and folk customs, entertainment industries, and traditions of playing of its own time; it is also interested in the reinvention, adaptation, citation, and appropriation of the plays (and, to a lesser extent, the poems), and the myths and histories that circulate around them, across a wide range of media in subsequent periods and cultures. Throughout history, Shakespeare's enduring high-cultural status has coexisted with a multiplicity of other Shakespeares, recycled in stage performance and cinematic adaptation, political discourse, literary and theatrical burlesque, parody, musical quotation, visual iconography, popular romance, tourist itineraries, national myth, and everyday speech. Shakespeare can be quoted in support of an individual declaration of love or an act of war; his works have acted as sources of inspiration for everything from high opera to the porn movie; his image turns up in the unlikeliest of locations. Versions of, or borrowings from, Shakespeare may be respectful or irreverent, they may be witty, acute, or scurrilous, delinquent, or just plain silly, and whether everything and anything that operates under the banner of Shakespeare can or should be afforded any value or significance, or is of more than passing academic interest, is a matter of debate; as is the desire of generations of educationalists, theatre practitioners, and film-makers for a truly popular "authentic" or mainstream Shakespeare, whether this is to be found in the classroom, on stage, or on the screen. The "popular" is itself hardly a singular or uncontested term or frame of reference: seen from some angles, it denotes community, shared values, democratic participation, accessibility, and fun; from others, the mass-produced commodity, the lowest common denominator, the reductive or the simplified, or the shoddy, the coarse, and the meretricious. When the transmission and appropriation of Shakespeare are at stake, considerations of taste and aesthetic value are also bound up with inevitably vexed questions of cultural ownership, educational attainment and class, and with issues of who the desired and actual consumers of "popular" Shakespeares may be, who these hope to include, and who they don't.

Whereas many recent studies of popular Shakespeare have tended to focus upon its contemporary manifestations, this volume aims at broader historical coverage. It addresses the ways in which Shakespeare has been consumed and reinvented, allowing for interface between cultural, literary, performance, and cinema studies, by means of focused and localized case studies as well as through the mapping of larger cultural logics of Shakespeare-making. In the first chapter ("From popular entertainment to literature"), Diana Henderson traces Shakespeare's journey from the early modern theatrical marketplace to the beginnings of literary lionization, outlining a career as a working dramatist within an emergent entertainment industry which belies his subsequent repositioning as an icon of elite culture. This chapter addresses the relation between the cultures of entertainment and performance (both learned and popular, aristocratic and plebeian) in which the plays of Shakespeare and his contemporaries originated and the fashioning of Shakespeare's dramaturgy into a literary oeuvre, a process definitively marked by the publication of the First Folio in 1623. Peter Holland ("Shakespeare abbreviated") offers a brief history of Shakespearean theatrical production, cultural dissemination and transmission, in terms of its logics of reduction, selection, and abbreviation; in the popular theatre, Shakespeare seen whole is anomalous and exceptional. Beginning with the shortened and streamlined performance texts of the seventeenth centuries, the chapter considers the durability of the burlesque, skit, spoof, sketch, and parody in the theatre and other media. Holland's performance history, which considers the factors which adjust Shakespeare's texts to the material contingencies of theatre-making and popular taste, is followed by Barbara Hodgdon's account ("Shakespearean stars") of the phenomenon of the "star" Shakespearean performer in both the theatre and cinema, from Richard Burbage to Ian McKellen, looking in particular at the ways in which the popular understanding of stardom is differently inflected on stage and screen, and, in relation to this, at the changing levels and types of cultural prestige afforded to the Shakespearean performer before and after the advent of mass media.

From Henry Peachum's extempore illustration of a sixteenth-century text of *Titus Andronicus* onwards, Shakespeare's works have provided ample material for artists of every description, serving as source material and inspiration for portraiture, genre painting, representations of scenes and characters, cartoons, caricatures, and prints. Tracing the ways in which Shakespearean visual iconographies both shape expectations of reading and performance and assume a life of their own, Stephen Orgel's chapter, "Shakespeare illustrated," examines how the changing relationship between the arts of performance and of illustration disseminates images of the drama beyond the limits of both page and stage. There are, as Orgel points out, only a handful of pictorial representations contemporary to Shakespeare which allude to performance; much more generally associated with the likeness of Shakespeare in popular consciousness is the portrait of the author, attributed to Martin Droeshout, that acts as the frontispiece for the 1623 Folio. This iconic, much-reproduced image is the point of departure for Douglas Lanier's essay, "Shakespeare^{TM}," which moves from a consideration of its status as a universally recognized trademark to an examination of Shakespeare's personal appearances, in various guises, in popular fiction. Addressing a range of media and cultural formats (theatre, film, the novel, comic books), this chapter investigates how biographical fictions trade with and transform the popular mythologies that circulate around the writer and the work. Like Shakespeare himself, Shakespeare's plays and characters have also provided material for narrative adaptation from an early stage, and in the following chapter, Laurie Osborne focuses upon recent novelistic appropriations of *Hamlet* to explore the ways in which popular fiction reworks dramaturgy as narration. Questions of genre, and of the effects of adjusting Shakespeare's works to a medium for which they were not conceived (in this case, television), are also the concern of Emma Smith's chapter, "Shakespeare Serialized." Looking at a pioneering instance of Shakespearean transposition to the broadcast medium, the BBC's serial adaptation of the First and Second History play cycles, *An Age of Kings* (1960), Smith identifies its generic affinities with the soap opera and historical epic, as well as comparing the forms and conventions of modern serialization with the original circumstances of composition and theatrical production of the multi-part play.

As Stephen Buhler observes in his survey of "Musical Shakespeares," the story of Shakespeare in music begins with the presence of music in Shakespeare; since then, across a range of musical genres, the language, narratives, dramatis personae, and mythology of Shakespeare's works have served as resources of musical inspiration, citation, allusion, and recycling, frequently in ways which blur the divisions between the serious and the popular, highbrow and lowbrow, minority and mass culture. Acknowledging the vast terrain of musical appropriations of Shakespeare, this chapter examines modern popular musical culture's enduring capacity to borrow or steal Shakespearean archetypes as a means of engaging concerns of race, generational conflict, and sexuality. Shakespeare's auditory presence is also the concern of "Shakespeare Overheard," in which Susanne Greenhalgh surveys Shakespeare's fortunes within one mass entertainment medium in which he has seemed remarkably at home: radio. Greenhalgh details a history of productions of the works, and their associated authorial fictions, that has remained largely invisible to performance critics. Following an itinerary which runs from Shakespeare's Stratford to "Juliet's balcony" in Verona, Nicola Watson's chapter, "Shakespeare on the tourist trail," examines the dissemination of Shakespearean mythologies and cultural memories across a range of key tourist sites, assessing both the official narratives that are available to the Shakespearean tourist, and the variety of ways in which these can be negotiated by the serious, agnostic, or casual visitor. If the tourist sites associated with Shakespeare can be regarded as specific, highly charged geographical locations in which popular myths and alternative narratives around Shakespeare flourish independent of scholarly concerns, the placeless, global space of the world wide web is another arena in which information – and misinformation – about Shakespeare can circulate regardless of academic boundaries and regulations. A number of recent accounts of Shakespeare on the internet have begun to focus upon the pedagogic and scholarly possibilities and responsibilities of the digital media with regard to the dissemination of archival, teaching, and research materials, to the exchange of information and to the management of critical debate. Once academic discourse is placed in the wider context of internet culture, however, it finds itself situated within a medium which does not necessarily differentiate between the responsible and the irresponsible use and circulation of information, between high and low cultures, and between what can be verified and what can be fabricated. Shakespeare on the internet is as much the provenance of the cultist, the crank, the conspiracy theorist, the parodist, and the pornographer as it is the domain of the professional researcher and pedagogue, in that it allows, even encourages, the proliferation of resources and viewpoints once confined to marginal groups of self-styled sectarians, heretics, and dissidents. In the penulti-mate chapter, "Performing Shakespeare in digital culture," W. B. Worthen takes up the challenge of Shakespeare in the newest media, suggesting that the extent of the impact of digitalization, the DVD, and the potential for interconnectivity, upon our understanding of how performance works, and what it is, has only begun to be realized. Finally, in "Shakespeare's popular face," Carol Chillington Rutter reflects upon both the beginnings and endings of performance by turning to an aspect of Shakespeare's visual presence within the cultural environment that has been strangely neglected as a source of evidence of how the theatre engages its audiences: the playbill and the theatre poster.

This *Companion* invites the reader to consider the singular case of Shakespeare in order to address wide-ranging questions of cultural transmis-sion, appropriation, authority, and pleasure. It asks what happens when Shakespeare is popularized, and when the popular is Shakespeareanized; it queries the factors that determine the definitions of and boundaries between the legitimate and illegitimate, the canonical and the authorized, and the subversive, the oppositional, the scandalous, and the inane; it investigates the consequences of what happens when cultural practices and vocabularies located within one zone migrate to another, as when popular performance becomes legitimized, or when aspects of elite or minority culture are ren-dered mainstream. Acknowledging the immense diversity of forms and activities adopted by, on behalf of, or under the name of, Shakespeare, it hopes to extend and enrich our continuing conversations with the works, and with the cultural legacies they have sustained and generated.

Quotations from Shakespeare are from the Oxford *Complete Works* (1988), edited by Stanley Wells and Gary Taylor.

I

DIANA E. HENDERSON

From popular entertainment to literature

Shakespeare's transformation from popular entertainer to literary lion was a complex, fascinating process, but it is only one of several plots in the drama of his ever-widening success and influence. Although it is undeniable that Shakespeare has become the Bard of high culture, he has never been exclusively or stably held aloft. Indeed, his story convincingly demonstrates the instability of the line dividing high and low, elite and popular, revealing the multiple (and sometimes colliding) meanings of those terms. Certainly never "unpopular," Shakespeare worked in a theatre that was attended by a broad cross-section of the London populace and drew on a range of ritual and folk elements; at the same time, his theatre belonged to an emergent proto-modern economy that arguably displaced oral and amateur traditions. Through greater attention to marketplace and medial transformations as well as distinct variations among non-elite groups, the last forty years of research have shown the inadequacy of simple, singular definitions of "the Elizabethan stage," "popular culture" – and even "Shakespeare." Thus, rather than engage in the potentially "futile endeavor" to "isolate what was purely popular" in the early modern period,[1] this chapter works outward from narrow signifiers to broader contexts, dancing through the evidentiary thickets. It thereby reveals both the importance and rich multiplicity of relationships between Shakespeare and popular culture.

The man and his theatre

To begin with the man William Shakespeare is already to signal his distance from traditional conceptions of popular culture: namely, those derived from folk practices that were immediate, oral, visual, and gestural, in which no individual or writer took precedence over the communal experience and the division between performers and audience was virtually non-existent. Naming Shakespeare serves as a useful reminder of our modern distance not only from those ritual practices but also from their traces in Shakespeare's theatre. Its popular inheritance included non-scripted performances (by clowns and dancers, as well as the gestural and rhetorical improvisations of other actors), collaborative scripting that made plays by "patchwork," lively interaction between actors and audiences, and the subordinated importance of the playwright.[2] But to get back there from here, let us start from modern assumptions, with the man.

If forced to place young William Shakespeare in one cultural location, it would not be among the elite. He was born neither noble nor "gentle," did not attend university, worked as an actor and provider of scripts for a professional theatre of such dubious status that it was not allowed to perform within London's city limits, and wrote in a vernacular with little enough belabored classicism to remain generally comprehensible to most English speakers centuries later. The earliest documentary reference to his presence in London makes clear that even within theatrical circles, he was perceived as an "upstart"; in lines attributed by Henry Chettle to Robert Greene, this "Shake-scene" threatens to undo the aspirations of those university-educated playwrights who strove to attain a higher status than the actors. He did so precisely by being a "Johannes factotum" who performed both roles.

Will had a way of blurring boundaries. His first and only definitively "authorized" publications were narrative poems on classical themes, dedicated to an earl; he circulated sonnets in a manuscript form associated with elite and would-be courtiers. Like the uneducated rustic (called, conventionally, a "clown") in *The Winter's Tale*, the adult Shakespeare became a "gentleman born" as an adult, when he acquired a coat-of-arms for his father. He used his earnings as a theatrical professional to buy the biggest house, New Place, in his hometown of Stratford-upon-Avon. His plays would be performed not only in Southwark alongside whorehouses and animal-baiting arenas but also before queens and kings at court, and would be published posthumously in an almost unprecedented, expensive format. In short, Shakespeare was exceptional and exceptionally hard to pin down, in the process forcing his audiences likewise to reconsider inherited ideas of hierarchy, propriety, and value. "Art thou base, common, and popular?" (*Henry V*); "Wherefore base?" (*King Lear*); "What is honor?" (*Henry IV, 1*); "What's aught but as 'tis valued?" (*Troilus and Cressida*). His art still prompts scrutiny of the meanings in, around, and behind those words.

To the extent that Shakespeare can be regarded as representative, it is in his socioeconomic background from a family of the "middling sort," the growing class of merchants, yeomen, and artisans from whence (*pace* Chettle and Greene) most theatrical professionals came. He and his cohort challenged a two-tier vision of high and low, and could on occasion move in either direction. As actors, moreover, their very appearance defied sumptuary (dress) codes designed to maintain old hierarchies: wearing robes donated by aristocrats as well as their own or cheaper garb, they played roles ranging from aristocrats and royalty down to beggars and country "clowns." The language Shakespeare would provide for them likewise ranged from rhyme to prose, from elegant textbook rhetoric to scurrilous jokes and insults. This mobility of perspective clearly contributed to the dynamic energy of their storytelling, and the potentially subversive popularity of their performances. They had to hope that King Lear was right when he said: "Robes and furred gowns hide all ... None does offend" (4.5.161–64). Their box office success, in turn, became Shakespeare's route to financial security and more elevated, if not elite, social status.

The acting companies that were the fundamental organizations of London theatre likewise challenged easy categorization as popular or elite. Officially they were liveried servants under aristocratic or royal patronage, and thus distinguished from the increasing number of socially disruptive "vagabonds" wandering across the English landscape in an era of land enclosures, staggering inflation, unpensioned armies, and expanding markets. From the courtly perspective, their performances in public amphitheatres in the "Liberties" outside London – free from the City Fathers' control, although not from supervision and censorship by the court-appointed Master of the Revels – were warm-ups, encouraging the development of skilled groups of professionals and an extensive repertory, the most successful of which would then be produced at court. Whereas many writers worked as freelancers for various acting companies, Shakespeare was from 1594 both a performing member of the Lord Chamberlain's Men and wrote exclusively for them; in 1599 with the construction of the Globe Theatre he also became a "sharer" or shareholder in that theatre and in their indoor one at Blackfriars, meaning that he was one of a limited number of actors sharing the risks – and profits – from performances in those spaces. He remained a "company man" when, with the ascension of James I, the Chamberlain's Men were renamed the King's Men.[3] Thus, while the company's daily lives and economic fortunes were reliant upon their popular success with those paying as little as one pence (more for a bench seat) to watch their shows in "lowlife" districts, the King's Men were court-affiliated and in Shakespeare's last years performed as well at the more expensively priced Blackfriars (minimum entrance 3–6 pence), for those who could afford it. Although aldermen and Puritan preachers regarded the theatre industry as distracting, disorderly, and even devilish, Shakespeare's career within it reveals the analogy between its incipiently bourgeois aspirations and the business models of its London critics. Whether we follow Paul Yachnin in emphasizing the "popu-luxe" character of this theatre's entertainment, or attend to its submerged expressions of the "popular voice," as does Annabel Patterson, the mobility of the middling sort and the middle term contributed – and continues to contribute – to Shakespeare's multifaceted appeal.[4]

The popular performance tradition

Both as performance scripts and within their dramatic fictions, Shakespeare's plays are infused with signs of popular culture. Perhaps easiest for the modern reader to discern are two character types identified chiefly by functional rather than individuated names: the Fool and the Clown. Peter Thomson rightly details the distinctions among fools, clowns, and knaves (such as Autolycus in *The Winter's Tale*).[5] Nevertheless, they all derive from what Joel Schechter represents as the origins of popular theatre in mime and clowning: "Their art lives in bodies and voices, in their memories and stage acts, and those of people who know them; their repertoire reposes in people."[6] Emphasizing the unruly body and the immediacy of performance, these figures move back and forth between the world of the fictional representation and that of its audience. Some argue that they follow in a secular satirical tradition tracing back to the ancients; certainly they brought to the professional stage the kinds of tricks and attention to the body common amongst medieval *jongleurs* and amateur folk players. Richard Tarlton, who most likely honed his skills at insults and jigging while working as a tavern host, became the biggest star of the Queen's Men in the 1580s playing (satirical) bumpkins such as Simplicity in *The Three Ladies of London* (1584) and Derrick in *The Famous Victories of Henry V* (1587?), plays with which Shakespeare was clearly familiar.[7] Thomson argues that soon after Tarlton's death in 1588 Shakespeare "resurrected him" as the rebellious Jack Cade in *Henry VI Part 2*.

Like his relative the Fool, the rustic Clown could, under guise of boorish incomprehension, make jibes at issues and authorities a "wiser" man would not dare broach. Although not their skill exclusively, Clowns were often associated with jigging and other forms of popular dancing. (After his stint with Shakespeare's company, Will Kemp would make a "Nine-Day's Wonder" out of his stunt of Morris-dancing from London to Norwich.) The jigs that concluded each professional stage performance seem to have involved not only dance steps but satire, libel, or scurrility – which may be another reason why none of them survive. They were thought "dangerous enough for an order for their suppression in all London playhouses to be issued in October 1612 after the 'tumultes and outrages'" they caused at the Fortune Theatre, where they drew "divers cutt-purses and other lewde and ill disposed persons in great multitude."[8] Here, as in so much official and anti-theatrical writing, unruliness onstage is held responsible for unruliness beyond it, with forms drawing on popular tradition being seen as particularly threatening. Similarly, in 1607, a Somerset Justice of the Peace complained that "shews" involving the folk plays of Robin Hood and St. George, performed in the streets of Wells, were slandering him.[9] Clearly the dukes and kings of Shakespeare's plays were not alone in suffering under the scrutiny of their social "inferiors." Robert Weimann contrasts this "disenchanting" function of clowning with the "enchanting" work of representational fiction-making, noting how it allows a structure of burlesque and parody within or alongside a more "elevated" plotline.[10]

The Fool figure has an especially rich history in this regard, and his multiple connections with both popular and courtly traditions have made him also among the most studied. Enid Welsford has traced the ways in which the "natural fool," whose lack of mental capability was regarded as having bawdy bodily compensations, contrasted with the "artificial fool" or witty court jester, and yet were mingled in the playing tradition. Medieval devils and the Vice figures from earlier popular plays such as *Mankind* (c. 1471) and *Cambises* (c. 1561) provided another analogue from the religious tradition for the Fool's outrageous behavior and unusually free speech: although within the fiction they would eventually be defeated in the name of morality, along the way they stole the show by running amidst the audience, announcing their pleasure in evil-doing, and otherwise wreaking havoc.[11] Weimann dubs the Fool the "heir of myth and the child of realism," calling attention to the flexible functionality of such topsy-turvy figures in performance.[12] Certainly the Fool's carnivalesque role in Shakespeare's *Twelfth Night* and *King Lear* includes turning the world "upside down" in language and behavior, but even more importantly within the fiction he reveals how much more inverted and "foolish" putatively civilized society can be: one witnesses the transfiguration of a popular performance tradition in the service of an artfully multifunctional dramatic production.

Shakespeare would have encountered actors in the popular Italian tradition as well, the *commedia dell'arte* actors who wore masks, played tricks, and improvised from action-based scenarios called *lazzi*. In *Love's Labour's Lost*, he creates his own versions of the pedant, the wily servant, and the braggart soldier, all popular figures from the *commedia*. The "rude mechanicals" in *A Midsummer Night's Dream* unwittingly combine the group performance antics of a bad *commedia* troupe with the clownish rustics of English tradition. The popularity of traditional types melded with (and was complicated by) the popularity of the particular actors for whom Shakespeare provided scripts. Not only did this mean "less need for any actor to work on issues of characterization" – a useful time-saver for repertory companies performing as many as six different plays within a week – but also provided a prompt for the busy writer, who "may have started writing a play for, say, King, Queen, Bastard, Fool, Braggarts … adding individual names later."[13] This granted, the combination of Shakespeare's storytelling interests with the particular talents and personalities of a changing cast of actors led to a far greater range of individuation than such typecasting might imply, and indeed has led to continuing uncertainty about who played which parts. (The first extant cast list matching actors to their roles did not appear until 1623, and then not in Shakespeare's First Folio but in the quarto publication of Webster's *The Duchess of Malfi*: beyond what we can glean from particular praises of exceptional performers such as tragedian Richard Burbage – creator of Hamlet, Brutus, Othello, and Lear – all is speculation.) But undoubtedly among the actors who were most popular with Shakespeare's audience were his Clowns and Fools, Will Kempe and later Robert Armin, who between them probably created Peter in *Romeo and Juliet*, Bottom in *A Midsummer Night's Dream*, Dogberry in *Much Ado About Nothing*, Touchstone in *As You Like It*, Sir Toby Belch and Feste in *Twelfth Night*, and – most popular of all – Sir John Falstaff.

Yet characters alone do not create a play, and in Shakespeare's theatre they cannot be separated from the larger patterns and narratives likewise derived from popular tradition. S. L. Bethell, C. L. Barber, François Laroque and others have traced the myriad ways in which Shakespeare's plays echo and borrow from the seasonal and religious rituals of the culture in which he was raised.[14] Puck and the fairies of *A Midsummer Night's Dream* are only the beginning. Among the most popular folk forms were Morris-dancing and Robin Hood skits. These latter built upon the four-part structure of Mummers' plays in which an actor addresses the audience, an heroic combat leads to the death or wounding of one fighter, an impudent servant assists in his healing or resurrection, and a comic conclusion again addresses the audience (with coins solicited). Linked with the agricultural calendar essential to group survival, these narratives were often performed at spring festivals of rebirth such as May Day: Robin Hood might in ballads become a figure redressing social injustice, but his consort Maid Marion was also linked with the Queen of May. In 1606 Nicholas Bownd remarked that "most people were more familiar with Robin Hood than with the stories in the Bible."[15] A few years after, Shakespeare created his most extensive scene of folk rituals signifying rebirth, complete with clowning, ballad-singing, and Perdita as Queen of the sheep-shearing. They are of course transformed through placement within a self-consciously artificial narrative shaped by psychosexual trauma among the elite: *The Winter's Tale* is a far cry from winter folk tales imagined by Mamillius or told by old women at the fireside. As this instance exemplifies, Shakespeare's dramaturgy can be seen as either a transformed tribute to popular culture and folk wisdom, or a sophisticated displacement of them.

Even at the top of the social pyramid, theatre's traditional connection with holiday and games shaped the performance schedule, producing such seemingly incongruous events as King James watching *King Lear* as a form of Christmas revelry. (Through the account left by a Clown, William Harrison, we know that a traveling company was also performing *King Lear* and *Pericles* at Christmastime in Yorkshire, 1608/9.) But this was indeed the time of year for topsy-turvy, when descendants of the carnivalesque Lord of Misrule were allowed to disrupt the conventional hierarchies of "everyday" social order. The setting up of such mock lords and ladies has been viewed by some as a playful or anxious parody of rebellious sentiments among the commons, perhaps even deployed consciously by the monarchy in its attempts to forge a post-feudal national consciousness. Others regard their appearance (at the law schools known as the Inns of Court, for instance) as devices for expressing dissent among elite factions. And many still argue that their religious and ritual associations trump any political potential or topicality at all. Yet Shakespeare makes much of the contrast between holiday and everyday not only in what C. L. Barber dubbed his seasonal "festive comedies" but also in his histories (Hal's opening soliloquy in *Henry IV, Part* 1 for example); and the Fool's song from *Twelfth Night* returns in the most dire of contexts, *King Lear*'s stormy heath scene.[16] Whether the plays' narratives and public performance served to bridge the social divisions, or to reveal them more starkly, thus remains a matter of lively interpretation.

Although the public amphitheatres undermined ritual occasionality by presenting their "holiday" worlds every day – hence raising the ire of London businessmen whose apprentices were thereby lured from work – Shakespeare's use of that theatrical space preserved elements of popular theatre's stagecraft. Robert Weimann most famously has emphasized the important multifunctionality of the *locus/platea* distinction derived from medieval and amateur performances. There the fictional world being represented, usually centering on social elites or religious figures, had been set off spatially. Weimann stresses the dynamic play between these elevated, defined *loci* and the more fluid, undifferentiated performance space of the *platea*, which was a place for clowning, popular or "lower" figures, and rich interaction with the audience. He further argues that, even with the combination of these figures and elements on the raised stage of the Elizabethan professional theatres, old associations persisted, encouraging such dramaturgical choices as Prince Hamlet's encounter with the gravediggers and the anachronism in *Lear*'s Fool's speech to the audience.[17] Although acknowledging how hard it is to unravel the popular from the elite in pre-Shakespearean drama, David Bevington and others have charted the structural continuities that lead from popular moralities to the sophistication of Marlowe's learned scripts, and hence to Shakespeare.[18] Without doubt, Elizabethan stagecraft was deeply indebted to popular traditions, genres, and performance conventions, and of its many script-writers Shakespeare – in his comic types, allusions, storylines and dramaturgical imagination – was as immersed as anyone.

The common people's perspective

In the pre-democratic society of Shakespeare's day, as in his drama, to be called "popular" or "of the people" was usually not a compliment. Nevertheless, the roots of theatre in popular entertainments and its primarily non-aristocratic audience in public amphitheatres encouraged representation of "lower class" experiences and opinions, at least in encoded or oppositional contexts. Indeed, theatrical performance provided an adaptable occasion to defend the common people's perspective within a culture that excluded them from governmental structures (other than their theoretical representation by gentlemen in Parliament, the election of whom only a small fraction of landowners determined). The audacious bodily expression of the clown literalized the ubiquitous metaphor of the people as the nation's body, and could challenge the elite's monopoly over the law. As early as Mary Tudor's reign, a proclamation linking "preaching, printing, and playing" testifies to official worries about the development of an unruly urban populace, and Master of the Revels Edmund Tilney's 1581 commission tried to make sure that "playmakers" did not foment dissatisfaction among the multitude.[19] The Elizabethan powers-that-be had even more reason to be concerned: their Protestant state was ruled by a woman, whose targeted assassination had been sanctioned by the Pope, at a time when bad harvests, inflation, enclosures, and religious upheavals all provided cause for popular anger and desperation.

Few scholars now would maintain the once orthodox (and wishful) argument that Shakespeare's drama was made possible by and expressed a unified, orderly world vision and nation-state, even if theatre's place within that society was unusually communal. The Church of England's regular reiteration of its Homily Against Rebellion testifies less to a shared ritual belief than to a sense of constant peril: even if the Earl of Essex would badly miscalculate in 1601 in thinking that "the people" would rise up against their Queen, he was not wrong to have identified deep strains of unhappiness, both economic and ideological, that manifested themselves in Elizabethan London in over thirty riots or uprisings, and would lead to the larger-scale Midlands Rising (alluded to in *Coriolanus*) in 1607.

In 1595, the Mayor of London argued to the Privy Council that plays were "a great cause of disorder in the Citie," perceiving "infection" from the theatre as a cause of mutinous servants.[20] And indeed, in the collaboratively written *Sir Thomas More* (among whose authors was Shakespeare), the discontent of "native" Londoners explodes in an anti-immigrant uprising. Whether this ever made it to the stage is another matter. Although the violence is defused and opposed by Sir Thomas, even this foiled insurrection was judged too provocative for representation in a city that saw at least four anti-immigrant riots under Elizabeth, and Tilney demanded it be cut. To draw a broad analogy, in *More* as in Martin Scorsese's 2002 film *Gangs of New York*, the underclass perspective of an earlier generation is presented as motivated, even when misguided: that understanding of the people's viewpoint could in itself threaten a rigid order that discounted the "multitude" as by definition irrational, bestial, and wrong.

In the most extensive argument for Shakespeare's sympathy with the popular voice, Annabel Patterson counters what she regards as an enduring Coleridgean view of the playwright as politically disinterested yet upholding a conservative, aristocratic social order. In addition to highlighting republican rhetoric involving the people's consent in the poems and plays set in ancient Rome (*The Rape of Lucrece*, *Coriolanus*), she argues that "in thematizing the popular and its role in earlier historical events (both Roman and English) Shakespeare made visible" the causes for official anxiety, and demanded attention to the "popular voice."[21] Conceding the obvious contempt for mob stupidity and violence in *Julius Caesar* (in which Cinna the poet protests his difference from Cinna the conspirator, to no avail), she argues against the standard reading of *Coriolanus* by stressing our distance from the perspective of its tragic hero. One may question (for instance) her utopian reading of *A Midsummer Night's Dream* as imagining "social play that could cross class boundaries without obscuring them, and by those crossings imagine the social body whole again";[22] but certainly she reveals the myriad associations involving the "popular" within Shakespeare's vocabulary, and their importance within his storytelling.

Among the richest and most contested plays in this regard remains *Henry V*. Pistol is its most obvious rogue in bandying about status: he dissociates himself from the "base, common and popular" (4.1.39), before he develops his base plan to "steal" back to England faking battle scars – "and there I'll steal" (5.1.83). But one must also wonder about the King who would "steel" his soldiers' hearts – especially given that his heroic Crispin's Day rhetoric rejecting monetary crowns in favor of royal ones is directly followed by

Pistol's seizure of just such base "crowns" on Agincourt's battlefield. The slipperiness of "name" and gentility returns relentlessly, from the Chorus's initial request for pardon from the London audience (hardly "gentles all") through Henry's offer to "gentle" the condition of his entire "band of brothers" (when his numbers are desperately inadequate), only for them to revert to being "none else of name" once victory has been achieved and he can again play practical jokes on his followers. The battle's eve sequence culminating in Henry's unresolved "quarrel" with the commoner Williams – that unexpectedly contentious "little touch of Harry in the night" (4.0.47) – likewise raises questions rather than presenting clear conclusions: Anne Barton argues that the reworking of the king-in-disguise motif from "the popular theatre and the popular imagination" in which it "was an archaic, utopian gesture" here is criticized "as attractive but untrue."[23] Patterson goes further in calling Henry "self-deluding" in his attempt at a populist gesture, and "self-justifying" in his subsequent soliloquy, in which "the common people are mindlessly irresponsible."[24] Others would say this is too harsh or at least too univocally radical a reading: the four pre-Branagh decades of veneration for Laurence Olivier's uncritical film Henry indicate that even far more democratically minded audiences can be seduced by a charming actor-monarch in performance. Nevertheless, Shakespeare's creation of the frank, sharp-tongued Williams does present a challenge unmatched in argument or emotional clarity by his social superior, and as such illustrates the playwright's powerful dramatization of at least one popular voice.

Less directly coded as popular are the many songs that enliven Shakespeare's plays: elite male characters were not singers in English drama at this time.[25] Rather, singing was associated with lower social status, and/or the supernatural – in other words, with those deemed less "rational" than were those with political power. Fairies, hired musicians, rogues, gravediggers, and madwomen sing – suggesting that when Desdemona intones a servant's "willow" song after Othello's mistreatment of her, she is on the verge of emotional collapse.

The dramatic genres in which Shakespeare worked also tended to be the ones already popular with his audiences: he produced almost all his English history plays in the 1590s, when they were playing well at Bankside theatres. Serving the company's interests by serving the public taste may have been as large a factor in Shakespeare's generic decisions as was his "authorial" personality. He shifted genres to match the times, writing a cluster of his most scathingly satiric plays (*Troilus and Cressida*, *Measure for Measure*, *All's Well That Ends Well*) on the heels of printed satire having become so popular that church authorities felt it required censorship (the Bishops' Ban of 1599). He often chose characters of established stageworthiness

(Hamlet, Henry V) or popularity in other forms (the "shrew" from ballads, Romeo and Juliet from print narrative).

In *Cymbeline*, Shakespeare mixes fairy tale tropes (the wicked stepmother, the imperiled princess) with contemporary questions concerning the location of nobility, in blood or behavior, and as ever allows multiple interpretations: this is a play in which the "natural" distinction of two princes raised in the Welsh wilds competes with the stupidity of another prince (Cloten) who is clearly less worthy than the commoner Posthumus Leonatus. If one associates the popular with the local, as some theatre historians do, the carved presence of Cymbeline and other ancient Britons on Ludgate, near Blackfriars Theatre, would be a reminder of this play's iconographic immersion in its audience's experience.[26] But like Shakespeare's other late plays, this one emphasizes artifice, seems written for the indoor theatre's more privileged audience, and draws on historical and literary works. It remains as difficult to establish stable boundaries between popular and elite culture here as it is to determine the playwright's exact "message" regarding noble birth.

Indeed, that very indeterminacy encourages us to consider other ideas of popularity connected not exclusively with loyalty to tradition or the lower classes but instead with the wide range of spectators, the emerging marketplace, and circulation. Even while some believe the professionalization of early modern theatre threatened inherited folk culture, theatre historians acknowledge that one could deem "popular" that "drama produced by and offered for the enjoyment or edification of the largest combinations of groupings possible in that society."[27] The loss of precision in such a definition is balanced by its recognition that there are always multiple competing ways of dividing a society: by wealth, gender, education, rank, political power, and more. Especially in a time of great social change, acknowledging breadth and variety of audience may be a more useful way to consider popularity than is using an inverted binary to seek out instances of the (oversimplified) "low" triumphing over (an equally simplified) "elite."

To say this, however, is to become involved in a modern political debate that extends well beyond Shakespeare scholarship. The desire to venerate old folk ways has its radical as well as conservative adherents: for those who see themselves upholding the better legacies of Marx, the early modern past is prologue to a vexed present in which the popular label can be stamped on forms of mass entertainment dedicated entirely to unindividuated commercial consumption.[28] Nevertheless, even if true, and even if the unexamined "self"-indulgence sometimes validated by pop culture studies warrants critique, hypothesizing a pre-Shakespearean society of unalienated labor and a unified "people" hardly seems defensible historically – or politically helpful, for those now wishing to create an authentic sense of community within a global economy. Thus it seems worth recognizing the potential for new forms of popular culture, both within commercial corporate models such as the early modern acting company and in their work of pleasing a heterogeneous audience.

New markets, new media

Long before Shakespeare, popular players were touring and performing for profit as well as pleasure: those two motivations never were, and still are not, necessarily at odds. The creation of purpose-built theatres in London did, however, increase the economic pressure and possibilities for professional practitioners. Moreover, Shakespeare's success in that arena has eclipsed interest in other local theatrical forms that persisted in his day. It is within a new commercial industry that Shakespeare became popular to a broad audience, and his continued popularity has in turn made that industry the site of English classical theatre.

Although London ranked among the largest European cities in 1600 (somewhere in the vicinity of 200,000), this was still a small population to sustain two or more companies performing in large (2,000–3,000 persons) amphitheatres six times weekly for large segments of the year – even if interrupted by plague, religious observances, and weather. Hence the need for a boom in play production, with new plays constantly added into rotation with revivals: "A reasonably popular play could expect up to twelve performances in all spread over two years; an extremely popular play might become 'stock' and be performed on a regular basis for a number of years."[29] Alterations and additions to old scripts and collaborative writing involving freelancers were essential to keeping these repertory-based companies afloat. The writers might be called "poets," but their works were definitely part of this popular industry, and became company property; the £6 earned for a completed play was "comparable with the annual wage of an artisan," yet "[f]or those with high cultural aspirations, the composition of plays was tainted."[30]

Recently, scholars have challenged the premise that Shakespeare was uninterested in the publication of his plays. Nevertheless, their primary and immediate value for him, both financially and communally, lay in performance.[31] He quickly became among the most popular playwrights, and remained so throughout his career. Although no one play of his matched the spectacular notoriety of Marlowe's *Tamburlaine* or the crowd-pleasing endurance of (the anonymously authored) *Mucedorus*, for nearly two decades Shakespeare regularly produced about two plays per year of which the majority were solidly successful. In print, single-play (quarto-sized) editions sold well and regularly, whether or not he had anything to do with their publication. Even compared to many of his professional contemporaries Shakespeare's style was less "elitist," less arcane or overt in advertising its book-learning. Yet it was only his two narrative poems that he saw fit to publish with his authorial imprimatur. These poems would in fact become among his more popular works – if we can now include "broadly read" in that word's many definitions.

Which brings us to the thorny question of the "literary" in relation to the performative, avoided until now in order to delay, if not defy, yet another oversimple twentieth-century opposition that still shapes the thinking of many academic and theatrical professionals. One unfortunate side effect of Shakespeare's exceptional textual success from the time of the Romantics onward has been the attempt to elevate his plays "above" the stage, which in the 1970s oddly coalesced with poststructuralist privileging of textual complexity. This provoked an equally dismissive tendency in performance studies (and, to a lesser extent, media studies of orality) which discounted or ignored the role of anything "literary" in performance. In the case of Shakespeare's scripts, the "text v. performance" debate fragmented precisely what made his plays – and those of his fellow-workers in early modern theatre – so fascinating: their ability to address an audience hungry for words *as* performance, their self-conscious artistry in melding once-"elite" reading matter with popular stage antics, and their evident delight in what Douglas Bruster and Robert Weimann call "the socio-cultural 'mingle-mangle' of the Elizabethan period."[32] By refusing to read backwards from the eventual enshrining of Shakespeare's texts as "literature" (a category not yet current in early modern England), we can better comprehend the multimedia phenomenon – and popularity – of his drama at a time of major change within manuscript, print, oral, and performance cultures.

About a century after the printing press came to England, its potential to reach a broader audience through "cheap print" was being realized, with sermon and ballads the most popular genres in circulation. Although rates of early modern literacy (itself a nineteenth-century neologism) are notoriously hard to determine, certainly the majority of the populace could not read.[33] Nevertheless, with literacy fast increasing among merchants, craftsmen, professionals, and others of the "middling" sort (especially in London), and in a context where much reading was done out loud and socially, a large segment of the populace benefited from printed texts. Trickle-down theories work better in the case of storytelling than economics: condensed chapbook versions of once "elite" romance narratives were among the most successful fictional forms, and plays likewise drew from these highly popular stories. The romance *Pandosto* went through at least forty printings and became one of the sources for *The Winter's Tale*; like most popular print forms (and published plays in quarto), these editions did not name its author, Robert Greene. Poetic aspirers such as Ben Jonson would mock Shakespeare for staging such "mouldy tales," and eventually the romance aesthetic would suffer through its very popularity among a "low" readership. But, as Lori Newcomb remarks, textual availability in multiple forms at different prices led to common story knowledge despite the efforts of those wishing to sort the forms hierarchically, and the "high" and "low" audiences "cannot have been mutually exclusive from the start."[34] Nor were the relationships between manuscript and print as simple as used to be claimed by those who – sometimes with opposing allegiances – affiliated the former with high and the latter with popular culture. Studies such as Margaret Ezell's and Julie Stone Peters's, for instance, reveal contextual variations across genders, decades, intellectual circles, and genres.[35] Not surprisingly, Shakespeare's writing shows signs of affiliation with both popular and learned textual traditions.

During the same years he was being attacked as an "upstart crow," Shakespeare had *Lucrece* (1593) and *Venus and Adonis* (1594) printed, the latter providing further testimony of his generic attention to Marlowe (specifically *Hero and Leander*). It became "probably Shakespeare's best-known composition between 1590 and 1616"; E. K. Chambers cited ten reprints by 1617.[36] Within a decade Gabriel Harvey noted this erotic epyllion's strong (some said pornographic) appeal among the "younger sort," although the scholarly Harvey and those whom he esteemed "the wiser sort" preferred *Lucrece* – and *Hamlet*. Frances Mere's *Palladis Tamia: Wits Treasury* praised both Shakespeare's plays and his "sugared sonnets," which would not be published until 1609 and hence had to be circulating in manuscript. Moreover, very early rebuttals to Greene's attack on the "upstart crow" which mention Shakespeare's "facetious grace in writing" may imply the plays also circulated in manuscript – although this, like the extent of Shakespeare's interest in print publication, is a source of ongoing debate.[37] The length of his playscripts, in some instances demanding much more than the "two hour's traffic" he attests to be their playing time, has led some to argue he wrote for readers as well as spectators. In his range of poetic forms, media, and reception, then, Shakespeare again blurred status boundaries from the start.

The year 1598 saw other signs besides Mere's often-cited testimonial that Shakespeare had "made it": a Marston satire mocks an obsessive playgoer who makes "a common-place book out of plays / And speaks in print" – "from whence doth flow / Naught but pure Juliet and Romeo." (Another 1598 satirist, Joseph Hall, attests to the absurdity of separating language from performative pleasure when he notes that the dramatic poet with "big-sounding sentences" and "pure Iambick verse ... ravishes the gazing Scaffolders.")[38]

1598 saw the publication of the first quarto which announced Shakespeare's name on its title page, not by any means a typical inclusion: it implies that the sales of the play (*Love's Labour's Lost*) would be improved by association with that writer. Indeed, if we can take Thomas Heywood's *Apology for Actors* at its word, in a later case of title-page attribution, Shakespeare was "much offended with M. Jaggard that (altogether unknowne to him) presumed to make so bold with his name": whether this testifies more to pride in his name and publication record (as Lukas Erne argues) or to concern at being credited with Heywood's poems, it shows clearly that in 1599 the publisher Jaggard had something to gain by invoking Shakespeare.[39] Similarly, the published play quartos more frequently named him (2 *Henry IV*, notably, as well as plays such as *A Yorkshire Tragedy* no longer attributed to him). According to Brian Vickers, "His name appears (by my count) on a total of forty-nine quarto and octavo editions of plays and poems published between 1598 and 1622, far more frequently than any other poet or dramatist, indeed, more often than most professional writers."[40] Such naming suggests the "personalization of print," and the gradual rise of the single authorial figure from the 1590s onward, as well as this man's particular success.[41]

Plays never made up more than a very small fraction of the book trade (below 4 percent), but even that estimate means that sometimes 20,000–50,000 play copies were published during a single year. Throughout Shakespeare's career, "publication of playbooks was at its peak" and included many editions of his individual plays, including numerous first editions in 1594, 1600, and 1607, and multiple reprints.[42] This would culminate, famously though posthumously, in a collection of thirty-six plays entitled *Mr. William Shakespeares Comedies, Histories, & Tragedies. Published according to the True Originall Copies*. Brought to the press by two of Shakespeare's friends and fellow-King's Men who had access to the company's papers, half of the plays in this First Folio were appearing in print for the first time. It was followed within a decade by the 1632 Second Folio, which included a tribute poem that was John Milton's first publication. This was a quicker turnaround to a second edition than greeted Ben Jonson's 1616 *Works* despite that poet's higher reputation among the elite (who could afford large books). A third Folio was issued soon after the Restoration (its second printing including seven new plays of which all but *Pericles* are no longer attributed to Shakespeare), and a fourth in 1685.

Shakespeare's popularity – both at the box office and on the page – was soon reflected in other playwrights' allusion and imitation, ranging from local citations (Dekker called his *Satiromastix* errata list a "short *Comedy of Errors*") to full-blown companion plays, such as John Fletcher's "sequel" to *The Taming of the Shrew* entitled *The Tamer Tamed*. A. R. Braunmuller notes that *Hamlet* was "an instantly influential play," prompting allusions in Marston's *Malcontent* and

Dekker's *Honest Whore* almost immediately, and more significantly in John Ford's *'Tis Pity She's A Whore* years after, showing "its popularity and its memorableness."[43] Borrowings continued throughout the Caroline reign and even after the theatres were closed, as in the interregnum tragedy *Fair Irene and Mahomet*'s reference to Romeo and Juliet. The plays themselves were also performed, Bentley citing ten recorded instances during the 1630s.[44]

It was for his characters especially that Shakespeare remained popular. In his copy of the Second Folio, King Charles I annotated *Much Ado About Nothing* with the marginal reminder, "Beatrice and Benedick." Hamlet, Brutus, and Othello were likewise among the memorable, as measured by frequency of seventeenth-century allusion. But of all his plays and characters, the most popular, from 1600 right through the next century, was Sir John Falstaff: Hal might banish him and Shakespeare kill him off, but plump Jack – like many another crowd-pleasing clown – refused to stay down. In performance, in allusions, and even (when the theatres were effectively closed at mid-century) in short "drolls," that madcap rogue, that "Vice, that grey Iniquity," that compendium of so many dimensions of popular culture rolled up into one "huge hill of flesh," continued to please.

Becoming literature

So how, given this rich and varied nexus of ways in which Shakespeare began and remained popular, did he become regarded as the acme of "high culture" and the crown prince of literature? How did Jack Falstaff's creator become "elite"? Although it was not until the mid-eighteenth century that Shakespeare was fully transformed into "The Bard," two publications are conventionally cited as watersheds in his elevation: the First Folio in 1623, and Nicholas Rowe's edition in 1709.

At the other end of the publishing spectrum from "cheap print" octavos, the First Folio (15 shillings unbound, £1 bound in leather) was designed as a book for the elite, and presented its contents as worthy of the same treatment as serious historical and philosophical works. No book in this format had ever contained plays exclusively – not even Jonson's groundbreaking *Works*. A new claim for the literary quality of English plays and for Shakespeare thus went hand in hand, at a time when theatrical tastes were likewise becoming more stratified between the indoor and outdoor venues. Selling upmarket products was of course good business, and it behooved those with access to Shakespeare's scripts to make a profit as well as remember an esteemed friend. What little we can glean indicates that buyers of the initial 750–1,000 copies were "noblemen and commoners of standing"; not until Congreve at the end of the century do we know of a playwright owning a First Folio.[45] Format alone might not override the objections of those such as Thomas Bodley who famously excluded from his library such "unworthy matters" as plays, but in time it contributed to the gradual elevation of the playwright as author, and by later in the 1600s even the Bodleian Library owned a copy (albeit preferring, like others after the Restoration, to replace the First Folio with the "improved" Third). Among William Prynne's many sources of indignation with theatricality in the 1630s was this new veneration of the text, that "Shackspeers Plaies are printed in the best Crowne paper, far better than most Bibles."[46] Perhaps not surprisingly, then, by mid-century we find numerous allusions to Shakespeare as "great," and after the publication of Beaumont and Fletcher's Folio in 1647, he becomes part of the most respected "triumvirate" (with Jonson and Fletcher) of the pre-war theatrical "giants."

It is easy to oversimplify the course of this historical elevation because of the past two centuries' much greater veneration for that First Folio and its author, when the Bible and Shakespeare have indeed vied as scripture. But for 120 years after his death, both onstage and among critics, Shakespeare in fact neither disappeared nor stood out above all others.[47] It is difficult to determine just how highly esteemed he was and by whom: the evidence we have is sketchy and anecdotal, and particular perspectives (such as that of quirky Samuel Pepys) are easily – and often falsely – generalized. And because editions remain while performance fades away, the particulars of this first collection may similarly be overemphasized. It is worth remembering, for example, that Restoration comments about Ben Jonson's superiority were written at a time when "Shakespeare" referred to the author not of the First Folio plays alone, but also of *The Widow* and *The Arraignment of Paris*; meanwhile, the popularity of *Macbeth* for Pepys, and of *Lear* for the next 150 years'-worth of stage audiences, would be based upon altered Restoration texts and performance additions. Even Rowe's groundbreaking editorial presentation in 1709, which featured illustrations and a (deeply suspect) biography of the now-venerated "author," included the extra plays from the Third Folio reprint.

We should be cautious, then, in retrospectively assuming Shakespeare became synonymous with "literature" upon the publication of, or even with the later eighteenth-century editorial return to, the First Folio. Similarly, while Restoration playwrights certainly catered to a particular courtly perspective, the theatrical audience was not so starkly "elite" as is sometimes presumed, and the fate of "Shakespeare" would continue to be deeply involved with the popularity of particular actors (Betterton's success as Hamlet being a notable example). Only in the studies of Romantic and twentieth-century academic critics – with the exaggerated split between textual and theatrical cultures – did Shakespeare ever become divorced entirely from the "hurly-burly" he created (both literally and figuratively), or from the crowds he wrote to please. Arguably, it is for that very reason that his "bifold authority" continues to draw a crowd. As the following chapters will demonstrate, there remains a popular Shakespeare, a pop culture Shakespeare, and a Shakespeare available to be claimed in the name of the popular ... today, tomorrow, and perhaps – like his social chameleon Henry V's paradoxically status-defying "happy few" – "to the ending of the world."

NOTES

1. Tim Harris (ed.), *Popular Culture in England, c. 1500–1850* (Basingstoke: Macmillan, 1995), p. 10.
2. Tiffany Stern, *Making Shakespeare: From Stage to Page* (London: Routledge, 2004), p. 42, uses "patchwork" (from Thomas Dekker's remarks on "playpatchers") to describe the composition and rehearsal practices of Shakespeare's day.
3. I borrow the memorable phrasing of Richard Dutton, "The Birth of the Author," in *Texts and Cultural Change in Early Modern England*, ed. Cedric C. Brown and Arthur F. Marotti (Basingstoke: Macmillan, 1997), pp. 153–78, p. 161, whilst acknowledging recent challenges to his conclusions about Shakespeare's attitude towards publication.
4. Anthony B. Dawson and Paul Yachnin, *The Culture of Playgoing in Shakespeare's England: A Collaborative Debate* (Cambridge: Cambridge University Press, 2001); Annabel Patterson, *Shakespeare and the Popular Voice* (Oxford: Blackwell, 1989).
5. Peter Thomson, "Clowns, Fools and Knaves: Stages in the Evolution of Acting," in *The Cambridge History of British Theatre*, vol. 1, ed. Jane Milling and Peter Thomson (Cambridge: Cambridge University Press, 2004), pp. 407–23.
6. Joel Schechter (ed.), *Popular Theatre: A Sourcebook* (London: Routledge, 2003), p. 3. See also Richard Beadle, "Masks, Mimes and Miracles: Medieval English Theatricality and its Illusions," in *From Script to Stage in Early Modern England*, ed. Peter Holland and Stephen Orgel (Basingstoke: Palgrave, 2004), pp. 32–42.
7. See David Wiles, *Shakespeare's Clown* (Cambridge: Cambridge University Press, 1987), and Scott McMillin and Sally-Beth MacLean, *The Queen's Men and Their Plays* (Cambridge: Cambridge University Press, 1998).
8. Cited in Peter Holland, "Theatre Without Drama: Reading REED," in Holland and Orgel, *From Script to Stage*, pp. 43–67, p. 59.
9. Carolyn Sale, "Slanderous Aesthetics and the Woman Writer: the Case of *Hole v. White*," in Holland and Orgel, *From Script to Stage*, pp. 181–94.
10. Robert Weimann, *Shakespeare and the Popular Tradition in the Theater*, ed. Robert Schwartz (Baltimore: Johns Hopkins University Press, 1978), p. 5.
11. Enid Welsford, *The Fool: His Social and Literary History* (London: Faber and Faber, 1935).
12. *Ibid.*, p. 11.
13. Stern, *Making Shakespeare*, p. 64.
14. S. L. Bethell, *Shakespeare and the Popular Dramatic Tradition* (London: King and Staples, 1944); C. L. Barber, *Shakespeare's Festive Comedy: A Study of Dramatic*

Form and its Relation to Social Custom (Princeton, NJ: Princeton University Press, 1959); François Laroque, *Shakespeare's Festive World: Elizabethan Seasonal Entertainment and the Professional Stage*, trans. Janet Lloyd (Cambridge: Cambridge University Press, 1991).

15. Cited in Weimann, *Shakespeare and the Popular Tradition*, p. 27.
16. C. L. Barber, *Shakespeare's Festive Comedy: A Study of Dramatic Form and its Relation to Social Custom* (Princeton, NJ: Princeton University Press, 1959).
17. See Robert Weimann, *Shakespeare and the Popular Tradition in the Theater: Studies in the Social Dimension of Dramatic Form and Function*, ed. Robert Schwartz (Baltimore: Johns Hopkins University Press, 1978).
18. David Bevington, *From "Mankind" to Marlowe* (Cambridge, MA: Harvard University Press, 1962).
19. Douglas A. Brooks, *From Playhouse to Printing House: Drama and Authorship in Early Modern England* (Cambridge: Cambridge University Press, 2000) argues that the same documents undermine Janet Clare's emphasis on censorship as a factor for playwrights; the combined presence and scarcity of such allusions makes it hard to generalize categorically. On antitheatricality and censorship, see my "Theatre and Controversy, 1572–1603," in Milling and Thomson, *Cambridge History*, pp. 242–63 and works there referenced.
20. Cited in Annabel Patterson, *Shakespeare and the Popular Voice* (Oxford: Blackwell, 1989), p. 9.
21. *Ibid.*, p. 85.
22. *Ibid.*, p. 69.
23. The first two quotations come from Patterson's paraphrase, the last from Barton herself as quoted by Patterson, *ibid.*, pp. 89–90.
24. *Ibid.*, p. 91.
25. I am indebted to musicologist Ellen Harris on this point.
26. On the local in popular theatre, see David Meyer, "Towards a Definition of Popular Theatre," in *Western Popular Theatre*, ed. David Meyer and Kenneth Richards (London: Methuen, 1977), pp. 257–77, and Schechter, *Popular Theatre*; on Ludgate iconography, see Stern, *Making Shakespeare*, p. 11.
27. Meyer, "Towards a Definition of Popular Theatre," p. 263.
28. On the association of popular theatre (itself an eighteenth-century French phrase) with twentieth-century "democratic, proletarian, and politically progressive theatre," see Schechter, *Popular Theatre*, p. 5 and throughout; for many practitioners this conflation seems enabling, although skeptics might query whether such work is what "the people" enjoy or choose to attend.
29. Stern, *Making Shakespeare*, p. 62. Andrew Gurr and Roslyn Lander Knutson are among the foremost authorities on the company, repertory, and material conditions of the theatre: see his *The Shakespearean Stage, 1574–1642* (Cambridge: Cambridge University Press, 1992) and *Playgoing in Shakespeare's England* (Cambridge: Cambridge University Press, 2004), and her *Playing Companies and Commerce in Shakespeare's Time* (Cambridge: Cambridge University Press, 2001), as well as the essays in Milling and Thomson, *Cambridge History*; John D. Cox and David Scott Kastan (eds.), *A New History of Early English Drama* (New York: Columbia University Press, 1997); and David Scott Kastan (ed.), *A Companion to Shakespeare* (Oxford: Blackwell, 1999).

30. Peter Thomson, "Conventions of Playwriting," in *Shakespeare: An Oxford Guide*, ed. Stanley Wells and Lena Cowen Orlin (Oxford: Oxford University Press, 2003), pp. 44–54, p. 45.

31. Building on Peter W. M. Blayney's groundbreaking studies of the London book trade, see Brooks, *From Playhouse to Printing House*; Lukas Erne, *Shakespeare as Literary Dramatist* (Cambridge: Cambridge University Press, 2003); Zachary Lesser, *Renaissance Drama and the Politics of Publication: Readings in the Early English Book Trade* (Cambridge: Cambridge University Press, 2004), and the essays by Blayney ("The Publication of Playbooks") and Heidi Brayman Hackel ("'Rowne' of its Own: Printed Drama in Early Libraries") in Cox and Kastan, *New History*. On the First Folio specifically, see Peter Blayney, *The First Folio of Shakespeare* (Washington, D.C.: Folger Publications, 1991) and Anthony James West, *The Shakespeare First Folio: The History of the Book. Volume 1: An Account of the First Folio based on its Sales and Prices, 1623–2000* (Oxford: Clarendon Press, 2001).

32. Douglas Bruster and Robert Weimann, *Prologues to Shakespeare's Theatre: Performance and Liminality in Early Modern Drama* (London: Routledge, 2004), p. 107.

33. On popular literary genres, see Diana E. Henderson and James Siemon, "Reading Vernacular Literature," in Kastan, *A Companion to Shakespeare*, pp. 206–22, and the works cited therein.

34. Lori Humphrey Newcomb, "The Triumphs of Time: The Fortunate Readers of Robert Greene's *Pandosto*," in Brown and Marotti, *Texts and Cultural Change*, pp. 95–123, pp. 96–9.

35. Margaret Ezell, *Social Authorship and the Advent of Print* (Baltimore, Johns Hopkins University Press, 1999); Julie Stone Peters, *Theatre of the Book 1480–1880: Print, Text, and Performance in Europe* (Oxford: Clarendon Press, 2000).

36. E. K. Chambers, *William Shakespeare: A Study of Facts and Problems*, 2 vols. (Oxford: Clarendon Press, 1930), I, 544; Gerald Eades Bentley, *Shakespeare and Jonson: Their Reputations in the Seventeenth Century Compared* (Chicago: University of Chicago Press, 1945), p. 41.

37. Patterson, *Shakespeare and the Popular Voice*, p. 92.

38. Cited in Stern, *Making Shakespeare*, p. 21, p. 29. Scaffolders could afford a seat.

39. Erne, *Shakespeare as Literary Dramatist*, pp. 1–2.

40. Brian Vickers, *Shakespeare, Co-Author* (Oxford: Clarendon Press, 2002), p. 6.

41. See Bruster and Weimann, *Prologues to Shakespeare's Theatre*, p. 83; Brooks, *From Playhouse to Printing House*; Peters, *Theatre of the Book*.

42. Erne, *Shakespeare as Literary Dramatist*, p. 15, pp. 250–51.

43. A. R. Braunmuller, "Shakespeare's Fellow Dramatists," in Wells and Orlin, *Shakespeare: An Oxford Guide*, pp. 55–66, p. 56.

44. Bentley, *Shakespeare and Jonson*, p. 45.

45. West, *The Shakespeare First Folio*, p. 6, p. 2.

46. *Ibid.*, p. 7.

47. See Paulina Kewes, "Between the 'Triumvirate of Wit' and the Bard: The English Dramatic Canon, 1660–1720," in Brown and Marotti, *Texts and Cultural Change*, pp. 200–21. See also W. B. Worthen with Peter Holland, *Theorizing Practice: Redefining Theatre History* (Basingstoke: Palgrave, 2003), especially the introduction, which illustrates more theoretically aware developments in theatre history.

2

PETER HOLLAND

Shakespeare abbreviated

> *Polonius.* This is too long.
> *Hamlet.* It shall to the barber's, with your beard.
> (*Hamlet*, 2.2.501–2)

> A heavily condensed version of Hamlet, still with Shakespeare's text,
> still with the same story line – but speeded up. Now there's
> no need to sit through the full 4 hours!
> (Gail from Surrey, UK, on Tom Stoppard's *The
> Fifteen Minute Hamlet*, on amazon.co.uk)

Henry IV in Kent

On 27 February 1623, Edward Dering noted in his "Book of expenses" a payment of 4 shillings to "Mr Carington for writing out the play of King Henry IV" at a rate of 1½ pence per sheet.[1] Edward, then a young man of twenty-five, recently widowed, was living at his family home in Surrenden in Kent and had a passion for plays. He regularly went to the theatre in London and caught performances by companies on tour in Kent. He bought plays at an extraordinary rate: over fifty a year, including, on 5 December 1623, the first recorded purchases of the Shakespeare First Folio as well as a copy of the *Works* of Ben Jonson. He also organized amateur productions at his home, often buying multiple copies of a play for the purpose, casting other members of his family and neighbours and their servants, including, for a proposed production of John Fletcher's *The Spanish Curate*, "Jack of the buttery."

But the payment to the rector of the nearby parish of Wootton for copying out *Henry IV* was different. Dering could have bought a number of copies of the fifth quarto of Shakespeare's *Henry IV Part 1*, published in 1613, or of the only published version of *Henry IV Part 2*. He certainly had at least one of each of these books. He chose not to buy more. He chose, too, not to produce one or the other play. Instead he saw the two plays as parts of a single whole and created his own version of both plays, conflating them into a single work, cutting scenes and characters and whole sections of the plot completely, adding a few bridge passages and adjustments consequent on the cuts or the problems of the printed texts, making a new, briefer, different Shakespeare play.

Edward Dering was a wealthy gentleman, the eldest son of Sir Anthony Dering and himself made a baronet by King Charles I in 1627. Perhaps, then, his adaptation of the two parts of *Henry IV* for performance at his country house is not exactly "popular culture." As so often, the boundaries of the category will slide according to the formulations and constructions for each of the two words. *Part 1* had at the very least proved itself remarkably popular with a reading public, as the mere fact of reaching a fifth edition by 1613 attests. *Part 2* seems to have been significantly less popular in print. But Falstaff and, from *Part 2*, Ancient Pistol had rapidly become remarkably potent figures in the cultural imagination.

From a number of perspectives the narrative of the two parts can easily be seen as cohering into a single whole, forming the central diptych of the four plays that construct Shakespeare's history cycle from the reign of Richard II to that of Henry V and charting Henry IV's defeat of the rebels and the crowning of his son as Henry V. But it is one that the theatre has by and large proved remarkably uninterested in creating. Augustin Daly, perhaps the most success-ful American producer of popular and spectacular Shakespeare at the end of the nineteenth century, conflated the two plays and published the results but, running out of money for the costumes, Daly abandoned the production itself, planned for New York in 1896.

More successfully and certainly more pragmatically as part of an attempt to remake Shakespeare into popular culture, John Barton created a three-part drama out of the two *Henry IV* plays and *Henry V* for the Royal Shakespeare Company's Theatregoround project, touring in 1969–70 and playing in London at the Theatregoround Festival at the Roundhouse in 1970. A thoughtful attempt by the RSC to take their work out of the grand venues of the Royal Shakespeare Theatre in Stratford-upon-Avon and the Aldwych Theatre in London's West End in order to find different, younger audiences, Theatregoround offered energized productions with minimal sets (to make touring easy and to increase the range of possible venues). Barton's text consisted of "The Battle of Shrewsbury" (ninety-five minutes long), "The Rejection of Falstaff" (seventy-five minutes), and an eighty-minute version of *Henry V* as "The Battle of Agincourt," with the first two parts usually being played together as a single evening show. Performing mostly one-night stands in schools, colleges, and town halls as well as theatres in towns that had never hosted the RSC and some of the new regional theatres of the postwar expan-sion (like the Nuffield Theatre in Southampton), Theatregoround deliberately sought to redefine professional Shakespeare (then rapidly vanishing from regional repertory) as a central part of popular culture rather than a high-cultural product which required the lengthy travel and high expenditure of a visit to Stratford-upon-Avon or London. Barton's version – with its adroit use of Shakespeare's own source, the anonymous *Famous Victories of Henry the Fifth*, a play which is fun in performance without in any way demanding to be seen as a part of high culture – is brilliantly successful in its resisting the popular image of Shakespeare drama (and especially Shakespeare's historical drama) as drearily long and dull.

But Dering's version is distinctly unusual, and I want to align it in this chapter with moments in the history of Shakespeare reception and performance where similar extensive abbreviation refashions Shakespeare plays outside the contemporary conventions, in varying kinds of assumed and actual relations to varying historical and geographical constructions of popular culture. Abbreviated Shakespeare becomes a deliberate intervention in a history of cultural reception that negotiates concepts of high/low and popular/elite cultural formations, often, though not always, as a means of burlesque of cultural pretension. It also constructs a history of an emerging concept of Shakespeare himself, for, for Dering and others, an author-function is effectively invisible. Many abbreviations redefine genre: *Hamlet* abbreviated in the late twentieth century is apparently no longer a tragedy, as "Gail from Surrey," in her comment on the amazon website, announces, "I never thought Hamlet could be funny, until I saw it condensed." They also move Shakespeare outside the conventional spaces of Shakespearean performance: abbreviated Shakespeare is often to be found in and created for fairs and fayres, as well as for performance on a double-decker bus and a terrace outside the National Theatre, London. Most particularly, abbreviated Shakespeare makes widely varying assumptions about what its audiences know of/about Shakespeare and what they assume "Shakespeare" to be, turning lengthy verse-drama into highlights and famous quotations, narrowed narratives and sentimentalized action, often recreating a memory of the agonies of the schoolroom and even more frequently acting as an emphatic sign of the audience's alienation from forms of high-cultural social approval.

Edward Dering's abbreviation, whatever its similarities to the texts that Daly and Barton created, had no such function. One might read it simply as a transfer of a metropolitan success to the context of early modern provincial gentry entertainment. But the nature of its abbreviation, the kind of narrative it chose to cull out of the two plays, could also be seen as an act of deliberate or unconscious political analysis. Whatever the popular importance of Falstaff and Prince Hal in 1622, Dering's version was far less concerned with the former's exploits and the latter's reformation and far more concerned with the defeat of the rebels and the death of the monarch. His *Henry IV* is a political drama of rule and rebellion, not a family drama of princely education nor a subversive drama of the comic commentary on political ambition. If Dering's wish to keep the cast size small was the primary impetus behind the decision to put the Gadshill robbery mostly offstage, the effect was to minimize the story of Falstaff more than any other stage version of the plays.

Dering's is also a version that places its emphasis on *Part 1* and turns to *Part 2* only as needed to end its action. George W. Williams and G. Blakemore Evans calculate that Dering cut only 11 percent of *Part 1* (347 lines out of 2,968) while cutting about 75 percent of *Part 2* (2,374 out of 3,180).[2] Dering's abbreviation reaches Part 2 only towards the end of his Act 4 – and it may be a sign of the cultural placing of the adaptation as the work of an educated gentleman that Dering divides his play into acts and scenes within a classical five-act structure, where the only published versions of the two plays had no act or scene divisions. Only two scenes of *Part 1* were entirely omitted (2.1 and 4.4, both removed to eliminate minor characters completely); only a few scenes of *Part 2* remain (the response of Northumberland to the death of Hotspur, the King's final illness, the rejection of Falstaff and a single comic scene of Falstaff and Mrs. Quickly).

Statistics only confuse. It may be easier to think of Dering's version of *Part 1* as significantly more complete than the versions usually performed in modern productions – and hence his text as whole longer than the playing texts in contemporary theatre, making for a long evening for the spectators in Kent. Almost all modern productions cut their Shakespeare texts, often extensively. *Cymbeline*, for instance, is often cut by anything up to a thousand lines. Other long plays, like *Richard III* or *Hamlet*, popular though they may be with audiences, are usually performed, including in productions by major companies like the RSC, in versions that freely and substantially cut lines, speeches, characters, and scenes. Kenneth Branagh's film version of *Hamlet* (1996) was made, at the backers' insistence, in two versions, one running 242 minutes (the full-text version Branagh wanted to make) and the other abbreviating it to what was assumed to be a more marketable 150 minutes simply by cutting and re-editing (with no shots taken specifically for that version). The reasonable assumption was that audiences would not come to a four-hour film of Shakespeare (and hence that it would not prove popular) or that, if they did come, most would be bored. The former proved surprisingly incorrect, though the film probably still lost money, and the second unsurprisingly accurate. But the backers' construction of a model for popular reception of Shakespeare had generated the need to reduce text to what the hypothesized audience would accept as tolerable proportions.

One aspect of the topic of this chapter that I shall not be pursuing is the radical abbreviation of Shakespeare plays for film. Branagh's *Hamlet* is remarkably unusual in its commitment to a full-text version. By comparison, the text for his film of *Love's Labour's Lost* (2000) used approximately 25 percent of the play's lines, partly because of the time taken with large-scale musical numbers using songs by Irving Berlin, George Gershwin, Cole Porter, and others and partly through a determination to have a running time well below two hours (released at ninety-three minutes). This meant that, for instance, though the "pageant of the nine worthies," the show-within-the-play in Act 5, was filmed, the release print carried only a performance of "There's no business like show business," while the DVD has the pageant as a bonus extra deleted scene. Signally unsuccessful and both a critical and box office disaster, Branagh's *Love's Labour's Lost* may seem to represent the opposite extreme of the abbreviation of the play from his *Hamlet* but such substantial reduction of the spoken text is frequent, even close to normative for film. By its nature film resists being word-heavy (early Tarantino being a striking exception) and Shakespeare plays have almost always been heavily cut for filming. Precisely because this degree of reduction is so much a fundamental feature of the form, like the lesser degree that is normative for contemporary theatre performance, I shall not be concerned with it.

Hamlet in Germany

Though sometimes assumed to be the earliest Shakespeare adaptation (let alone abbreviation), Dering's collapsing of *Henry IV* into one play was antedated by the first versions of Shakespeare plays to be performed by the English Comedians playing across continental Europe. These troupes, initially groups of English actors (Fynes Morison, an Elizabethan traveler, called them "some of our cast and despised stage-players"[3]), soon became mixed companies of English with German and Dutch performers and later wholly non-English groups, though still often managed by Englishmen. Their performance language altered too, from English through a polyglottal mixture and general linguistic flexibility to vernacular texts: in 1602 one troupe was in Münster playing comedies in English but with their clown performing in German to cover Act-breaks and costume changes; one of Robert Browne's company, Thomas Sackville, played his character of John Posset in Dutch while in the Netherlands and in German when the troupe moved on to Wolfenbüttel. Certainly, by the early seventeenth century some troupes were performing wholly in German and, though still performing as "English Comedians," trading on their tradition and reputation, there was little English about them. The actors were also dancers and musicians and singers, talented performers who could and would do anything. Though most troupes were small (there were eleven in the company at Münster), John Spencer's group played to the Emperor in Regensburg in 1613 on a specially constructed large stage and numbered nineteen actors and fifteen musicians.

Many of the plays the English Comedians performed were adaptations or rethinkings of the most popular plays from the London stage, not because their audiences were eager to see the triumphs of the London theatre, as Dering's cast and spectators may have been, but because they were good plots that were adaptable and effective. Among other plays, there were performances of (versions of) *Titus Andronicus, The Merchant of Venice, King Lear, Romeo and Juliet, The Taming of the Shrew, A Midsummer Night's Dream, Julius Caesar*, and *Hamlet*. At no point do any of the performances or the published versions of the adaptations mention Shakespeare's name. Where in England by the early seventeenth century Shakespeare's name was a marketing device for the sale of playtexts (hence its appearing on the title pages of plays not by Shakespeare), in Germany the play functioned as a form of entertainment disjunct from a concept of authorship. If some among the company knew the identity of the playwright whose work they were abbreviating, audiences certainly did not. Shakespeare was a resource as a collection of plot-materials, narratives out of which a new drama that is somewhere between English and German/Dutch, defined by Bosman as "intertheatre,"[4] might be made. Difficult to date, the surviving versions were often not printed until later: though a *Titus Andronicus* adaptation was printed in 1620 and companies had performed their own versions of the workers' play of "Pyramus and Thisbe" from *A Midsummer Night's Dream* by that date, the earliest printed German version of the rehearsal and performance of "Pyramus," Andreas Gryphius's *Master Peter Squentz* (= Shakespeare's Peter Quince), appeared in 1660; players performed a German comedy of *The Jew of Venice* in 1611 but the earliest manuscripts to survive, with the play now called *The Well-Spoken Judgment of a Female Student*, were probably written eighty years later in connection with court performances at Dresden.

Professional German and Dutch theatre at this period had barely begun. The touring companies could not have found purpose-built playhouses as they traveled but performed in town squares and inn yards, tennis-courts and palaces, on temporary structures created anywhere an audience might be found. The earliest plays have the quality of variety show, demonstrations of performance skills (acting, clowning, singing, dancing, and other musical numbers), that characterize certain major strands of English theatre before the early modern period. They are also short. *Hamlet* was performed by John Green's company at Dresden in 1626 but the only German adaptation to survive, *Der Bestrafte Brudermord (Fratricide Punished)*, probably performed before 1695, is one-fifth the length of Shakespeare's play, and the same principle of approximately 80 percent reduction can be seen in a number of other abbreviations and rewritings for this performance context. Quite what text the author(s) of *Fratricide Punished* knew is unclear. He/they might have used any of the published Shakespeare texts: the first quarto of 1603, itself usually regarded as some kind of abbreviation, perhaps for touring, of a longer, earlier Shakespeare text; the second quarto of 1604, announced on its title page as "Newly imprinted and enlarged to almost as much againe as it was"; or the Folio of 1623. The author(s) might have known a pre-Shakespearean version or some post-Shakespearean adaptation. The result is a play too often seen only in some vexed relationship to its probable Shakespearean origins, as in the major revival by William Poel in Oxford and London in 1924 as part of Poel's attempt to recreate, for an educated audience, the performance conditions of early modern theatre; the audience in 1924 found the production, unintentionally, hysterically funny, with one critic calling it "funnier than any burlesque on Hamlet that one can recall, with the solitary exception of Gilbert's much less primitive *Rosencrantz and Guildenstern.*"[5]

Transposed to a sophisticated theatre, *Fratricide Punished* might well be received as parodic but we can see it as a successful piece of popular theatre, for an audience less concerned with the philosophical musings of a neurotic aristocrat than with the entertainment of clowns and comedy. There is no playing-time here for introspection and only one of Hamlet's soliloquies is kept, deriving from "Now might I do it pat" (3.2.73–96), with Hamlet's refusal to stab Claudius at prayer now a carefully articulated moral act: "But pause, Hamlet! Why do you wish to take his sins upon yourself? I shall permit him to say his prayer, and I shall now depart, granting him his life. But at another time I shall surely exact my revenge."[6] After a short prologue for Night and the Furies, neatly setting out the drama's back-story, *Fratricide Punished* moves swiftly through the Shakespeare plot, its prose quickly substituting for Shakespeare's slower-moving, densely imaginative poetry. There is, though, ample room for comic additions. The frightened sentry not only sees the Ghost but has his ears supernaturally boxed. This mad Ophelia shares with Shakespeare's the release of sexual desire but is now fixated on the ever-retreating Phantasmo, a clown courtier adapted from Osric but with a more substantial role, for one major cause of the success of the English Comedians and their successors was the work of their clown roles, like John Green's Nobody or the famous character of Pickleherring, whose role in *The Merchant* adaptation, full of dirty jokes and impro-derived by-play, is one of the largest in the play. If we cannot read *Fratricide Punished* without reading it against *Hamlet*, measuring its differences usually as failures and inadequacies, we also to have to see it as a text whose brevity and form is a direct response to a performance context that had no knowledge of a complex, psychologized drama of the family and geopolitics. Not lesser but different, its abbreviation speaks of a culture of popular theatre that was unmarked by the ponderous length of later German or earlier English forms.

Illegal Shakespeare

At exactly the same time that some at least of the work of the English Comedians was being created for the new audience for popular theatre across continental Europe, the state's closure of the theatres in England moved some performances into private productions in country houses and into public spaces like fairs or other venues where brief extracts from pre-Commonwealth plays might be performed. These drolls, published in 1662 as *The Wits* with a second volume in 1673, included snippets from a number of plays by Beaumont and Fletcher, one by Jonson (*The Alchemist*), and two by Shakespeare: Hamlet's meeting with the gravediggers and a Falstaff dramaticule called "The Bouncing Knight," derived from *Henry IV Part 1*. Where Dering had underemphasized Falstaff, the droll creates a mini-plot out of the Gadshill robbery and the Battle of Shrewsbury. The published text's table of contents identifies the source-plays for "the several Droll-Humours" (not always accurately: "The Bouncing Knight" does not come from *Edward IV*) but not the playwrights.

Often performed surreptitiously – Francis Kirkman, the publisher of the second volume, writes that these "pieces of Plays" were "all that we could divert our selves with ... and that but by stealth too, and under pretence of Rope-dancing or the like" – the drolls were created, Kirkman claimed, by Robert Cox, "not only the principal actor but also the contriver and author of most of these farces," and played on tour "in halls and taverns" and in London at the ostensibly closed playhouses like the Red Bull as well as at the great fairs like Bartholomew Fair and at temporary locations for street theatre ("on several mountebanks' stages at Charing Cross, Lincoln's Inn Fields and other places").[7] Cox himself is a shadowy figure but the fact that he was the author of a number of original drolls, four of which were published in 1656, the year after his death, as *Actaeon and Diana* makes Kirkman's attribution probable.

More significant than authorship is Kirkman's analysis of these shows. He noted, admiringly, that at these fragmentary performances (or performances of fragments),

> these being all that was permitted us, great was the confluence of the auditors; and these small things were as profitable and as great get-pennies to the actors as any of our late famed plays. I have seen the Red Bull playhouse, which was a large one, so full, that as many went back for want of room as had entered, and as meanly as you may now think of these drolls, they were then acted by the best comedians then and now in being.[8]

The drolls of *The Wits* are a response to an audience deprived of public theatre performance by the state but still wanting to see parts at least of the stock plays that had become familiar staples of London's repertory theatre. Filling the Red Bull is outstanding box office, even for occasional performance, and Kirkman conjoins here the financial success and the artistic one, identifying the outstanding quality of the actors. Yet he also marks a temporal shift. By 1673, more than a decade after the King's restoration and with the professional theatres of London flourishing in an entirely new mode (with spectacular scenery and female performers), the drolls might be seen by his middle-class readers as trivial. They also represent the location of drama outside theatre (or inside a theatre no longer functioning), a sign of a displacement into a community of performance in which theatre's social function is radically different from its normative (i.e. pre-interregnum) placing. Theatre in fairs or street platforms, performed by "several strolling players, fools and fiddlers, and the mountebanks' zanies," as the title page to the second volume of *The Wits* (1673) describes them (however inaccurate such a description of the cast might be), suggests a resistance both to the state's denial of performance and to the forms of professionalism (both location and personnel) that the institutions of early modern theatre had achieved.

The playlets can only be social gestures towards the forms and practices of the theatre from which they were derived but which were now closed. They can also barely be seen as actions with narrative plots. The half-dozen pages of "The Grave-Makers" (i.e. *Hamlet* 5.1) are exactly what Kirkman's or Cox's summary describes: "While he is making the grave, for a Lady that drowned herself, Hamlet and his friend interrupt him with several questions."[9] Such scenes resonantly echo the complete texts to which they witness but they also signify that these drolls are aimed, at least in part, at an audience that is fully aware of their sources.

The second volume of *The Wits* included a third example of Shakespeare abbreviated but one that had already been published by Kirkman in 1661. *The Merry Conceited Humours of Bottom the Weaver* is a more substantial abbreviation (if that is not an oxymoron) than "The Bouncing Knight." Nearly three times as long as that abbreviated *Henry IV Part 1*, the play reduces the multiple plots of Shakespeare's play simply by choosing to ignore everything irrelevant to the workers and their experiences. There is no sign of the lovers, and Theseus and Hippolyta, left unnamed as Duke and Duchess, appear only as audience for "Pyramus and Thisbe," along with two lords, who are given Lysander's and Demetrius's comments on the workers' play. Tiny fragments of the conflict between Oberon and Titania are left in, sufficient to provide the explanation for Bottom's transformation. Once "Pyramus and Thisbe" is over the play ends. What is left is a comic farce lasting less than an hour, simplified carefully and purposively to make a drama for performance by a cast of at least eleven, with some doubling thoughtfully noted so that Oberon and Titania double as Duke and Duchess, Pugg (= Puck) as a lord, and three of the workers – Snout, Snug, and Starveling – "likewise may present three fairies."[10]

The text of the play as it was reprinted in *The Wits* in 1673 gave no clue why the play was both much longer and required a larger cast than the other drolls, too substantial a piece for the performance conditions of the rest of the collection. But the 1661 edition states that the play "hath been often publicly acted by some of his majesty's comedians" (presumably a reference to pre-Commonwealth performances) "and, lately, privately presented by several apprentices for their harmless recreation." The publishers announce their text as ideal for amateur performance, a play "which we know may be easily acted and may be now as fit for private recreation as formerly it hath been for public."[11] Amateur performance by a group of apprentices is remarkably like the context within which *A Midsummer Night's Dream* is now most often to be found, as the school play. The emphasis here is on theatre as harmless fun for workers, as it is for the workers within the play, for this text mirrors performers and performed in complex ways, imaging its own performance. Barely a year after the theatres had reopened this might be a legitimate anxiety but it is also about theatre's being recreational for the performers rather than for the audience, the pleasure of making theatre taking precedence over the pleasure of watching it as a form of popular cultural consumption of drama. There can here be no question about the location of this text within popular culture, its class-basis firmly demarcated as apprentices.

Shortened dreams

Bottom the Weaver is a first step in the history in England of *A Midsummer Night's Dream* as adapted play. Its fortunes over the next century chart a range of responses to the complexities of the play, a recognition that what had to be performed could only be a part, an abbreviated segment, for, though the full play was performed in London in the 1660s, it was not a success again at such length on the professional stage until well into the nineteenth century. I use it as an example of a play modulating between different concepts of popular culture across the period from 1660 to the mid eighteenth century.

By the 1690s, as the United Company, the only professional theatre company in London, searched for audiences, it took the dangerous step of mounting spectacular productions, full of enormous sets and extravagant machines, with large-scale musical numbers. These "semi-operas," as they are usually known, were a desperate marketing device and a catastrophic failure. *The Fairy Queen*, the adaptation of *A Midsummer Night's Dream* probably written by Thomas Betterton, cost over £3,000 to mount, a vast sum (a modern equivalence might be well over a million pounds) which could not possibly be recouped. The playtext was cut by half so that there would be time for the massive masque-like sequences at the end of each Act written by Henry Purcell and stretching the scenic and performance resources of the theatre to the limit. The cuts from Shakespeare are often intelligently compensated for and balanced by material in Purcell's settings so that, for instance, Titania's account in 2.1 of the disordered seasons consequent on her dispute with Oberon becomes reversed in the ordered pageant of the seasons in Purcell's scene in Act 4, a parade for Oberon's birthday. The result is a complex and coherent drama, play, and masque carefully interwoven into a whole.

The Fairy Queen is not much concerned with Bottom and his co-workers and "Pyramus and Thisbe" is entirely eliminated. This is Shakespeare transformed into an operatic form that is increasingly defined as high culture and there is no concern with popular cultural forms either within the play or in its reception. Indeed, the text carefully ensures that the narrowed social range of its concerns privileges the aristocratic culture in the play. Where Shakespeare's Theseus is remarkably imperceptive, failing to know that his joking comment "Lovers, to bed; 'tis almost fairy time" (5.1.357) will be swiftly followed by the arrival of the fairies in his palace, Betterton's Theseus is educated out of his error. No sooner has he scorned the lovers' account of their night in the wood than Oberon appears, announcing that the music Theseus can hear, " 'Tis fairy music, sent by me / To cure your incredulity. / All was true the lovers told. / You shall stranger things behold," before he reveals a "transparent prospect of a Chinese garden, the architecture, the trees, the plants, the fruit, the birds, the beasts quite different from what we have in this part of the world."[12] The only group excluded from this vision is the workers. This reassuring vision of the hierarchies of Restoration society is offered only to those gentry capable of comprehending it both on stage and in the audience.

Purcell's work did, however, make a transition to an unequivocally popular cultural location, being performed in 1711 as a puppet-show performed by the marionettes of Martin Powell, and four human actors in the Little Piazza at Covent Garden. But *A Midsummer Night's Dream* soon became a resource for contemporary parody. Richard Leveridge's *The Comick Masque of Pyramus and Thisbe* (1716) used the playlet not to mock Bottom but as a means of mocking the new fashion for Italian opera and events in recent plays. In 1745 John Frederick Lampe took up the same part of Shakespeare's play for the same purpose, this time mocking Handel. Lampe, for the first time in this stage history, makes clear that his text is taken from Shakespeare, using Shakespeare's cultural authority as the support for his text. Shakespeare becomes a convenient basis for cultural opposition, bourgeois mockery of a fashionable high-cultural form, played to the same audience that flocked to the operas.

A Midsummer Night's Dream's ambivalent position in relation to opera (nearly turned into one in *The Fairy Queen*, used to mock opera by Leveridge and Lampe) would continue in David Garrick's version of the play as *The Fairies* in 1755. *The Fairies* is full-scale eighteenth-century opera, using barely 500 of Shakespeare's 2,100 lines, adding innumerable songs and through-sung with full-scale recitatives. Garrick cut Bottom and the workers completely, eliminating almost all of Shakespeare's fifth Act: only two and a half of its 420 lines survive. This is *A Midsummer Night's Dream* refocused on the lovers, not the workers. Throughout his career, try as he might, Garrick could not make anything approximating to full texts of Shakespeare's comedies work commercially on stage. The tragedies posed no problem but the comedies were sedulously resisted. *The Fairies* was his first attempt to find a solution. He followed it with the greatly successful abbreviation of *The Taming of the Shrew* as *Catherine and Petruchio* (1756), a three-Act afterpiece, designed to be played after a five-act drama. Removing the induction and the complete Tranio plot leaves behind a neat and constricted account of the taming, a drama of male control. Garrick paired this half a play (in length and in what it contained of Shakespeare's multiple action) with an abbreviation of *The Winter's Tale* into another afterpiece, *Florizel and Perdita* (1756), following the lead of Macnamara Morgan's adaptation as *The Sheep-Shearing* (1754) by starting the action halfway through – and after the sixteen-year time-gap – and managing to keep it entirely in Bohemia by bringing Leontes there shipwrecked. The two were regularly played as a double-bill with a prologue making Shakespeare both a shop-sign guaranteeing good quality products ("To draw in customers our bills are spread; / You cannot miss the sign: 'tis Shakespeare's Head") and a "fountainhead divine" from which "For different palates springs a different wine."[13] The "wide gap of time" that Shakespeare charts in *The Winter's Tale* needed abridging to be saleable alcohol:

> The five long acts from which our three are taken
> Stretched out to sixteen years, lay by, forsaken.
> Lest then this precious liquor run to waste,
> 'Tis now confined and bottled for your taste.
> 'Tis my chief wish, my joy, my only plan,
> To lose no drop of that immortal man![14]

Cutting a play in half is then a salvage operation on the principle that half a bottle is better than no wine or that some of the drops can be lost to return others to the stage.

But *A Midsummer Night's Dream* did not work in this guise. Garrick explored the possibility of making the play a full-length five-Act version acceptable to his audiences, and worked with George Colman on such a version before leaving for a grand tour of Europe. The production lasted only one night in November 1763. William Hopkins, the theatre's prompter, noted in his diary: "Upon the whole, never was anything so murdered in the speaking ... Next day it was reported: the performers first sung the audience to sleep and then went to sleep themselves. Fairies pleased – serious parts displeased – comic between both."[15] Recognizing how little had worked, Colman followed the critics' advice and within three days produced a two-act afterpiece, *A Fairy Tale*. After versions centered on Bottom and *The Fairies* centered on the lovers, it was inevitable that the fairies should, sooner or later, become the focus of an abbreviated *Dream*, and Colman cut all the Athenians except as much of Bottom as was needed for the fairy action. At the end of *A Fairy Tale* Puck hauls Bottom offstage still asleep, never, apparently, to be awakened.

These desperate attempts to make the play work commercially, driven by Garrick's commitment to Shakespeare, reached their climax in the tiniest part of the play to be performed onstage. Garrick lost a great deal of money on the Stratford Jubilee of 1769, the first celebration of Shakespeare in his home town, bedevilled by torrential rain and with no play performed at all (though with a horse-race and a costume ball). He recouped by turning the events into an afterpiece, *The Jubilee*, performed at Drury Lane an unprecedented eighty-eight times in a single season. At its climax came a grand procession of Shakespeare's characters and scenes, representing nineteen plays, including *A Midsummer Night's Dream*, consisting simply of "Bottom with ass's head and banner, sixteen fairies with banners, chariot drawn by butterflies, king and queen of the fairies in the chariot" with Garrick's notes suggesting a moment of action: "suppose Bottom and Q. of Fs asleep in the chariot – and K of F drops her eyes with the flower, turns out Bottom and takes his place. Bottom and she awake, etc."[16] It is difficult to abbreviate the play much further.

Singing *Macbeth*

Garrick's versions of Shakespeare were all prepared for Drury Lane, one of the two patent companies, the only theatre companies allowed to perform serious drama, including Shakespeare. In 1809 Robert Elliston, an actor turned manager in the aftermath of the burning down of Drury Lane that year, took over control of the Royal Circus in London and decided to stage a version of *Macbeth* written by J. C. Cross, one that would satisfy both his patrons and the law. Illegitimate Shakespeare, that is, Shakespeare in the theatres outside the patent houses, was necessarily restricted. Since his actors could not perform spoken drama, he advertised the production as "a grand ballet of action, with recitative, founded on *Macbeth*" and published "a full description of the scenery, action, choruses and characters of the ballet ... with ... every information to simplify the plot and enable the visitors of the circus to comprehend this matchless piece of pantomimic and choral performance."[17] Since the actors could not legally speak, they had to depend on action and some singing, mixing mime with rhyming couplets (and with only the witches speaking any lines of Shakespeare other than scenes' final couplets). As a prologue made clear,

> Though not indulged with fullest powers of speech,
> The poet's object we aspire to reach ...
> To prove we keep our duties full in view
> And what we must not *say*, resolve to *do*,
> Convinced that you will deem our zeal sincere,
> Since more by *deeds* than *words* it will appear.[18]

Sheridan, manager of Drury Lane, complained to the Lord Chamberlain but no legal action was taken. Cross's doggerel verse may have protected Elliston from being accused of performing spoken drama. So too did Elliston's adroit use of banners with speeches or titles for scenes written on them (rather like the intertitles of silent film) and his use of music as a means of conveying action and thought, with, for instance, a chorus of spirits explaining what is happening when Macbeth "appears revolving somewhat in his mind."[19]

A huge commercial success – and a major step in the breaking of the patent theatres' monopoly – Elliston's *Macbeth* surprised the critics not least because of the nature of the audience. Though the elite culture's belief was still firmly that Shakespeare's plays were "but little calculated for the multitude,"[20] *The Times* found the packed audience at the Royal Circus to be "altogether as respectable and brilliant as we have ever beheld in the best days of our winter theatres."[21] If commercial success is a mark of popular success, Elliston's *Macbeth* is a fine piece of popular culture. In its attitude to the texts as well as its use of a new form of performance to create that financial triumph, it also strikingly anticipates the cinema's early excitement over Shakespeare, for, from 1899, when a small part of Tree's production of *King John* was filmed, to the end of the silent era, there were hundreds of Shakespeare films, ranging in length from two to over 100 minutes in length, all marked, of necessity, by a radical abbreviation of the language to what could be mouthed by the actors and read off the intertitles. Silent Shakespeare also demonstrates the globalization of this abbreviated Shakespeare for it was comparatively easy to transfer the films across language barriers simply by translating the intertitles, denying the kinds of linguistic otherness that dubbing and subtitles would later manifest. An extraordinary phenomenon and one whose traces are themselves fragmentary – most of the films not having survived – silent Shakespeare would deserve a chapter to itself.[22]

Hamlet abbreviated

Elliston's solution to legal restrictions abbreviated and transformed the play as the sole means of performing it at all in his theatre. But by the late twentieth century, what constitute the reasons for abbreviating Shakespeare? I want to use a specimen group of abbreviated *Hamlets* to stand for the kinds of popular cultural work that abbreviated Shakespeare has recently been intended to achieve.

In 1976 Tom Stoppard's *The Fifteen Minute Hamlet* or, to give it its non-abbreviated title, *The (Fifteen Minute) Dogg's Troupe Hamlet*, received its first performance on the terraces of the National Theatre in London, presented by Ed Berman's fringe company Inter-Action Productions. Originally "written (or rather edited) for performance on a double-decker bus,"[23] – and Stoppard's definition here of editing as an act of writing in abbreviating is significant – the piece was later twice enlarged by additions: first, as *Dogg's Hamlet*, by being combined with his earlier short piece *Dogg's Our Pet* (1971), also written for Berman's company, a brief dramatization of the problem of false perceptions of apparently shared languages from Wittgenstein's *Philosophical Investigations*; then, in 1979, by being linked to Stoppard's transformation of Pavel Kohout's abbreviated *Macbeth* into *Cahoot's Macbeth*.

Like Elliston's, Kohout's version of *Macbeth*, reduced to seventy-five minutes' playing-time with a cast of five, was a response to legal restrictions, in Soviet-controlled Prague in 1977. Prevented from working in theatres, Pavel Landovsky, Kohout and three others formed a "Living-Room Theatre," bringing a show in a suitcase to people's homes in the hopes that thereby they would be able to continue performing without intervention and arrest. As Kohout commented to Stoppard, "I think, [Shakespeare] wouldn't be worried about it, it functions and promises to be not only a solution of our situation but also an interesting theatre event. I adapted the play, of course, but I am sure it is nevertheless Macbeth!"[24] Stoppard's version intersperses his own abbreviation of *Macbeth* with the arrival and comments of a secret policeman, punningly and viciously controlling the performance. The performance of *Macbeth* is here less important than the negotiations between theatre workers and the threatening state, Shakespeare's play only a pretext for that terrifying situation.

Abbreviated *Macbeth* is functional here, a sign of Czech struggles. Stoppard's abbreviated *Hamlet* is little more than a comic display of virtuoso theatre skills, created for Ed Berman's Fun Art Bus, a double-decker converted into a theatre and part of a belated countercultural attempt to move performance out of conventional high-cultural theatre spaces and towards the hypothesized popular culture that radical theatre yearned to engage with. Its eventual first performance, adjacent to the National Theatre, by it but not in it, permitted by that central institution of socially approved theatre, signals its uneasy status. Stoppard's version is clever, witty for what it manages to keep (though there is no room for Fortinbras) and for the extremely compacted two-minute encore, all played "at a shortened version of Elsinore Castle,"[25] but it also depends on a knowledge of a complete text: this is abbreviated *Hamlet* for those who already know *Hamlet*, not for those who might define themselves as excluded from the elitist culture Shakespeare now signifies. Nonetheless, "Gail from Surrey, UK" enjoyed seeing it: "I never thought Hamlet could be funny, until I saw it condensed into 13 minutes – and then in 2 ... With 6 people playing all the characters, it is both a challenge for the actors and a visual spectacle for the audience. Hilarious in every aspect – has to be seen/done to be believed!" Her emphasis on it as a piece of theatre virtuosity, a demonstration of performance skills, suggests its strong echoes of the work of the English Comedians performing, singing, and dancing in early modern Germany.

Where the English Comedians performed in towns during fairs, the most successful modern abbreviated stage Shakespeare began life at one example of those extraordinarily popular pan-American phenomena of cultural nostalgia for an imagined "Merrie England," the "Renaissance Pleasure Faire," this one at Novato, California, in 1981. The Reduced Shakespeare Company's *The Complete Works of William Shakespeare (Abridged)* was directly inspired by Stoppard's *Fifteen Minute Hamlet* and started as a four-person half-hour *Hamlet*. It became a three-person *Hamlet* and then a two-person *Romeo and Juliet*, performed at "fairs, festivals, weddings, bar mitzvahs, car dealership blowouts, shopping mall openings, Young Republican bake sales; no venue was left unsullied."[26] The *Complete Works* version was created for the Edinburgh Festival Fringe in 1987 for a cast of three and toured successfully, ran for nearly nine years at the Criterion Theatre in Piccadilly Circus from 1996, was shown on television and released as audiotape and DVD, as well as a published text, and was the cause of the company's creating further shows, including an abridged Bible and equally condensed Complete History of America.

The Shakespeare show, with *Titus Andronicus* as a cookery lesson, *Othello* as a rap number and the English histories as a sports broadcast, reaches its intermission when there is a sudden realization that they have managed to avoid *Hamlet*, and Adam, one of the cast of three, terrified at the prospect, races for the exit and has to be found and brought back. The *Hamlet* performance, which ends with a rapid forty-five-second encore (less than half the length of

Stoppard's), even more rapid second encore, and then encore in reverse ("Silence is rest the. Thee follow I."), has as its centerpiece the problem of Ophelia. This involves forcing a member of the audience up on stage to scream and, when she fails to scream adequately, getting the whole audience involved in workshopping the "subtext" or "inner monologue."[27] One man plays Ophelia's Ego, which "is flighty, it's confused" and is therefore symbolized by his running "back and forth across the stage in front of her." The front three rows become her "wishy-washy" Id: "So everybody, hands in the air, wave them back and forth, kind of undulate, and say, (*in falsetto*) 'Maybe . . . maybe not . . . maybe . . . maybe not'." The rest of the audience, her "Superego," is divided into three: one section, "the masculine part of Ophelia's brain, the animus," chants "Get thee to a nunnery!"; the second, "the voice of vanity," calls "Paint an inch thick!"; while the third, the voice of modern relevance ("maybe she wants power . . . but she doesn't want to lose her femininity"), cries "Look, cut the crap, Hamlet, my biological clock is ticking and I want babies now!"[28]

On the page it seems ineffective. In performance it is superbly managed and very funny (as I know from the three performances I have seen). In its mockery of modern fake Freudian acting theory and its search for a relevant Shakespeare it is a superbly comic parody of the difficulties posed by Shakespeare in current American acting training and in contemporary American culture. It also has intriguing resonances with the radical experiment of a four-person *Hamlet* developed by Cambridge Experimental Theatre in a 1987 production and the subsequent video *Making Shakespeare*, a production that sought to investigate concepts of subjectivity by refusing to allocate roles to particular performers: any and every actor played each "character" as the performance opened out the text as a collage of voices, denying narrative and creating non-linear theatre.[29] Highly theorized and, for all its brilliance as performance, hardly popular culture, the CET *Hamlet* was a theatrical exploration of critical anxiety about the political complicities of conventional Shakespeare representation – and, at an opposite extreme both of theory and practice, the Reduced Shakespeare Company's workshopped scream works as a subversion of the kinds of assumption about rehearsal and performance, Freud and Stanislavski, gender and relevance, that could be seen as a broadly held cultural perception of the template within which the elite culture's possession of Shakespeare is placed. It also, predictably, wants to dissociate *Hamlet* from that culture in one of the Reduced Shakespeare Company's less successful gags:

> *Adam*. Shakespeare didn't write "Hamlet," did he?
> *Jess*. Of course he did.
> *Adam*. I thought it was a Mel Gibson movie.[30]

The Reduced Shakespeare Company's *Hamlet* uses every cliché of ham acting and stays close to Shakespeare's lines in shortened form, except when Jess cannot manage "To be or not to be":

> To die; to sleep;
> Or just to take a nap and hope you wake up
> In time for dinner because you gotta make guacamole for twelve and
> you just can't take the pressure of this speech!!![31]

As, repeatedly, the show veers from Shakespeare to gags (carefully indicating the moments when the published version leaves Shakespeare by closing quotation marks), so it signs its own controlled refusal to be controlled by the authoritative text, its pleasure in resistance.

Animating abbreviation

If the twentieth-century *Hamlet* examples I have so far used have been marked by their repeated status as parody, it seems especially ironic that the most carefully crafted abbreviations have been driven by the twin aims of respect for Shakespeare and the need to find new Shakespeare audiences among children. Twelve plays were chosen for *Shakespeare: The Animated Tales*, developed by S4C, the Welsh-language TV channel, animated by Russian film-makers working for Soyuzmultfilm, and voiced by major British actors (including many from the "other" RSC), in two series of six first broadcast on UK's Channel 4 in 1992 and 1996. The texts were abbreviated by Leon Garfield, author of *Shakespeare Stories*, a series of short prose narrative adaptations of Shakespeare in the tradition of the *Tales from Shakespeare* by Charles and Mary Lamb and intended for young children.[32] Garfield, required to cut each play to a running time of just under thirty minutes, added brief voice-over links but left all lines spoken by characters as unaltered Shakespeare. The animators used a broad range of techniques: traditional cel animation (e.g. for *Macbeth* and *Othello*), stop-frame animation (e.g. for *The Taming of the Shrew* and *The Tempest*), painting on glass (*Richard III* and *Hamlet*), and watercolor (*As You Like It*). The effects range from superbly detailed movement of the figures in stop-frame work (including Katherine's Medusa-like hair in *Shrew*) to a sequence for Jaques's "Seven Ages of Man" that seems to animate early woodblocks, from the cels that show the thoughts in Macbeth's head bursting into armed men as the head splits apart to the titanic Julius Caesar that dominates the conspirators.

The oil on glass technique used by Natalia Orlova for *Hamlet* was the least familiar to TV audiences. The animators painted an image onto a glass sheet which could be lit from behind, producing a lustrous glow. Before the slow-drying paint had set, parts could be scraped away and repainted for the next frame. It is an irreversible process: unlike cel animation, which produces a huge stack of transparencies, the end of the process of filming glass-painted animation is still only one sheet of glass. Again unlike cel, it cannot move at twenty-four frames per second and each image is shot for a number of frames before dissolving into the next, the result being oddly both fluid and static. The result is consciously painterly. It was also, for *Hamlet*, often deliberately made to echo images from Grigori Kozintsev's Russian film of 1964 and Laurence Olivier's of 1948. The Claudius, for instance, looks strikingly like Basil Sydney in Olivier's film while the vast billowing cloak of the ghost recalls Kozintsev's. The images move in ways that suggest the transposition of camera movement from conventional non-animated feature films. The effect is of a filmed painting, with a distinctly realist representation of action that is capable of intense emotion and, in the fragile transitoriness of its metamorphic method, something embedded in a structure of memory and loss that movingly echoes the play itself.

The effect of the sources in other films and its appearance as painting is also to make the animated *Hamlet* oddly old-fashioned, the novelty of its technique offset by its deep allegiance to traditional views of the play and of how Shakespeare might be understood. Almost sentimental in its tonalities, certainly stereotyping in its characterization, Orlova's *Hamlet* images exactly the reverence of Garfield's abridgement. For, where so many of the abbreviations use Shakespeare as material to consider other aspects of their culture, *The Animated Tales* seek to present Shakespeare, to educate their audience into an appreciation and love of Shakespeare, out of a conviction of Shakespeare as a cultural artifact available to all, not restricted to a narrowly defined social or educated class nor to a narrowly defined form of performance. Screened in dozens of countries (and easily dubbed since animation creates no need for subtitling), *The Animated Tales* is Shakespeare as cultural educational television available to all, Shakespeare in the classroom or, more often, as much in the modern home as Dering's adaptation of *Henry IV* had belonged in his home in a Jacobean country house.

NOTES

1. Laetitia Yeandle, 'The Dating of Sir Edward Dering's Copy of "The History of King Henry the Fourth"', *Shakespeare Quarterly* 37 (1986), 224–26, p. 224.
2. George Walton Williams and Gwynne Blakemore Evans (eds.), *The History of King Henry the Fourth, as revised by Sir Edward Dering, Bart.* (Charlottesville: University Press of Virginia, 1974), p. ix.
3. Ernest Brennecke (ed.), *Shakespeare in Germany 1590–1700* (Chicago: University of Chicago Press, 1964), p. 5.
4. See Anston Bosman, "Renaissance Intertheater and the Staging of Nobody," *ELH* 71 (2004), 559–85 and "History Between Theatres," in *From Performance*

to *Print in Shakespeare's England*, ed. Peter Holland and Stephen Orgel (Basingstoke: Palgrave Macmillan, 2006), pp. 191–207.

5. J. Isaacs (ed.), *William Poel's Prompt Book of "Fratricide Punished"* (London: Society for Theatre Research, 1956), p. xiv.

6. Brennecke, *Shakespeare in Germany*, p. 273.

7. John James Elson (ed.), *The Wits, or Sport upon Sport* (Ithaca NY,: Cornell University Press, 1932, pp. 267–8.

8. *Ibid.*, p. 268.

9. *Ibid.*, p. 111.

10. *Ibid.*, p. 316.

11. *The Merry Conceited Humours of Bottom the Weaver* (London, 1661), sigs. [A]1r–2r.

12. [Thomas Betterton], *The Fairy Queen* (London, 1692), pp. 47, 48.

13. David Garrick, *The Plays*, ed. Harry William Pedicord and Frederick Louis Bergmann, 7 vols. (Carbondale: Southern Illinois University Press, 1980–82), III.223.

14. *Ibid.*, III.225.

15. Quoted by George Winchester Stone, Jr., "*A Midsummer Night's Dream* in the hands of Garrick and Colman," *PMLA* 54 (1939), 467–82, p. 474.

16. Garrick, *Plays*, II.118.

17. See Jane Moody, *The Illegitimate Theatre in London, 1770–1840* (Cambridge: Cambridge University Press, 2000), p. 130; James Cartwright Cross, *The History, Murders, Life and Death of Macbeth* (London, 1809).

18. Quoted in Moody, *Illegitimate Theatre*, pp. 130–31.

19. Quoted in *ibid.*, p. 132.

20. *Theatrical Inquisitor* 1814, quoted in *ibid.*, p. 130.

21. Quoted in *ibid.*, p. 130.

22. See Robert Hamilton Ball, *Shakespeare on Silent Film* (London: Allen & Unwin, 1968) and William Uricchio and Roberta E. Pearson, *Reframing Culture* (Princeton, NJ: Princeton University Press, 1993).

23. Tom Stoppard, *Plays One* (London: Faber and Faber, 1996), p. 141.

24. *Ibid.*, p. 143.

25. Tom Stoppard, *The Fifteen Minute Hamlet* (London: Samuel French Ltd, 1976), p. iii.

26. Jess Borgeson, *et al.*, *The Reduced Shakespeare Company's The Compleat Works of Wllm Shkspr (Abridged)* (New York: Applause Books, 1994), p. 117.

27. *Ibid.*, p. 84.

28. *Ibid.*, pp. 84–89.

29. See Nigel Wheale, 'Scratching Shakespeare: Video-teaching the Bard,' in *Shakespeare in the Changing Curriculum*, ed. Lesley Aers and Nigel Wheale (London: Routledge, 1991), pp. 204–21.

30. Borgeson, *Compleat Works*, p. 59.

31. *Ibid.*, p. 79; see footnote 193, which helpfully provides a recipe for guacamole for twelve.

32. See Leon Garfield, *Shakespeare Stories* (Boston: Houghton Mifflin, 1985) and *Shakespeare Stories II* (Boston: Houghton Mifflin, 1995). On *The Animated Tales*, see Laurie Osborne, "Poetry in Motion: Animating Shakespeare," in *Shakespeare, the Movie*, ed. Lynda E. Boose and Richard Burt (London: Routledge, 1997), pp. 103–20 and "Mixing Media and Animating Shakespeare Tales," in *Shakespeare, the Movie II*, ed. Richard Burt and Lynda E. Boose (London: Routledge, 2003), pp. 140–53.

3

BARBARA HODGDON

Shakespearean stars: stagings of desire

I begin with the desire to see Michael Gambon play Falstaff – a desire initiated by memories of his past performances and fueled by Michael Cordner's description of a South Bank Show's fly-on-the-wall recording of rehearsing *1 Henry IV*'s great tavern scene:

> Gambon [is] playful and full of power ... When recounting how he had dispatched in one fell swoop a posse of nocturnal attackers, he adroitly spears several with his sword, then spins on his foot and immobilizes another with a back-kick, spins again and repeats the trick in a different direction, then kills a few more with his sword before continuing blithely with his narrative. (He has obviously been studying films like *Hero*, *House of Flying Daggers*, and indeed *Kill Bill*.)[1]

Dancing the role, inflecting Falstaff with movements borrowed from Asian warrior figures in recent award-winning films, writing Jet Li, Lucy Liu, or Uma Thurman over "Shakespeare," adapting the part, one might say, to contemporary understanding or popular taste. (Gambon: "I try to move like a dancer. If I had been born again ... I would be a ballet dancer."[2]) Whether or not these moves travel from rehearsal to performance, I anticipate a Falstaff so light on his feet that he makes me want to dance with him, a Falstaff performed by the actor Ralph Richardson dubbed "The Great Gambon" and whom Deborah Warner called "heavenly, super great."[3] A star, yes, but is Gambon a *Shakespearean* star? He has played Macbeth, Othello, King Lear, and Antony, but he probably is better known – in the sense of being "popular" – for *The Singing Detective*'s Philip Marlow (1986), *Inspector Maigret* (1993–94), Lyndon Johnson in *Path to War* (2002), Dumbledore in *Harry Potter and the Prisoner of Azkaban* (2004), or even the voice of the washing machine in a Wisk television commercial. Does the starring role "make" the Shakespearean star actor? Certainly staging the *Henry IV* plays means casting an actor who can masterfully command Falstaff's role, but in the present-day theatrical firmament, as in Newton's or Hubble's expanded universe, there are no fixed Shakespearean stars.

Theatrical history, however, obeys more Ptolemaic thinking. In that sphere, one encounters a more or less finite number of "stars" – outstanding performers of protean skill and exceptional talents who manifest an illusion of "absolute presence" – at times appearing in constellations.[4] And just as physicists can tell a star's temperature from its thermal spectrum, from the light it throws off, what constitutes stardom is calibrated differently in any one historical moment, its "presence" determined in part by the surrounding culture, in particular by the values it accords to and desires from the star performer. Moreover, since stardom looks both forward and back (stars are announced but also recognized retrospectively), is conferred on the very new and on the veteran performer, and folds in on itself in elaborate hauntings, exploring theatrical history's galaxy, reading one history in terms of another, offers one way of discerning intimations of the star phenomenon, stardom, and the star system. How, then, I want to ask, does that history construct the Shakespearean star? Such an investigation straddles a paradox of desires, moves between the historian's desire to uncover the past and the complex mechanisms of fantasy that drive the present-day star phenomenon, the desire to see – even to *know everything about* – an extraordinary actor. Indeed, the very term "Shakespearean star" is misleading, for the idea of the star is associated less with classical theatre than with the rise of modernity and mass communication and with the politics of large-scale industrial cultures: the star is a product, well-paid (and paying) merchandise destined for mass consumption ("Look at me!" say the stars, putting themselves on offer, making commodities of themselves).[5] In such a climate, not only can starring roles make stars of non-stars but such roles are written in hopes of attracting stars to them (if you write it, they will come); financing a production often depends on a star-property's interest and notice of his casting (think Denzel Washington as Brutus in New York's 2005 *Julius Caesar*) can pre-book and sell out a play's run, regardless of the notices.

(Re)seeing Stars

Arguably, Richard Burbage (1568–1619), the leading actor in the Chamberlain's/ King's Men, was the first Shakespearean star: according to his eulogist, who mentions his performances of Hamlet and Lear in particular, he "suit[ed] the person which he seemed to have ... so lively" as to amaze spectators and fellow-actors alike, even to evoke in them a kinesthetic response.[6] And Thomas Middleton writes him into stardom's first heavenly metaphor:

> Astronomers and star-gazers this year
> Write but of four eclipses; five appear,

> Death interposing Burbage; and their staying
> Hath made a visible eclipse of playing.[7]

Middleton's eulogy aside, Burbage achieves stardom as understood today only through a kind of back-formation, for the notion of stardom is alien to early modern thinking: when Shakespeare's company staged *Hamlet*, *Othello*, or *King Lear*, those roles went to Burbage because he was their most celebrated performer. In the early modern universe, a performer's success depended on his status as a sharer, a player who shared the proceeds equally with his fellows; even if financial arrangements were an ensemble affair, then as now, "show me the money" was the bottom line. Celebrity, however, had a modicum of social significance, at least for clowns: Richard Tarleton was so well known that, as one contemporary writer remarked, tavern owners used him for their signs.[8] Building on his success as a stage clown, Will Kempe took his show on the road, performing a Morris dance from London to Norwich; and, like Robert Armin, who wrote pamphlets, ballads, jestbooks and a play, he not only advertised his dependence upon audiences but also carried his fame into print.[9] All three can be considered prototypes of the "personality performance," where the actor's persona and idiosyncratic performing style overwhelm the role (think Robin Williams, Billy Crystal).

Like Burbage before him, Thomas Betterton (1635–1710) was dubbed "our English *Roscius*"[10] – the period's honorary epithet for "star quality"; perhaps the first great actor-manager deeply associated in the public's mind with Shakespeare, he not only was the most popular but the most remarkable (and remarked upon) actor of his generation. Appearing in roles as various as Hamlet, Macbeth, Brutus, Othello, Mercutio, Hotspur, Henry VIII, Thersites, Antony, Sir Toby Belch, and Falstaff (to name a few), in addition to starring in non-Shakespearean roles, notably Dorimant in George Etherege's *Man of Mode* (1676), crafted expressly for him, his powers, and his reputation, threaten to eclipse Burbage.[11] He could, writes Colley Cibber, "vary his Spirit to the different character he acted," moving with ease from "those wild impatient Starts, that fierce and flashing fire" of his Hotspur to the "unruffled Temper of his Brutus."[12] Whereas today's stardom depends at least in part (especially for women actors) on stage beauty, this mattered less to Restoration spectators, who flocked to see the actor Anthony Aston describes (possibly from hearsay) as "labour[ing] under an "ill Figure"; Cibber, who saw Betterton in his prime, notes his "serious and penetrating Aspect, his Limbs nearer the athletick, than the delicate Proportion; yet however form'd, there arose from the Harmony of the whole a commanding Mien of Majesty"[13] – comments which support

Joseph Roach's suggestion that audiences looked past Betterton's physical body to his "other body, the one that existed outside itself," consisting of "actions, gestures, intonations, vocal colors, mannerisms, expressions, customs, protocols, inherited routines, authenticated traditions – 'bits'."[14]

In an age when audiences were especially tuned to *hearing* an actor's performance, Betterton's vocal musicality invites comparison with Sir John Gielgud's incomparable attention to elocution and phrasing.[15] Waxing rhapsodic, Cibber speaks of hearing Shakespeare's words "rising into real Life, and charming [the] Beholders"; and in "all his Soliloquies of moment," he writes, "the strong Intelligence of his Attitude and Aspect, drew you into such an impatient Gaze, and eager Expectation, that you almost imbib'd the Sentiment with your Eye, before the Ear could reach it." Further evidence of Betterton's ability to control and manipulate an audience's response comes from Cibber's report of his sense of "what was true or false Applause": Betterton "never thought any kind of it equal to an attentive Silence; that there were many ways of deceiving an Audience into a loud one; but to keep them hushed and quiet was an Applause which only Truth and Merit could arrive at."[16] Just such a moment occurred when, in the closet scene, the Ghost appears to Hamlet:

> every Article of his Body seem'd to be affected with a tremor inexpressible ... this was felt so strongly by the Audience that the blood seemed to shudder in their Veins likewise, and they in some Measure partook of the Astonishment and Horror, with which they saw this excellent Actor affected. And when Hamlet [spoke] *See – where he goes – ev'n now – out at the Portal*: The whole Audience ... remain'd in a dead Silence for near a Minute, and then – as if recovering all at once from their Astonishment ... joined as one Man, in a Thunder of universal Applause.[17]

Not surprisingly, such performances persisted in memory. Walking in the cloisters of Westminster Abbey at Betterton's funeral, *The Tatler*'s Richard Steele recalled the terrifying life-likeness of his broken speeches during Othello's jealous rages and the "moving and graceful" energies as "he tells the manner of winning the affection of his mistress" to the Venetian Senate. "I thought of him," Steele writes, "with the same concern as if I waited for the remains of a person who had in real life done all that I had seen him represent."[18] Betterton left behind a public who had returned again and again to watch his performances; ravished by his stage presence, the diarist Samuel Pepys set a precedent for a centuries-later fandom obsessed with knowing stars as people, as "picture personalities," by trying to find out more about the private life of his favorite performer from intimates of the theatre.[19]

A star is born

If the *cult* of the star began with Betterton, the language of stardom appeared soon afterwards, with reference to David Garrick (1717–79). Writing in 1761, Benjamin Victor looked back twenty years to 19 October 1741, the opening night of *Richard III*, and remembered "the arrival of a bright luminary in the Theatrical Hemisphere . . . That Luminary soon after became a Star of the first Magnitude and was called GARRICK."[20] And for Thomas Davies, "Mr. Garrick shone forth like a theatrical Newton."[21] What struck audiences was the vitality of his performance, his vivid eyes, his constantly changing facial expression, his total physicality: "The moment he entered the scene, the character he assumed was visible in his countenance; the power of his imagination was such that he transformed himself into the very man; the passions rose in rapid succession, and, before he uttered a word, were legible in every feature of that various face."[22] Although the language of metamorphosis joining star-to-character recalls Burbage, Garrick's stardom derived in part from the bourgeois theatrical culture of which he was a part, for the star was tied to that theatre as a viable economic enterprise and a respectable profession: wrote Dr. Johnson: "his profession made him rich and he made his profession respectable." No actor before him had been so written of and – predating fan discourse – written to. He was the first actor to promote his public image in tandem with Shakespeare's, a doubled individuality that, in anticipating the star phenomenon, adds a fillip to the notion of desire, for part of that desire is the performer's own. Exceeding Betterton, Garrick saw himself as Shakespeare's disciple (erecting a temple to him at his Thames-side villa): linking his status to Shakespeare's already established centrality in the English national imaginary earned him funeral and burial in Westminster Abbey, where his statue's inscription reads: "Shakespeare and Garrick like twin stars shall shine / And earth irradiate with a beam divine."[23] No occasion for a performer on a similar scale would occur until the late twentieth century, with Laurence Olivier's memorial service in the same space.

The eyes have it

Fixed in paintings – forerunners of the theatrical or cinematic still – Garrick, despite his small stature, is a compelling presence: his face and eyes a site of wonder, astonishment, terror, and power. Subtly and psychologically nuanced, "face-acting" not only pre-exists realism – Thomas Davies said of Sarah Siddons (1755–1831) that her eye is "so full of information that the passion is told from her look before she speaks"[24] – but points towards the camera's invention, to Gloria Swanson's Norma Desmond ("We didn't need

1 James Scott, Mezzotint after Thomas Gainsborough, *Garrick with a Bust of Shakespeare*, 1750s–80s.

dialogue. We had faces"),[25] and to a distant future where the cinematic close-up could close the distance between spectator and star, giving fresh emphasis to the precise articulation of Shakespearean speech. Although Siddons lacked such close-up advantage, to William Hazlitt, "She was Tragedy personified. She was the stateliest ornament of the public mind. To have seen Mrs Siddons was an event in everyone's life": the same would be said, generations later, of Sarah Bernhardt (1844–1923). Just as the century's emphasis on the value of the individual was wrapped up in Shakespearean characters, through the star's powerful presence, women spectators came to the theatre in large numbers whenever Siddons performed. Seeing their own material conditions as abject subjects to the legal and social frameworks of late eighteenth-century middle-class culture – lacking civil rights, control over income, property, and custody of children – mirrored in the roles she played, they sobbed aloud, screamed, went into hysterics, and fainted. Forerunners of present-day fan culture, their kinesthetic response resulted less from her technical skill than from empathy for her powerful portrayals of more or less helpless women who suffered at the hands of men.[26]

At the age of ten, after seeing Siddons perform, William Henry West Betty (1791–1874), known as Master Betty or the Infant Roscius, declared that he would expire if he did not become an actor. Engaged to play Hamlet at Covent Garden for high fees, he rose like a nova, causing a sensation that swept London into "Bettymania": William Pitt even suspended Parliament so that members could see him perform Hamlet.[27] Hailed as the wonder of the age (he supposedly memorized Hamlet's role in three hours), prints of him appeared in every shop window (just as Joe Cocks's shop on Stratford-upon-Avon's Sheep Street, nearly three centuries later, would feature photographs of the RSC's star actors, either in current role or in autograph-ready "star shots").

Yet even Master Betty could hardly compete with the blazing star of Edmund Kean (1787/9–1833). Citing his "great powers" and "fine sensibility" in his debut performance as Shylock, Thomas Barnes evoked genius: "It was this that gave fire to his eye, energy to his tones and such a variety and expressiveness to all his gestures, that one might almost say, 'his body thought'" (writing of Mel Gibson's 1990 Hamlet, John Lahr would echo the latter phrase). According to Hazlitt, "He filled every part of the stage … His style of acting is … more significant, more pregnant with meaning, more varied, alive in every part, than any we have almost ever witnessed. The character never stands still; there is no vacant pause in the action; the eye is never silent."[28] Calling his Othello "the finest piece of acting in the world," a performance in which Kean "bore on his brow the mark of fire from Heaven," Hazlitt placed him "far beyond the touch of Time," and worthy of Shakespeare's own genius.[29] And writing in the *Examiner*, he goes further: "We wish we had never seen Mr. Kean. He has destroyed the Kemble religion and it is the religion in which we were brought up." That Hazlitt and others thought of the rage for actors as a "religion," endowing performers with heavenly metaphors and iconic status, offers a fascinating comment on star quality – if one reads "religion" as a term for "stardom." No writing before or since matches the eloquence with which these writers re-performed, in lovingly detailed descriptions, the performer's emotional affect and ability to reproduce bodily sensations. Reading like love letters to their gods and goddesses, or odes to joy (and desire), they position the actors of whom they speak in the realm of the Sublime.[30] In a sense, Kean was *their* creation, their commodity. Yet perhaps the most famous statement on Kean comes from Samuel Taylor Coleridge: "His rapid descents from the hyper-tragic to the infra-colloquial, though sometimes productive of great effect, are often unreasonable. To see him act, is like reading Shakespeare by flashes of lightning." Read in their contemporary context, Coleridge's words edge away from Hazlitt's effulgent praise ("lightning" was code for gin), but it was his phrase that Adrian Noble would evoke to describe Gambon's acting, his skill at moving from situation to situation, playing each moment with energy and force.[31]

If Kean's 1814 Shylock effectively erased all memory of previous performers in the role, overturning an eight-decade-long stereotype of "the Jew that Shakespeare drew" by displaying a "conflict of passions" through rapid transitions from one tone and feeling to another,"[32] memories of Kean were more long-lasting, even making their way into burlesque, the nineteenth century's popular performance form, through its most celebrated star, Frederick Robson. Performing in Francis Talfourd's *Shylock; or, the Merchant of Venice Preserved* (1853), Robson echoed Kean's "swift and perplexing changes": Robson was adept at convulsing spectators with laughter, then "hushing them into awe-struck silence," then holding them "midway between terror and laughter as he performed some weirdly grotesque dance."[33] His ability to move from emotional depths to comic heights, from despair to exultation, spinning from one to another with lightning speed, brought surprised acclaim: citing his "real and very serious power," Henry Morley wished that Robson had "made trial of Shakespeare's [Shylock] in preference" to Talfourd's, that he would turn to the "legitimate" stage. Yet if Robson's performance served to reawaken Kean's stardom through mimicry, it also was the case that even – or perhaps most especially – in travesty performances, which relied on intimate knowledge of the plays and their past and current performers, Shakespeare remained the abiding star.[34]

In the nineteenth century, spectators thrilled to archaeologically correct revivals: as the taste for spectacular Shakespeare boomed – from Charles Kean's elaborate historical reconstructions at the Princess's Theatre (1851–59) to those at Herbert Beerbohm Tree's His Majesty's (1897–1915) – décor became a star in its own right (think Franco Zeffirelli's Italianate Shakespeare films). Moreover, nineteenth-century stagings of Shakespeare made star roles even starrier, rewriting the plays to have act curtains fall on "big" speeches or emotional climaxes in order to draw full focus to the star actor, often surrounded (as in a musical finale) in a tableau of supernumeraries standing at respectful distances from the "great man." Audiences who crowded Henry Irving's Lyceum theatre (1878–1901) came to see, as with *Richard III*, what Irving the actor-manager did best: make, "for the setting, a big brave general picture, and then, for the figure, play on the chord of the sinister-sardonic, flowered over as vividly as may be with the elegant-grotesque." Observers considered Irving's movements graceless and undignified, his speaking extravagant and often inarticulate: commenting on this lack of technique, Bernhardt thought him "a mediocre actor but a great artist" but praised his "profoundly thoughtful expression" – as with Garrick, Siddons, and Kean, the agile part of his body was his face – his mask.[35] Although critics such as Dutton Cook questioned Irving's stage business – why, he asked, does Hamlet, meditating on murdering Claudius, "wave about a lighted torch within a few feet of him, as though expressly to rouse him to a sense of his peril, as a danger-signal warns a coming train of a possible accident? ... Or why, bidding good-night to his mother, [does] Hamlet so involve himself with the chamber candlesticks?"[36] – sometimes such realistic "innovations" paid off, especially in his performance of Shylock. The *Spectator*'s critic describes his "cold, slow smile, just parting the lips and touching their curves as light touches polished metal" which passed over the lower part of his face but did not "touch the eyes or lift the brow" as one of Irving's most remarkable facial effects. And his portrayal of Shylock's return to his house after Jessica's elopement has become one of the role's hallmarks. Following her exit with the carnival crew with Lorenzo and other Christians, a "very quick curtain" rose almost immediately: "the stage was empty, desolate, with no light but the pale moon, and all sounds of life at a great distance – and then over the bridge came the wearied figure of the Jew. As Shylock was about to enter the house, the act drop fell."[37] Al Pacino is only the most recent Shylock who has borrowed Irving's moment of isolation, transposing it to the play's end: the penultimate shots of Michael Radford's 2005 film show him standing in a small Venetian campo, a solitary outcast, the doors of the Jewish ghetto closing behind him as the camera pulls away.

Whether playing to mixed reviews or traveling to America with the Lyceum company, less to seek more fame than to sell himself and his product in order to save his London operation, Irving was alert to the paradox of his own greatness. "How strange it is that I should have made the reputation I have as an actor, with nothing to help me – with no equipment. My legs, my voice – everything has been against me. For an actor who can't walk, can't talk, and has no face to speak of, I've done pretty well." In conversation with Ellen Terry, his co-star, he gave the equivalent of a celebrity interview: "What makes a popular actor? Physique! What makes a great actor? Imagination and sensibility." Musing as to whether Irving ever was really popular, Terry concludes that most people disliked his acting, found it strange. "But he forced them, almost against their will and nature, out of dislike into admiration. They had to come up to him, for never would he go down to them."[38] And so they did. Not only did Irving create, at least in the public mind and sentiment, a prototype for England's national theatre, he also, in 1895, became the first theatrical knight. If not a blazing Shakespearean star (his signature role was Mathias in *The Bells*), Irving's honor marked not only his own achievements but also those of the proto-stars who had preceded him.

"Who's on next?": a twentieth-century pantheon

In the generation following Irving, Laurence Olivier (1907–89), John Gielgud (1902–2000), and Ralph Richardson (1902–1983) were unquestionably the "greats" – and Gambon's acknowledged idols. For that generation, entry to playing the big roles, the stairway to the stars, was directly straightforward: drama school, work at the Birmingham Rep, then to the Old Vic – and on from there to film stardom. Among the three, Olivier courted stardom from the outset, desired the panoply of public adulation accompanying it: already starring in the West End in 1930, by 1939, he was a Hollywood icon. In an age where theatrical roles made stars who became film idols and where the star, dispersed between stage and screen, mirrored modernity's dystopic culture, the making of a star was a collaborative enterprise built by agents, producers, casting directors, and image-makers; by this time, an entire mass-media machine, where everything publicly available contributes to the star image – pre-performance build-up, back- and front-stage gossip, what's said and written about the star, what the star says and writes – was ready and waiting. No theatre star has attracted so much public press, as many biographers; and, like many film stars past and present, Olivier took agency over his own image. His autobiography, *Confessions of An Actor* (1982), followed by *On Acting* (1986), offer anecdotal catalogues of his success in roles, with enough titillating personal revelation (sexual anxieties, domestic scandal, public accomplishments) to convey the impression of a personable "ordinary guy" – like the reader.

Taking ownership of Shakespearean roles – perhaps most famously Henry V, Hamlet, Richard III, and Othello – his presence – and voice – haunt performers present. Studying Richard III's role, Anthony Sher writes: "'Now is the winter ...': God ... You don't like to put your mouth to it, so many other mouths have been there. Or to be more honest, one particularly distinctive mouth. His poised, staccato delivery is imprinted on those words like teeth marks."[39] As with James Earl Jones, the original voice of *Star Wars*'s Darth Vader (1976) and then that of CNN, Olivier's voice on the Polaroid television commercial needed no identification other than stardom's authority, an authority that, in Olivier's case, embraced his country's culture. Charles Laughton remarked of his stage Henry V (1937), "Do you know, Larry, why you're so good in this part? Because you *are* England!"[40] And Olivier's ensuing film, famously dedicated to the RAF, wrapped role, play, and author ("I had a mission," wrote Olivier, "... my country was at war; I felt Shakespeare within me, I felt the cinema within him"[41]) into England's – and America's – patriotic imaginary, winning him an Oscar (1946) for his "outstanding achievement as actor, producer and director in bringing *Henry V* to the screen." Linked, like Garrick before him, to the national imaginary, which would eventually result in a knighthood (at thirty in 1947) and a life peerage, Olivier could claim lasting international stardom. Indeed, Olivier's *Hamlet*, which won Oscars (1948) for his portrayal and for best picture, still represents to many the epitome of high-culture Shakespeare: a signature role embodied by a great classical actor (wearing puffy-sleeved dueling shirts and tights, his hair dyed blond so as to disassociate his active, sexually alert matinee idol persona from that of "a man who could not make up his mind") in a black-and-white art film. (Given Olivier's shirt as he was rehearsing Hamlet [1990] Mel Gibson tried it on, found it fit "well enough"; hailed by some as Olivier's putative heir, Kenneth Branagh [1996] also played Hamlet as blond.)

Perhaps the greatest present-day fabricator of disguise, Olivier admits his own delight at surprising an audience ("My God, is *that him*?") – in putting on the face of the part ("my face has always been a blank canvas ready to be shaped as I wished").[42] Remarked Peter Brook, "Everything was there except the soul of Olivier, which nobody saw because he was always working to disguise it."[43] Yet the home page for his official website, which shows an image of his Hamlet, framed by one of him as *Rebecca*'s Maxim de Winter (1940) and an iconic publicity shot, is dominated by picture perfect images of an elegant, gentlemanly Olivier – the very model of a (post)modern major celebrity. Following in Irving's footsteps as actor-manager, he ran the National Theatre in London from 1962 to 1973, reluctantly ceding it to Peter Hall; his name is stamped on the largest performing space at the present Royal National Theatre and on London's reigning theatre awards, he was honored by a special Oscar (1979) for his full body of work and celebrated with royal panoply at a memorial service in Westminster Abbey, where actors of his own generation – Gielgud, Alec Guinness, Peggy Ashcroft, Douglas Fairbanks, Jr. – and those bridging to the next – Maggie Smith, Paul Scofield, Derek Jacobi, Ian McKellen – paid tribute to him in a cere-mony that Joseph Roach considers the most recent surrogation (with Garrick's the precedent) of the funeral never accorded to Shakespeare;[44] his chosen epitaph, "Goodnight, sweet Prince." On the occasion of Olivier's Richard III (1944), John Gielgud presented him with the sword carried by Edmund Kean as Richard, which Kean had given to Irving, who passed it to the Terry family. Asked to whom he would give it, Olivier replied, "No one. It's mine." At least in Olivier's mind, his star would reign for ever; like Elizabeth I, he refused to name a successor.

"No one today," writes Michael Blakemore, paying tribute to the past, "can make an iambic pentameter thrill as Olivier did, or phrase one as gracefully as Gielgud" – who "played Shakespeare as if in unending rapturous tribute, the language harrowing him like fire."[45] And Lee Strasberg, the famous teacher of Method acting, said of Gielgud, "When he speaks, I hear Shakespeare think."[46] Although Olivier studied his craft by listening to recordings of Irving, Gielgud, the grand-nephew of Ellen Terry and thus the last surviving link to Irving's age, often was accused of relying too much on rhetorical flourishes and elocutionary models deriving from that earlier age. Yet he achieved the affection of fellow-professionals in a way Olivier never quite did. Like Olivier, Gielgud wrote about his craft (Stage Directions, 1963; An Actor in his Time, 1979; Acting Shakespeare, 1991); he was an intensely private man, in part to cover his homosexuality, which was known but cloaked by convention and silently accepted by all. Even his recently published letters, which reveal a biting, even wicked wit aimed in part at rivals or detractors, show him modest about his considerable accomplishments. Knighted in 1953, he remained a working actor until his death; measuring his Shakespearean performances against those past, he continually sought "innovations" – the new "bit," mannerism, cos-tume, or décor that would set his own stamp on a role and, as director, on a play, yet it was his performance as the butler Hobson in Arthur (1981), with Dudley Moore, that brought him Oscar fame.

And whereas Olivier fantasized his oneness with Shakespeare, Gielgud saw himself as Shakespeare's servant. Although teasingly described as being the greatest living actor from the neck up, his voice echoes in memory. Simon

Callow writes of a gala Harold Pinter organized, some twenty years ago, to raise funds for imprisoned writers, where Gielgud was to speak Richard II's prison soliloquy. After rehearsing their own speeches, the actors assembled in the darkened theatre to listen:

> He stood on the stage of the Duke of York's theatre with that inimitably erect posture of his, head held high at a slight angle as if he were listening to an inner voice, and spoke again the words he had first acted more than 50 years earlier. As he spoke, he wept, and as he wept, so did we all, knowing that we were in the presence of a kind of purity and perfection of the art we all struggle to practise. Pinter commented, "Lovely, John. Bit sentimental." "Oh dear," said Gielgud briskly, "that's always been my downfall. Thank you, Harold, I do so need to have people to tell me these things." On the night, the speech was more restrained and finally more effective; but the over-generosity of that private performance was of the essence of the man. It was nothing to do with impressing us – why on earth would he want or need to do that? – it was simply that in speaking the familiar text, he fell in love with it all over again.[47]

Said Peter Hall, "The first time I saw him, he was starring as Hamlet in Cambridge. I was 12, and I felt I knew him already, as one does with God."[48] If Olivier's latter-day box-office popularity was as the Olympian Zeus in *Clash of the Titans* (1981), Gielgud's god-role was Prospero, the theatrical magus most associated with Shakespeare and with his farewell to the stage. Fittingly, in Peter Greenaway's *Prospero's Books* (1991), he speaks not just Prospero's part but all the lines, co-creating the play-as-film – and, within Greenaway's fiction, speaking as well as writing Shakespeare's book.

By the mid-1970s, however, Olivier and Gielgud were no longer acting Shakespeare in the theatre; moreover, theatrical culture as they knew it – the classiness of professional stardom, classical acting as a gentlemanly game, the ability to fill a theatre on name alone, had changed. So had audiences, who now were more likely, as Michael Pennington writes,

> to be caught by argument and irony than by the ring of a beautiful line. An instinctive populism draws them from the heroes to the victims; watching Claudius [through a filter of the nightly news], they may reflect that he's a far better decision-maker and political leader than either the late King Hamlet or his son, for whom life seems inordinately complex.[49]

Moreover, although it always had been the case, from Burbage forward, that performers were never exclusively "Shakespeareans," there was increasingly less demand for classical acting. "Shouting in the night" – Gambon's definition of stage acting –[50] clearly was being displaced by "whispering to the camera" – and despite Hollywood's fond epithet for "Billy Big Boy" as founding father and ultimate plot source, Shakespeare films were being made in Cinecittà's studios, not California. If there once had been a formula for the Shakespearean star presence, that particular combination of body and role, face, voice, reputation, and person(ality) no longer ruled.

Yet the possibility of becoming a nova – a slightly older Master Betty – still existed. Cast shortly out of RADA as the RSC's Henry V (1984), Kenneth Branagh rejected the company's directorial dominance, wrote an autobiography (*Beginning*, 1989), set up his own acting company, Renaissance, and, transferred his stage performance to film (grossing $10,161,099 worldwide). When Judi Dench, his far more famous Mistress Quickly, saw rushes of *Henry V*'s opening scene – Branagh's Henry emerging in loomingly backlit silhouette from massive doors – she asked him, "Who do you think you are?" Branagh retorted, "The film is not called Mistress Quickly the Fourth." If not an out-and-out bid for stardom, it came close: "King Ken Comes to Conquer," read Richard Corliss's *Time* review (13 November 1989), predicting Branagh's trajectory as the next Olivier and, like him, linked to the nation. *Much Ado About Nothing* (1993) enhanced his popular appeal, a phrase that sorts well with his desire to make films of the classics with mass media appeal: like Olivier, he speaks of "realistic Shakespearean acting," of his obligation to be truthful, to go for spontaneity, freshness, and naturalism – no "fake Shakespeare" voices.[51] Certainly Branagh possesses an extraordinary gift for making Shakespearean language sound not strange or estranged but "natural" – a talent which has made him more of a star in America than in England, where he is perceived as perhaps too pushy, too ambitious – ironically, "too American." Whereas Irving published annotated acting editions of his Shakespearean stagings as well as co-edited the *Henry Irving Shakespeare*, screenplays constitute Branagh's print memorials. Yet even the most elaborately detailed, that for his full-text Hamlet (1997), itself an "original" of a sort, has not destined him to inherit Olivier's star status. Noticeably absent among theatrical culture's luminaries at Olivier's funeral, Branagh would not – at least in revered national space – challenge the crown or life peerage of Lord Olivier of Brighton.[52]

But if the slippery term "Shakespearean star" has undergone something of a sea change, residues of Shakespearean stardom persist as stars cross over from Shakespeare into television or mainstream blockbuster films. Patrick Stewart, a brilliant Shylock (1978) and Henry IV (1982), becomes *Star Trek*'s Captain Jean-Luc Picard, a role in which he, as well as the aliens he encounters, channel Shakespeare's lines, Picard to prove his authority, the aliens to prove their humanity – anticipating, in the popular imaginary, the arrival of Harold Bloom's *Shakespeare: The Invention of the Human* (1998). And in *X-Men 2* (2003), comic-book-made-blockbuster-film, Stewart's Professor Charles Xavier (endowed with telepathic abilities) is joined by

Ian McKellen (Richard II, Romeo, Macbeth, Iago, Richard III) as Magneto and Brian Cox (Titus, Lear, frozen fish commercials) as the genocidal General William Stryker: the favored roles for English stage actors on blockbuster screens are those of villains (star go-to guys: Anthony Hopkins or Alan Rickman), and film and television salaries fund their stage work.

In November 1995, *Vanity Fair* published "Empire of the Stage": written by John Heilpern and lavishly embellished with forty-four photographs by Lord Snowdon, the reigning British celebrity photographer, its come-on phrase reads, "From London's footlights, the monarchs of British theater rule the cultural seas. Broadway and Hollywood bow before their talents." Gielgud leads off (photographed in his garden seated by a classical Cupid); images of Helen Mirren (in her dressing room, more or less *en negligée*), Jonathan Pryce (the voice and body of the Lexus commercial seen in a red Mercedes), Jeremy Irons (black T-shirt, motorcycle), Vanessa Redgrave – but not Judi Dench – follow, ending with Richard Harris and Peter O'Toole ("hellraisers" having tea in the Dorchester). There are Highbrows (Adrian Noble and Richard Eyre); Middlebrows (the people who brought you *Cats*, among them Andrew Lloyd Webber and Trevor Nunn); a panoply of knights – Alec Guiness, Derek Jacobi, Anthony Hopkins, Nigel Hawthorne, Ian McKellen – and playwrights (Tom Stoppard, Harold Pinter, Alan Bennett); the Next Generation – directors Simon McBurney, Sean Mathias, Katie Mitchell, Sam Mendes, Declan Donnellan, and Nick Ormerod; Kenneth Branagh (on a tanning bed) – and the Next Wave (Alan Cumming, Paul Rhys, Joseph Fiennes, Rupert Graves, and Simon Russell Beale), young executives photographed in the Virgin Upper Class departure lounge at Heathrow Airport, prepared to take their product on tour. Pretending to wrap an elaborate advert for classical theatre – England's "primary way of self-definition, like movies in America," remarks Stephen Daldry[53] – in glossy high-hype style, this gallery of performers with "It,"[54] that magical, sought-after, immediacy of presence, puts bodies and faces on offer, consumer-ready. Captions function like puff career capsule bios, star status quantified by the numbers: how many plays, films, TV commercials has your favorite done? Which have *you* seen? Although sixteen mention Shakespeare in passing, this plays second fiddle to popular taste and to film and television work; of the six photographs showing performers in costume, only two – Fiona Shaw as Richard II and Nigel Hawthorne as Clarence in *Richard III* – feature a Shakespearean role. If the spread directs its gaze towards a future (now the present), what is even more striking is a pervasive nostalgia for an Edwardian past, right on the cusp of Empire's collapse. It's there in Redgrave's romantic white-gowned figure, seen at Eton College on the set of *The Wind in the Willows*; in the ascots and velvet jackets of Alan and

Benedick Bates; the school uniforms of Jane Horrocks, Iain Glenn, and Imogen Stubbs; in Peter O'Toole's elegant tailoring; and, perhaps most specifically, in its celebration of the beloved theatrical form of pantomime, showcasing John Hurt as a fantastical panto Dame and Diana Rigg, a resplendent Principal Boy.

However deeply imbued with nostalgia for another age, *Vanity Fair*'s piece serves to position Shakespeare firmly within the massive machinery of the star industry – within, to borrow Christine Gledhill's apt title, an industry of desire.[55] And after all, as Anthony Lane, writing of Branagh's *Much Ado*, remarks: "for all the long shadows of Burbage and Kean and Garrick and Irving, there are times when what you really want from Shakespeare is Denzel Washington in leather pants."[56] Yet if the term "classical actor" as well as any idea that there is one single authoritatively *classical* interpretation of a role have fallen into disrepair, roles still draw stars and stars bring audiences. Until Peter Brook's *Hamlet* with Adrian Lester (2000), no recent New York performance had been as excitedly anticipated as Ralph Fiennes's Hamlet – recuperating his image from *Strange Days* (1995). There, spectators' first sight of the star was neither that of Gielgud's romantically passive prince, Mel Gibson's action hero via Mad Max, or Branagh's buttoned-up (or unlaced) Edwardian but of "a tragic antihero alone, his back turned on us. A Hamlet without princeliness: unregal, unshaven, unkempt, a dark, contemporary grunge Hamlet on the precipice. In isolation, he might have been a rock star about to explode in klieg lights and smoke, hurling his black topcoat aside to turn and shout to his fans, 'Love ya, Cleveland!' "[57]

Surfing with Sir Ian

Ian McKellen also may be playing Cleveland – at least virtually. What is the position, place, and work of the star in the age of digital reproduction, on the internet? Whereas the official Sir Laurence Olivier website, managed by a corporation, CMG Worldwide, not only carefully selects what it reveals but also preserves his iconicity in perpetuity: the "image, name and voice of Laurence Olivier is a protected property right owned by the estate,"[58] the Sir Ian McKellen official site offers users The Compleat McKellen.[59] Billed as an online autobiography, it is more than that, for it shows McKellen in total control of an image that extends from Shakespeare everywhere. As the home page opens with a shot of his Richard III, speaking "Now is the winter of our discontent made glorious summer," that image dissolves into one from *Neverwas* ("Neverwas . . . is where you will find your strength, your purpose, your reason for being" [2005]), then to James Whale in *Gods and Monsters*

(1998), Gandalf in *The Lord of the Rings* (2001–03), and X-*Men*'s Magneto, whose words – "We are the future, Charles, not them" – offers an apt trope for what the site itself enacts: a slow drift towards film and away from classical theatre, the performance form that, a decade or so ago, Richard Schechner called "the string quartet of the 21st century."[60] And McKellen even says so: capping the shifts between image and sound bites, his smoothly timbred tones assert, "Making movies is the most wonderful thing in the world ... entertaining people."

What most star bios offer – a "backstage" look which functions as a guarantor of truth, generating a rhetoric of sincerity that produces an illusion of the authenticity, meaningfulness, and genuineness of the star[61] – has become the website's province. Most are managed by fans, but McKellen's is his alone (or that of his webmaster Keith Stern) and his footprints are everywhere. Public and private McKellen collide in this world of infotainment: consummate actor (a full index of all his stage and film roles); author of several one-man shows (his marked-up script can be downloaded); theatrical archivist-historian ("Tears in Bratislava: Richard II in Czechoslovakia" [1982]; his dresser's notes for Romeo [1976]); theatre activist (arguing for preserving the foundations of the Rose [1989]); gay activist (coming out; speaking against Clause 28, marching in Stonewall rallies). Prefaced by a guarantee of regular expansion with "archival materials from personal files," the site's content swings between the informative – discussions of Shakespearean plays and stagings from the 1590s to the present – and the promotional – "Media Lounge" (exclusively for the working press, requires registration). Here is the perfectly postmodern form for self-adulation: the star as the product of his own writing about himself (and of this essay as well), purposefully caught up in a self-perpetuating web of factual detail (including rehearsal diaries, the theatrical equivalent of *The Making of "The Lord of the Rings"*); "Rumours False and True" (did he *really* kiss Orlando Bloom? And was Bloom annoyed?); and "E-post," where McKellen answers questions (providing recipes for veggie soup; teasers and promos for films – *The Da Vinci Code* – and future roles – King Lear; "Bits and Bobs"). Links direct users to Shopping (videos, DVDs) and to Ian on eBay, where (as of 10 June 2005) one could bid, among other items, on a signed 8 × 10 photograph of his Gandalf with Elijah Wood's Frodo ($7.95).

Photo galleries include childhood pictures, the expected star shots, posters and programmes for productions in which he had either a supporting or starring role. But what is most astonishing is the archive of theatrical stills accompanying each performance: eleven from his famous *Macbeth* with Judi Dench (1976) at the RSC's intimate Other Place, nearly as many for other past roles, ranging from his early student days at Cambridge for the Marlowe Society to present and future work. The "New" section features some forty to fifty backstage photos of McKellen transforming himself into Widow Twankey in *Aladdin* (2005), including a pose, in full panto Dame regalia, with co-star Roger Allam's "Allam Abbanazer"; a range of stills show him as Mel Hutchwright, the "dodgy novelist" and author of the steamy bodice-ripper *Hard Grinding*, with the cast of ITV1's soap, *Coronation Street*; video clips document the filming of *Asylum* (2005) co-starring Natasha Richardson. *Everything* – images as well as documents – can be downloaded. Whether as person or protean persona, McKellen *is* his roles, a postmodern showbiz Roscius who takes delight in his own magnificent showmanship: putting him on offer, the site is tempting enough to convert even the most skeptical anti-theatricalist to fandom, ready to shout "McKellen – or Richard, Gandalf or Magneto – Forever!" Or as McKellen, tongue in cheek, remarks: "After all these years, [who would imagine that] Dame Maggie [Smith] would end up being best known as the Harry Potter Lady, Tony Hopkins best known for eating people's faces, and they'd make me into an action figure! I love my action figures. I play with them all day long."[62]

Epilogue: looking back, looking at now

By way of a conclusion – and also in anticipation of a desired, yet-to-be-seen performance[63] – I want to pause for a moment over Snowdon's image of Michael Gambon, who sees himself as "the carthorse to Ian's thoroughbred."[64] Photographed in Poets' Corner, Gambon wears a blue custodian's uniform jacket, its logo reading Westminster Abbey; one elbow rests on a mop handle, the opposite foot on an overturned bucket. Just behind him, Shakespeare's statue takes up a more gentlemanly pose, one elbow on a stack of folios, one hand displaying a scroll with Prospero's words ("The Cloud capp'd Towers ... The Great Globe itself ... Shall vanish"); at the foot of the pedestal, the heads of crowned monarchs. If Gambon's image teasingly mocks Shakespeare's (Shakespeare loose, one might say), it more specifically evokes – and recycles – Gainsborough's portrait of a gentlemanly, bewigged Garrick in a romantic setting, one arm wrapped around a bust of Shakespeare on a pedestal, the other arm akimbo, the hand resting on a slim cane. There is something entirely appropriate about such recycling, not only because it gestures towards Gambon's obsession with restoring English eighteenth-century firearms but also because, if time travel were possible, he would wish to be among the generation that followed Garrick, in "a time of bombast, and the theatre of Drury Lane and Covent Garden and Macready and Kean and all those people, those massive great actors."[65] If Garrick's portrait is all about Garrick the gentleman (Shakespeare emerging from tangled roses as a prop for his figure), Gambon's is all about another "great," posing as an ordinary worker: playing clean-up next to Shakespeare, a proud if glowering custodian capable of transforming tradition. In a recent interview, Mel Gussow told Gambon that Simon Russell Beale wanted to play Falstaff. "Who," he asked, "is going to get to it first?"

> *Gambon.* Well, I probably won't. He'd better do it. He'll speak it more clearly than I will, and maybe he'll get more sense out of it.
> *Gussow.* But you would be funnier and more moving in the end.[66]

That's what a Shakespearean star can do. And that's what I want to see.

NOTES

My deep thanks to Richard Abel, Peter Holland, William Ingram, and Robert Shaughnessy for conversations and information that have traveled into this essay.

1. Michael Cordner, personal communication, 3 May 2005.
2. Mel Gussow, *Gambon, A Life in Acting* (London: Nick Hern Books, 2004), p. 154.
3. *Ibid.*, p. 216, p. 218.
4. Michael L. Quinn, "Celebrity and the Semiotics of Acting," *New Theatre Quarterly* 22 (1990), 154–61, p. 156.
5. Edgar Morin, *Paris Seuil* (1957), trans. Richard Howard (New York: Grove Press, 1960), pp. 134–35.
6. Attributed to John Fletcher, cited in E. K. Chambers, *The Elizabethan Stage*, 4 vols. (Oxford: Clarendon Press, 1923), II. 309. See also Alexander Leggatt, "Richard Burbage: A Dangerous Actor," in *Extraordinary Actors: Essays on Popular Performers: Studies in Honour of Peter Thomson*, ed. Jane Milling and Martin Banham (Exeter: Exeter University Press, 2004), pp. 8–20.
7. Edwin Nungezer, *A Dictionary of Actors and of Other Persons Associated with the Public Representation of Plays in England before 1642* (New Haven, CT: Yale University Press, 1929), p. 73.
8. Chambers, *Elizabethan Stage*, p. 345.
9. Nora Johnson, *The Actor as Playwright in Early Modern Drama* (Cambridge: Cambridge University Press, 2003), pp. 17–19.
10. After Quintus Roscius Gallus, a celebrated Roman comic actor known for his painstaking rehearsal of the fine points of each role he played and for his improvisational gifts. He supposedly tutored Cicero in elocution.
11. My thanks to Mike Cordner for reading an earlier draft of this essay and urging me to reconsider my assessment of Betterton.
12. Robert W. Lowe (ed.), *An Apology for the Life of Mr. Colley Cibber, Written by Himself* [1740] 2 vols. (London: John C. Nimmo, 1888), I. 103.
13. Anthony Aston, *A Brief Supplement to Colley Cibber, Esq; His Lives of the late Famous Actors and Actresses*, in *ibid.*, II. 299; *ibid.*, I. 116–17.
14. Joseph Roach, *Cities of the Dead: Circum-Atlantic Performance* (New York: Columbia University Press, 1996), p. 93; see also Jane Milling, "Thomas Betterton and the Art of Acting," in Milling and Banham, *Extraordinary Actors*, pp. 21–35, p. 26, p. 31.
15. Michael Dobson, "Improving on the Original: Actresses and Adaptations," in *Shakespeare: An Illustrated Stage History*, ed. Jonathan Bate and Russell Jackson (Oxford: Oxford University Press, 1996), pp. 45–68, p. 54.

16. *An Apology*, I. 109–10.
17. *The Laureat* (1740), p. 31; cited in Philip H. Highfill, Kalman A. Burnim, and Edward A. Langhans (eds.), *A Biographical Dictionary of Actors, Actresses, Musicians, Dancers, Managers & Other Stage Personnel in London, 1660–1800*, 16 vols. (Carbondale: Southern Illinois University Press, 1973), II. 95.
18. Cited in R. W. Lowe, *The Life and Times of That Excellent and Renowned Actor Thomas Betterton . . .* (London: Reader, Orange Street, 1888), pp. 130–31.
19. Milling, "Thomas Betterton," p. 30.
20. Simon Varey, "A Star is Born," *Notes and Queries* 40. 3 (September 1993), 335.
21. Thomas Davies, *Memoirs of the Life of David Garrick* (1780), (Georg Olms Verlag, 1972), I. 3. I also draw on Jean Benedetti, *David Garrick and the Birth of Modern Theatre* (London: Methuen, 2001).
22. Arthur Murphy, *Life of Garrick*, (London, 1801), I. 23.
23. Peter Holland, "The Age of Garrick," in Bate and Jackson, *Shakespeare: An Illustrated Stage History*, pp. 69–91, p. 69.
24. Thomas Davies, *Dramatic Miscellanies*, (Dublin: S. Price, 1784), III. 147.
25. *Sunset Boulevard* (1960), dir. Billy Wilder.
26. William Hazlitt, *Examiner*, 16 June 1816; Michael R. Booth, John Stokes, and Susan Bassnett, *Three Tragic Actresses: Siddons, Rachel, Ristori* (Cambridge: Cambridge University Press, 1996), pp. 28–31.
27. Michael Dobson and Stanley Wells (eds.), *The Oxford Companion to Shakespeare* (Oxford: Oxford University Press, 2001), p. 44.
28. Thomas Barnes, *Examiner*, 26 January 1814; Raymond Fitzsimmons, *Edmund Kean: Fire From Heaven* (London: Hamish Hamilton, 1976), p. 56.
29. Fitzsimmons, *Edmund Kean*, p. 73.
30. Hazlitt, *Examiner*, 27 October 1816. I draw on Lucy Fischer, "General Introduction: Back Story," in *Stars: The Film Reader*, ed. Lucy Fischer and Marcia Landy (London: Routledge, 2004), pp. 1–9, p. 7.
31. Samuel Taylor Coleridge, *Table Talk*, 27 April 1823.
32. William Hazlitt, *Morning Chronicle*, 27 January 1814, cited in Richard W. Schoch, *Not Shakespeare: Bardolatry and Burlesque in the Nineteenth Century* (Cambridge: Cambridge University Press, 2002), p. 101, n. 86.
33. Cited in *ibid.*, p. 100.
34. Henry Morley, *Examiner*, 9 July 1853. See Schoch, *Not Shakespeare*, for a brilliant analysis of the relations between burlesque Shakespeare and its supposedly legitimate "other."
35. *Harper's Weekly*, 23 January 1877; Sarah Bernhardt, *The Art of the Theatre*, trans. J. J. Stenning (London: Geoffrey Bles, 1924), p. 65.
36. Dutton Cook, *Nights at the Play: A View of the English Stage* (London: Chatto and Windus, 1883), pp. 201–02.
37. *Spectator*, 8 November 1879; Alan Hughes, *Henry Irving, Shakespearean* (Cambridge: Cambridge University Press, 1981), p. 232, p. 69, cited in Russell Jackson, "Actor-Managers and the Spectacular," in Bate and Jackson, *Shakespeare: An Illustrated Stage History*, pp. 112–27, p. 121.
38. *Ellen Terry's Memoirs, with a Preface, Notes, and Additional Biographical Chapters by Edith Craig and Christopher St. John* (New York: G. P. Putnam's Sons, 1932), p. 173. For another description of Irving's strange movements, see William Archer, *Henry Irving, Actor and Manager: A Critical Study* (London: Field & Tuer, 1883).

39. Anthony Sher, *The Year of the King* (London: Methuen, 1985), pp. 28–29.
40. Cited in Peter Holland, " 'Some of you may have seen him': Laurence Olivier's Celebrity," in *Theatre and Celebrity in Britain 1660–2000*, ed. Mary Luckhurst and Jane Moody (London: Palgrave, 2005). My thanks to Holland for sending me his essay in manuscript.
41. Laurence Olivier, *On Acting* (New York: Simon and Schuster, 1986), p. 275.
42. *Ibid.*, p. 30.
43. Peter Brook, quoted in Michael Billington, " 'I hate nothing more than art and culture' " (8 June 2005); www.guardian.co.uk, accessed 8 June 2005.
44. Roach, *Cities of the Dead*, p. 83.
45. Michael Pennington, "The Kingmakers" (21 May 2005); www.guardian.arts.co.uk, accessed 2 June 2005.
46. Simon Callow, " 'When he speaks, I hear Shakespeare think' " (14 April 2005); www.guardian.co.uk, accessed 6 June 2005.
47. *Ibid.*
48. *Ibid.*
49. Pennington, "The Kingmakers."
50. Gussow, *Gambon*, p. 128.
51. Kenneth Branagh, *Much Ado About Nothing by William Shakespeare, A Screenplay* (London and New York: W. W. Norton, 1993), pp. x–xi.
52. For a brilliant reading of Olivier, see Holland, " 'Some of you may have seen him'."
53. Quoted in John Heilpern, "Empire of the Stage," *Vanity Fair* 423 (November 1995), p. 192.
54. On the "It" phenomenon, see Joseph Roach, "It," *Theatre Journal* 56 (2004), 555–68.
55. Christine Gledhill, *Stardom: Industry of Desire* (London and New York: Routledge, 1991).
56. Anthony Lane, "Tights! Camera! Action!" *New Yorker* (25 November 1996), p. 72.
57. Heilpern, "Empire of the Stage," p. 225.
58. See www.laurenceolivier.com
59. See www.mckellen.com
60. Richard Schechner, "A New Paradigm for Theatre in the Academy," *The Drama Review – The Journal of Performance Studies* 36:4 (1992), 7–10.
61. See Richard Dyer, *Stars* (London: BFI Publishing, 1982), p. 11.
62. Opening monologue, *Saturday Night Live,* 16 March 2002; see www.mckellen.com
63. Gambon's Falstaff in Nicholas Hytner's productions of *1* and *2 Henry IV* at London's Royal National Theatre (May–August 2005).
64. Gussow, *Gambon*, p. 42. Snowdon's portrait can be found in *Snowdon on Stage: With a Personal View of the British Theatre, 1955–96* (London: Pavilion Books, 1999), p. 156.
65. Gussow, *Gambon*, p. 85.
66. *Ibid.*, p. 173.

4

STEPHEN ORGEL

Shakespeare illustrated

The earliest illustration of a Shakespearean subject, and the only one surviving from Shakespeare's lifetime, is a drawing related to *Titus Andronicus*. (Figure 2) It appears on a single sheet preserved in the collection of the Marquess of Bath at Longleat; it is inscribed with the name of Henry Peacham, presumably the emblem writer and author of *The Complete Gentleman*, and a date that has been interpreted as either 1595 or (more persuasively) 1614/15. The picture is so well known that to reproduce it yet again would be superfluous were it not for its uniqueness as the sole visual testimony of a spectator contemporary with Shakespeare – this is where any discussion of Shakespearean illustration must begin.

The drawing shows Queen Tamora pleading with Titus for the life of her two sons, who kneel on the right, guarded by Aaron the Moor, as two soldiers watch. These are all characters in the play, and they are certainly performing a scene; but the scene is not in the play – or at least, not in any version that survives. There is a portion of the opening scene that includes all the figures depicted in the drawing, but at this point Aaron is a prisoner along with the two sons, and could not be standing over them with drawn sword. Below the drawing is a dramatic extract. It is this that identifies the drawing as relating to Shakespeare's *Titus*, but the passage transcribed is not simply a quotation from the play. It combines passages from two separate scenes: an exchange between Tamora and Titus from Act 1 is answered by a speech of Aaron's from Act 5 – both the scene and the text represent a conspectus or epitome of the drama.

This drawing is not, then, an eye-witness sketch of Shakespeare on the stage; but it shows how a contemporary imagined Shakespeare in action, and is certainly informed by a theatregoer's experience. The costumes are especially notable. Titus is in Roman dress, and Tamora is in some sort of generalized royal dress, neither Elizabethan nor Roman, but vaguely medieval. The sons and Aaron are in ambiguous costumes: the sleeves are Elizabethan, and they wear either Elizabethan pants or Roman military

2 Henry Peacham, a scene from *Titus Andronicus*, c. 1614–15. The only illustration of a Shakespeare play surviving from Shakespeare's lifetime.

skirts, though the sash on the son on the left is the same as Titus's, and is presumably intended as Roman. But the guards are fully outfitted Jacobean soldiers. This all looks inept and unconvincing to us, but the inconsistency and anachronism are clearly essential elements, and not included casually or thoughtlessly. The costumes are designed to indicate the characters' roles, their relation to each other, and most important, their relation to us. A few elements are included to suggest the classical setting, but there is no attempt to mirror a world or recreate a historical moment. The anachronistic details serve as our guides, accounting for the figures, locating them in relation to our world, and locating us in turn in relation to theirs.

We are always told that the Renaissance stage performed history as if it were contemporary, but images such as this render such a claim untenable. On the contrary, the drawing provides a good index to the limitations on the imagination of otherness. Our sense of the other depends on our sense of its relation to ourselves; we understand it in so far as it differs from us, and conversely, we know ourselves only through comparison and contrast, through a knowledge of what we are not – we construct the other as a way of affirming the self. The anachronisms here (and, indeed, throughout Shakespearean drama), far from being incidental or inept, are essential; they are what locate us in history. The meaningful re-creation of the past requires the semiotics of the present. Indeed, the concept of anachronism may be considered essential to the very notion of historical relevance itself, which assumes that the past is in some way a version of the present.

Only two other Shakespeare illustrations survive from the seventeenth century, both relating to the most perennially popular of his characters, Falstaff. A quick costume sketch by Inigo Jones for a 1635 masque shows a portly soldier labeled "like a Sir John Falstaff"; and Falstaff and Mistress Quickly appear among a group of famous clowns on the engraved title page to *The Wits* (1661), an anthology of comic skits. Aside from these examples, the Shakespeare visualized by the seventeenth century was confined to various versions of the playwright's portrait: the engraving by Martin Droeshout introducing the first four folios, adapted also for the title page to John Benson's 1640 edition of the *Poems*; the bust on the Stratford funeral monument sculpted by Gerard Janssen the younger; and several dubious revisions and rationalizations of the famous Chandos painting (the "standard" portrait of Shakespeare, now in the National Portrait Gallery, London), which is almost certainly a portrait of somebody else.

The first illustrated Shakespeare was also the first attempt at a systematic edition, Nicholas Rowe's *Works of Mr. William Shakespear*, published by Jacob Tonson in 1709. This was, for the English market, a significant innovation. Dramatic texts on the continent had been illustrated, often by major artists, throughout the sixteenth and seventeenth centuries; but the English tradition was exceedingly meagre. A small number of early play quartos had frontispiece or title page illustrations, for the most part crude woodcuts. The only fully illustrated play was Elkanah Settle's heroic tragedy *The Empress of Morocco* (1673). The volume was a real attempt to locate Settle's text in the theatre: it had as a frontispiece the façade of the Dorset Garden (or Duke's) Theatre, where the play was performed, and included five engravings of stage settings and action. These look, however, much more like book illustrations than theatrical performances; even at their most imaginative their decorative frames overwhelm them, and particularly a sensationally gory conclusion, with the body parts of executed victims displayed hanging on a grillwork, is much too neatly contained – the stage, for this artist, is clearly constrained by the page. Dryden, who called the play "a rhapsody of nonsense,"[1] was especially contemptuous of its publication with illustrations, and attacked it in a pamphlet called *Notes and observations on The empress of Morocco, or, Some few errata's to be printed instead of the sculptures with the second edition of that play* (1674) – the second edition, thirteen years later, was indeed published without illustrations, as was the third in 1698. The play was a success, but London publishers clearly felt that playtexts would do well enough on their own. When seventeenth-century English publishers did issue elegant and expensive books of plays, collected (and usually memorial) volumes, they embellished them not with dramatic scenes, but with portraits of the author – Shakespeare, Jonson, Fletcher (no portrait of Beaumont was available), Cartwright, Killigrew, Sir Thomas Howard. So plays became literature, visualizing the author rather than the stage.

But for Rowe's Shakespeare, Tonson provided every play with a frontispiece, for the most part reflecting contemporary stage practice. The *Hamlet* illustration, for example, shows the bedchamber scene with the ghost appearing, and an overturned chair, which Hamlet has toppled in his excitement. Betterton had introduced the overturned chair into his productions; and the Hamlet in the illustration is doubtless Betterton. Even in the frontispieces to plays that had not been performed for more than a century, such as *The Two Gentlemen of Verona*, the stage was modern. The illustration to *Troilus and Cressida* (figure 3) nicely encapsulates the assumptions guiding Rowe's imagination of Shakespeare. The scene depicted is 5.2, in which Cressida, watched from behind the stage curtain by Ulysses, Troilus, and Thersites, gives Diomede the sleeve, or decorative armband, that Troilus had given her as a love token. The theatre represented is an early eighteenth-century one, with a proscenium and artificial lighting. The play had never been staged before the Restoration, and thereafter was presented only in Dryden's revision, in which Cressida gives Diomede not a sleeve, but a ring – a

3 Frontispiece to *Troilus and Cressida*, from Nicholas Rowe's edition of Shakespeare, 1709. The scene illustrated is 5.2: Troilus, Ulysses and Thersites watch from behind the curtain as Cressida gives Diomede the love token she has received from Troilus.

less chivalric and medieval, more romantic and modern token. The artist is scrupulous about adhering to Shakespeare's text, but his stage is Dryden's. The costumes, too, are enlightening: the men are in an approximation of classical armor, but Cressida is clothed as a modern courtesan – the conventions of costuming are unchanged from those of the Peacham drawing a century earlier. The same sense of the virtues of anachronism is evident in the frontispiece to *Henry VIII*, in which the King appears in a costume based on Holbein's famous portrait, but his courtiers are in eighteenth-century frock coats and wigs.

For Rowe's second edition, published in 1714, the illustrations were redone – Tonson now had a group of French engravers in his service, and most of the plates were simply copied more stylishly, the point being not to reflect the stage more accurately, but to produce a more elegant book. The move towards reconceiving Shakespeare as a bibliophile classic, with the plates as a primary attraction, had begun; and as the eighteenth century progressed, through the talents of such artists as Louis du Guernier, Michael van der Gucht, and Francis Hayman, Shakespearean illustration grew increasingly independent of the stage tradition, less concerned with realizing the plays in action than with devising an artistic style appropriate to Shakespearean poetry. The first edition of Pope's Shakespeare (1723–25) included only two engraved frontispiece portraits; but for the second edition (1728), Tonson commissioned a full suite of thirty-six scenes. Similarly, the second edition of Theobald's Shakespeare (1740) and Hanmer's Shakespeare (1744) were handsomely illustrated in the French style – the plates suggest not the theatre but the paintings of Watteau and Boucher. All these editions were major scholarly efforts, but the pictures were clearly felt to add significantly to their value – Shakespeare was a book to be embellished.

For the first time, too, painters were finding in Shakespeare a suitable subject. One of the earliest examples was Hogarth's version of a scene from *The Tempest*, a baroque, sentimental fantasy costumed in the style of Van Dyck and Rembrandt, not at all related to the stage tradition. Ferdinand emerges from the sea bowing before an enthroned Miranda, watched by Prospero, resembling a Rembrandt rabbi, while a cherubic Ariel hovers above with a lute, and a deformed, malevolent Caliban carrying logs crushes one of a pair of linked doves beneath his clawed foot. The painting was done around 1735 – at this period the theatrical *Tempest* was that of Davenant and Dryden, in which Prospero's household includes a sister to Miranda named Dorinda, and a youth named Hippolito; Ariel has a spirit-girlfriend named Milcha; and the comic Caliban is supplied with a lumpish sister named Sycorax. Hogarth's visual repertory, in contrast, is that of classic annunciation and nativity paintings; his vision of *The Tempest* was derived from his artistic

4 William Hogarth, *Mr. Garrick in the character of Richard the 3d*, 1746, engraving by
Hogarth after the painting.

heritage, not from his playgoing. It was also heavily dependent on his reading –
if this was not Shakespeare's *Tempest*, it was nevertheless the play of the new
editorial and bibliophile tradition, the *Tempest* of Rowe, Pope, Theobald, and
the increasingly elaborate illustrated Shakespeare.

Hogarth's next Shakespearean painting, however, was explicitly theatrical: the superb portrait of Garrick as Richard III, recording and celebrating
the actor's first great success, at the Goodman's Fields Theatre in 1741,
repeated thereafter innumerable times throughout his career at Drury
Lane. (Figure 4) The painting conveys brilliantly Garrick's strikingly original
conception of the character, not the half-comic machiavel of Shakespeare's
text, but a figure of magnificent will and passionate intensity, satanic but
also heroic and even glamorous. Through the combined efforts of Garrick
and Hogarth, this became the standard interpretation of the role. The
engraving Hogarth made from this painting was phenomenally popular,
and for generations of English audiences, well into the next century, it
depicted less Garrick in a particular role than a portrait of Richard III; so
that in 1801 Charles Lamb could criticize the actor George Frederick Cooke
for emphasizing the villainous and grotesque aspects of the part, elements that
are certainly not underplayed in Shakespeare's text. Hogarth places this dramatic

moment, however, not on a stage but on a minutely rendered battlefield – the play is realized in action.

Garrick's career was chronicled and celebrated through painting and engraving – the paintings were often commissioned by Garrick himself. These included not only scenes from his productions by Zoffany, Reynolds, Benjamin Wilson, and Zuccarelli, but also (perhaps more significantly for the history of theatre) portraits of Garrick as a gentleman – for example, at home at his country estate at Twickenham, or as an avatar of Shakespeare, contemplating the playwright's bust and attended by the admiring allegorical figures of comedy and tragedy. At the same time Henry Fuseli was recording Garrick's *Macbeth* and *Richard III* in brilliant eye-witness drawings that constitute an invaluable record of the eighteenth-century stage. The dagger scene in *Macbeth* particularly, as performed by Garrick and Mrs. Pritchard, served as a touchstone for Fuseli throughout his life – he sketched it in performance in 1766 with a feverish energy that brilliantly renders the production's explosive tension; did a classicized version of the scene in 1774; and as late as 1812 did a ghostly, eerily powerful recollection of the same moment.

From Garrick's time on, Shakespearean illustration was increasingly concerned with depictions of famous actors in their roles. Zoffany's paintings provide the best record we have of Macklin's Shylock, and Bell's popular editions of Shakespeare (published from 1774 onward) were illustrated with scenes from contemporary productions and portraits of individual performers. The market for Shakespeare had become a market for theatrical stars. But it had become a market for artistic innovation as well. Paradoxically, depictions of Shakespeare also moved increasingly away from the stage, towards creative realizations of the dramatic action in a world unconstrained by actors or theatres. These rarely expanded the imaginative horizon. From 1781 to 1786 Robert Smirke and Thomas Stothard published forty plates comprising *The Picturesque Beauties of Shakespeare* – the pictures were issued both by themselves and accompanied by the texts of the plays. One could, that is, see the plates either as realizing the texts, or as embellishing them; but in either case, Shakespeare is construed exclusively in terms of picturesque beauties – a century and a half earlier Milton had similarly diminished Shakespeare's breadth and power, imagining, in *L'Allegro*, "Sweetest Shakespeare, fancy's child / Warble his native woodnotes wild":[2] Shakespeare the artless free spirit, at home with fancy and nature; even more reductive, Shakespeare the *child*. The sentimentalization and miniaturization are part of a bucolic and disarming fantasy about Shakespeare, who is, after all, not only the author of the sweet, fanciful, picturesque *Midsummer Night's Dream*, but of *Richard III*, *Macbeth*, *King Lear*, *Coriolanus*, daunting models for even so self-confident a poet as Milton, to say nothing of artists like Smirke and Stothard. It is, however, a fantasy that starts very early – "O Sweet Master Shakespeare," says a character named Gull in a satiric academic play called *The Return from Parnassus* in 1600, "I'll have his picture in my study."[3] Sweet master Shakespeare becomes the contemplative muse: Milton in 1631 treats this as already a commonplace, and it continues to be an integral part of the legend.

A critical figure in the transition described here was John Boydell, engraver and publisher, alderman, sheriff, and ultimately Lord Mayor of London, who in 1786 announced his intention of commissioning a series of paintings illustrative of Shakespeare, and the creation of a Shakespeare Gallery, which he duly opened in Pall Mall. The grand motive behind this scheme was to found and encourage a native British school of history painting – this was considered the most serious kind of painting, but it had found few practitioners and fewer patrons in England. British artists, Boydell believed, had the technical skill and the genius necessary to compete with history painters on the continent; what they lacked was a suitable subject. And the one national subject about which there could be no disagreement, Boydell concluded, was Shakespeare.

There is a significant slippage in Boydell's proposal, from Shakespeare as a national subject to Shakespeare as a historical subject. As a way of regarding Shakespearean drama, this constitutes a radical departure from the stage tradition. Garrick's Hamlet and Macbeth, Macklin's Shylock, Spranger Barry's Romeo, were costumed in modern dress. In 1786, however, Boydell conceived Shakespeare as no longer our contemporary, but history. There were, in fact, some premonitions: the first Shakespeare production in Elizabethan dress had already been presented three years earlier, John Philip Kemble's *Hamlet*, and Talma was about to launch a similar movement on the Paris stage. It was clearly an idea whose time had come.

History painting as Boydell and the age conceived it implies relatively little in the way of archaeological fidelity, though it does tie the expression of noble sentiments and general truths to particular historical moments or incidents, and therefore consistency and credibility are central to it, providing the drama with a seriousness that is maintained in great measure precisely through the move into history. Tragedy and the heroic were in the past, historic. Comedy posed less of a problem (as it was also, for artistic theorists, of less interest), but in both cases the crucial point was the removal of the plays from the distractions and trivialities of present time. The real issue was, however, *whose* history was evoked in the plays, Shakespeare's or those of the characters. Kemble's Hamlet was clothed as an Elizabethan; Talma's Hamlet, a sixteenth-century German university student, wore a historically correct academic gown.

Boydell's artists, who included some of the major figures of the age – Reynolds, Romney, Wright of Derby, Fuseli – found the Shakespearean subject matter attractive, but responded only indifferently to the historicizing aspects of the project. *As You Like It* and *Much Ado About Nothing* are, in Boydell's collection, entirely modern, populated by young people out on a party, modishly dressed in the fashions of the 1790s; and plays like *Cymbeline* and *The Merchant of Venice* are located in a generalized romantic past, not even specific enough for anachronisms to be noticeable. The costumes in James Barry's *King Lear* include a medley of antique styles, from Roman helmets to Elizabethan housedresses, and the only gesture towards history is a view of a pristine Stonehenge in the background. *Measure for Measure* and *All's Well That Ends Well* maintain a fairly consistent sixteenth-century look; and though the Roman plays are classical enough, the English histories tend to be historical only in detail – fifteenth-century armor and ecclesiastical garb, gothic backgrounds. In fact, the most impressive of Boydell's pictures are those that ignore the historical premise entirely – Fuseli's Prospero, modeled on Leonardo da Vinci, facing down a diabolical Caliban with the magnificent body of a classical Hercules; or his Macbeth, naked and heroic, invoking the witches, who appear hovering in midair, impossibly out of scale (figure 5). Boydell's Shakespeare also, moreover, included pictures that did not illustrate

5 James Caldwell, after Henry Fuseli, *Macbeth, Banquo and Three Witches*, from John Boydell, *A collection of prints, from pictures painted for the purpose of illustrating the Dramatic works of Shakespeare, by the artists of Great-Britain*, London, 1803.

the plays at all, but realized moments in the poetry. For example, in Robert Smirke's series of canvases showing the Seven Ages of Man, from the "All the world's a stage" speech in *As You Like It* – the lover, a young man composing his love poems, is shown at a table beneath two pictures of Cupid, on the right seated triumphant atop the globe, on the left performing the balcony scene from *Romeo and Juliet*. The lover is not a character in the play; he is part of a rhetorical set piece recited by Jaques for the entertainment of the exiled Duke Senior and his companions. Shakespearean poetry is here detached from Shakespearean drama, in a way that literary criticism was not to attempt until Coleridge in the next century. Fuseli went on to provide brilliant, disturbing, often surreal illustrations for Rivington's Shakespeare in 1805. The plates were engraved by William Blake, who was himself producing a series of astonishing visual meditations on Shakespearean imagery – pity like a naked newborn babe (from *Macbeth*); the triple Hecate (mentioned in *A Midsummer Night's Dream*); Oberon and Titania nestled in two giant lilies; Queen Katherine's dream (described in *Henry VIII*); a strikingly beautiful, not at all comic, view of Jaques and the wounded stag (from *As You Like It*); a powerfully attenuated Brutus confronted by the ghost of Caesar; and many more. The plays' poetic imagery was a similar source of free-floating invention for John Flaxman, whose sketches on Shakespearean themes are scarcely less imaginative.

Boydell's Shakespeare Gallery in Pall Mall was a failure, but its significance was immense; it contributed, through engraved versions of the paintings, an iconography of Shakespearean drama that remained influential for more than a century (indeed, the engravings are still being reproduced). Moreover, despite the fact that the iconography was for the most part not historical, the stage began to follow Boydell's principles rather than his artists' practice: increasingly in the nineteenth century theatre was seen as a kind of history painting. The first historically correct productions were those of Charles Kemble (younger brother of John Philip Kemble, who forty years earlier had done the first *Hamlet* in Elizabethan dress), with sets and costumes based on the researches and designs of James Robinson Planché. Playbills and advertisements for such productions always stressed, as a primary attraction, the historical seriousness of the event. The playbill for Kemble's 1823 *King John*, an originary moment for stage archaeology, declares that the play will be presented "with an attention to costume never before equalled on the English stage. Every character will appear in the precise habit of the period, the whole of the dresses and decorations being executed from indisputable authorities" – the authorities cited are not textual but material, visual, documentary: tomb effigies, royal seals, manuscript illuminations. These were the models Planché provided for Shakespeare. They served first as the basis for the costumes of

Kemble's *King John,* and, two decades later, in 1842, for those of Macready's production of the same play – the costumes remained unchanged because they stamped the productions as authentic. This is what Planché did to theatre. It also gives a striking sense of what the attractions of theatre were now conceived to be. The underlying assumptions here are not new. Kemble and Planché reassert Addison's claim a century earlier, in his treatise *On Medals* (1708), that the truth of history is not to be found in literature, which is too prone to misrepresentation on the one hand and misinterpretation on the other, but in objects, the material remains of culture. And Addison, in his turn, was refining and refiguring the ideology of a long line of Renaissance humanist antiquarians. But this *is* a new idea for the stage, and the most striking part of it is the assumption that the truth of both theatre and drama is the truth of history.

Planché's work was a manifesto, backed by a genuine historical impulse and informed by an impressive body of scholarship. His several histories and encyclopedias of British costume, published in increasingly enlarged editions from the 1840s, remain useful reference works today. He also published a series of historically correct costume designs for a number of Shakespeare plays, to serve as models for "authentic" productions. Figure 6 shows his costume for Queen Anne in *Richard III*; the plate is accompanied by a detailed account of the sources for each item of dress, as well as a critique of Shakespeare's historical errors in relation to Richard's and Anne's marriage. Planché not only laid down rules for the histories and corrected their facts; he also published "correct" costume designs for *Hamlet, Othello, As You Like It,* and several other plays, for which he selected appropriate, if arbitrary, historical eras.

Shakespeare could not, of course, be appropriated for history in any simple way. It is both ironic and characteristic that the first Shakespeare production to claim serious historical credentials should have been *King John*, a history of the reign that does not mention Magna Carta. Kemble apologized in his playbill for Shakespeare's omission, though he stopped short of rectifying it. (Herbert Beerbohm Tree, in his 1899 *King John*, finally supplied the lack with a sumptuous pantomime of the king signing the elusive document.) Shakespeare, in fact, was always insufficiently historical – for *Henry V* Charles Kean included a number of spectacular reconstructions of events and places that are only described or alluded to in the play, or, in some cases, that are not in the play at all, but only in the chronicles on which the play is based. The most lavish of the historical spectacles was devised for Henry's triumphant return to London after the victory at Agincourt, an event that is dispatched in ten lines of the Chorus's prologue to Act 5. This was a tremendously effective scene, duly illustrated in the major papers. Such mute addenda do more than "correct" Shakespeare. They acknowledge an

Anne Queen of Richard 3.

6 James Robinson Planché, costume design for Queen Anne in *Richard III*. From
C. F. Tomkins, after J. R. Planché, *Twelve Designs for the Costume of Shakespeare's
Richard the Third*. London, 1830. Colored engraving.

increasing problem in both imagining and elucidating the plays: the fact that Shakespeare's concerns often simply do not coincide with ours. The Magna Carta scene, the entry into London, therefore rectify not only history, but Shakespeare's imagination as well.

To locate the plays in history was thereby to enable the theatre to present an entirely consistent stage picture. Consistency was an issue throughout the period, in all aspects of Shakespearean realization. Characters were given not merely motivations, but psychologies, pasts and futures. Charles and Mary Lamb's *Tales from Shakespeare* recount, rationalize, humanize (and sometimes, as in the account of *Measure for Measure*, sanitize) their originals; and the idea that characters have a life beyond, and not dependent on, their dramas is one that extends far beyond the nineteenth century and dramatic criticism – psychoanalytic critics have rarely been clear about whether their subjects were, say, Hamlet and Othello, or Shakespeare. The great Victorian monument to this way of conceiving Shakespearean character was Mary Cowden Clarke's *The Girlhood of Shakespeare's Heroines* (1851, and many subsequent editions and revisions). We feel very far from this famous and influential work now, but we are not at all, in our critical and editorial practice, free of its assumption that the essence of drama is character, that characters have consistent psychologies determining their motivations, and that what we see of them is only part of a larger whole that exists outside the play. Shakespeare's knowledge of human psychology has always been claimed to be beyond praise, but in fact the plays have always required a good deal of help in this department, and much of the commentary in editions since Pope's has been concerned with explaining why the characters say what they say, justifying lines that look obscure or inconsistent, when they have not been editorially "rectified" by outright emendation. The character is thus conceived to be something different from the lines, prior to the dialogue we are elucidating or emending.

This seems to us a logical and perhaps even inevitable procedure (the characters, after all, are surely supposed to behave like people); the issue is only how far beyond the play the life of its personnel may be said to extend. Clarke's fictions were illustrated with putative portraits of her heroines in their youth. For example, a serenely meditative Isabella, her head demurely covered with a shawl, long before the events of *Measure for Measure* seems already destined for the convent. Of course, psychologists with even minimal clinical experience might find such an implied narrative simplistic, inadequate to account for the fierceness and coldness of her behavior to her condemned brother; and an actor might conceive a more satisfactorily complex Isabella by imagining the move towards the convent not as assured and untroubled but as, say, the product of a painful adolescent rebellion, or as a flight from her own passionate nature. Representation brings the text to life, but it also closes down options. Clarke continued her focus on Shakespeare's heroines in her subsequent edition of Shakespeare's works, which was illustrated exclusively with pictures of the female characters. She has therefore been claimed as a prototypical feminist; but the point is surely not the mere fact that women, rather than men, are represented, but *how* the women are represented; and here Clarke offers nothing to disturb her society's notions of what women are or should be.

Enterprises such as Planché and Kemble's, or as Clarke's, suggest that what is real about Shakespeare is not the dramatic action and the poetry, but what is being represented – the characters, versions of real people with pasts and futures; the events, increasingly conceived as historical, that the plays record. Hence the attempt to correct Shakespeare by reference to chronicles or archeology. The great illustrative version of this movement is found in Charles Knight's *Pictorial Edition of the Works of Shakespeare*, issued in eight volumes from 1838 to 1843. This vast, extraordinary work undertakes to translate everything in the text of the plays into pictorial form – not dramatic action only, but allusions and poetic imagery. When, in *The Taming of the Shrew*, Tranio identifies himself as coming from Pisa, a view of the Duomo and the Leaning Tower is appended; a reference to an argosy is glossed with a picture of a merchant ship; Gonzalo's reference in *The Tempest* to "mountaineers / Dewlapped like bulls" is accompanied by an image of a Swiss peasant with a goiter; Petruchio's characterization of Kate as his falcon is illustrated with an engraving of King James I hawking. There is hardly a page in this huge compilation without multiple images, tying the imaginative world of the plays to a world of fact and history – or at least, to whatever in that world could be represented visually. The illustrations in part serve as footnotes and running commentary, but often, as with the last of my examples, they are pointless, an index primarily to the intensity of the editorial conviction that everything in the text requires a visual counterpart – the pictures, indeed, were the point of the enterprise. Knight's edition created a vast pictorial repertory for Shakespeare that is still being mined today to sell cheap reprint editions.

Knight's Shakespeare was a genuine sign of the times, addressed to a middle-class audience with a growing, carefully educated, taste for paintings in their homes, and an enthusiasm for theatre as a thoroughly proper entertainment – as everything that is implied in the epithet "the legitimate stage." The Shakespearean stage was now respectable, educational, increasingly evoking a world of historical and factual re-creation; and the key element in that re-creation was pictorial: setting, costume, a world of visual detail, which often crowded out the dialogue in favor of spectacular tableaux. (The *Saturday Review*, after praising the décor of Charles Kean's 1857 *Tempest*, remarked that "as for the acting, there is not very much room for it" [4 July 1857].) Tragedies and even comedies were increasingly located securely within historical time – spectacle guaranteed the popular appeal, but historical authenticity guaranteed the seriousness of Shakespearean theatre. Boydell's reinterpretation of Shakespeare as history painting had been realized by the stage – Shakespeare showed us what life was like in olden times. Of course, plays like *Hamlet* and *Macbeth* pose real problems: what time do you locate them in? John Philip Kemble's 1783 Elizabethan *Hamlet* was a logical start, placing the play in the world of Shakespeare and his audiences; but for directors like Charles Kemble and Charles Kean, the logic was irrelevant: the history had to be not Shakespeare's but Hamlet's, not the history of the play but that of its fictive hero – it was not until a century later that William Poel would realize the possibilities inherent in Kemble's historical experiment, and undertake to present the plays as Shakespeare's audiences would have seen them. As the nineteenth century began, however, the stage *Hamlet* moved backward in time to become a generalized medieval world, though the prince himself retained Kemble's Elizabethan puff-pants until the 1830s, when Charles Kean introduced the more properly medieval tunic. Delacroix's famous series of lithographs of the play, published in 1844, is obviously influenced by an older stage practice – the only time he saw *Hamlet* was apparently on a visit of the English players to Paris in 1827, in a production which had a rather generalized Renaissance style. The lithograph in figure 7, done almost twenty years later, is his version, or recollection, of the bedchamber scene, just before the murder of Polonius (whose feet are visible beneath the curtain). The medieval Queen's costume is a good two hundred years earlier than her son's. Talma, in Paris, had already, several decades before, presented his archeologically correct Hamlet as a sixteenth-century German university student.

There is no reason to feel that Talma's décor is more appropriate, more authentic, than Delacroix's – Shakespeare, even in the history plays, is full of anachronisms – but the trend in both production and illustration was increasingly towards Planché's and Talma's kind of literalism; and the text, in this enterprise, often had to be radically adjusted. Charles Kean's 1856 *Winter's Tale*, for example, set the play (entirely arbitrarily) in an archeologically correct Sicily of the fourth century BC, and all anachronisms in the text were excised. There were therefore no references to the emperor of Russia, Giulio Romano, Whitsun pastorals, saint-like sorrows, and the like. An eminent archeologist was engaged to provide authentic costumes and properties, which were derived from the palpable evidence of vase paintings and ancient artifacts. Shakespeare's fairy tale became a re-creation of the ancient world, historically rationalized. Kean dealt with the fact that

7 Eugène Delacroix, the bedchamber scene in *Hamlet* (3.4), 1844. Lithograph.

Bohemia did not exist in the fourth century (as well as with the notorious problem of its seacoast) by emending the locale of the pastoral scenes to Bithynia – authenticity can always be invented. Book illustration was not far behind: figure 8 shows the statue scene, from an exquisitely produced art book of "authentically" classical scenes from the play published around 1860: this imagined world has nothing to do with Giulio Romano, and little enough to do with Shakespeare. The book, moreover, gives no information

8 Anon., the statue scene from *The Winter's Tale* (5.3), from *Scenes from The Winter's Tale*, London, n.d. (*c.* 1860). Colored lithograph.

about either its artist or date, nothing that would locate it in the world of modern art or commerce – authenticity can go no further.

By the beginning of the twentieth century, tastes on the stage had changed. Productions were beginning to take their cue not from archeology but from modern art and technology – Henry Irving's spectacles in the 1880s and 1890s, especially *King Lear* and *Macbeth*, though they relied heavily on a sophisticated electric lighting system, were the last of the great historical re-creations. Herbert Beerbohm Tree's 1905 *Tempest* was no less spectacular, but it was a different sort of spectacle, far more concerned with the subtle and shifting impressionistic visual effects enabled by electric light than with reviving the past. Harley Granville Barker's 1912 *Winter's Tale* was genuinely innovative, setting the play on a thrust stage with settings that recalled post-impressionist painting, Léon Bakst's sets for the Diaghilev ballet, and the styles of Charles Rennie Mackintosh and the incipient art deco movement. At the same time, the Shakespearean art book – elegantly produced volumes of Shakespeare illustrated by well-known contemporary artists – now, analogously, offered a fertile field for a broad range of artistic innovation, and, for the book trade, such volumes now constituted a recognizable genre. These for the most part made no reference to the theatre; the illustrations did not realize the dramatic action, but retold the story or imaginatively refigured the poetry. Notably successful examples were Arthur Rackham's *Midsummer Night's Dream* (1908), W. Heath Robinson's *Midsummer Night's Dream* (1914), and Edmund Dulac's *Tempest* (1908). All were several times reprinted in both elaborate limited versions and cheap editions.

Dulac's *Tempest*, in its selection of subjects and the conspectus it presents of the play, may serve as an epitome of Shakespearean book illustration at the beginning of the twentieth century. Even the trade edition of the book is handsomely produced, in a light green binding with elegantly varied typography and gold-stamped decorations – a bird and a dragon (perhaps some creature of Shakespeare's inhospitable isle) flank the title, and a large central medallion shows Ariel raising the storm that opens the play. The illustrations consist of forty watercolors, reproduced in color and tipped onto dark green cardboard inserts throughout the book. Each plate has a tissue guard with a caption, generally citing the line illustrated, but sometimes giving simply the name of the character depicted. The volume includes a full text, with no notes, but with a plot summary and brief commentary by Arthur Quiller-Couch. This introduction is entitled "The Story of *The Tempest*" – the drama is firmly narrativized. Quiller-Couch was a Cambridge don, a prolific writer in many genres, especially the retelling of folk and fairy tales, though he was not yet the distinguished Shakespearean scholar he was eventually to become. He was surely chosen as much for his academic respectability as for his narrative talent. The general design of the volume, however, gives the impression less of a bibliophile edition or an art book than of a lavish children's book. Quiller-Couch's introduction, indeed, concludes by observing that for most readers *The Tempest* was their earliest Shakespeare (this would surely not be the case today), the first "to open our children's eyes and catch their fluttering imaginations," and even asserting that "for the child, Shakespeare in this his closing work becomes a child again."[4] The idea of "Sweetest Shakespeare, fancy's child" was as potent in 1908 as it had been for Milton in 1630.

Quiller Couch's "Story" of the play is skillfully told, with the problematic elements (such as the issue of Prospero's dubious right to the island and the justice of his treatment of both Caliban and Ariel) suppressed – until, surprisingly, at the very end, a brief commentary questions Prospero's authority and insists on the validity of Caliban's claims. The play is not, after all, simply a fairy tale, and Prospero is not Shakespeare:

> Irony, wise and resigned, underlies all the romance of the story. The island is, after all, not Prospero's ... This bookworm Prospero is a hard master, reaping where he has not sown and gathering where he has not strawed; abominably

potent, to be kneeled to because he can afflict Caliban's bed with hedgehogs; and Ariel has been enlarged for a season to play his tricks.[5]

The play is, finally, a political and moral parable with a distinct sting.

It is a striking double vision, but none of its negative side informs Dulac's images, in which the fairy tale remains paramount throughout. Of the forty paintings, only twelve may be said to depict dramatic action at all. Some illustrate narrated scenes from the past: Prospero "rapt in secret studies" (1.2.77) a conventional magician surrounded by alchemical retorts and books; his arrival on the island twelve years before with the infant Miranda, watched from a cliff by the unseen Caliban; the long dead witch Sycorax, Caliban's mother, confining the angelic, recalcitrant, Ariel in a cloven tree (not, in Dulac's rendering, the pine of the text). Other images are inspired by poetic conceits, analogies, bits of description, pictorial moments in the verse: a group of musical spirits produce the "sounds and sweet airs that give delight and hurt not" (3.2.139) which Caliban tells Stephano and Trinculo are his only comfort on the island; a proleptic vision of an adult, domestic Miranda educating her future children in an Italian garden is extrapolated from Juno's wish, in the masque, that the young couple be "honoured in their issue"(4.1.105); a surreal, almost abstract vision represents Prospero's "We are such stuff / As dreams are made on" (4.1.136–37); Prospero's great renunciation speech in Act 5, "Ye elves of hills, brooks, standing lakes and groves" (5.1.33–57) elicits (disappointingly) only a wispy group of fairy creatures flying off into the moonlight.

Dulac's watercolors are for the most part richly imaginative, at times recalling Redon, Böcklin, or Klimt. Prospero and Miranda watching the storm stand perilously on a precipitous cliff overlooking a wild sea. They seem to grow out of the sheer rocks and mountains, to be part of that inhospitable nature. Prospero, bearded, dignified and alert, is in a robe adorned with magic symbols; he holds the terrified Miranda, her hair starting on end, in a firm and comforting embrace. Their garments echo the colors of the sea and rocks. Sea birds are the only other visible creatures. It is a powerful and beautiful composition. For Ariel's song "Full fathom five," Alonso drowned, on the ocean floor, his white hair and beard splayed, his hands and feet turning to coral, his red robe merging with the red rocks, becomes "something rich and strange" (1.2.404) before our eyes. He is watched by red-haired mermaids atop an undersea cliff; strange shapes of seaweed tower above him, and the largest area of the page is filled with the subtle, beautifully modulated bluish-grey wash of the watery atmosphere (figure 9). Not all the plates are as successful as these. The drama often loses out to the fairy tale, as in Prospero's "elves of hills" speech, cited above – the

9 Edmund Dulac, *Full Fathom Five Thy Father Lies*, color plate from *Shakespeare's Comedy of The Tempest*, London, 1908.

magician is here, after all, speaking the words of Ovid's Medea, the terrible, murderous sorceress, and the passage is as much an assertion of fearful power as it is of renunciation. Ferdinand throughout remains very much a fairy tale prince, much less individualized than Miranda (though Dulac's conspirators and clowns have a good deal of personality); and many of the drawings are content with simply inventing a cast of Prospero's spirits. For both artist and publisher here, the lavish children's book was clearly an inescapable model for the illustrated Shakespeare.

The greatest monument of Shakespearean illustration, and surely one of the most beautiful books ever produced, was the Cranach Press *Hamlet*, published in a German edition in 1928, and in an English edition in 1930. This tremendously ambitious project was conceived by Count Harry Kessler, founder of the Press, and took many years to complete. For it Kessler commissioned a new type based on a font used in the Mainz Psalter of 1457. Edward Gordon Craig, the stage designer, theorist and apostle of modernist theatre, and a brilliant printmaker (he was also Ellen Terry's son) was engaged to produce illustrative woodcuts; the book was printed in a strictly limited edition on handmade paper, with a few copies also on vellum.

In 1910 Craig had collaborated with Stanislavsky on a *Hamlet* for the Moscow Art Theatre. For this he designed a non-realistic stage, the central element of which was a set of complex, moveable screens. The collaboration was, from the outset, not a success – Craig's abstract theatre was the wrong vehicle for Stanislavsky's intensely psychologized, character-centered, view of drama; moreover, the screens could not be got to work properly, and kept falling down. But the concept remained with him, and the stage he could not create for Stanislavsky he realized in large measure for Kessler.

Kessler's conception was to present *Hamlet* in a Renaissance setting; the book would be a reflection of the historical *Hamlet* – not, however, the *Hamlet* of the quartos, or the Shakespeare folio, and least of all the putative "real" Hamlet; but a bibliographic embodiment of the towering monument to Renaissance culture that *Hamlet* had become. So the models for the book were the masterpieces of the great fifteenth- and sixteenth-century presses – the Nuremberg Chronicle, the *Hypnerotomachia*, the Gutenberg and Koberger bibles, the great Estienne and Plantin editions of the classics. It is significant that Kessler's typeface was based not on a font from Shakespeare's age, but on the grandest of the early German models: this Hamlet was the German intellectual, the Wittenburg student, the humanist philosopher and scholar. The design of the book was that of a very grand late fifteenth- or early sixteenth-century scholarly edition: the text was in the center of the page, and in the margins around it, in smaller type, related material was placed. In the original editions, the marginal material would have consisted of commentary and notes; Kessler's marginalia were the play's main sources, the Hamlet story in the Latin chronicle of Saxo Grammaticus and the *Histoires Tragiques* of François de Belleforest – these were printed in both the original languages and in translation. For the German edition, the text was the standard translation of August William Schlegel, embellished by Gerhardt Hauptmann, who supplied several brief additional scenes (such as the confrontation between Claudius's emissaries Voltimand and Cornelius and the Norwegian king) to fill in what he conceived to be gaps in the plot. (Schlegel's version itself was not unproblematic: for example, it moves the "To be or not to be" soliloquy to the fifth act.) For the English edition, J. Dover Wilson prepared a more sensible text based on the second quarto.

Craig provided seventy-two woodcuts for the German edition, and five additional ones for the English version. The deployment of these on the page resembles more the format of the Nuremberg Chronicle than any illustrated scholarly edition of drama (figure 10): the images are not contained by the typography, but are in a full partnership with it, and sometimes seem even in control. Hamlet and Horatio await the ghost, dwarfed by a setting composed of a combination of Craig's woodcut screens, Shakespeare's text, and Saxo's chronicle. Throughout the book, Craig's images are superbly attuned to the play's changes of mood. Several of the woodcuts had to be printed in two stages, to register lighter and darker blacks. For the Play Scene, a cast of *commedia dell'arte* characters in black silhouette appears in various formats – free-standing across the bottom margin, within whole scenes incised with white on black and grey backgrounds, in a tiny roundel in the center of a page, and most startling, for the Dumb Show, two elaborately masked and costumed silhouettes replacing the central text on two facing pages, with the description of the pantomime printed in red beneath them. Ophelia's last appearance is as a tiny white waif-like form within a grid of pale blue flanked by two of Craig's massive black woodcut screens, with a silhouetted mob beyond them – this is the only use of color in the woodcuts, and it is tremendously affecting. There is no illustrated Shakespeare in which the images are so thoroughly integrated with the typography, and in which text, book, and performance are conceived so completely as a whole.

The Cranach Press *Hamlet* is a good place to end this survey, not because it represents a conclusion in any sense, but because it undertakes to rethink the relation of drama, book, and image – in short, the nature of dramatic representation on the page – from the beginning; reconceives the book of the play as a performance. The most innovative of the subsequent developments in Shakespearean book illustration are probably the recent comic book versions, the most striking aspect of which is their presentation of a complete text to accompany the cartoon panels. Of these by far the most

ERSTER AKT
VIERTE SZENE

DIE TRAGISCHE GESCHICHTE VON

DIE TERRASSE

Ham. Die luft geht scharf, es ist entsetzlich kalt.
Hor. 's ist eine schneidende und strenge luft.
Ham. Was ist die uhr?
Hor. Ich denke, nah an zwölf.
Mar. Nicht doch, es hat geschlagen.
Hor. Wirklich schon?
  Ich hört es nicht. So rückt heran die stunde,
  Worin der geist gewohnt ist, umzugehn.
  Trompetenstoß und geschütz abgefeuert hinter der szene.
  Was stellt das vor, mein prinz?
Ham. Der könig wacht die nacht durch, zecht vollauf,
  Hält schmaus und taumelt den geräuschgen walzer.
  Und wie er züge rheinweins niedergießt,
  Verkünden schmetternd pauken und trompeten
  Den ausgebrachten trunk.
Hor. Ist das gebrauch?
Ham. Nun freilich wohl.
  Doch meines dünkens (bin ich eingeboren
  Und drin erzogen schon) ist's ein gebrauch,
  Wovon der bruch mehr ehrt, als die befolgung.
  Dies schwindelköpfge zechen macht verrufen
  Bei andern völkern uns in ost und west;
  Man heißt uns säufer, hängt an unsre namen
  Ein schmutzig beiwort; und fürwahr, es nimmt
  Von unsern taten, noch so groß verrichtet,
  Den kern und ausbund unsres wertes weg.

Der geist kommt.

AUS DES SAXO GRAMMATICUS DÆNISCHER
GESCHICHTE. DRITTES BUCH. ÜBERSETZUNG
der auf seite vier bis zehn wiedergegebenen auszüge.
Horwendil und Fengo, die söhne Gerwendils, wurden
von Rorik, könig von Dänemark, an ihres verstorbenen
vaters stelle zu statthaltern über Jütland gesetzt. Nach

28

10 Edward Gordon Craig, Hamlet and Horatio await the ghost, 1.4. Woodcut illustration
for the Cranach Press *Tragische geschichte von Hamlet prinzen von Dænemark*, Weimar,
1928, p. 28. The running titles are printed in red.

successful is Ian Pollock's *King Lear*, published in 1984, an amazing, surreal vision, beautifully drawn, and with a visual momentum genuinely expressive of the play's energy. The focus here is not on character, but on the full repertory of pictorial imagery required to realize the text.

But the most significant and far-reaching modern developments in Shakespearean illustration have surely been in cinema. What Shakespeare has looked like to film-makers over the course of the past century is a subject requiring a separate essay; but some examples will indicate the extent to which film has not recapitulated the visual history of Shakespearean theatre or adopted the conventions of illustration, but has devised a visual language of its own. The camera's realism lent itself easily to the sort of detailed historical re-creation that had been popular on the Victorian stage, but Shakespeare was just as often a fantasy world, freed from the constraints of both history and theatre. Max Reinhardt's *Midsummer Night's Dream* (1935), filmed in a subtle and beautifully modulated black and white, was a notably imaginative cinematic interpretation of Shakespeare's poetic imagery, and was widely admired. The less successful, and largely miscast, 1936 *Romeo and Juliet*, also in black and white, with a preposterously mature pair of lovers in Leslie Howard and Norma Shearer, and an elderly John Barrymore as a stagey Mercutio decades out of date, is all soft focus and sympathetic lighting. In contrast, Franco Zeffirelli's very successful 1968 version of the play is full of beautiful young people, and the camera, and the lush technicolor, make the most of their sexual energy and good looks. The costumes are those of Renaissance Verona, but the city is as clean and uncluttered as a movie set. Baz Luhrmann's 1996 film, now titled *William Shakespeare's Romeo + Juliet*, despite the claim of authorial sanction, sees the play as a contemporary teen-age rave – the ball scene is a pool party, with the lovers in the pool, in each other's arms, by the scene's end. Mercutio is brilliantly played as a drag queen, and the visual conventions are largely those of porn films. Transgressive as this sounds – and as it was certainly intended to be – it was nevertheless an exciting and largely successful version of the play.

The cinema's Shakespeare, indeed, is a vivid reflection of the culture's view of itself. The re-creation of the Globe Theatre at the beginning of Olivier's *Henry V*, made just at the end of the war in 1944, depicted it as a neat, quaint, sociable place, full of courteous, clean, friendly people. The Elizabethan theatre in *Shakespeare in Love* (1998) – not the Globe, which had not yet been built at the time the film is set – is a crowded, scruffy, vaguely threatening place, liable to erupt in violence at any moment. Film says, far more clearly than pictures or the stage, that we see Shakespeare as we see ourselves. As the age of the book seems about to come to an end, Shakespearean illustration has reached some kind of logical culmination.

NOTES

1. John Crowne, John Dryden and Thomas Shadwell, *Notes and observations on The empress of Morocco, or, Some few errata's to be printed instead of the sculptures with the second edition of that play* (London, 1674), sig. A2r.
2. John Milton, *Poetical Works*, ed. Douglas Bush (Oxford: Oxford University Press, 1966), pp. 88–92, p. 91.
3. *The First Part of the Return from Parnassus*, 1. 1201, *in The Three Parnassus Plays (1598–1601)*, ed. J. B. Leishman (London: Ivor Nicholson and Watson, 1949).
4. *Shakespeare's Comedy of The Tempest. With illustrations by Edmund Dulac and an introduction by A. T. Quiller-Couch* (London: Hodder and Stoughton, 1908), pp. xxii, xxiii.
5. *Ibid.*, p. xxiv.

5

DOUGLAS LANIER

Shakespeare™: myth and biographical fiction

Shakespeare™'s face

The name of an author, Michel Foucault famously observed, does not simply refer to a specific historical person who lived and wrote; "more than an indication, a gesture, a finger pointed at someone," he writes, "it is the equivalent of a description."[1] That is, attaching an author's name (and image) to a text (or product) predisposes us to interpret it in a certain manner, to classify it with certain texts (or products) and not with others, to expect it to have certain qualities, themes, ideas, or formal traits. For an example, one need look no further than Shakespeare. In culture generally, but certainly in popular culture, the name and image of "Shakespeare" has become a byword for a set of qualities that have been attached to an astonishing variety of texts and products – bank cards, £20 notes (from 1970–93), beer, crockery, fishing tackle, book publishing, cigars, pubs, and breath mints, to name a few. "Shakespeare" has come to serve as an adjective, a tool potentially for reshaping the associations of objects that become linked with his name. The phenomenon to which Foucault points bears interesting affiliations with the phenomenon of branding, in many ways the popular counterpart of the critical operation he describes. Like an author's name, a brand is a sign that is instantly recognizable, distinctive, transferable (that is, capable of being attached to an array of products), and powerful and productive in its connotations. The significance of a brand (or author's) name is not controlled by a single marketer or critic, but rather emerges from myriad interactions between producers, consumers, and various cultural intermediaries and contexts. Brands have become ubiquitous elements of contemporary popular culture, functioning like authors' names as principles for classifying texts and products.[2]

If, then, Shakespeare is the Coca-Cola of canonical culture, its most long-lived and widespread brand name, the face of Shakespeare, familiar from the Droeshout portrait that graces the First Folio, has become its trademark. Like all trademarks, that single image telegraphs what have been widely taken as certain key qualities of the franchise. The engraving's now antique style has come to communicate Shakespeare's status as a figure for aesthetic tradition-ality (and by extension, time-tested trustworthiness), that is, for art before (and to an extent opposed to) the advent of mass media and identified with traditional British rural life or "merrie old England." Shakespeare's high-domed forehead, the face's most recognizable feature, bespeaks his work's association with intellectuality and by extension with elite culture. The com-paratively unadorned quality of the portrait (no crown of bays or allegorical accoutrements) and the somewhat naive quality of the rendering accord with Shakespeare's reputation as a natural genius whose work has its roots not in study but in God-given talent or as a poet writing for and about "the people," about a shared human nature and not the experience of the privileged few. Yet like all brand icons, the Shakespeare trademark is an open signifier. The correspondences I've just described are not *necessarily* inherent in the details of the Droeshout portrait and are certainly in no simple way intended. Rather, the portrait serves as a widely shared memory device, a visual anchor for a body of connotations historically accrued by the name "Shakespeare," some of which are contradictory. That field of established associations is a powerful cultural resource precisely because it is so well established, but the particular associations within that field are open to appropriation, rearticulation, exten-sion, even negation and parody, its meanings transferable to other arenas of cultural production depending upon the needs and purposes of the user and always open to re-branding should the need arise. To put this another way, adding Shakespeare's face to a product has become a means for adding value, both of certain connotations and, consequently, of commodity value, but in the process of adding value to other products, the value (and values) of the Shakespeare brand have been preserved, extended, and transformed.

The appropriation of Shakespeare's face in marketing has a long history stretching back to the late nineteenth century, when his face adorned some of the earliest advertisements featuring graphics. To take one example, Horlick's Malted Milk, a baby formula created in late nineteenth-century Wisconsin and aggressively marketed throughout the early twentieth century, featured Shakespeare's face in its turn-of-the-century advertisements, a campaign which ran from 1905 to 1908. Part of the attraction was its sheer recognition value, but another was that face's rich set of associations. On the one hand, Shakespeare's face signified that which is well established, wholesome, and trustworthy, connotations particularly important for a product that aspired to replace a mother's natural milk. Shakespeare's face also promised a product whose usefulness, like his plays, might be appreciated by and available to those in all walks of life. In the Horlick's campaign (as in many other turn-of-the-century advertisements), that association was reinforced by inclusion of a version of the "seven ages" speech, rewritten so that the product became linked to every stage of life, an attempt – a successful one, it would turn out – to extend Horlick's market beyond infants. On the other hand, the Shakespeare trademark also exemplified "quality," not only the product's well-crafted and healthy nature (a major concern for mothers replacing their milk with a commercial product), but also its deluxe associations. The product's Shakespearean trademark thus promises a vicarious experience of elitism, a taste of the cultural good life and intimation of upward social mobility.

The advent of modern mass media in the early twentieth century (particularly film and radio) led to the displacement of the stage as the dominant popular performance medium. The theatre was the medium closely identified with Shakespeare and served in many ways as the basis for his claim to popularity, and its move from a dominant to a residual form within the panoply of pop cultural offerings precipitated a decisive shift in the meaning of the Shakespeare trademark in popular culture, a meaning which accentuated nascent tensions and contradictions in the field "Shakespeare." This shift in significance was played out against the backdrop of the disciplinary institutionalization of English in the academy (with Shakespeare at its symbolic center), the cult of the modern with its narratives of technological progress and fears about dehumanization and urbanization, and concerns about newly dominant forms of popular culture which, so critics feared, presaged the fall of traditional artistic canons and the rise of working-class, immigrant, and (particularly in Europe) American cultural clout. Within mid-twentieth century popular culture the Shakespeare trademark takes on an increasingly ambivalent cast. Though Shakespeare's face continues to evoke traditionalism, learnedness, hand-crafted quality, and high art, those associations signify in the context of popular culture's self-advertised qualities of instantaneous accessibility, newness, "democratic" inclusiveness, and anti-elitism. Shakespeare comes to signify what modern popular culture defines itself against, becoming in effect popular culture's symbolic "Other." And, as is often the case with the cultural "Other," in many cases Shakespeare also becomes an object of ambivalent desire for popular culture – a source of still potent cultural capital and thus of legitimation, a mark of social mobility, or even a vehicle for self-critique. Nevertheless, we should be quick to notice that in these invocations popular culture was, for all its putative hostility to the elite tradition for which Shakespeare came to stand, invested in affirming, even enhancing Shakespeare's "high" cultural status, for that association was a powerful resource which mass producers could invoke and manipulate in order to articulate the "popular" nature of their products. That is, one especially long-lived paradox of the Shakespeare trademark is that it is popular culture's favorite sign of high culture.

Something of this mid-century ambivalence can be seen in his cameo appearance in *Time Flies*, a routine if oddball B-picture produced by Gainsborough Pictures in 1944, the same year as Laurence Olivier's *Henry V*. This bizarre time-travel comedy features popular British radio comedian Tommy Handley as a flim-flam man who, with a dotty professor and American show-biz duo Susie and Bill Barton, accidentally travels back to Elizabethan England, where the group encounters Sir Walter Ralegh, John Smith and Pocahontas, Elizabeth and her court, and (briefly) Shakespeare. After ducking into the Globe Theatre to hide and donning the period attire she finds there, Susie climbs into a balcony where she spies Shakespeare writing. As he struggles with a speech, she supplies the crucial line: "He jests at scars that never felt a wound." When he asks her her name, she replies "What's in a name?," and in the exchange that follows, she, knowing Shakespeare's famous lines from the future, ends up dictating to him much of the balcony scene while Bill interrupts with quips. This sequence affirms, indeed depends upon, the monumental quality of Shakespeare's writing, lines so powerful that Susie would have committed them to memory. But at the same time, the scene plays out a persistent pop cultural fantasy of appropriation, maintaining the cultural authority of Shakespeare's work while comically transposing the source of that work from Shakespeare (now rendered inarticulate by writer's block) to the mouth of a modern popular entertainer. The scene's second half develops the juxtaposition of popular and Shakespearean, this time shifting to the realm of music. At the end of Susie and Shakespeare's exchange, a group of musicians gather on the Globe stage and rehearse a short Renaissance ditty about ringing bells; in response, Bill plays a jazz riff on a recorder, launching Susie into a song-and-dance number, "Ring Along Bells," a performance that quickly gathers a crowd who sway with the syncopated rhythms and appreciatively toss pennies Susie's way. In one shot we see Shakespeare in merriment, pictured somewhere between directing the musicians (now suddenly playing swing music) and simply enjoying the show and realizing its commercial potential. Again, the opposition of "classical" and "popular" dominates – the period recorder tune functions as the equivalent of Shakespeare's text and is set against big band swing, in the forties the epitome of modern popular culture. Susie's impromptu swing update of the Globe musicians' song points the way to "classic" culture's popular survival – it demands being jazzed up, brought in line with the protocols of modern pop. One part of that process includes Shakespeare and "Shakespearean" music becoming Americanized, a quality made all the more striking given the British provenance of this film and strongly shaped by the wartime context; another, more subtle element is the sweeping away of a signature feature of Shakespearean theatrical practice, the stricture against women performing onstage and the consequent cross-dressed performance of female parts, a stricture which, in this context, marks the Elizabethan theatre as quaint, artificial, and sexually restrained. Even so, it is striking that the sequence "popularizes" only "Shakespearean" music and not Shakespeare's words. For all its emphasis upon the need for updating the glories of England's cultural past, a culture revealed elsewhere in the film to be comically superstitious, classist, and credulous, the film retains a respect, albeit an ambivalent one, for the Shakespearean text.

The postwar triumph of mass media precipitated a crisis in long-standing schemes of cultural stratification and thus in the significance of the Shakespearean trademark. The mediatization of culture accelerated the absorption of icons of traditional high culture into the pop mediastream, a process already begun with film and radio but hastened by television and ever more ubiquitous forms of visual culture. Many have argued that by the third quarter of the twentieth century traditional distinctions between "high" and "pop" culture had collapsed into a postmodern array of decontextualized signs and styles, all equally available for producers to mix and match for their own purposes. In such a scheme, the Shakespearean trademark is emptied of any foundational claim to special authority and threatens to represent little more than the face of yet another celebrity, akin to Marilyn Monroe or Mao Tse-Tung, albeit with a more "retro" feel than most. Such a view underestimates, however, the recuperative capacity of stratificational schemes and the residual usefulness of connotations of exclusivity, learnedness, and quality long attached to the Shakespeare trademark. In postmodern culture yet another significance of Shakespeare's image emerges: it comes to function as a marker of a self-ironized mode of cultural connoisseurship. Shakespeare is attached to products capable of being appreciated by a special class of consumer capable of appreciating *both* the subtleties of pop allusion and consumption *and* reference to a different cultural register, though that register has been largely emptied of (and is sometimes actively mocked for) its traditional claims to moral authority or aesthetic superiority. The result is a form of reciprocal irony: by attaching the Shakespeare trademark to an inappropriately pop object, the act of engaging in pop consumerism by buying or collecting it becomes self-consciously ironic; by attaching kitsch to Shakespeare, any residual hint of bardolatry or snobbery involved in the invocation of Shakespeare becomes self-protectively parodic. In this context, the Shakespeare trademark marks a distinction between the run-of-the-mill consumer simply immersed in pop mediastream and the connoisseur conversant with two cultural registers at once and thus capable of a knowing distance from each. This dual cultural literacy, what Josef Gripsrud has dubbed "double access," implies a privileged access to education and leisure time and thus serves as one marker of a newly emergent "high" cultural strata, the college-educated intelligentsia that came of age in America and Europe after World War II.

Consider, for example, the Shakespeare beanie baby, the Shakespeare bobble-head, the Shakespeare action figure, or the Shakespeare celebriduck (a rubber bath duck adorned with the face of Shakespeare). Though all are toys, none are intended for the "educational" children's market. Rather, they are intended as upmarket fetish commodities for educated adults. The suggestion of cultural superiority communicated by Shakespeare is ironically infantilized, the heart of each item's appeal its ironic distance from mainstream pop capitalism. The Shakespeare celebriduck mocks celebrity culture even as it trumpets its owner's sophisticated taste in culture heroes (the other "celebrities" in this product line tend to be "classics" – the Mona Lisa, the Marx Brothers, the Lone Ranger – rather than current mainstream celebrities); the Shakespeare action figure and bobble-head attach an intellectual icon to a genre of objects more typically associated with male bodily pastimes, sports and combat; the Shakespeare beanie baby, a parodic riff on the ultimate in pop collectibles, is one of several campy items produced by the Unemployed Philosophers Guild to, their website proclaims, "fulfill the materialistic desires of the funny and sophisticated everywhere,"[3] the company name sardonically celebrating the marginal place of the disaffected intellectual in the pop marketplace. What these Shakespeare-trademarked objects provide for their consumers is a differentiated relationship to the pop marketplace and an opportunity to display that "sophisticated" differentiation; what one buys is a set of air quotes one can place around consumerism even as one participates in it. Such mutual lampooning of highbrow and lowbrow has its roots in nineteenth-century Shakespearean burlesque, in which Shakespearean theatre and popular melodrama were melded in order to mock the conventions and clichés of both. Of course, Victorian Shakespearean burlesque, often sharing the bill with straight performances of the bard, was directed not to a market niche but to a wide audience, and it served as a carnivalesque reassertion of Shakespeare's popularity. By contrast, these contemporary Shakespop objects acknowledge the hegemony of the pop marketplace and recuperate Shakespeare's status as a mark of high culture only by camping up his commodification.

Though the three modes of Shakespearean branding I have detailed here – what we might call appropriative, juxtapositional, and ironic uses of Shakespearean cultural capital – emerge from particular historical moments in the relationship between pop culture and Shakespeare, nevertheless, they are not mutually exclusive nor do they fully displace each other. Earlier uses of the Shakespeare brand co-exist in contemporary pop culture with later ones, all still potent resources for reshaping the connotations of products for various audiences and purposes. Their continued potency depends upon the tenacious (albeit ambivalent) opposition between Shakespeare and mass-produced culture inherited from late nineteenth-century cultural theory, an opposition that has been periodically reinflected in response to pop culture's erosion and recontouring of cultural strata in the last century. Behind the various re-brandings of Shakespeare in the last century lies a fundamental continuity – Shakespeare as pop's Other. Within pop culture Shakespeare's face remains the sign of that culture which pop proclaims it isn't, old-fashioned, elitist, artisanal, intellectual, moralistic "proper" art promoted by official educational and cultural institutions, but it also remains the sign of pop's desire, its desire for the kind of cultural authority, quality, legitimacy, and upward mobility that Shakespeare continues to symbolize. For that reason, despite a concerted attempt within recent scholarship to rethink Shakespeare's cultural standing, pop has been a countervailing force for preserving Shakespeare's privileged status even as, paradoxically, pop has ever more aggressively assimilated his work and image.

A case in point might be found in Shakespeare's cameos in *Looking for Richard*, Al Pacino's 1996 cinematic paean to *Richard III*. As part of the film's introduction, Pacino strides onto the stage to perform as Richard III only to encounter Shakespeare as the only member of his audience, to which Pacino responds with an anxious expletive. Here Shakespeare serves as a standard-bearer of cultural propriety and authority before which Pacino, working as a film actor and popularizer, is doomed to fall short. At film's end, immediately after Pacino's staging of Richard's death dissolves into horseplay with his co-director Frederic Kimball, the opening scenario in the theatre returns, this time with Shakespeare shaking his head with disappointment, as if completing the actor's nightmare with which the film began. By this time, however, Shakespeare has become a figure for the theatre, a mode of production which Pacino's film, with its increasingly cinematic approach (the death of Richard is nearly wordless), has left behind. Indeed, Shakespeare is cited as both a symbol of academic and historical correctness that Pacino's "popular" approach consciously pushes against and a source of legitimation that Pacino only half-mockingly appropriates. The film's final conversation, between Pacino and John Gielgud, turns on Hamlet's final line. During the interview, Pacino, milking a momentary silence, asks, "After silence, what else is there? What's the, what's the line?" With delicious *sang-froid* Gielgud, ever the keeper of the "proper" Shakespearean text, supplies "the rest is silence." Pacino's reply, "Silence is . . . Whatever I'm saying, I know Shakespeare said it," underlines how he, an American film actor and spokesperson for the popular, in many ways

Gielgud's and Shakespeare's antithesis, nevertheless lays wry claim to a genuinely Shakespearean spirit, even though he hasn't gotten the lines quite right. Partaking of elements of bardolatry, iconoclasm, and postmodern irony all at once, the bard's cameos in *Looking for Richard* aptly illustrate the signature doubleness with which contemporary popular culture invokes its Shakespearean other.

Shakespeare™'s mythic biographies

Like the Shakespeare trademark, fuller pop treatments of Shakespeare the man – in fictional biography, in children's literature, in genre fiction, period costumers, musicals, comic books, TV and film biographies – dwell in the long shadow of nineteenth-century conceptions of Shakespeare, in particular the outsize mythos surrounding Shakespearean authorship which had its roots in the cult of Romantic genius. As Shakespeare was elevated to a literary master of all aspects of human nature and experience, Shakespeare the Author simply outstripped the known facts of his mundane bourgeois life. Given the predominantly biographical orientation of nineteenth-century literary criticism, with its assumption that writing springs from and expresses the personal experience of its author, the yawning gap between Shakespeare the Author and Shakespeare the man presented (and continues to present) a considerable problem. Throughout the twentieth century pop representations of Shakespeare the man persisted in this post-Romantic vein, even in the face of evidence that Shakespeare's writing was shaped by the commercial needs and collaborative atmosphere of the playhouse, most of his sources to be found in other works, his presentation of erotic passion poorly fitted to conventional heterosexuality, his writing attuned to the hurly-burly of early modern cosmopolitan London rather than bucolic Stratford. One explanation of this persistence is that, as Richard Burt observes, "mass culture narratives rely on dated scholarship."[4] Another is that what Pierre Bourdieu calls the "popular aesthetic" is founded on "the affirmation of the continuity between art and life"[5] rather than treatment of art as an autonomous realm, with its own history, conventions, and modes of connoisseurship. Thus, one issue linking pop's myriad treatments of Shakespeare the man is how to bring that biography in line with all that the Shakespeare trademark has come to represent, and nowhere is that challenge more vexed than in pop culture's treatment of Shakespearean authorship. For that reason pop versions of Shakespeare's life are typically concerned less with historical fidelity and more with adjusting (or fabricating) details of Shakespearean biography and reinflecting the mythic stature of Shakespeare the Author so that man and myth are in congruence. Some pop representations, particularly in contemporary works of an iconoclastic or parodic bent, emphasize the mundane or sordid nature of Shakespeare's life in order to cut the mythic author down to size, but far more typical for pop culture is to construct scenarios that locate the genesis of Shakespeare's writing in fabricated details of his personal experience, while never seriously challenging the extraordinary cultural authority accorded his work. Whatever the approach, pop representations of Shakespeare are not merely one more instance of the postmodern availability of biographical figures for fictional citation. Rather, they are instances of ideological negotiation and recuperation, in which the Shakespeare brand is fleshed out and adjusted. Through this process, the mythic Shakespeare can address changing social conditions that potentially challenge it, including, paradoxically, mass media culture itself.

Two venerable popular traditions involving Shakespeare the man have especially deep roots in nineteenth-century bardolatry. One is the "Shakespeare country" motif, stressing the ways in which Shakespeare the Author was definitively shaped by and thus symbolizes traditional British village life. This nostalgic association, an assertion of Shakespeare's affiliation with populist origins and folk culture, is a pronounced feature of tours of Stratford landmarks (and their various replicas around the world), as well as a mini-industry of Shakespeare-themed household goods (such as crockery, tea towels, and the like). The second tradition extends the biographical assumptions surrounding Shakespeare's writing by imagining his engagement with his own characters, who are presented as if they have lives of their own. In those versions clustered around the tercentenaries of Shakespeare's birth and death, the characters gather to praise their creator, allowing an often amazed Shakespeare to see the scope of his literary legacy. (Of course, this motif also admits of parody, in which Shakespeare's characters demand revisions or berate their author.) A variation on this theme can be found in the first talkie featuring Shakespeare as a character, *The Immortal Gentleman* (1935), in which he, Ben Jonson, and Michael Drayton gather to share a pint in a Southwark tavern. Passers-by prompt Shakespeare to think of his own characters and crucial passages from his plays, suggesting that Shakespeare drew his most famous creations from observation of contemporary Londoners. A third tradition, that of fictions of Shakespeare the lover, owes its fascination with Shakespeare's erotic life to his reputation as the preeminent poet of love in English, a reputation tied particularly closely to two works, his sonnets and *Romeo and Juliet*, the biographical catalyst for both serving as fodder for popular speculation.

Several strains of fictional Shakespearean biography bear a family resemblance to these long-lived traditions. Since popular culture so firmly locates the origins of Shakespeare's writing in his childhood in bucolic Stratford, popular novelists and playwrights have imaginatively filled in the particulars of Shakespeare's early life, especially those tantalizing lacunae in his early biography, his romance with and early marriage to Anne Hathaway and the so-called "lost years" between his Stratford adolescence and his debut as a London player. These works tend to fall into two groups. The first, exemplified by Emma Severn's *Anne Hathaway* (1845), Sarah Sterling's *Shakespeare's Sweetheart* (1905), and more recently Pamela Berkman's *Her Infinite Variety* (2001), paints an idyllic picture of Shakespeare's romantic and domestic life in Stratford, typically with his passionate relationship with Anne as its centerpiece. Targeting a female audience, these pieces recast Shakespeare in the mold of a romantic hero, with Anne serving as a surrogate for the reader. The second group, rather more common as the twentieth century progressed and exemplified by Anthony Burgess's *Nothing Like the Sun* (1964), William Gibson's *A Cry of Players* (1968), and more recently in Grace Tiffany's *Will* (2004), evoke a Shakespeare dissatisfied by the limits of village life and dreaming of theatrical adventure or poetic fame elsewhere.[6] In these works, Anne often hardens into a shrew, Shakespeare's parents and siblings come to personify rural provinciality, and only the young poet's children give him pleasure. Of interest in these latter group, however, is the prominent element of nostalgia and regret which haunts the Shakespeare of so many of these pieces, particularly so as he looks back in his retirement, as he does in *The Best House in Stratford* (1965), the final volume of Edward Fisher's biographical trilogy on Shakespeare, and in Neil Gaiman's evocative comic book treatment "The Tempest" (1996). In addition to locating the power of Shakespeare's work in personal loss, a frequent motif in Shakespearean pop biography, this strain recasts Shakespeare as a figure of modernity, drawn away from traditions of the past into an exhilarating but alienated existence in the city. Both groups of biographies situate Shakespeare's early life in Stratford at the center of his authorial power, either as the wellspring of his inspiration or the stultifying strictures of tradition against which he pushed.

Shakespeare's stature as a love poet, a long-standing centerpiece of his authorial mythos, provides ample material for pop fictionalization, and nowhere more fruitful than in speculation about another biographical lacuna, the identity of the Dark Lady of the sonnets and her various romantic avatars. A favorite plotline, stretching back at least as far as Alexandre Duval's influential, much translated play *Shakespeare Amoreaux* (1804), involves Shakespeare's passion for a clandestine lover who ignites his romantic eloquence and thus becomes the catalyst for the sonnets, *Romeo and Juliet*, or one of his heroines. This beloved becomes Shakespeare's erotic muse, a participant in the writing of his works, their inspiration, the secret hermeneutic key that unlocks their true meaning (which the reader comes to share), and their first, most privileged audience. The roster of Shakespeare's imagined beloveds is remarkable for its variety. Besides several candidates for the Dark Lady (in, for example, Karen Sunde's 1988 and Michael Baldwin's 1998 novels, both entitled *Dark Lady*; Leonard Tourney even builds a mystery novel around their affair in *Time's Fool* [2004]), it includes Rebecca Lopez, a Spanish Jew, in Faye Kellerman's *The Quality of Mercy* (1989); Lady Viola Compton, an orphaned aristocrat and ward of Queen Elizabeth, in Caryl Brahms and S. J. Simon's *No Bed for Bacon* (1941); and, through the magic of time travel, Jessica Pruitt, an aging actress filming *The Merchant of Venice* in Erica Jong's *Serenissima* (aka *Shylock's Daughter*, 1987). A recurrent romantic fantasy pairs Shakespeare with Queen Elizabeth, imagining a potential union of political and cultural power, two icons of British national culture. This fantasy too has its roots in nineteenth-century narratives (Ambroise Thomas's 1850 opera *Le Songe d'une nuit d'été*, a melding of biographical fantasy and the Bottom–Titania plotline from *A Midsummer Night's Dream*, is the most memorable example), but vestiges of it persist well into the twentieth century.

Given the homoerotic content of the sonnets and the gender-bending romances of Shakespeare's cross-dressed heroines, it is striking how little pop culture is willing to entertain the possibility of a male erotic muse for Shakespeare. There are isolated, largely post-Stonewall examples – Casimir Dukahz's pornographic novel *Shakespeare's Boy* (1991) features pedophilic trysts involving Ruy, a boy player, and Stephanie Cowell's *The Players* (1997) imagines a love triangle between Shakespeare, the Earl of Southampton, and Emilia, an Italian servant girl. But most of those pop presentations that acknowledge the possibility of Shakespeare's homoeroticism do so in order eventually to efface it. The blockbuster *Shakespeare in Love* (1999), a fine example of the erotic muse narrative, flirts with the homoerotic possibilities of its heroine's cross-dressing – Will kisses his beloved Viola de Lessups, for example, when she is in male disguise – only forcefully to reassert the heterosexual nature of his passion (his Sonnet 29 is addressed in the film to a woman, not a man); in *Serenissima*, it is the heroine's affair with Shakespeare that rescues him from the sterile love of Southampton (and gives the couple a child). These examples suggest how powerfully Shakespeare is identified with and functions as a mainstream icon for heteronormative sexuality, at least until relatively recently. Another indication of that ideological function can be seen in the recurrent opposition of Shakespeare and Marlowe in biographical fictions. Marlowe is often portrayed as homoerotic, promiscuous, hedonistic, recklessly drawn to political and religious intrigue, doomed by his passions – everything the mythic Shakespeare is not. The first episode of the 1978 TV mini-series *The Life of Shakespeare* (1978) uses this opposition to establish

Shakespeare's apolitical, bourgeois character, and the subsequent episodes featuring his relationship with Southampton confirm that his interests in his patron are less in sexuality than in material comforts. In *Young Will* (2004), Bruce Cook iconoclastically presents a Shakespeare who falls for Marlowe and is progressively drawn into a life of libertinism (young will, indeed), eventually becoming Marlowe's murderer. Tellingly, Cook's Shakespeare is no love poet but rather a literary hack cravenly pursuing aristocratic privilege and stealing his fellows' work. Even though Shakespeare is an object of erotic fantasy in popular culture, his authorial myth, it would seem, still remains incompatible with unconventional sexuality.

Of greater generic range are those fictionalizations which imagine Shakespeare's life in the theatre – the vicissitudes of stage performance, the playwright's rivalries and friendships with fellow-players and writers, the stage's participation in contemporary political machinations. Typically these works do not primarily focus on Shakespeare, in part because the minutiae of playwriting and stage production offer limited opportunities to sustain a narrative. Instead, Shakespeare and his plays serve as a historical backdrop for a genre narrative that becomes woven into the playwright's works. Historical mysteries, for example, with their evocation of period detail and their concern with hidden hermeneutic keys and the exercise of intellectual acumen, make a potentially fruitful match with Shakespeare's reputation for literary complexity, though, interestingly enough, he is rarely cast as a detective, perhaps because Shakespearean citation in mysteries is most often associated with villainy. Each installment of Philip Gooden's Elizabethan detective series – *Sleep of Death* (2000), *Death of Kings* (2001), *The Pale Companion* (2002), *Alms for Oblivion* (2003), *Mask of Night* (2004), *An Honourable Murderer* (2005) – is structured around a single Shakespearean play (with murders linked to their performances) and features a member of the Lord Chamberlain's Men, Nick Revill, as its narrator and sleuth; Shakespeare appears only as a recurring minor character, even serving as a murder suspect in *Mask of Night*. Simon Hawke's Shakespeare and Smythe series – *A Mystery of Errors* (2001), *Much Ado About Murder* (2002), *The Slaying of the Shrew* (2002), *The Merchant of Vengeance* (2003) – pairs the aspiring playwright with an erudite ostler and actor, Symington Smythe, in effect casting Shakespeare as Watson to Smythe's Holmes, though the novels are peppered with lines that eventually end up in Shakespeare's work; the final novel of the series even offers an ingenious rationale for the writing of *The Merchant of Venice*.

One body of popular material where fictionalizations of Shakespeare's playhouse activities thrive is children's literature. Portrayals of Shakespeare for children are designed to introduce them to Shakespeare's mythic stature as playwright, and they focus on his theatrical life because the pleasures of play and fantasy are among his key appeals for children. Typically children's narratives present Shakespeare as a substitute father or mentor for the young protagonist, who is often orphaned or alone and taken in by the bard and his stage compatriots. Shakespeare is by turns intimidating and nurturing, and being in his company helps initiate the child into the wider social world of adults represented by stage performance of his plays, acting a means for the child to overcome the traumas and developmental crises of youth. Gary Blackwood's *The Shakespeare Stealer* (1998) chronicles the maturation of Widge, an orphaned boy with special skills in reading and writing, from professional plagiarist to resourceful apprentice in Shakespeare's company. At first under the thumb of his authoritarian owner Simon Bass, who forces the boy into using his skill at writing to transcribe performances for piracy, Widge soon gives up his life of crime and becomes an apprentice in Shakespeare's troupe, his new surrogate (and far more benevolent) family. Interestingly, it is Robert Armin who serves as Widge's father-figure; Shakespeare is portrayed as an aloof, intimidating figure, rendered quick-tempered by the loss of his own son. (That Widge will eventually serve as that lost son's replacement is strongly suggested by the fact that the boy first sees Shakespeare in a mirror.) Although children's narratives typically paternalize Shakespeare's authority, they also take pains to de-monumentalize the man and his productions, emphasizing how the child protagonist (and vicariously the reader) becomes an active participant in the making of his plays – a co-creator, with a distant affinity to the erotic muse. In *The Shakespeare Stealer* Widge uses his talents for charactery to create a fake script that pirates pilfer, a ruse that saves the day. In subsequent installments in the series – *Shakespeare's Scribe* (2000) and *Shakespeare's Spy* (2003) – Widge's reading and writing talents allow him to move from an apprentice to a scribe and a sleuth who uncovers playhouse piracy, in effect becoming the guardian of the textual integrity of Shakespeare's work. In Don Freeman's *Will's Quill* (1975), a fatherly Shakespeare offers encouragement, artistic recognition, and comfort to orphaned Willoughby the goose, who is alone and frightened by London crowds; in exchange, the playwright receives a boon from his new friend, the quill-feather he needs to complete *A Midsummer Night's Dream*, thereby enabling Shakespeare's first literary triumph. The Shakespeare-themed contribution to Mary Pope Osborne's popular Magic Tree House series, *Stage Fright on a Summer Night* (2002), also imagines an exchange of boons: Jack and Annie help Shakespeare by playing parts when two boy actors don't appear, and Shakespeare returns the favor by adopting a maltreated bear on which Annie took pity and supplying Jack with pithy lines for his journal.

Though these narrative templates and motifs form the basis for most popular fictionalizations of Shakespeare, they are often freely varied and recombined, particularly in contemporary examples. Such is the case for Sarah A. Hoyt's *Ill Met by Moonlight* (2001), the first volume in her fantasy trilogy starring Shakespeare. Combining the Stratford and erotic muse narratives, Hoyt makes Shakespeare's awakening as a writer and lover the result of his encounter with Quicksilver, a shape-changing fairy prince whose brother Sylvanus has usurped his rightful title and exiled him from the supernatural world. The resemblances between *Hamlet* and the fairy court intrigue are deepened by Quicksilver's discovery that Sylvanus arranged the death of their parents, Titania and Oberon, and by Quicksilver's unwitting part in the death of Pyrite, his friend and brother of his Ophelia-like beloved, Ariel (also echoed are *A Midsummer Night's Dream* and *Romeo and Juliet*). Will, a milquetoast schoolmaster and dreamer, becomes drawn into the plot when Sylvanus kidnaps Anne Hathaway ("Nan") to be his bride and nursemaid for his child. Seeing an opportunity for revenge, Quicksilver engages Will to kill Sylvanus in order to save Nan from assimilation into Faerie. One of Hoyt's more provocative conceits is that Quicksilver, in his female guise as the Dark Lady, uses his erotic power to seduce Shakespeare and cement their relationship. Quicksilver, we learn, has had previous sexual dalliances in both female and male form, the latter with Christopher Marlowe, with the result that his homoerotic passions and fantastical imagination were inflamed beyond his control. That is, in this fiction the two beloveds of the sonnets, the young man and the dark lady, are the same person (actually, fairy), though Hoyt is careful to insist that Will's tryst with Quicksilver is, at least from his perspective, strictly heterosexual. In the end, Will's brief affair only serves to revitalize his love for Nan and his domestic life, and with Quicksilver's help he heroically rescues her during a fairy dance, thereby quieting the storms raised by Sylvanus's violation of the natural order. But, as the narrator notes in a coda, Will's contact with Quicksilver has tacitly awakened the poet's fancy, a fancy that will inevitably lead to the loss of his hard-won tranquillity and prompt the writing of "fantastical tragedies and mad farces" that draw upon his supernatural adventures: "Quicksilver's love had its price, after all . . . And is Will – who will leave wife and daughter and mother and father behind and trade his small domestic happiness for a spotlight in a world made stage – better or worse off than if he had never come across the unexplained marvels of elvenkind?"[7] In the sequels, *All Night Awake* (2002) and *Any Man So Daring* (2003), Will is haunted by his recognition that his artistic genius springs from a potentially self-destructive bargain, a self-destructiveness borne out by Marlowe's premature death, and he struggles twice, as an aspiring playwright in London and again in his

Stratford retirement, to defend his fidelity to family and bourgeois comfort against the dangerously seductive and politically volatile world of faerie.[8] Hoyt engages the gap between man and authorial myth by emphasizing it, recasting the wellspring of Shakespeare's imaginative potency as a threat to his otherwise quotidian life and reinventing the bard as a hero rising to meet that threat.

A very different body of popular works eschew entirely concern with fictional biography, instead using time travel or magic to bring Shakespeare in contact with modernity. There are instances in which Shakespeare makes an un-ironic cameo appearance as an authority on human nature or literary craft to offer advice at a moment of crisis, as in "The Power of the Pen" (1990), an episode of *A Different World* in which Shakespeare appears in a dream to defend the value of poetry, or the Norwegian film *Sofies verden* (1999), where Shakespeare offers the heroine Sophie a crucial clue to her mysterious identity. Far more often, however, the encounter between Shakespeare and the present is an instrument of critique. Parting company with Victorian presentations of Shakespeare worshiped by his own living creations, one group of works stages a comic confrontation between Shakespeare and the contemporary myth he has become. When Blackadder, that popular antithesis of British heritage, time-travels from the present to the Elizabethan past in *Blackadder Back & Forth* (1999), he bumps into Shakespeare (literally) as the bard rushes with his latest creation, *Macbeth*. Blackadder promptly decks him, offering this explanation:

> That is for every schoolboy and schoolgirl for the next four hundred years. Have you any idea how much suffering you're going to cause? Hours spent at school desks trying to find *one* joke in A *Midsummer's Night Dream*, wearing stupid tights in school plays and saying things like, "What ho, my Lord," and, "Oh, look, here comes Othello, talking total crap as usual."

Of course, the suffering is not caused so much by the man himself as by those official institutions that promulgate "proper" Shakespeare, in this case one of popular culture's favorite targets, academia. As Blackadder leaves, he strikes a blow against another highbrow institution, the heritage cinema, kicking Shakespeare for "Ken Branagh's endless, four-hour version of *Hamlet*" and in the process resisting the importation of high cultural notions of quality and reverence into the cinematic popularization of Shakespeare in the 1990s.[9] Nonetheless, ever the craven materialist, Blackadder recognizes the commercial value of the Shakespeare myth, and so he makes sure to get Shakespeare's autograph before thrashing him.

Another group uses Shakespeare as an indisputable standard of cultural achievement against which to criticize (or to celebrate, with tongue in cheek) the failings of contemporary pop culture. One episode of the American radio show *Favorite Story*, "Mister Shakespeare" (1947), imagines how a resurrected Shakespeare might fare in modern Hollywood. Finding his poetic talents universally rejected by the studios as hopelessly uncommercial, he is forced to work on a genre picture, *The Capulets*, and becomes discouraged by pop's reliance on mass-produced formulae. In effect endorsing radio's emphasis on the spoken word, Shakespeare ruminates that "after three centuries, I thought maybe people would learn to appreciate beautiful words by themselves without having them strung on stale plots. I was wrong." Though he is delighted to find a romancing couple who appreciate the erotic power of his language ("the old stuff still works!," he observes), in the end the vapidity of popular culture overwhelms Shakespeare, and he chooses simply to fade away. More recently, "Death Trek 100, Part Two," an episode of the comic book *Lobo* (number 36, 1997), offers a more ambivalent, postmodern mode of critique. It intercuts an adventure of the ultra-violent hero Lobo with a lecture by Shakespeare, analyzing a story where the writer runs out of plot. Though the tale includes skewed allusions to *Romeo and Juliet* (in this version, the star-cross'd lovers treacherously kill their parents and betray Lobo in order to be together and enjoy the movie rights to their story), Shakespeare repeatedly observes that the comic's scant narrative is padded out with visual spectacle and gratuitous violence, echoing long-standing highbrow complaints about the empty sensationalism of superhero comics. What Shakespeare and his highbrow students discover is that they are merely plot devices to fill up space until the final pages where Juliet has constructed a secret narrative fail-safe device: if all else fails, blow everyone up. In the end, it is bad-boy Lobo who gets his revenge upon high culture by actively embracing pop culture's commercialized, sensationalistic values. After killing the lovers, he sells their story of "murder, sabotage, forbidden love – everything" to the highest bidder, and he is the only one to survive the final fireball, exiting with the pun "write on, dudes."[10]

Yet another means of negotiating the gap between man and authorial myth is entirely to reassign the identity of the man, a strategy which has the added frisson of resisting conventional scholarly wisdom about the playwright's identity in which official Shakespeare-dom is so invested. A number of fictional works playfully reimagine the true author of Shakespeare's plays as a gay black slave (as in Farrukh Dhondy's novel *Black Swan* [1993]) or a woman (as in Snoo Wilson's play *More Light* [1987] or Malia Martin's romance novel *Much Ado About Love* [2000]) as a way of suggesting that Shakespeare's penetrating portrayals of female or black psychology spring not from the author's imagination or his sources but from personal experience.

(This approach also lends itself to parody, where the "real" Shakespeare is imagined as a fool.) Such reassignments of Shakespeare's identity marshal the considerable cultural authority associated with his works to lend legitimacy and dignity to groups historically denigrated. It is for that reason, for example, that the gay popular press has been concerned to claim Shakespeare as one of its own, even though Shakespeare's depictions of sexuality, unconventional though they may be, do not line up well with modern notions of homosexuality.

In the same family of appropriations, though far less progressive in its implications, is the phenomenon of anti-Stratfordianism. This popular conspiracy theory, which first surfaced in late nineteenth-century America, rejects the possibility that Shakespeare, with his provincial background and lack of formal education, could have written the sophisticated, politically informed works that bear his name. Instead, anti-Stratfordians have proposed a series of alternative figures with biographies that better match the dimensions of the authorial myth. Nearly all the candidates, not coincidentally, are aristocratic or university-educated and thus, so the logic runs, were personally acquainted with the privileged milieu – the trials and tribulations of kings, cosmopolitan European locations – depicted in the plays. This hypothesis casts the man from Stratford as a front to protect the real aristocratic author from the taint of the playhouse and requires elaborate conspiracies among members of the court and theatrical companies. Anti-Stratfordianism has emerged as official Shakespeare's *Doppelgänger*, the basis of a considerable counter-industry of amateur scholars and a periodic favorite of popular journalism. Not surprisingly, then, it has also spawned works in pop genres that advance (or occasionally parody) its cause, including Amy Freed's *The Beard of Avon* (2001), a comedy that dovetails the erotic muse narrative with the hypothesis that Edward de Vere, Earl of Oxford, penned Shakespeare's plays; Lynne Kositsky's young adult novel *A Question of Will* (2000), an Oxfordian variation on the time-travel tale in which Shakespeare is revealed to be a drunken boor; and Sarah Smith's *Chasing Shakespeares* (2004), which grafts Oxfordianism and a critique of literary academia onto a *Da Vinci Code*-style suspense narrative. Anti-Stratfordianism reveals the lengths some have been willing to go to preserve the axiom of biographical expressivity, but it also provides evidence of a popular hostility towards Shakespearean professionals who have sought to become exclusive hermeneutic gatekeepers for (and drawn their own cultural authority from) "official" Shakespeare.

Though this survey of Shakespearean sub-genres might suggest that much of pop culture's representation of Shakespeare the man is self-serving and predominantly conservative in its orientation, a handful of examples suggest more progressive potential. Pamela Melnikoff's *Plots and Players* (1988), a young adult novel modeled on the familiar child-meets-the-bard narrative, engages the question of Shakespeare's liberal humanist sensibilities, a key ideological component of the authorial myth. Early in the book, Robin Fernandez, a Jewish Portuguese boy actor living in London, auditions for Shakespeare and gains a part in *Romeo and Juliet*. At that point, the narrative makes a break with generic convention – Robin becomes aware of a conspiracy to frame the Queen's Jewish physician and Fernandez family acquaintance, Doctor Lopez, for treason. In an early discussion with Robin about bear-baiting, Shakespeare displays a historically uncharacteristic sensitivity to the oppressed when he observes that "a poor beetle suffers as much when you tread on him as a giant suffers when he does." But as Robin recognizes the extent of Renaissance anti-Semitism, he also comes to recognize the limitations of Shakespeare's sympathies and his art. When Marlowe's *The Jew of Malta* whips Londoners into an anti-Semitic frenzy, Robin confronts Shakespeare about his unwillingness to depict Jews as heroes. When the playwright replies that "no audience would accept such a thing," Robin replies, "Then if we can't be heroes, why can't we at least be human beings? . . . You won't let us be giants, but why do we have to be horned beasts?" Only later does he learn that, chastened by their conversation, Shakespeare destroyed an earlier, more virulent draft of *The Merchant of Venice* and wrote another:

> You taught me that Jews are human beings, to be presented as such on the stage. And so, after leaving you, I went home and burnt my play. I have rewritten it, and more to your taste, I think. No, there is no need to look so happy. I would not make the Jew a hero . . . such a thing would not be allowed . . . no audience would accept it. He is still the villain of the piece, but a human villain, I think. He may not be a giant, but at least he is less of a horned beast.[11]

This portrayal of the genesis of *The Merchant of Venice* is remarkable for its frank acknowledgment of Shakespeare's ideological blindspots, the extent to which his plays were profoundly shaped (though not entirely determined) by popular prejudices to which the commercial theatre played. Shakespeare's sketch of Shylock underlines the limits of liberal humanism in the play that has come down to us – Shylock is a villain but a human one, less of a horned beast, but a beast nevertheless.

Harry Turtledove's *Ruled Britannia* (2002) is an equally remarkable revisionary work, but for different reasons. Turtledove, a writer renowned for well-researched alternate histories, imagines an Elizabethan England in which the Spanish Armada succeeded in forcing it back into the Catholic fold, an England under Spanish occupation where Elizabeth is imprisoned in the Tower, spying, suspicion, and brutal oppression are rife, and the theatre is subject to censorship. Shakespeare, the novel's protagonist, is presented as a respected playwright-for-hire, engaged by the Spanish to write a play in honor of the dying monarch Philip II at the same time that he is hired by Burghley and his allies to write a history play about Boudicca, the ancient Briton queen who resisted Roman occupation, a play designed to rouse Britain to rebellion. Shakespeare's two foils are Marlowe, portrayed as an impish, nihilistic provocateur who regards politics as a game, and Lope de Vega, depicted as a hedonistic connoisseur of women and words, a fellow man of the theatre who appreciates Shakespeare's verbal craft but who because of his egotism fails to nose out the bard's true political affiliation. Besides the sheer daring of Turtledove's premise and his detailed (and hardly idealized) portrait of London life, the novel is unusual for how it depicts the nature of Shakespeare's authorship. First, Turtledove uncouples the link between Shakespeare's personal experience and the content of his plays by emphasizing Shakespeare's process as a wordsmith crafting speeches, not as an imaginer of original plots and characters from his personal experience. Shakespeare's London experiences, all pointedly mundane, have nothing to do with his plays. For both of those he is contracted to write, he is given the sources from which to work, and the playhouse scenes stress how much Shakespeare's writing reflects give-and-take with his fractious company. As is often the case with Shakespearean fictional biographies, the novel is peppered with familiar Shakespearean bons mots, but since so many are spoken out of earshot of Shakespeare, the effect is to suggest that these phrases were simply in the Elizabethan air, not the bard's original creations. Second, Turtledove presents Shakespeare's playwriting as a fundamentally political and potentially subversive activity. Sensitivity about the application of plays to the immediate political situation Turtledove treats as a cultural given, even though Shakespeare himself is not portrayed as a political insider; his *Boudicca* prompts an immediate response, the bloody rebellion against the Spanish and restoration of the British crown that forms the book's climax. If popular culture often portrays Shakespeare's works as repositories of timeless if abstract truths, Turtledove's portrayal restores their political effectivity and historical specificity. The novel's premise also cleverly shifts the political orientation of Shakespeare's identification with British nationalism. Where recent scholarship has tended to see that identification as a mark of Shakespeare's alliance with conservative politics and outmoded notions of British identity, Shakespeare's British propagandizing takes on a revolutionary color in Turtledove's alternate history – not to recuperate conservative notions of British nationhood but to demonstrate the strategic, potentially politically transformative uses of Shakespeare's art.

Conclusion

In his study of branding, Douglas B. Holt observes that brands achieve iconic status by maintaining a sense of continuity of brand identity while reinventing themselves to speak to current collective fears and aspirations that spring from acute cultural tensions. "Icons," he writes, "come to represent a particular kind of story – *an identity myth* – that their consumers use to address identity desires and anxieties."[12] Holt's paradigm goes a long way towards explaining Shakespeare's continued iconic status in modern popular culture. Once Shakespeare's face had been established as a widely recognized sign of cultural power by the nineteenth century, it was available for popular culture to rearticulate its central qualities – its association with "culture," quality, Britishness, tradition – to serve its own often contradictory needs and to respond to social changes, not least of which was pop's emergent cultural hegemony and the erosion of inherited high–low cultural oppositions. The fleshing out of the Shakespeare trademark with fictions of Shakespeare's life has been one of pop's mechanisms for accomplishing that rearticulation, in the process (and with relatively few exceptions) reaffirming Shakespeare's mythic status and one of the foundational axioms of the popular aesthetic, the continuity of biography and art. It is beside the point, then, to chastize popular representations of Shakespeare the man for their myriad and often willful factual inaccuracies, for they are less concerned with historical fidelity than with the ideological work of servicing, extending, reorienting, and at the same time drawing upon Shakespeare's inherited cultural authority, one of pop culture's most valuable resources. One difference lies, however, between corporate brands and the Shakespeare trademark, a difference that is perhaps one key to its continued strength. The Shakespeare trademark is never under the control of a single institution or cultural (re)producer. It thus remains ever a contested object of value, a body that, despite Shakespeare's warning about moving his bones, remains always in motion.

NOTES

1. Michel Foucault, "What is an Author?," in *The Foucault Reader*, ed. Paul Rabinow (Harmondsworth: Penguin, 1986), pp. 101–20, p. 105.
2. For a fuller discussion, see John Frow, "Signature and Brand," in *High/Pop: Making Culture into Popular Entertainment*, ed. John Collins (Oxford: Blackwell, 2002), pp. 56–74.
3. www.philosophersguild.com
4. Richard Burt, "*Shakespeare in Love* and the End of the Shakespearean," in *Shakespeare, Film, Fin de Siècle*, eds. Mark Thornton Burnett and Ramona Wray (Basingstoke: Macmillan, 2000), pp. 203–31, p. 216.

5. Pierre Bourdieu, *Distinction*, trans. Richard Nice (Princeton, NJ: Princeton University Press, 1984), p. 32.
6. A contemporary feminist corollary of this group are those works which, using Virginia Woolf's portrait of Judith Shakespeare in *A Room of One's Own* as inspiration, imagine a female relative or acquaintance of Shakespeare as an aspiring poet or player frustrated by patriarchal restrictions and seeking relief in London, sometimes through Rosalind-like male disguise. Examples include Laura Shamas's *The Other Shakespeare* (1981), Doris Gwaltney's *Shakespeare's Sister* (1995), Judith Beard's *Romance of the Rose* (1998), and Grace Tiffany's *My Father Had a Daughter: Judith Shakespeare's Tale* (2003). Mollie Hardwick's *The Shakespeare Girl* (1983) and Peter W. Hassinger's *Shakespeare's Daughter* (2004) provide examples written for young adults.
7. Sarah A. Hoyt, *Ill Met by Moonlight* (New York: Berkley, 2001), p. 274.
8. Hoyt's trilogy, particularly its final novel, merits close comparison with Neil Gaiman's "The Tempest," the final installment of his *Sandman* comic book series, with which it shares many motifs and thematic concerns.
9. *Blackadder Back & Forth*, dir. Paul Welland, 1999, my transcription.
10. "Death Trek 100 Part Two," script by Al Vidal, *Lobo* 36 (January 1997), pp. 19, 22.
11. Pamela Melnikoff, *Plots and Players* (New York: Peter Bedrick Books, 1988), pp. 49, 153, and 157.
12. Douglas B. Holt, *How Brands Become Icons* (Boston: Harvard Business School Press, 2004), p. 2.

6

LAURIE OSBORNE

Narration and staging in *Hamlet* and its afternovels

In [genre fiction], the relationship between individual work and formula is somewhat analogous to that of a variation on a theme, or of a performance to a text. To be a work of quality or interest, the individual version of a formula must have some unique or special characteristics of its own, yet these characteristics must ultimately work toward the fulfillment of the conventional form. In somewhat the same way, when we see a new performance of a famous role like Hamlet, we are most impressed by it if it is a new but acceptable interpretation of the part. An actor who overturns all our previous conceptions of his role is usually less enjoyable than one who builds on the interpretations we have become accustomed to. But if he adds no special touches of his own to the part we will experience his performance as flat and uninteresting.[1]

[Cawelti] compares the publication of a new detective story by a talented mystery writer with a successful revival of *Hamlet*; in each case the public wants the new work to exhibit some special character of its own without violating the familiar original form.[2]

This comparison between popular fiction and stage revivals, which John Cawelti makes in 1976, and which George Dove reworks in 1990, equates the predictable conventions of genre fiction with the familiar contours of Shakespeare's play, the excellent fiction of the "talented mystery writer" with the renewed performance of Shakespeare's well-known characters. While the comforts of genre fiction emerge from its familiar, sometimes Shakespearean forms, its potential artistic value derives from the "special character of its own." The impulse to yoke Shakespeare, and particularly *Hamlet*, with popular fiction recurs in criticism as well as the novels themselves. One concern then becomes how these collusions between narrative and performance, between novel and theatre, employ the original form and, without violating it, establish their "special character." Another equally important issue, invoked by Cawelti's persistent metaphor, is why Shakespearean performance is so deeply implicated in popular fiction.

The temptation to narrate Shakespeare is long-standing, starting with the well-known apocryphal tales of his composition of *The Merry Wives of Windsor* because the Queen requested a play about Falstaff in love, the speculations about his relationship with Anne Hathaway deriving from his bequest of the "second-best" bed to her, and the old story of Shakespeare's expulsion from Arden for poaching the king's deer. Such tales enter the fabric of twentieth-century novels, when, for example, Mrs. Shakespeare tells her own tale about her husband's fecklessness in Robert Nye's *Mrs. Shakespeare: The Complete Works* (1993) or Leon Rooke narrates Shakespeare's flight from Arden from his hound's perspective in *Shakespeare's Dog* (1981). However, the history of novelistic adaptations of Shakespeare is considerably more multifaceted.

In the early 1800s, the storytelling surrounding Shakespeare moved beyond historical anecdote into published fiction, like Robert Folkestone Williams's 1838 *Shakespeare and His Friends*, which actually recounts Queen Elizabeth's command that Shakespeare write *Merry Wives*. Other authors began to draw on Shakespeare's plays for narrative, especially for youthful audiences, as Charles and Mary Lamb did in their 1810 *Tales from Shakespeare*. While novels like Charles Dickens's *Nicholas Nickleby* (1838–39) incorporated Shakespearean staging in their plots, Mary Cowden Clarke's novellas elaborated the early lives of Shakespeare's female characters in *The Girlhood of Shakespeare's Heroines* (1851). By the mid nineteenth century, there were four distinct modes of narrating Shakespeare: fictionalized bard biographies; simplified stories for young readers; character novels; and contextual narratives that invoke Shakespeare on stage. To this last category, we could add current novels that employ academic rather than theatrical Shakespearean contexts. Each of these narrative strategies promotes characteristics in fiction that merely staging the plays cannot, supposedly, supply.

For example, the enormous array of novels that follow *Shakespeare and His Friends* (1838) with fictionalized accounts of Shakespeare's life all assume that Shakespeare himself is a mystery that the stage productions cannot resolve. Most often the "Friends" are crucial to the narrative. Seldom does Shakespeare's perspective govern; much more frequently a child actor or a hapless apprentice or a fellow actor or even a dog drives the narrative perspective and fleshes out indirectly the relatively sparse biography of Shakespeare available. Shakespearean novels in this mode offer narration as the necessary substitute for the unavailable, constantly re-imagined staging of his life.

In *Tales from Shakespeare* (1810), the Lambs' strategies suggest that narrative can sort out, clarify, and thus simplify Shakespeare's characters and their actions. The Lambs offered children, particularly girls, early access to Shakespeare with *Tales* that present an explanatory, omniscient narration even as they abbreviate the plots. Although most critics would dismiss the idea that narrative is intrinsically less complex and difficult to understand than staged drama, the purpose of the Lambs' simplification – to intrigue youthful would-be Shakespearean readers – remains a cogent purpose for narration in current popular fiction. While radical simplification now resides chiefly in lavishly illustrated Shakespeare-for-children picture books, the use of narrative to lure young readers, especially teenagers, to Shakespeare pervades young adult fiction which, in turn, embraces author narratives, Shakespearean contexts, and character histories.

Mary Cowden Clarke's novellas and subsequent Shakespearean character novels offer their readers insight into Shakespeare's characters, usually through first-person or limited third-person narration. Following Cowden Clarke's lead, recent writers often use the Shakespearean novel to explain the interior psychological motives of particular characters, like Gertrude in *Hamlet*, whose ambiguous staged behavior invites the novelist's as well as the audience's imaginations. Whereas the Lambs' *Tales* imply that narration can simplify Shakespeare enough to make his plays accessible to young readers, Shakespearean character novels reflect the assumption that narration can flesh out the motivations and the history behind actions presented in merely "two-hours' traffic of our stage" (*Romeo and Juliet*, Prol. 12).

Late twentieth- and twenty-first-century popular novelists also use Shakespeare as the occasion that informs their own plots. The novels that incorporate the plays as context – in stage productions or academe – position staging and teaching Shakespeare as apparently neutral contexts that very often become meaningful counterpoints to the central plot. Mystery fiction, in particular, subordinates theatre to narrative in ways that then, paradoxically, re-establish Shakespeare as key to recreating the narrative of the murder. From Michael Innes's *Hamlet, Revenge* (1937), to P. M. Carlson's *Audition for Murder* (1985), to David Rotenberg's *The Hamlet Murders* (2004), Shakespeare's *Hamlet* on stage situates the mystery. Innes's Hamlet actor has indeed killed the person playing Polonius but for political reasons, the actress playing Ophelia in P. M. Carlson's novel dies but did not commit suicide, and the murdered director of *Hamlet* in Rotenberg's novel was killed by the actors playing Ophelia and Laertes, in part because he seduced "Ophelia." While these novels treat Shakespearean performances as less important than the central narrative, the eternal return of the plays onstage yokes theatrical action with narrative's ability to reveal psychologically complex motives.

The recent proliferation of Shakespearean novels in these several modes has provoked much contemporary criticism. As critics like Marianne Novy and Julie Sanders have pointed out, distinctive traditions of cross-cultural and gendered fictional reworkings of Shakespeare have emerged in the literary novel. In analyses of Shakespeare in genre fiction, Susan Baker has explored how Shakespeare marks both social class and innocence in classic detective fiction, while Linda Charnes locates Shakespeare – and specifically *Hamlet* – as intimately linked with noir detectives. Martha Tuck Rozett explores how authors use fiction and drama in *Talking Back to Shakespeare*. In my work, I argue that contemporary romance novelists use Shakespeare to register complex class and gender tensions.[3] These considerations of Shakespearean fiction typically pursue ideological readings of Shakespeare's fictional deployment. Either Shakespeare himself or his constrained characters provoke appropriative responses that validate new artistry or expose ideological contexts.

However, the ideological stakes in narrating Shakespeare are only one aspect of popular fiction's engagement with Shakespeare. The contending artistic powers of narration and drama are equally important to Shakespeare's influence in popular genre fiction. *Hamlet*'s novelistic afterlives, especially in the flood of popular novels in the last fifteen years, explore provocatively the tensions between theatrical and narrative representation in all four modes: fictional reconstruction of Shakespeare's life, young adult fiction, character novels, and Shakespearean contextual fiction. Recent fiction illuminates and exacerbates the tensions between narrative and theatre in these "familiar forms" of the Shakespeare novel, possibly due to increasing cultural tensions between literature/reading and media/watching performance.

The most important aspect of *Hamlet*, for my purposes, is its emphasis on the competition between narration and action, between telling a story and staging it. This play grapples with the same questions that popular fiction implicitly raises about the powers of narration: its access to individual point of view, its ability to sequence causes and effects, and its susceptibility to alternate versions and authorities. Telling a story imbeds it within a perspective, which has both limitations and advantages; staging an action yields perspective and judgment to an audience with necessarily multiple viewpoints. *Hamlet* offers several narrations; one, the ghost's narration of his death, is obviously important while the others almost disappear in the text. However, taken together, these narratives reveal an unresolvable struggle between narrative and theatre that re-emerges within current Shakespearean popular fiction.

All storytelling within *Hamlet* illustrates both the advantages and deficiencies of narrative point of view. The ghost's story, hedged around with his experiences in purgatory, reveals his clear bias against his brother Claudius, "that incestuous, that adulterate beast" (1.5.42). Surrounded by flourishes of personal perspective, his essential message is succinct: "The serpent that did sting thy father's life / Now wears his crown" (1.5.39–40). However, Old Hamlet's story is a counter-narrative from the start, challenging the current report of his death: "'Tis given out that, sleeping in my orchard, / A serpent stung me. So the whole ear of Denmark / Is by a forged process of my death / Rankly abused" (1.5.35–38). From the beginning, the ghost reminds us that there is an alternative narrative, one that he deems false.

As the ghost elaborates his story, its perspectival details proliferate. After much commentary on Gertrude, the ghost senses the morning:

> Brief let me be. Sleeping within my orchard,
> *My custom always in the afternoon,*
> Upon my secure hour thy uncle stole,
> With juice of cursed hebenon in a vial,
> And in the porches of my ears did pour
> The leperous distilment; *whose effect*
> *Holds such an enmity with blood of man*
> *That swift as quicksilver it courses through*
> *The natural gates and alleys of the body,*
> *And with a sudden vigour it doth posset*
> *And curd, like eager droppings into milk,*
> *The thin and wholesome blood. So did it mine;*
> *And a most instant tetter barked about,*
> *Most lazar-like, with vile and loathsome crust,*
> *All my smooth body.*
> Thus was I, sleeping, by a brother's hand
> Of life, of crown, of queen at once dispatch'd. (1.4.59–75)

Excluding the italicized commentary about his personal habits and about the poison's effect on his body, the "brief" story takes only seven lines. The difficulties of perspective emerge in narrative excess. Old Hamlet is sleeping when the "leperous distilment" enters his ears, the poison has "sudden vigour," and "a most instant tetter" covers his body with a "vile and loathsome crust." This nicely specific forensic description creates a paradox. Given these features of the event, how does the sleeping king, instantly paralyzed, know who poisoned him? How, for that matter, does he know that he has been poisoned, given that the poison's effects invoke the natural, if inexplicably swift, details of leprosy? The play pits Old Hamlet's narrative against the story as "given out" and offers no explanation of his curious, contradictory narrative perspective: both asleep and awake, both dying instantly and alert to complex medical diagnosis. According to the narrative, Old Hamlet is dead before he can actually perceive the events that he recounts; like the story of his "natural death," his narrative is post-mortem.

These odd narrative conflicts might be unremarkable, dismissible as a consequence of ghostly omniscience, if Gertrude's narrations did not reveal comparable emotional bias and temporal confusions. When Gertrude describes her son's behavior in her closet, her narration does not match the scene that she has just experienced; though technically accurate, her account omits most of her interaction with her son and elides his responsibility, both by insisting on his madness and by omitting his name. The difficulties in her narrations become more obvious when she tells Laertes of his sister's death. Her first account, like her husband's, is brief: "One woe doth tread upon another's heel, / So fast they follow. Your sister's drowned, Laertes" (4.7.135–36). However, Gertrude's subsequent description reveals more significant limitations in narrative perspective. Her lengthy narrative of how "an envious sliver broke" (4.7.145) works admirably as a story that justifies Ophelia's burial in the churchyard and that might soften Laertes's vengeful grief. At the same time these lines create difficulties comparable to those in the ghost's narrative. Gertrude's narrative is beautifully detailed, as if she were present. However, if she is watching, why does she not save Ophelia before "her garments, heavy with their drink, / Pulled the poor wretch from her melodious lay / To muddy death" (4.7.153–55)? After all, George Eliot's hero in *Daniel Deronda* (1876) both witnesses and rescues his suicidal "Ophelia." Gertrude's failure to save a girl "incapable of her own distress" (4.7.150) is, at least, problematic.

Gertrude's narration of the closet scene proves incomplete, self-serving, and exculpatory from a maternal perspective, as invested in personal perspective as Ophelia's earlier account of Hamlet's "lovesick" visit to *her* closet. Moreover, if Gertrude recounts Ophelia's drowning as one present, she becomes partially guilty of the death through neglect. If she was not a direct, conscious witness, she reconstructs Ophelia's drowning in the most palatable narrative possible to insure her some burial rites, although "her death was doubtful" (5.1.221). Both Ophelia and King Hamlet's deaths become doubtful because of the ways that they occur within narration.

Partly because of the doubts that invested perspectives create, narration never fully succeeds in *Hamlet*; however, neither does theatre. The ghost's vexed perspective prompts Hamlet to test the story by using theatre, specifically the players who inspire him with the speech he has requested: "One speech in it I chiefly loved: 'twas Aeneas' tale to Dido, and thereabout of it especially where he speaks of Priam's slaughter. If it live in your memory, begin at this line – let me see, let me see" (2.2.448–52). This performance of storytelling apparently motivates Hamlet's decision to commission a staged version of his father's narrative: "Dost thou hear me, old friend? Can you play the murder of Gonzago?" (3.2.539–40). However, which came first, the play Hamlet recalls or his ghost father's narration of the same plot? A preexisting play that Hamlet knows well and that closely resembles the ghost's narrative significantly complicates the sequential relationship between narration and "actions that a man might play"(1.2.84).

Moreover, despite his plans to use the performance of *The Murder of Gonzago* to gauge the all-important audience responses, Hamlet compulsively narrates. First, the dumb show performance collides with Hamlet's summary: "This play is the image of a murder done in Vienna: Gonzago is the duke's name; his wife, Baptista: you shall see anon; 'tis a knavish piece of work" (3.2.232–39). When the actors finally perform the murder, Hamlet again interjects his own narration: "He poisons him i' the garden for's estate. His name's Gonzago: the story is extant, and writ in choice Italian: you shall see anon how the murderer gets the love of Gonzago's wife" (3.2.255–58). This troubled persistence of narrative and its presumed authority challenges the representational power of the play that Hamlet himself has requested. Whereas neither Old Hamlet nor Gertrude acknowledge the implicit conflicts in their narrative perspectives, Hamlet's encounters with narration propel him into performance even while he challenges the performance he himself has designed by telling the story.

By the time the play reaches Hamlet's final plea to Horatio, "Absent thee from felicity awhile; / And in this harsh world draw [his] breath in pain / To tell my story" (5.2.352–54), narration and theatrical performance are mutually compromised and functionally interdependent. Narration promises secret truths beyond overt events and retrospective "truth" but falters because of limited individual perspectives; performance offers an open, current display of the actions but neglects "that within which passeth show" (1.2.85), especially the crucial motives of several characters. These narrative dynamics in *Hamlet*, which extend to the stories told by Ophelia, Gertrude, Claudius, and Horatio, are one crucial reason that this particular play has generated such a wide array of popular fiction.

In all four modes of Shakespearean fiction-making I offered at the beginning of this essay, *Hamlet* has served, either directly or indirectly, as an important "formula" through which Shakespearean novels explore the "special character" of the relationship between making stories and making theatre. Recent literary novels, young adult fiction, and murder mysteries all include illuminating negotiations with *Hamlet*. The structural contention between narrative and theatrical performance that literary novels present as "high art" to literate adult audiences, young adult fiction exposes in blatant terms to its adolescent readers. Taking up similar issues and strategies, detective fiction reframes most explicitly the dynamic interaction between narrating and staging as well as the problematics of perspective and sequence in narration because "detective fiction – with its streamlined structure, its emphasis on interpretation at all levels of plot and narration, and its peculiar focus on the writer and reader – represents narrativity in its purest form."[4] Taken together, these three genres of Shakespearean novel demonstrate how Shakespeare's play continues to enable narrative in current popular fiction and how theatre still challenges the conditions of narrative.

The implied priority of perspective and resulting artistic power of narration anchor the numerous popular novels that pursue Shakespeare's own identity. These fictions typically reveal both the "true" author of the plays and the deepest motivations and/or literary artistry of those pursuing the mystery. Recent literary novels like Sarah Smith's *Chasing Shakespeares* (2003) and Alan Wall's *School of Night* (2002) employ the mystery of who really wrote the plays as the key to their characters' self-understanding. *Chasing Shakespeares* works through the class struggle and desire between Joe Roper, working-class graduate student who favors Shakespeare as the author despite his lower-class origins, and Posey Gould, the graduate student of privilege who favors the Earl of Oxford and finances their joint travels to London to verify – or debunk – the archival letter Joe has found wherein "WS" reveals de Vere's authorship.

Like *Chasing Shakespeares*, Wall's *School of Night* opens with a character stealing early modern documents. Wall's Sean Tallow discovers as much about himself, his relationship to his friend Dan Pagett and the School of Night as he does about Shakespearean authorship. The narrator's preoccupations with Shakespeare's failure to leave any books in his will and his growing conviction that Christopher Marlowe wrote the plays finally provoke him to decode Ralegh's encrypted text. As Ralegh supposedly puts it, Shakespeare is a "rainbow man." When Sean investigates how Marlowe and his conspirators could have been controlling Shakespeare, he discovers that "[Shakespeare had] not been controlled by them; instead they'd been resurrected in him. He has taken his fire from their flames. And because he had been a nobody, the man from nowhere, he had been able to become everyone. Shakespeare was Shakespeare after all."[5] As Tallow finds, his own apparent cowardice, smallness, and malleability in the face of his friend's felonious daring resonates in Shakespeare, who can richly represent the dead voices because his own will does not intervene.

Novels in this mode, though not categorized as detective fiction, nonetheless treat Shakespeare as the mystery that generates their narratives and thus expose their own validation of narrative structure over staged performance. Martin Stephen's historical mystery *The Conscience of the King* (2004) overtly plays out how Shakespearean author novels attempt to validate narrative over theatre. Even though the question of who wrote the plays matters less than tracking down the syphilitic former spy Kit Marlowe and King James's all-too-revealing private letters, Sir Henry Gresham uncovers the secrets of Shakespeare's authorship. The novel opens with a "literal" rendition of *The Mousetrap* in *Hamlet* in which old Ben stands in for Shakespeare as the player-king of Hamlet's dumb show and dies when the poison substituted by Kit Marlowe enters his ear instead of Shakespeare's, as intended. In Stephen's novel, Marlowe, after staging his death and escaping to France, has sent his plays back to England to be performed under Shakespeare's name. Murderous and crazed with venereal disease, Marlowe returns to England to avenge himself on those who exiled him and to reclaim his reputation as a playwright, usurped by Shakespeare. Initially, the novel seems to offer the most conventional of explanations for Marlowe's authorship beyond the grave, while establishing that Gresham's narrative supersedes staged performance.

However, rather than presenting the single rival claimant and then elaborating one alternative narrative of Shakespeare's artistry, Stephen's novel peels off layers of potential authorship. Gresham discovers that the supposedly volatile letters he must recover are not the most crucial documents that Marlowe has stolen – he also took the original drafts of Shakespeare's plays in their authors' own hands. In Stephen's second solution to the "authorship" mystery, Shakespeare has apparently functioned as the early modern equivalent of a nom de plume for several aristocratic would-be playwrights. Stephen's novel thus authorizes all the rival playwrights proposed over the years and more: Kit Marlowe, Edward de Vere, Francis Bacon, Launcelot Andrews, the Countess of Pembroke (as the author of *Twelfth Night* and *As You Like It*), and even King James himself. These aristocrats and clergymen, eager to dabble in the new literary form but protective of their status, have used Shakespeare as their conduit to the stage and now risk scandalous exposure as playwrights. This compound conspiracy theory fully accounts for the enormous array of legal, medical, and political knowledge in Shakespeare's plays, often cited as evidence he could not have written them.[6] It also effectively raises the stakes for Gresham's quest, already intensified by Marlowe's personal hatred of Gresham.

Stephen moves beyond this gentle mockery of authorship conspiracy theories when Gresham actually recovers the documents, reads them, and realizes that the aristocratic pseudo-playwrights have written terrible, unstageable plays. Shakespeare has taken and transformed their work through his own linguistic and theatrical artistry. These authors may have supplied narratives, characters, details of law, religious doctrine, medicine, and current science in their fledgling works, but Shakespeare created their poetic beauty and their theatrical power. Ultimately, Gresham protects his aristocratic patrons and secures Shakespeare's status as author by destroying both Marlowe and the drafts during the Globe production when Marlowe planned to claim the glory for himself.

As Stephen's mystery demonstrates with its kaleidoscopic survey of possible authors for the plays and Gresham's ultimate "rescue" of Shakespeare as playwright, such novels empower the hero/narrator and the newly established (or re-established) author of the plays simultaneously. In the contest between narrative and stage, the "author" novels validate the superiority and prior claims of an individual perspective and narrated history over the limited residue of William Shakespeare's life. However, as Stephen's novel also shows, such validated narrations paradoxically rely on the actual stage performances and must acknowledge fraudulent and therefore "staged" performances of Shakespearean authorship.

The mystery of Shakespeare's identity also serves as a popular lure for teenaged readers of young adult fiction. For example, the pseudo-superhero adolescent of *The Blue Avenger Cracks the Code* (2000), like Sean in *School of Night*, deciphers the code of Shakespeare's plays, but he discovers de Vere's authorship. However, young adult author novels most often involve Elizabethan or time-traveling adolescents who discover Shakespeare or his surrogates within theatrical contexts. In *A Question of Will* (2000), by Lynne Kositsky, Perin Willoughby – known as Willow during her time at the Globe – uncovers de Vere's authorship, persuades a fellow player to let everyone else know after de Vere's death, and returns to the present to discover that everyone is now studying the world's most famous author – Edward de Vere. In Gary Blackwood's young adult novel, *The Shakespeare Stealer* (1998), a dictation-taking orphan named Widge becomes apprentice to Simon Bass and receives an unusual job: he must attend a play at the Globe Theatre and transcribe it word for word. This theft will benefit his master, who intends to stage the play with his own company. Thus piracy theories about the quartos of Shakespeare devolve onto an orphan who learned "charactery" from his first apprenticeship with an apothecary. Thwarted in his theft, first by the distractions of the play itself and later by a cutpurse who steals his tablet, Widge signs on as an apprentice with the company when they catch him searching for the missing document. Predictably he comes to value his new theatrical "family," including the moody Shakespeare, more than he fears the punishments of his previous master. Shakespeare and the adolescent narrative perspective prove equally important.[7]

Blackwood's hero follows a characteristic narrative arc from theatrical outsider to awkward actor/boy-actress to associate/friend of Shakespeare, the dominant pattern in much contextual Shakespearean fiction. Current young adult novels in this mode – J. B. Cheaney's *The Playmaker* (2000) and *The True Prince* (2002), Gary Blackwood's sequels, *Shakespeare's Scribe* (2000) and *Shakespeare's Spy* (2003), Susan Cooper's *King of Shadows* (1999) – generally take their narrative perspective from the experiences of an apprentice, sometimes a boy-actress. These narrators often become the source of lines, plots, characters, and even plays. Widge, for example, finishes off and sells a play that Shakespeare abandons in frustration – with Shakespeare's permission, however. Claiming part authorship for *Timon of Athens* may not be as influential as providing whole plot sources for Shakespeare as does Tuck Smythe in Simon Hawke's mystery series. However, Widge puts his unusual literacy skills to important tasks. After all, the play he must steal in *The Shakespeare Stealer* is, again, *Hamlet*.

These young adult novels embrace even more directly than do Shakespearean author novels how living in Shakespeare's theatre, as Nat Field does in Susan Cooper's *King of Shadows* or Perin Willoughby does in *A Question of Will*, enables narration. In *King of Shadows*, Nat Field's miraculous transportation into *A Midsummer Night's Dream* in Shakespeare's company not only saves Shakespeare from catching the plague from the "real" Nat Field but also encourages the twentieth-century Nat to tell his story of parental loss to his new father-figure, Will Shakespeare. Shakespeare, in turn, takes Nat as the model for the Ariel of his *Tempest*, a character Nat only discovers when he returns to his own time. Thus young adult fiction also embraces the Shakespearean stage, past and present, as context or counterpoint to the important task of narrating adolescent experience.

In addition to recording apprentice narratives, contemporary theatrical situations, and even academic Shakespearean contexts (see Laura Sonnenmark's *Something Rotten in the State of Maryland* [1990]), several young adult novels incorporate pre- or alternative histories of characters. Bruce Colville, well known for his picture-book narrations for still younger readers, also offers a slightly older audience *The Skull of Truth* (1997). This novel recounts the afterlife of a piece of *Hamlet*, resembling the Shakespearean artifacts in adult novels and the magical "tokens" that appear in other young adult fiction. In Colville's novel, Yorick's skull compels its possessor, currently Charlie Eggleston, to tell the absolute truth in answer to all questions. This talent may wreak havoc in Charlie's friendships and family, but it elicits the truth from developers who unwillingly reveal the problems with their proposed destruction of a local park. The magic compulsion of Yorick's skull echoes the way Shakespearean artifacts across many popular genres, including the revered documents in the Shakespeare-quest novels, compel or enable narration.[8]

Young adult fiction also translates the Cowden Clarke character narrative into the conventions of current young adult genres. Consider David Bergantino's young adult horror novel, *Hamlet II: Revenge of Ophelia* (2003), in which a swamp-like, monstrous Ophelia haunts and destroys numerous friends of Cameron Dean, Hamlet's descendant. Cameron has inherited a version of the plot (the death of his father and remarriage of his mother to his paternal aunt Claudia), half of Hamlet's ghost (the family curse), and Elsinore itself (including Ophelia's murderous ghost). More closely allied to the Cowden Clarke model, Leslie Fiedler's revisionist *Dating Hamlet* (2002) takes Ophelia's perspective, endows her with herbal knowledge of near-poisons from her dead mother, and gives her a different father, the gravedigger, who becomes her co-conspirator. This novel reworks *Hamlet* into a successful *Romeo and Juliet*, with a decisive Ophelia and a Hamlet who really does love her so much that "forty thousand brothers / Could not with all their quantity of love / Make up [his] sum"(5.1.264–66). Not only does Ophelia see Old Hamlet's ghost and ally herself with Hamlet from the start, she also feigns madness to torment and escape the villainous Claudius, who has, she thinks, sent her Hamlet to his death. She stages her own death, and, using the same potion, she arranges with her brother to stage his and Hamlet's deaths and subsequent revivals in the same way. The virtuous (Hamlet and Laertes) and the repentant (Gertrude) receive the antidote after the duel scene, but Fortinbras decides that Claudius does not merit revival. Fiedler's retelling/rewriting of *Hamlet* through Ophelia's first-person narrative re-imagines the play through the invested, revisionist perspective of an individual character.

This novel presents in much more blatant terms the gynocentric perspectives that critics have begun to track in Shakespearean contemporary fiction. In its perspectival shift and investment in female agency, *Dating Hamlet* takes up contemporary feminist ideology much as George Gross has argued that Mary Cowden Clarke's novellas about Ophelia and other Shakespearean female characters engage with Victorian perceptions of women.[9] By reworking the "truth" underlying familiar performances of *Hamlet*, Fiedler positions Ophelia's decisive narrative as more central than Hamlet's performances. At the same time, however, Ophelia's narrative power relies on her greater awareness of the performances going on in Denmark: she participates in Hamlet's performance of madness, stages her own drowning, and manipulates Claudius's fraudulent duel so that neither he nor Hamlet realizes that they do not genuinely face death. Her narration thus preserves not only Hamlet's life but also his "genuine" love and heroism – he declaims his love for her and justifiably kills his murderous uncle at long last without knowing that Ophelia has enabled his actions by her staging.

In similar but less obvious ways, "literary" novelists have consistently recast the narrative point of view in *Hamlet*, echoing the contentions between narrative perspectives we have seen in the play itself. As far back as Lillie Buffum Chace Wyman's *Gertrude of Denmark: An Interpretive*

Romance (1924) and James Cabell's *Hamlet Had an Uncle: A Comedy of Honor* (1940), novelists have embraced these alternative narrative perspectives. As Rozett implies in her analysis of Wyman's personally revelatory novel, these novelists explore how narration's psychological interiority can outdo and even rewrite *Hamlet* as staged. In *Gertrude and Claudius* (2000), John Updike validates narration in multiple ways while embracing Gertrude and Claudius's perspectives. Updike alternates his limited third-person narrative principally between Gerutha-Geruthe-Gertrude and Feng-Fengon-Claudius. Throughout its three acts, the novel shifts the spellings of its characters' names in ways that invoke the source narratives preceding Shakespeare's play:

> Part I is based on the oldest Hamlet legend of *Historia Danica* of Saxo Grammaticus, a late text of the twelfth century, published first in 1514, with its tone of the old saga; Part II is related to the French version of Francois de Belleforest's *Histoires tragiques* (Paris, 1576) of the Saxo original with Updike's embroidered version of medieval romances, while Part III presents the events of Hamlet just before the play begins.[10]

Despite this slow approach to *Hamlet* and the telling use of Shakespearean character names in the title (one wonders how well *Gerutha and Feng* would work as a title), *Gertrude and Claudius* never actually arrives; Updike positions his novel as a prequel while its shifting nomenclature implies both the priority of *Hamlet*'s narrative precursors and its universality in reiterable narrative.

However, even within this overdetermined narrative framework, the novel reveals its connections to theatre. The exterior performances of dialogue and behavior help create intimacy in the limited third-person narrations of Gertrude and Claudius. Such intimacy, and its concomitant involvement in staged behavior, pervades the adulterous relationship Geruthe and Fengon pursue:

> "I make no claims, Geruthe, I am a beggar sheerly. The truth is simple: I live only in your company. The rest is performance."
>
> "This is not performance?" Geruthe said dryly, brushing his tingling hair with a hand gone cold in the fatality of her commitment. "We must find a better stage – one not borrowed from our king."[11]

Although performance and the stage become metaphors in Geruthe and Fengon's conversation, the figurative theatre pervades the roles that the secret lovers must play in public and, increasingly, with each other. The individual, psychological reality reveals everything else as mere performance, as Claudius's meditations about Gertrude reveal: "Whenever he saw her afresh … he realized what was, simply, real, all the rest being an idle show of theatrical seeming."[12] Unlike the perpetually sulky and self-dramatizing Amleth-Hamblet-Hamlet throughout *Gertrude and Claudius*, Gertrude possesses "that within which passes show" (*Hamlet*, 1.2.85), at least for Updike's Claudius. The irony of Claudius's final thought, "all would be well,"[13] derives ultimately from the ways in which repeated stage *Hamlet*s both underwrite and undo Updike's novel.

As *Gertrude and Claudius* illustrates with its layered yet unitary narrative, the very "pastness" of Shakespeare's plays exposes the conflicted position of time in narration. Staging *Hamlet* "revives" the play and the character, as the epigraphs to this essay imply. The play occurs live onstage, and its sequential performance develops in actors and audiences who are actually moving through time. However, the play, with its internal narrations, also invokes the complexities of narrative time which detective fiction best exposes:

> Narratives are read consecutively from beginning to end, and often over a gradual period of time; their plots inevitably concern the sequential nature of events and the influence of the past upon the present; and their narration usually recounts what has already happened in a third- or first-person point of view that implies temporal distance between action and narration … Detective fiction, which begins ex post facto, and in which the detective must reconstruct the past, exacerbates this temporal relationship.[14]

Detective fiction underscores not only the perspectival stakes espoused in narration but also narration's crucially conflicted involvement with both priority and sequence.

By offering Shakespearean character novels as detective fiction, Alan Gordon underscores the temporal complexities that Shakespearean novels like *Gertrude and Claudius* expose so delicately. Gordon set his first historical mystery, *Thirteenth Night* (1999), in the medieval period, significantly predating Shakespeare. Yet the central characters of the novel and of the series, Feste and Viola, appear in Shakespeare's *Twelfth Night*; Gordon's master fool Feste and widowed Viola thus presumably function as the prior and "authentic" narrative that Shakespeare only partially presents. At the same time, as the title suggests, the narrative picks up *after* the play's events, which Theophilos, alias Feste, has manipulated because the Guild of Fools dispatched his "admirable fooling" to insure social stability in Illyria. Whereas Fiedler gives Ophelia the governing perspective and Updike recasts Hamlet through the point of view of "Claudius … as able and worthy king and husband [and] Gertrude a loving queen and mother,"[15] Gordon liberates Shakespeare's fools from their ironic isolation and gives Feste's/Theophilos's narration as evidence that the guild functions as the true unacknowledged legislator of the world. At the end of *Thirteenth Night*, when Theophilos has married the widowed Viola and initiated her into the guild as well, the series apparently moves beyond its Shakespearean origins into medieval politics and social instabilities.

Gordon returns to Shakespeare in his recent novel, *An Antic Disposition* (2004), which, like *Thirteenth Night*, underscores the problematic temporal relationships imbedded in narration. Since the birth of their daughter Portia, Viola/Claudia and Feste/Theophilos spend their time with the Fools' Guild listening to stories, including a story told by Gerald, an elder fool, of Denmark's Feng (Claudius), Ørvendil (old Hamlet), Gerutha (Gertrude), Amleth (Hamlet), and, of course, Yorick, the fool that the guild has sent to the troubled Danish court. In this retrospective telling, Yorick is the crucial figure, fool to the doomed Ørvendil and friend to Amleth, whom he trains in self-protective madness and foolery. The narrative recasts Amleth's madness and his duel with Lothar/Laertes as the work of apprentice fools who escape their grisly ends with the guild's help and become fools themselves.

However, Gerald's story does not include the key details that Theophilis recounts to Claudia afterwards when he admits he was Lothar/Laertes; he completes the story of his youthful relationship to Amleth and his sister Ophelia/Alfhild. After Amleth reveals to Lothar that his real father was Yorick, murdered by the jealous Gorm/Polonius, Lothar, in turn, confesses that he let Gerutha die from the poisoned cup because she drowned Ophelia herself. Thus Gordon takes the potential guilt in Gertrude's story about Ophelia's drowning and recasts her entirely as the villain. In fact, not only did she drug Ørvendil's drink before he went to duel Feng, but she also killed Lothar's mother with a potion. Her thwarted ambitions and violent jealousy of other women have driven all the events from behind the scenes. This secondary narrative further complicates the underpinnings to the staged behavior in *Hamlet*. Gordon's nested narratives not only rework the narrative underlying the superficial staged events of *Hamlet*, much as other character novels do, but also draw attention to the medieval origins of the play, as Updike does.

By turning Shakespeare into fiction, popular novelists rework Shakespeare's own creative process. As many of *Hamlet*'s afternovels recall, Shakespeare reworked novellas, prose romances, and histories as drama. Geoffrey Bullough's magisterial and still authoritative *Narrative and Dramatic Sources for Shakespeare* lists "narrative" first for a reason. When Gordon's novel authorizes the narrator of his series, Theophilos, as both Feste and Laertes, he effectively recasts Shakespearean theatre within narration that both precedes and follows the plays while simultaneously locating narration originating in the always-performing fool.

The wide array of detective fiction that actually takes place in the theatre also asserts the advantages that narration supposedly has over staging. Some of these detective novels imply that their narrations provide the events and sometimes actual lines that Shakespeare incorporates into his plays, as in Simon Hawke's amusing titled mysteries, most recently including *The Merchant of Vengeance* (2003). Others, like Michael Innes's *Hamlet, Revenge!* (1937) or Marvin Kaye's *Bullets for Macbeth* (1976), offer narrative co-opting of theatrical effects (Hamlet killing Polonius as the Hamlet actor killing the Polonius actor) or theatrically inspired resolutions for textual problems (the Third Murderer in *Macbeth*). Turning theatre into background neatly affirms the greater importance of narration while the detective genre itself explores the "temporal distance between action and narration."[16]

Philip Gooden's *Sleep of Death* (2000), which takes place in the Shakespearean theatre, effectively illustrates how detective fiction engages issues of both perspective and sequential priority. At the same time that Gooden includes multiple retellings of the *Hamlet* murder from several perspectives, sometimes in dialogue, sometimes in narrative, the novel also oscillates between narrative to performance. The very first "narration" records in italics the perspective of the murderer and his actions in the enclosed garden. Italicized accounts from the perspective of the murderer serve as prologues to each of the book's five "Acts." The subsequent narrations of the play compete with and complement the murderer's version. Actor Nick Revill recounts the eventful murder in Shakespeare's play during his erotic encounter with his prostitute lover Nell. Thus, the "high points" of the murder plot are punctuated with reminders of the simultaneous sexual action. Even while Nick's perspective seems to dominate the narrative, Nell's asides remind the reader that action counterpoints narrative. Just as important, the story of *Hamlet* soon proves to be more generally possessed by other perspectives, as Master William Eliot asks Revill to stay at his home in order to investigate the odd coincidences in his own family narrative – his father's death and his mother Lady Alice's swift remarriage to his Uncle Thomas. The issue rapidly becomes one of priority since the death occurred before Shakespeare's play was performed.

Like most detectives, Revill soon finds that there are competing narratives that could explain the death of Sir William Eliot – perhaps the lady committed or commissioned the murder or possibly the father-uncle killed the brother whom he was cuckolding regularly. However, the signature of William Shakespeare is also all over the death – he is the man who wrote the play resembling Eliot's death and representing that death as murder, and the initials W. S. appear carved in the pear tree where Revill deduces that the murderer hid. As S. E. Sweeney notes, the detective seeks the authoritative narrative among several possible narratives, the revelation of the murderer, and his perspective and motives.[17] In the structure of Gooden's novel, this quest emerges also in the contest between the italicized narratives from the murderer's point of view and the ongoing exploration of our detective-actor, whose judgments rest in part on his understanding of how people on and off stage play roles and stage their own public displays.

As Shakespeare's *Hamlet* shifts uneasily between narrative and staging to establish truth, so, too, does Shakespearean detective fiction. To resolve these multiple possible narratives and, most important, to test whether Shakespeare is guilty of committing the murder in actuality rather than just in drama, Revill uses the play to catch the conscience of the murderer, rewriting some of the lines in the play within the play where he acts the role of Lucianus. He discovers the murderer in front of him, the actor playing the Player-King, rather than the author. Thus *Hamlet* both provokes the multiple narratives Revill contemplates and becomes the theatrical occasion that reveals the actual killer, a company member who knew the play while it was being written. Gooden's *Sleep of Death* negotiates the relationship between narration and staging of Shakespeare in ways that identify both perspective and temporal priority as crucial.

Shakespearean detective fiction's interrogation of narrative time reaches a bizarre pinnacle of literary self-examination in Jasper Fforde's *Something Rotten* (2004), his fourth novel about Thursday Next. Fresh from her adventures living in literary texts and running Jurisfiction, Fforde's heroine returns to the supposedly real world with Hamlet as one of her companions. On leave from his play out of his concern for his "real-world" reputation, Hamlet stumbles upon several displacements of himself: the numerous familiar film and stage productions that represent him; a "Hamlet WillSpeak machine," which recites "to be or not to be" for two shillings; and an impromptu *Hamlet* contest, in which his rendition of the same soliloquy comes in last. The trauma of Hamlet's encounters with his representations sends him to a conflict-management specialist and result in a (temporarily) decisive and active Hamlet. Partaking in Thursday's adventures, Hamlet finally realizes that his public reputation as "a mouthy spoiled brat who can't make up his mind" is less important than his new understanding that "my play is popular because my failings are *your* failings, my indecision is the indecision of you all." A combination of time-travel and extra-literary experiences puts Hamlet in touch with his own inner universality.[18]

Something Rotten's other *Hamlet* crises appear more serious since they include both character insurrection and the troublesome "conjoinment" of

Hamlet and *Merry Wives* into *The Merry Wives of Elsinore*. The insurrections parody character novels as the Polonius family petitions for "Internal Plot Adjustment requests" (p. 114) to rewrite the play from their own perspectives – starting with "*The Tragedy of the Fair Ophelia Driven Mad by the Callous Hamlet, Prince of Denmark*." These "minor" difficulties in Jurisfiction lead to the less tractable problem of the book merger, "where one book joined with another to increase its collective narrative advantage."[19] To ensure that *Hamlet* will continue to exist, Thursday must find one of the Shakespeares secretly cloned by the novel's corporate villain and commission a new "original" manuscript. With Hamlet and *Hamlet* under pressure on several plot levels, Fforde playfully exposes the problems of Shakespearean priority – both priorness and authority – in a vertiginous literary time travel paradox. Moreover, Hamlet's various interactions with performances of himself turn out to be crucial in restoring him to his literary self, once Thursday has freed the play from its entanglements with *Merry Wives*.

Fforde's self-conscious narration of Hamlet's encounters with theatre and performance offers a thoroughly postmodern metaphysics of literary reality. Despite its persistent relationships with both detective and science fiction, *Something Rotten* escapes genre fiction and typically appears on literature and fiction shelves. In Fforde's novels literary criticism becomes detective work and "Jurisfiction" while both drama and fiction are indiscriminately enfolded into "BookWorld." The Shakespeare in Fforde's literary universe bridges the several modes of Shakespearean fiction I have been exploring: narratives of authorial (re)construction, with the author literally cloned; the character novel, with Hamlet's "extra-literary" adventures; and the ultimate combination of theatrical and quasi-academic contextual novels.

Despite Fforde's fantasy of the vulnerability of Shakespearean forms, both Shakespeare's plays and his life have become important formulas in genre fiction. In responses to those fixed forms, Shakespearean popular fiction actively wrestles with what it can offer as the "special character" of its own. Most often the answer is narrative perspective, valued throughout popular culture and courted in the niche marketing of current genre fiction. Given that "popular fiction" now covers an array of increasingly specific genres that appeal to audiences identified by age (young adult), gender (chick lit. and lad lit.), and status ("Book Review" novels versus science fiction, romance, and detective fiction, to name the big three), both narrative perspective and established forms have become ever more important. Shakespearean novels, of course, have always courted and perhaps created niche audiences, as when Mary Cowden Clarke's *Girlhood of Shakespeare's Heroines* embraced fictional perspectives aimed largely to appeal to women readers. The very recent novels which I have been exploring here bear out Shakespeare's place in fiction-making and tailored audience appeal. The plays themselves, like *Hamlet*, often use multiple narratives and perspectives that in turn provoke later fictional development of those perspectives and plot sequencing. As a result, the stressful interplay between narrative and drama that pervades Shakespeare's plays continues to inform their novelistic afterlives and participates in larger current cultural struggles between narrative/reading and media/performance.

In the author novels, perspective challenges staging because narrative point of view reveals the author even while Shakespeare's highly publicized persona depends upon theatrical performance. The shift from *Tales* to young adult fiction exposes our investment in the adolescent perspective, in youthful time-travelers, apprentices, or Shakespearean characters who contend with an adult world that always seems staged. While Shakespearean contextual novels embrace the theatre in order to subordinate it, often incompletely, to the behind-the-scenes power of the back story, character novels expose most clearly how celebratory validation of narrative provokes conundrums comparable to Hamlet's. Which comes first, the ghost's narrative or the play that already staged his death, narration or performance? Is access to personal perspective crucial enough to outweigh biased narrative? Twenty-first century Shakespearean popular fiction embraces these conflicts surrounding perspective, while also exploring the temporal paradoxes of Shakespeare's priority: the pre-existence of his plays enables the subsequent explanatory adaptations which in turn present themselves as precursors. Throughout its various narrative modes and generic forms, Shakespearean popular fiction re-enacts an ongoing, cyclical struggle between narrating events and enacting them, a struggle over perspective, priority, and power.

NOTES

1. John G. Cawelti, *Adventure, Mystery and Romance: Formula Stories as Art and Popular Culture* (Chicago: University of Chicago Press, 1976), p. 10.
2. George Dove, "The Detection Formula and the Act of Reading," in *The Cunning Craft: Original Essays on Detective Fiction and Literary Theory*, ed. Ronald G. Walker and June M. Frazier (Macomb, IL: Western University Press, 1990), pp. 25–37, p. 27.
3. See Marianne Novy's *Engaging with Shakespeare: Responses of George Eliot and Other Women Novelists* (Athens: University of Georgia Press, 1994) and Julie Sanders's *Novel Shakespeares: Twentieth-Century Women Novelists and Appropriation* (Manchester: Manchester University Press, 2001); Susan Baker, "Shakespearean Authority in the Classic Detective Story," *Shakespeare Quarterly* 46 (1995), 424–48; Linda Charnes, "Dismember Me: Shakespeare, Paranoia, and

the Logic of Mass Culture," *Shakespeare Quarterly* 48 (1997), 1–16; Martha Tuck Rozett, "American Hamletology: Two Texts," in *Talking Back to Shakespeare* (Newark: University of Delaware Press, 1994); Laurie E. Osborne, "Sweet, Savage Shakespeare," in *Shakespeare Without Class: Misappropriations of Cultural Capital*, ed. Donald Hedrick and Bryan Reynolds (New York: Palgrave, 2000), pp. 135–51. See also Laurie Osborne, "Harlequin Presents: That 70s Shakespeare and Beyond," in *Shakespeare After Mass Media*, ed. Richard Burt (New York: Palgrave, 2001), pp. 127–49, and "Romancing the Bard," in *Shakespeare and Appropriation*, eds. Christie Desmet and Robert Sawyer (New York: Routledge, 1999), pp. 47–69.

4. S. E. Sweeney, "Locked Rooms, Detective Fiction, Narrative Theory, and Self-Reflexivity," in Walker and Frazier, *The Cunning Craft*, pp. 1–14, p. 3.

5. Alan Wall, *The School of Night* (New York: St. Martin's Press, 2002), p. 290.

6. See William Rubinstein, "Who Was Shakespeare?," *History Today* 51 (August 2001), 28–35, p. 30.

7. See also Megan Lynn Isaac, *Heirs to Shakespeare: Reinventing the Bard in Young Adult Literature* (Portsmouth, NH: Boytowcook Publishers Inc., 2000).

8. See Susan Baker, " 'Comic Material: Shakespeare' in the Classic Detective Story," in *Acting Funny: Comic Theory and Practice in Shakespeare's Plays*, ed. Frances Teague (Cranbury, NJ: Associated Press, Inc., 1994), pp. 71–73.

9. George Gross, "Mary Cowden Clarke, The Girlhood of Shakespeare's Heroines, and the Sex Education of Victorian Women," *Victorian Studies* 16 (1972), 37–58.

10. Henry D. Janowitz, " 'Master Eustace' and *Gertrude and Claudius*: Henry James and John Updike Rewrite Hamlet," *Hamlet Studies* 25 (2003), 189–99, p. 193.

11. John Updike, *Gertrude and Claudius* (New York: Ballantine Books, 2000), pp. 91–92.

12. *Ibid.*, p. 208.

13. *Ibid.*, p. 210.

14. Sweeney, "Locked Rooms," p. 7.

15. Janowitz, " 'Master Eunice', " p. 197.

16. Sweeney, "Locked Rooms," p. 7.

17. *Ibid.*, pp. 4–5.

18. Jasper Fforde, *Something Rotten* (New York: Viking, 2004), pp. 68, 371.

19. *Ibid.*, pp. 114, 115, 159.

7

EMMA SMITH

Shakespeare serialized: *An Age of Kings*

Shakespeare has suffered the final indignity ... *Romeo and Juliet* has been rewritten by a woman novelist as a serial in an American newspaper.
(*Evening Standard*, February 1937)

Writing with exquisite scorn – that cluster of denigration in "woman," "novelist," "serial" and "American," the implied bathos of the contrast between these lowbrow signifiers and "Shakespeare" – the *Evening Standard*'s "Londoner" ridicules the idea that Shakespeare might be serialized, quoting the cliffhanger from the penultimate episode: "Will Friar John overtake Romeo on the road? Or will Romeo reach Juliet's tomb before he can be saved? Don't miss to-morrow's concluding chapter!"[1] This short, snide review takes as a given the aesthetic mismatch between the commercial practices of serialization and the exalted cultural status of Shakespeare. In this chapter, however, I want to start from a different premise in order to engage with the question and practice of Shakespearean serialization, juxtaposing eight of the plays based on medieval English history written by Shakespeare during the 1590s with their publication in chronological sequence in the First Folio text of 1623, and their performance as a cycle or series during the twentieth century, in particular in the television series *An Age of Kings* broadcast by the BBC in 1960. What can the formal practices of the construction and consumption of television serialization tell us about original serial or cycle composition of the plays? Rather, therefore, than engaging with the television adaptation of Shakespeare as always and already parasitic and secondary, I want to invert the order of priority. By focusing on the specifically televisual aspects of *An Age of Kings* I hope to reveal something about the functions of serial narrative in Shakespeare's plays, as well as something about their adaptation onto the small screen. In discussing parallels between television scheduling and the rival programming of the early modern theatre, and in comparing the consumption of Shakespeare's plays in the theatre and on television, this chapter uncovers some reciprocal relations between Shakespeare, serialization, and popular culture in the 1590s and the 1960s.

Shakespeare on television

Studies of televisual Shakespeare have tended to stress its inadequacy. While recent criticism, riding the wave of stylish Hollywood Shakespeare films of the 1980s and 1990s, has been highly responsive to Shakespeare in the cinema, the routine disparagement of the "dull" BBC television series (1978–1985) has come to stand in for the apparently inevitable disappointments of Shakespeare on television.[2] Laurence Kitchin's 1965 denunciation of television as a medium chronically inadequate to Shakespeare's plays has been indicative of subsequent critical approaches. Attributing viewing figures of three million to the British broadcast of *An Age of Kings*, Kitchin sees this popularity as a regrettable means by which "a drastically limited image of Shakespeare gains enormous circulation, infecting audiences in particular with television's allergy to lyricism and rhetoric, in fact to any form of heightened speech." Resistance to television per se is an important component of Kitchin's argument: "compared with the medium's routine output [Shakespeare adaptations on television] are excellent; compared with a good stage production they are cramped and perfunctory."[3] However, even sympathetic subsequent commentary has continued to struggle with this disproportion of scale and sense of visual and thematic restriction in an attempt to address H. R. Coursen's question: "how to establish a scale and a style for Shakespeare on television. It is like playing with toy soldiers." Writing in 1981, Sheldon Zitner offered two related methodological problems in the adaptation of Shakespeare into television which we might conceptualize as difficulties of consumption and production: the "maimed rites" of televisual viewing, in which a "deritualized" audience is both passive and isolated, and the difficulty of "defining the locus of dramatic action" in the translation of Shakespeare's virtual, theatrical space into the more "real" space of television.[4] Coursen proposes that the "scale of TV insists upon a diminution of the images and an erasure of any background. It lacks any depth of field."[5] Elsewhere he argues that television's hospitality to language, particularly when compared with the largely visual tradition of film, ought to make the transition from text to small screen easier, but admits that "Shakespeare encounters difficulties when he confronts the tube," including commercial scheduling, an expectation of realism and of entertainment, and a relation to the "masses" about which Coursen seems ambivalent.[6] Michèle Willems's "Reflections on the BBC Series" is more cautious, arguing that the small screen actually accentuates the problem of the dominance of the visual already found in film, and that the "naturalistic and even domestic" scale of television is inimical to many of Shakespeare's dramatic effects. Reviewing the different approaches of the BBC series, Willems concludes that "the naturalistic approach often aggravates the tensions between the two media instead of resolving them" and that stylized productions eschewing television's habitual reliance on realism were the more successful.[7] Amid these doubts, the more favorable commentary on the possibilities and achievements of Shakespeare on television tends to be by academic consultants to television productions. Thus John Wilders, literary advisor to the BBC series, argues that "television can restore to Shakespeare's plays the unbroken flow and continuity they almost certainly achieved in the Renaissance theatre," and Maurice Charney, consultant to the American PBS *The Shakespeare Hour* series, argues that "televisionary Shakespeare has the potential to enlarge our vision of Shakespeare's plays"; both statements seem conditional rather than descriptive.[8] Just as television studies has lagged behind film studies, so the serious study of Shakespeare on television, hampered in large measure by restricted access to television texts, has yet to approach the extent, subtlety, and sophistication of Shakespeare on film.

An Age of Kings

An Age of Kings was broadcast in fifteen episodes, most lasting sixty minutes but with three seventy-five minute episodes. It thus covered the sweep of plays – *Richard II*, 1 and 2 *Henry IV*, *Henry V*, 1, 2 and 3 *Henry VI*, and *Richard III* – with each play, except for a heavily cut 1 *Henry VI*, divided into two episodes.[9] It was an ambitious project, widely considered, as a review in *The Times* put it, as "monumental," and claimed as "a landmark in the BBC's Shakespearian tradition."[10] It was heir, however, to more than two decades of Shakespeare on television, stretching from the screening of one scene from *Henry V* in 1937. These early broadcasts were sourced from contemporary theatrical productions, and have not been preserved. Nor was *An Age of Kings* the BBC's first foray into Shakespeare serialization. During the early part of 1959 a seven-part series adapted from Shakespeare by Ronald Eyre, *The Life and Death of Sir John Falstaff*, was broadcast in half-hour episodes, aimed at schools. The budget and scale of *An Age of Kings* were, however, distinctly more ambitious than anything previously attempted.

Viewing *An Age of Kings* now, it is striking how little the series concedes to our structural expectations of serial narrative. Sarah Kozloff has identified a number of formal properties particular to television serials, including the needs to "bring up to date viewers who do not usually watch the show or who may have missed an episode. To this end, many begin by offering a flashback recap of ongoing storylines" and to generate "enough viewer interest and involvement to survive their hiatus. Some offer flashforwards to tease the viewer with bits of upcoming action; frequently, they also turn to the technique made famous by movie serials – the cliffhanger."[11] While *An Age of Kings* utilizes the regular schedule slot – the episodes were screened fortnightly on Thursdays at 9pm between April and November 1960 – it conforms to very few other formal properties of the serial. There are, for example, no interpolated recapitulations, reminders, or plot summaries to bring audiences up to date with events or encourage those who may have missed an episode, and nor do these seem to have been part of television listings or print media at the time. There is no attempt to identify or differentiate the protagonists, nor to give an indication of the date or place of events, nor to explain potentially puzzling tussles for power. An accompanying booklet published by the BBC does give a synopsis of each episode and an explanatory genealogical tree, but it is difficult to know how widely this publication was circulated. I have not, for example, come across any reference to it in the reviews or listings for the series.

The series does make use of a few explicit instances of "flashforward" or prolepsis, particularly in the closing images of particular episodes. At the end of *Richard II* the episode closes with an image of Northumberland's dagger stabbing into a sheaf of King Henry's papers, its unexpected small-scale violence "a calculated image of inconclusiveness" and an indicator of Northumberland's forthcoming rebellion.[12] The first episode of *Henry V*, "Signs of War," ends with a literal signpost: a marker pointing the way to "Agincourt." The compositional gap between 1 *Henry VI* and *Henry V* is happily bridged as the Chorus speaks the epilogue to "The Band of Brothers" over the King's catafalque with which the next episode, "The Red Rose and the White," is to open. In turn, "The Red Rose and the White" gestures towards ongoing civil conflict in ending with Suffolk picking a red rose on the prophetic line "I will rule both her, the King, and the realm" (1 *Henry VI*, 5.7.107). The final sequence of the penultimate episode, "The Dangerous Brother," shows Richard of Gloucester watching his sleeping nephews, ending with his smile as he snuffs out the candle. Crucial to serialization is the "ability to construct 'open' rather than 'closed' narrative forms ... like the soap opera the continuous nature of serial drama means that resolution is frequently delayed, conclusion is evaded, and the neat tying up of all major storylines generally avoided"; in ending episodes with open or proleptic forms rather than closed ones, *An Age of Kings* attempted to engage viewers in a longer-term narrative than the immediate unit of the episode.[13] Head of BBC Drama Michael Barry described the structural intention: "a strengthened purpose is added to the narrative when it is wholly seen, and we are able to look forward to 'what happens next'."[14] Writing in *The Listener* Irving Wardle noted with approval these devices to interconnect the different episodes: "the rearrangement of the text in the final scene [of *Richard II*] was an entirely admissible device for stretching the narrative line."[15]

But if the endings of the episodes occasionally gesture towards a cliffhanger, the openings of the episodes do not offer any clearly complementary structure of analepsis. The narrative movement is decisively forward-looking rather than retrospective. Even where nostalgic recollection is explicitly invited by the text – in the reminiscences of Falstaff in the *Henry V* episodes, for example – there is no use of flashback or recapitulation. This teleological impetus – towards an endpoint and towards a final resolution, links the ideology of *An Age of Kings* with the orthodoxies of contemporary criticism. E. M. W. Tillyard's highly influential reading of the plays in his *Shakespeare's History Plays* (1944) established sequential interpretation as a norm. Tillyard's subdivision of the history play as two tetralogies stressed their cumulative unfolding of the "Tudor myth," by which the accession of the Tudors on the defeat of *Richard III* was narrativized as a providential restitution of rightful sovereignty interrupted by the usurpation of Richard II and expiated through the bloodletting of the Wars of the Roses. Tillyard's argument is less convincing when the history plays are viewed in order of composition, but its logic may succeed when the plays are seen in historical sequence as in *An Age of Kings*. Thus the series mobilizes both the preference for deferred conclusion typical of serial narration and the narrative telos of Tillyardian providentialist historiography. These ideologies may, however, be in a subtle tension. *An Age of Kings* is both serial – a segmented narrative structured towards a final conclusion, the accession of Henry VII after his victory at Bosworth field – and series – an ongoing and potentially inconclusive unfolding of historical process. John Ellis's insight into serial as television's "characteristic form of repetition" with "no end in view" sees that "the TV series repeats a problematic. It therefore provides no resolution of the problematic at the end of the run of the series."[16] Why should this Henry's coronation provide a final narrative conclusion?

In this context, it is intriguing to see what scriptwriter Eric Crozier has done with Shakespeare's own most explicit subversion of serial narrative continuity: the opening of 2 *Henry IV* with the personage of "Rumour," dressed in a robe "painted full of tongues." We might expect the start of a play apparently always called "Part 2" to make some reference to the foregoing part, particularly given the way in which 1 *Henry IV* ends decidedly in the middle of events rather than with complete narrative resolution. In the play's closing words, the King, victorious at Shrewsbury, dispatches his armies to other points of conflict and vows to march on Wales: "since this business so fair is done, / Let us not leave till all our own be done" (5.5.44–45). The opening of 2 *Henry IV* alludes to the business at Shrewsbury, but, rather than filling in the audience about the outcome and recapitulating the previous play, Rumour mystifies it. First he tells us of

"King Harry's victory" (1.0.23), but then immediately retracts: "My office is / To noise abroad that Harry Monmouth fell / Under the wrath of noble Hotspur's sword' (1.0.28–30). The first scene continues this confusion of information. Lord Bardolph tells Northumberland "certain news from Shrewsbury": that Prince Henry is dead, Prince John and the other noblemen fled, and Falstaff in captivity. "Came you from Shrewsbury?," Northumberland asks: the reply is "I spake with one, my lord, that came from thence" (1.1.12–25). A sequence of messengers enter bringing different information, until the picture of events, already known to those who had seen 1 *Henry IV*, is made clear to the wracked Northumberland, who functions here as a kind of onstage substitute for those audience members who have not witnessed at first hand what happened at Shrewsbury. By beginning the sequel play in confusion about what has gone before, rather than with an omniscient expository clarity, Shakespeare dramatizes the unknowability, the pastness, of the previous play in the theatre. In the television presentation, however, this episode, "The New Conspiracy," follows a fortnight after "The Road to Shrewsbury," and the role of Rumour is cut entirely. Given the serial's wariness of authoritative narrative analepsis, it is perhaps inevitable that this dramatically complex and disorientating version of alternative flashbacks should be excised.

Serialization works to yoke together plays which may have been written or experienced in the theatre achronologically. Thus, in serial performance, 1 *Henry VI* precedes parts 2 and 3, whereas most scholars feel the composition date for the play is later than that for its apparent sequels. But the format of the television serial also works to divide single plays into two episodes, sometimes with particular narrative effect. In *Richard II*, for example, the splitting of the play into the episodes "The Hollow Crown" and "The Deposing of a King" serves to separate out a culpable Richard from a tragic one, as if the time-lapse between the broadcasting of the two episodes works to erase the memories of Richard's faults. The first of the episodes, which finishes with Richard's intimation of the transfer of power, 'Let them hence away / From Richard's night to Bolingbroke's fair day' (3.2.213–4), stresses Richard's failings and focuses on speeches against him. A shift in sympathy occurs just at the close of the episode, with a close-up on Richard's recognition of death's reign within the "hollow crown / That rounds the mortal temples of a king" (3.2.156–57); the second episode leaves behind all of the previous recriminations, does not recapitulate the reasons for Bolingbroke's claim to the throne, and within this silence about the immediate past establishes Richard as an almost sanctified tragic victim, murdered in the manner of a crucifixion, with an extreme close-up of his face and bloodied lips at the moment of his execution. In dividing up single plays, the serial is able to separate out potentially problematic shifts of mood: the attitude to Falstaff in the two episodes from 1 *Henry IV* is another case in which the likeable rogue is confined to the first episode, while the second stresses the necessity for Hal to reform.

The only substantial and thoroughgoing conformity to formal conventions of serial narrative is in the opening title sequence, a major factor in the unity or branding for the cycle. John Ellis has written of the semantic significance of the "highly organised and synoptic" title sequence for the marketing and consumption of serial television, as "in effect a commercial for the pro-gramme itself."[17] Against music by Sir Arthur Bliss, Master of the Queen's Musick, an opening synecdoche for the historical terrain to be covered in *An Age of Kings* was established with a shot of a stone table bearing a sequence of five crowns decorated with the heraldic symbols representing the dynasties of Richard II (deer), Henry IV (swan), Edward IV (rose and dagger), Henry VI (sun), and Richard III (boar). Tracking along this table at the start of each episode, the camera symbolically recapitulates the regal upheavals of the previous episodes, orients the current episode in the historical sequence, and implicitly suggests that there will be more upheaval in the future. Implicitly, the sequence and its steady tracking shot serve to stress historical movement rather than individuation or stasis. In this it inscribes a serial narrative of repetition and change, echoing contemporary critical readings of the plays as a political sequence, discussed in more detail later. The final episode ended by tracking right along the table to show all five crowns in their order. Series continuity was also aided by the existence of a permanent set and cast: figures and spatial relations are thus repeated. The series producer Peter Dews described in the accompanying booklet "a large permanent setting; plat-forms, steps, corridors, pillars, and gardens, which will house nearly all the plays' action and which will, despite its outward realism, be not very far from Shakespeare's 'unworthy scaffold'." In this, as in his "permanent company of about twenty young men who will be going right through the series playing a variety of ages and parts," Dews may have been influenced by Anthony Quayle's similar practice for his cycle of *Richard II* to *Henry V* at Stratford-upon-Avon in 1951.[18] Thus the practices of serial television are spliced with the traditions – and some of the status – of repertory theatre.

Rival programming and televisual "flow"

Introducing an argument about the relations between the two dominant playing companies in the 1590s, the Admiral's Men and the Chamberlain's Men, Andrew Gurr makes an analogy with "primitive times in Britain when there were only two TV channels": "It was better, or at least safer, to be imitative rivals than to offer a radically different choice."[19] Gurr's suggestions about this imitative rivalry in the early modern period have some particular application to the history plays: Henslowe's company lists a play called *Richard Crookback*, for instance, presumably drawing on Shakespeare's *Richard III*, and another called "sir Pierce of Exton," a version of *Richard II*. The relation between a "Henry V" play at the Rose and Shakespeare's play at the Globe or between "King John" plays in both companies suggests a pattern of mutual derivation and replication. Most famously, of course, Henslowe's *Oldcastle* plays capitalized on the furore over the naming of Shakespeare's fat knight. This interplay between the rival companies suggests that the broader serial of English history on stage was not constructed around a single author or playing space, and that, for early modern audiences, consuming plays across these categories was a more usual form of theatrical spectatorship.

The two rival television channels that form the analogy for Gurr's argument are, of course, highly significant to the broadcasting of *An Age of Kings*. Its broadcast in 1960 coincided with the launch of the commercial television channel ITV, the first time the BBC had had to share its broadcast monopoly; the rival stations each transmitted a significant serial during the year. ITV's was the soap opera *Coronation Street*, set in a working-class Northern community, and still a mainstay of the station's programming almost fifty years later. We might contrast this with the BBC's own serial *An Age of Kings*. It is much too simplistic an analysis to contrast the soap opera of commercial television with the high-culture product of public service broadcasting – ITV had its own cultural mission and also broadcast two plays by the playwright Harold Pinter during its first year, for example: what is more interesting is the ways in which both series share certain narrative structures, particularly of characterization.

Using *Coronation Street* as her major example, Christine Geraghty has identified three types of character in serial narrative. The first is the "individuated character," a unique individual often marked by one specific trait and whose function in the serial is to "reinforce the notion that it is giving us an endlessly rich pattern of life and people." The second is the "serial type," a character understood as existing "within the serial rather than outside it" as a way of identifying a key theme of that serial world. Geraghty's examples in relation to the soap opera are its dominant female serial types: the impulsive, foul-mouthed, ultimately decent, sexually predatory women who recur in *Coronation Street*. Her third type is of characters "holding a certain status pattern": characters whose role is defined in relation to their position in terms of sex, age, and marital position, including, for example, the unmarried young men and women who are available for plots about courtship and marriage.[20]

We can see that this method of character analysis is remarkably applicable to Shakespeare's history plays as presented by *An Age of Kings*. As privileged "individuated" characters we can see Prince Hal, Falstaff, or Hotspur, all played by specific named actors who do not double elsewhere in the serial, marked by individual identifying markers, such as Falstaff's girth or the slight stammer Sean Connery gives to his speeches as Hotspur. But as the ensemble principles of the series' casting suggest, more significant to the texture of *An Age of Kings* as a serial are the character types Geraghty labels "serial" and "status": those essentially unindividuated noblemen playing out treacherous or loyal or conflicted plots, the uncertain and troubled kings and their rash, overconfident challengers, the cursing mothers and widows, the choric soldier figures. Polish theatre director Jan Kott writes that "when we read the Histories in their entirety, the faces of kings and usurpers become blurred, one after the other. Even their names are the same. There is always a Richard, an Edward and a Henry. They have the same titles ... the drama that is being played out between them is always the same."[21] This effect of repetition is amplified when watching rather than reading the sequence. Thus the specific patterns of repetition in the structure of soap opera serial narrative are correlated with the patterns of echo and duplication within and across Shakespeare's history plays.

Related to this experience of soap opera character types is what John Caughie has discussed in terms of the relation of audience to television narrative as distinct from that of cinema: "lacking the concentrated forms of identification which the articulation of point of view invites in the cinema, television drama substitutes familiarity for identification, a familiarity which depends on recognition, repetition, and the extension of time."[22] This analysis offers a way of recognizing our particular, temporary engagement with the characters of Shakespeare's history plays, as the narrative of political power takes up specific protagonists and discards them. Unlike the more characterological trajectory of the genres of comedies and tragedies which depend on a consistent personnel and a developed sense of engagement with their narratives, therefore, history plays are already significantly serialized in the segmented forms of identification they mobilize. By offering us provisional, serial identification with a changing cast of characters, Shakespeare's history plays engage their audience through a dynamic articulated as a temporal, rather than an intersubjective, relation. They are already prototypically televisual.

The comparison with the techniques of soap opera is intended to suggest that television Shakespeare needs to be seen in the context of television, rather than just of Shakespeare. Shakespeareans, as has been shown, have been reluctant to engage with television versions of the play; the discipline of television studies has tended to be ideologically committed to more demotic programming. However, Raymond Williams's influential concept of the experience of television as textual "flow" rather than as distinct programmes requires that *An Age of Kings* be seen alongside other television output; Sarah Kozloff amplifies in arguing that "television narratives are unique in the fact that all texts are embedded within the metadiscourse of the station's schedule."[23] The first episode of the series was sandwiched between an anthropological documentary by David Attenborough, a news bulletin, and the highbrow discussion programme *The Brains Trust*. There are, however, any number of examples of different televisual idioms in *An Age of Kings*, from soap opera to the new accessibility of royal events to television audiences: 1960 also saw the first televised royal wedding, that of Princess Margaret to Lord Snowdon. Laurence Kitchen identifies two of the medium's habitual topoi in connection with the limited successes of the Shakespeare series: "at their best, perhaps, when the camera can hold one character at a crisis of emotion or a group round a conference table. The first fits the groove of hysteria in close-up, a cliché of television plays. The second conforms to a familiar layout in discussion programmes."[24] Examples of the former might include Richard's soliloquy in the second episode, "The Deposing of a King," and of the latter the opening scene of 1 *Henry IV* in "Rebellion from the North," when Henry IV addresses his nobles sitting round a table.

We might also add to this list another topos of television broadcasting which has a suggestive parallel with early modern stage praxis: the "talking head" direct to camera familiar from news programming, the television analogue of an address direct to the audience. Ellis argues that, in its reliance on "continuous updating on the latest concatenation of events rather than a final ending or explanation," the television series is closely allied to the form of television news reporting.[25] There are some speeches direct to camera early in the series – this technique is used particularly with Falstaff, for example – but it takes on a new impetus for the ending of the sixth episode, "Uneasy Lies the Head," which covers the second half of 2 *Henry IV*. Dews translates the particular mode of Shakespeare's Epilogue into television terms. As the credits roll for the end of the episode, we see the actors disrobing and removing their beards and makeup "backstage." The actor William Squire steps forward after the credits to deliver the Epilogue straight to camera: "One word more I beseech you." The technique – and the actor – is carried forward into the Chorus to *Henry V* in the next episode. Writing in the *Daily Mail* in the following year, Peter Lewis acknowledged that television had "created an art-form that did not exist before: the one-hour play": *An Age of Kings* shows that this one-hour format can adopt any number of other specifically televisual styles.[26] Although *An Age of Kings* was criticized for adopting a single performance style – a middle-shot default perhaps reminiscent of the view from the average-priced seats in a conventional theatre – as these examples show it in fact makes use of a range of televisual idioms, interpolating its audience by a range of specifically small-screen representational strategies.

Serial publication and serial performance

Serial performance of Shakespeare's history plays was not a feature of their stage history until the twentieth century. Seeing a number – but not all – of the plays directed by Frank Benson at Stratford in 1901, W. B. Yeats felt that they "have, when played one after another, something extravagant and superhuman, something almost mythical."[27] Versions of serial performance were mounted again in 1906, in 1933, and in 1951, against the increasing critical interest in the history plays as a grand narrative sequence. Both critical and performance exploration of the histories as a series take their cue, belatedly, from the First Folio publication of the collected works of Shakespeare in 1623, which arranges the history plays as a sequence. John Heminges and Henry Condell's tripartite generic division of their volume as "A Catalogue of the severall Comedies, Histories, and Tragedies contained in the Volume" institutes the Shakespearean history play as a distinct genre, allocating *King Lear* and *Macbeth*, both plays based on historical source material, to the tragedies along with the Roman history plays and thus establishing the principles of Englishness and sequentiality at the heart of the "Histories." This narrative of sequentiality is achieved through the order and titling of those plays. In place of the inverted chronology of Shakespearean composition, in which the plays on the reign of Henry VI predate those written about his predecessors Henry IV and V, the Folio orders the plays chronologically. Two temporal outriders, *The Life and Death of King John* at the head and *The Life of King Henry the Eight* at the end, flank a sequence of chronologically titled eponymous monarchs, rather as Shakespeare's own source Raphael Holinshed's *Chronicles of England* carries the reigning monarch as a running header on each page.

In the Folio, a sense of sequence and equivalence is achieved through consistent titling formulae. Thus the play published in 1598 as *The History of Henrie the Fourth; With the battell at Shrewsburie betweene the King and Lord Henry Percy, surnamed Henrie Hotspur of the North, With the humorous conceits of Sir John Falstaffe* is both abbreviated, losing the specifics of its plot and the generically diverse reference to the comedy of Falstaff, and set into a sequence or historical serial by being retitled for the Folio. The quarto text of the play was followed by the publication of *The Second part of Henry the fourth, continuing to his death, and coronation of Henrie the fifth. With the humours of sir John Falstaffe, and swaggering Pistoll* (1600). The design-ation "second part" and the verb "continuing" suggest that this play exists in relation to its predecessor, but that predecessor retains an autonomous life in print: subsequent quartos of the play now called part 1 do not so describe it. For consistency, however, the Folio follows *The First part of King Henry the fourth*, followed by *The Second part of K. Henry the fourth*. Part one thus only becomes part one by virtue of the proximity of part two. These new titles, like the others in the Folio catalogue, focus attention on the monarch as the organizing principle of historical narrative: the titles of the quarto texts suggest, rather as the plays themselves do, that the king must always share top billing with the historical events of his reign and the dramatic effective-ness of rival characters.

A similar, but more complicated, process can be seen in the case of the plays the Folio catalogue calls *The First part of King Henry the Sixt, The Second part of King Hen. the Sixt* and *The Third part of King Henry the Sixt*. Here the Folio compilers reallocate as a three-part play a previous two-part play plus a single play. The Folio's parts two and three were initially pub-lished as *The first part of the contention betwixt the two famous houses of Yorke and Lancaster with the death of the good Duke Humphrey: and the banishment and death of the Duke of Suffolke, and the tragicall end of the proud Cardinall of Winchester, with the notable rebellion of Jacke Cade: and the Duke of Yorkes first claime unto the crowne* (1594) and *The true Tragedie of Richard Duke of Yorke, and the death of good King Henrie the Sixt, with the whole contention betweene the two Houses Lancaster and Yorke* (1595). In 1619, these two plays were published together as *The Whole Contention betweene the two Famous Houses, Lancaster and Yorke. With the Tragicall ends of the good Duke Humfrey, Richard Duke of Yorke, and King Henrie the sixt. Divided into two Parts: And newly corrected and enlarged*: the title "Whole Contention" suggests that the two parts comprise a single narrative movement rather than two distinct and separate plays, although it will be seen that the same phrase was also attached to the 1595 quarto. The play the Folio prefixes to this pair as part one was not previously published, and thus both compositional chronology and titling have been redrawn in order to produce the three-part play in the Folio. One of the functions of the Folio's sustained retitling here is to fore-ground the character of Henry VI and perhaps even to consolidate his hold on his throne, despite – or perhaps because – that king's relatively minor role in the three plays to bear his name, and the fact that the business of the three plays is the dramatic and political challenges to Henry's own sovereignty.

It is the extent, rather than the fact, of this sequentiality that is significant. In the context of Thomas Kyd, Lukas Erne has discussed "a real vogue for two-part plays" in the two decades after 1587.[28] For the most part, these two-part plays are not published together, although the edition of Marlowe's two *Tamburlaine* plays printed by Richard Jones in 1590 as *Tamburlaine the Great* "devided into two tragicall discourses, as they were sundrie times shewed upon Stages in the Cittie of London" is a notable exception. Here seriality is a feature of print as much as, or more than, performance. But there are also indications that playing schedules made some accommodation for paired plays. Henslowe's diary gives us a number of examples of two-part or sequel plays being performed on consecutive days. Plays called "j pte of hercvlos" and "2 pte of hercvlos" were regularly performed in tandem, for example on 27–28 May, 12–13 June, 1–2 September, 12–13 October, and 12–13 November 1595; similar entries for parts one and two of "tamberlen" and "seaser" during the same period make it clear that consecutive programming was common. Henslowe's diary also makes it clear, however, that paired or sequel plays could also be performed independently: there are numerous entries, separated by days or weeks, for each part of *Tamburlaine*, for "seaser," and for the first and "2 pte of godfrey of bullen."[29] The evidence from performance scheduling thus suggests both that there was a commercial space for consecutive programming, and that both parts of the two-part plays were also seen as autonomous and self-standing.

We do not have any evidence, however, that Shakespeare's history plays were performed serially. Rather, we can see that seriality in the Folio is an editorial process rather than a theatrical one. The specific editorial interventions of the Folio text serve to build a sequence of plays out of a number of previously separately printed, individually titled, works. This structuring principle is clearly different from more recent collected editions of the plays: Stanley Wells's and Gary Taylor's influential Oxford edition, for example, instates an organization based on putative compositional chronology rather than following the generic categories of Folio. Thus the Oxford edition gives us the second and third parts of *Henry VI*, titled according to their quarto publications, then *Titus Andronicus*, then "*The First Part of King Henry the Sixth*" followed by *Richard III*, with the narrative poems and early comedies interspersed before *Richard II*, and *Merry Wives of Windsor* interposed between parts 1 and 2 of *Henry VI*. This fractured experience of the English history plays gives full structural and dramatic significance to the individual plays as complete theatrical experiences and reinstates history as a popular genre amid other types of play during the 1590s. But there are clearly ways in which Shakespeare's history plays themselves, not just their titles or their bibliographic history, lend themselves to the Folio's form of serial reading.

Shakespeare has worked on his history plays to carve out a narrative shape from the historical sweep in his chronicle sources; his earliest editors work to reinstate that sweep. Nicholas Grene argues that Shakespeare's researches always took him beyond the end point of the particular historical story he was following so that the characters who are needed for the next part of the story are introduced. The sudden mention of a wayward son to the newly crowned King Henry IV at the end of *Richard II* is a good example: the son who has not been seen for "full three months" (5.3.2) will emerge as the central protagonist of the next play. Grene also suggests, however, that Shakespeare "developed a structure in which no play was complete in itself, each part required a narrative sequel." This "Sheherezade technique to keep the audience narrative-hungry" is, Grene proposes, most prominent in the *Henry VI* plays and *Richard III*, "planned as an interlocking series with a narrative rhythm building across the parts rather than in the individual plays."[30]

It is this kind of reading that the Folio catalogue encourages us to adopt. A play designated "The First Part" is inevitably incomplete in itself, since its title suggests that its ending will be only provisional and that there is more to come. We know from our experience of contemporary sequel cinema that a work titled "The Second Part" or, as the serial epics *Star Wars* (George Lucas, 1977–2005) or *The Lord of the Rings* (Peter Jackson, 2001–03) would have it, "II," registers even more potential incompleteness, because of the expectation that this is, as the 1600 quarto of 2 *Henry IV* articulates, a continuation of an earlier story. The Folio encourages the experience of reading serially, an experience in which the endings of individual plays are subordinated to the onward movement of the sequential narrative. Like the television series convention in which a minor conclusion is reached at the end of each episode, but in which such a conclusion is designed to be superseded by the expectation of the next episode, the Folio works to engage the expectations and consumption practices of serial, rather than singular, fiction. In this it anticipates and shapes a further editorial intervention in the shaping of the plays for television transmission. In reading *An Age of Kings* simultaneously within television studies and Shakespeare studies as I have begun to do here, we have an opportunity to see how serial television contrasts and complements the narrative structures of the plays – and, perhaps most importantly – vice versa. Far from being a clash of registers, the juxtaposition of "Shakespeare" and "serialization" enables us to articulate some significant questions about narrative production and consumption in the sixteenth and twentieth centuries, to challenge the hegemony of historicism in the study of the early modern theatre, and to reassess the role of Shakespeare in and on television, the medium that above all has defined the notion of "popular culture."

NOTES

1. "Shakespeare is Now a Serial," *Evening Standard*, 17 February 1937, p. 6.
2. "Dull" is Martin Banham's word, from his "BBC Television's Dull Shakespeares," *Critical Quarterly* 22 (1980), 31–40, p. 31.
3. Laurence Kitchin, "Shakespeare on the Screen," *Shakespeare Survey* 18 (1965), 70–74, pp. 70–71.
4. H. R. Coursen, *Watching Shakespeare on Television* (Rutherford, NJ; London: Fairleigh Dickinson University Press; Cranbury, NJ: Associated University Presses, 1993), p. 22; Sheldon P. Zitner, "Wooden O's in Plastic Boxes," reprinted from *University of Toronto Quarterly* 51 (1981) in *Shakespeare on Television: An Anthology of Essays and Reviews*, ed. J. R. Bulman and H. R. Coursen (Hanover, NH and London: University Press of New England, 1988), pp. 31–40.
5. Coursen, *Watching Shakespeare*, p. 21.
6. H. R. Coursen, "The Bard and the Tube", in Bulman and Coursen, *Shakespeare on Television*, pp. 3–10, p. 7.
7. Michèle Willems, "Verbal-Visual, Verbal-Pictorial or Textual-Televisual? Reflections on the BBC Shakespeare Series," in *Shakespeare and the Moving Image*, ed. Anthony Davies and Stanley Wells (Cambridge: Cambridge University Press, 1994), pp. 69–85.
8. John Wilders, "Shakespeare on the Small Screen," *Shakespeare-Jahrbuch* 117 (1982), 56–62, p. 61; Maurice Charney, "Televisionary Shakespeare: Working with *The Shakespeare Hour*," *Shakespeare Quarterly* 36 (1985), 489–95, p. 495.
9. The entire series is archived in the National Film and Television Archive at the British Film Institute. Short extracts from a number of episodes are available at Screen Online (http://www.screenonline.org.uk/tv/id/527213/index.html), accessed 2 September 2005.
10. *The Times*, 29 April 1960; Michael Barry, "Presenting our Epic Pageant," in BBC, *An Age of Kings Presented by BBC Television* [1960].
11. Sarah Kozloff, "Narrative Theory and Television," in *Channels of Discourse, Reassembled: Television and Contemporary Criticism*, ed. Robert C. Allen (London: Routledge, 1992), pp. 67–100, pp. 91–92.
12. Irving Wardle, *The Listener*, 19 May 1960, p. 899.
13. Glen Creeber, *Serial Television: Big Drama on the Small Screen* (London: BFI Publishing, 2004), p. 4.
14. Michael Barry, "The Age of Kings," *Radio Times*, 22 April 1960.
15. Irving Wardle, *The Listener*, 19 May 1960, p. 899.
16. John Ellis, *Visible Fictions: Cinema, Television, Video* (London: Routledge and Kegan Paul, 1982), p. 122, p. 154.
17. *Ibid.*, pp. 119–20.
18. BBC, *An Age of Kings Presented by BBC Television*, [1960]; Quayle's production is discussed by Sally Beaumann in *The Royal Shakespeare Company: A History of Ten Decades* (Oxford: Oxford University Press, 1982), pp. 205ff.
19. Andrew Gurr, "Intertextuality at Windsor," *Shakespeare Quarterly* 38 (1987), 189–200, p. 189.
20. Christine Geraghty, "The Continuous Serial – A Definition," in Richard Dyer *et al.*, *Coronation Street* (London: BFI Publishing, 1981), pp. 9–26.

21. Jan Kott, *Shakespeare Our Contemporary*, trans. Boleslaw Taborski (1965; London: Methuen & Co., 1981), pp. 8–9.
22. John Caughie, *Television Drama: Realism, Modernism and British Culture* (Oxford: Oxford University Press, 2000), p. 205.
23. Raymond Williams, *Television: Technology and Cultural Form* (1975; London: Routledge, 1990), especially chapter 4, "Programming: distribution and flow"; Kozloff, "Narrative Theory and Television," p. 89.
24. Kitchen, "Shakespeare on the Screen," p. 71.
25. Ellis, *Visible Fictions*, p. 120.
26. Peter Lewis, *Daily Mail*, 18 April 1961.
27. W. B. Yeats, "At Stratford-on-Avon," in *Essays and Introductions* (London: Macmillan, 1961), p. 109.
28. Lukas Erne, *Beyond "The Spanish Tragedy": A Study of the Works of Thomas Kyd* (Manchester: Manchester University Press, 2001), pp. 37ff.
29. R. A. Foakes (ed.), *Henslowe's Diary*, 2nd edition (Cambridge: Cambridge University Press, 2002), pp. 27–33.
30. Nicholas Grene, *Shakespeare's Serial History Plays* (Cambridge: Cambridge University Press, 2002), pp. 21–23.

8

STEPHEN M. BUHLER

Musical Shakespeares: attending to Ophelia, Juliet, and Desdemona

> The generally accepted theory is that the mood was specific.
> Duke Ellington

From grand opera to hip-hop, the language, narratives, dramatis personae, and mythology of Shakespeare's works have served as resources of musical inspiration since their earliest performances and publication. Composers and songwriters have quoted from the plays and poems, have alluded to them, and have recycled them in ways that regularly call into question accepted divisions between serious and popular culture; between highbrow, middle-brow, and lowbrow artifacts; between mass-market and minority or emergent expression. In this essay, after briefly surveying Shakespeare's presence in musical theatre and other forms of popular music since the mid twentieth century, I will focus on the pivotal role of Shakespeare's Ophelia in marking and inspiring popular culture's enduring investment in Shakespearean texts. In *Hamlet* and in responses to the plays, Ophelia is implicated in materials that engage with societal concerns involving gender, generational conflict, racial identity, and sexuality.

Such concerns may still seem to speak more to our own times than to Shakespeare's; Terence Hawkes has connected this view of historicity with a residual tendency to set Shakespeare away from (and to set him "above") popular, non-elite concerns, while also asserting his "eternal relevance" to the maintenance of the status quo.[1] This tendency, however, did not fully emerge until the nineteenth century, although it grew more pronounced over time. Throughout the early twentieth century, Shakespeare continued to be shifted away from any categorization as popular entertainment: Lawrence Levine has charted the split as applied to Shakespeare specifically in United States culture into the categories of "highbrow" and "lowbrow";[2] some of the same dynamics, however, can be seen at work throughout Britain and Western Europe. Interestingly enough, a similar shift occurred mid-century with jazz music, which had once been dismissed as the lowest of the low by mainstream arbiters, as well as elite ones. Jazz musicians, however, first garnered general acceptance and then assiduously cultivated the stance that they were engaged in producing high art. While this similar movement might suggest that Shakespeare and jazz might regularly intersect, the reverse has been the case. For the most part, only jazz artists dedicated to reaching general audiences have continued to borrow from Shakespeare. Such artists include Duke Ellington and Billy Strayhorn, whose *Such Sweet Thunder* was recorded by the Ellington Orchestra in 1957, and John Dankworth, who wrote material for the 1964 album *Shakespeare – and All That Jazz* and 1978's *Wordsongs* (which added lyrics by other canonical poets), for his wife, singer Cleo Laine. *Such Sweet Thunder*, as the title punningly suggests, is a jazz suite, consisting of instrumentals, most of which respond to selected Shakespeare characters in dramatic, formalistic, or thematic contexts. For example, "Sonnet to Hank Cinq" is a portrait of King Henry V expressed in fourteen melodic lines, a musical analogue to the sonnet form. Although the phrase "Such Sweet Thunder" comes from *A Midsummer Night's Dream*, the composition itself explores how Othello's autobiographical stories must have sounded to Desdemona's ears. "Madness in Great Ones" concludes with an aural invocation of Hamlet running rhetorical rings around Polonius, Rosencrantz, and Guildenstern.[3] By contrast John Dankworth's recordings employ actual Shakespearean texts, providing jazz settings for several songs in the plays. On both *All That Jazz* and *Wordsongs*, he goes so far as to add the words of Shakespeare's sonnet to Ellington's "Hank Cinq": for this track, Laine contributes a persuasive vocal to Sonnet 40, "Take All My Loves."

A later conjunction of jazz with Shakespeare was the musical *Play On!*, an adaptation of *Twelfth Night* set during the Harlem Renaissance and featuring several standards by none other than Duke Ellington and his collaborators. In the musical's book, written by Cheryl L. West, the character of Duke Orsino in Shakespeare's play becomes Duke Ellington himself, while Viola becomes a young woman who adopts male attire in order to be accepted in the male-dominated world of jazz composition and performance. While the Ellington songs, the generally Shakespearean plot, and the gender-role dynamics complement each other well in the music, there are some unsettling aspects about *Play On!* The show's creator, Sheldon Epps, has claimed to have introduced the Duke and Shakespeare to each other, completely erasing *Such Sweet Thunder* from Ellington's canon. During the show, audiences can hear, once again, "Take the A Train" and "I've Got It Bad (And That's Not Good)," but are not treated to any of Ellington's own encounters with Shakespeare, either with lyrics that could be provided for the instrumentals (as Dankworth had done) or in dance sequences (which were choreographed by Ellington's granddaughter Mercedes). The new play's transformation of Ellington's real-life collaborator, Billy Strayhorn, from a gay man to the Viola figure from Shakespeare similarly suppresses what some clearly see as inconvenient truths in the Duke's biography. Some of the vitality of the sources seems to have been lost along with some of the life of Ellington. After a successful run in 1997 at the Old Globe Theatre in San Diego, California, *Play On!* moved to Broadway, where it received lukewarm reviews at best and closed far earlier than expected.[4]

Bards on (and Off-)Broadway

Long before *Play On!* made its brief visit to New York, however, Shakespeare had already been both embraced and shunned by Broadway musical audiences. What often determined the reaction was in part the amount of Shakespeare involved and in part the persons involved in presenting him. *The Boys from Syracuse* was the successful production, *Swingin' the Dream* the commercial failure. Based on Shakespeare's *The Comedy of Errors*, *The Boys from Syracuse* features songs from Lorenz Hart and Richard Rodgers, with a book by veteran playwright, director, and producer George Abbott. The script follows Shakespeare's plot closely, following the confusions that arise when two sets of identical twins begin to bump into each others' lives, but almost completely avoids Shakespeare's language. The exception is a speech from the character of the Abbess, who delivers two lines of Shakespearean blank verse: "The venom clamours of a jealous woman / Poisons more deadly than a mad dog's tooth" (5.1.70–71). Abbott even underlines the direct allusion by having one of the Dromio twins suddenly reappear on stage to announce, "Shakespeare!" The musical introduced two standards to the popular and jazz repertoires: "Falling in Love with Love," one of Rodgers's most charming waltzes, and the jaunty "This Can't Be Love," which highlights Hart's deft language and ironic view of romantic inevitability. As Fran Teague notes, the play was also highly successful due to its sly use of Shakespearean authority to permit the kinds of bawdry and risqué banter associated with the mid twentieth-century burlesque-show.[5]

While *The Boys of Syracuse* garnered audience and critical acclaim, with an original 1938–39 Broadway run of 235 performances, and regular revivals (including a 2002 production, with a new book by the usually darkly satiric Nicky Silver), *Swingin' the Dream* closed within two weeks of its 1939 opening. This adaptation of *A Midsummer Night's Dream* was written by Gilbert Seldes and Erik Charell, had music composed by the prolific Jimmy Van Heusen, among others, and performed by artists including the Benny Goodman sextet and the magnificent trumpeter Louis Armstrong. Armstrong himself, in fact, played the role of Bottom. With choreography by Agnes de Mille and dancers including the legendary Bill Bailey, the project seemed destined for a success that quickly eluded it. In her analysis of the show's poor reception, Teague points to repeated complaints by the critics that the show kept too much of Shakespeare's language, as well as plot.[6] While Teague points to race as an additional factor in audience impatience with the musical, Alan Corrigan has gone further in noting how many critics and audience members of the time had difficulty accepting African American performers doing any Shakespearean material that was not overtly parodistic or completely "translated" into what were considered culturally appropriate modes for African Americans. Corrigan finds critics using the term "mongrel" to describe the show, as well as the less overtly charged "hybrid."[7] I would add that a parallel case is provided by the very mixed reception of Duke Ellington's *Black, Brown, and Beige* suite, which debuted in Carnegie Hall just a few years later, in 1943: even some of Ellington's strongest advocates (such as record producer John Hammond) decried what they perceived as the inauthenticity involved in Ellington's engagements with longer – and European-influenced – musical forms. *Swingin' the Dream* quickly faded into legendary status as a box-office disaster, but nevertheless contributed one enduring standard to jazz: "Darn That Dream," which would provide the only track that Miles Davis made with a vocal (by Kenny Hagood) as he presided over the 1949–50 recordings later collected under the title *Birth of the Cool* and very deliberately helped jazz move away from the "pop" status that artists such as Ellington hoped to sustain.

The presence of Shakespearean language offered no challenges to audiences in *Kiss Me Kate*, which debuted on Broadway in 1948. For one thing, race was no longer a concern in plot or casting; for another, Shakespeare is again employed as a cover (or "Beard," as Teague astutely terms him) for exploring sexuality in public entertainment. In addition, the show "explains" the recurring blank verse by including scenes from a fictional production of *The Taming of the Shrew* with which several of the musical's characters are involved. This allows other characters to comment on Shakespeare's cultural authority, most notably when two gangland enforcers tell members of the audience to "Brush Up Your Shakespeare." In a vaudevillian, soft-shoe tour de force, the gangsters gradually up the stakes in each example of Shakespearean quotation, moving from seduction, to sexual assault, to physical attack, to utter submission to one's (male) physical prowess: if the lady is unimpressed, one can "flatter 'er" with "what Tony told Cleopatterer"; if she is resistant about undressing, clothes are "Much Ado About Nussing"; if she is angrily judgmental, one can "Kick her right in the Coriolanus"; and when she finally is "pleading for pleasure," one can allow her to "sample your Measure for Measure." Shakespeare can become a sexual weapon because he is universally perceived as a cultural weapon. The "dese and dose" wiseguys dispatched to collect gambling debts acknowledge the bard as a force, like them, to be reckoned with; all one has to do is "Brush up your Shakespeare," we are told, "And they'll all kow-tow" – that is, others will bow down in homage to our mastery of his masterpieces.[8] With irresistible and supremely subversive songs by Cole Porter and an effective book by Sam and Bella Spewack (who were inspired by the backstage wrangling of actors Alfred Lunt and Lynn Fontaine during a run of *The Taming of the Shrew*), *Kiss Me Kate* was an immediate success and enjoys frequent revivals.

What made it possible for Shakespeare to become a more constant presence in twentieth-century popular music was the incredible appeal of *West Side Story*, an adaptation of *Romeo and Juliet* set amidst gang rivalries in contemporary New York City. A formidable array of talent was involved in the project: the book was written by Arthur Laurents (who had written such stage plays as *Home of the Brave* and *The Time of the Cuckoo*, along with Hollywood screenplays); the music and choreography were created, respectively, by Leonard Bernstein and Jerome Robbins (who had worked together on the musical *On the Town*); the lyrics were crafted by a precocious Stephen Sondheim. The phenomenon of *West Side Story*, which was first staged in 1957, depended not only on its creators fulfilling the promise of their collaboration and their source materials, as such songs as "Somewhere," "I Feel Pretty," and "Maria" quickly became pop standards and Bernstein's symphonic treatment of especially the dance music themes entered the repertoire for orchestra. The musical's impact also depended on a concomitant rise in what came to be known as "youth culture" and on an increased sense of Shakespeare's play as being for young people as well as about young people.[9] As we will see, young audiences who might never attend a performance of *West Side Story* could nevertheless accept that the musical's conflation of classic theatre and street life lent Romeo and Juliet no small credibility for them. As a result, the play's title characters made increasingly frequent appearances in pop and rock music lyrics and continue to do so.

Meanwhile, amid several failed attempts to replicate the success of *West Side Story* in adapting Shakespeare for the Broadway stage, only two successful productions emerged. Significantly, both capitalized on association with youth culture and especially with rock music. *Your Own Thing*, a completely "young generation" take on *Twelfth Night*, opened in 1968, one year after *Hair* first asserted the compatibility of pop-rock with the musical stage. The book was written by Daniel Driver, with songs by Hal Hester and Danny Apolinar that played things even more safely than many of the tunes appearing in its predecessor. For the time, the treatment of gender ambiguity and (at least latent, to use the terminology of the era) homosexuality was moderately daring; Shakespeare's language was for the most part scrupulously avoided; and the musical was accordingly rewarded with a run of nearly three years. Again, the bard's own investigation into the arbitrariness and social utility of gender roles authorized the show's version of the same. In a kind of thanks, lyrics from two of the original play's songs received updated settings, while none of the show's songs have ever inspired covers (even the bland Cowsills, a pre-Partridge Family ensemble comprised of actual siblings and, at least once on record, their mother, garnered a hit with the title song from *Hair*) or warrant close listening today. While the songs from the 1971 musical version of *Two Gentlemen of Verona* have aged only somewhat more gracefully, the production overall remains revered for its deliberate engagement with issues of race and sexuality (and their interrelation), for featuring glowing performances by Raul Julia, Clifton Davis, Diane Davila, and Jonelle Allen, and for letting Shakespeare's original dialogue do much of the talking. Times had certainly changed since the brief run of *Swingin' the Dream*; here, a multiracial cast was applauded for negotiating both blank verse and the latest grooves. A contributing factor to acceptance may have been the show's development under the aegis of Joseph Papp's New York Shakespeare Festival. John Guare (long before *Six Degrees of Separation*) wrote new lyrics for the songs and adapted Shakespeare's text with director Mel Shapiro; Galt MacDermot, who wrote the music for *Hair*, was also the composer for *Two Gentlemen*. Even had the music for the show held up better, it likely would not have been embraced by other performers. In the 1970s, pop music moved on into arena anthems, disco, and the punk reaction those trends inspired. Broadway, for its part, generally shunned overt rock music for two decades (except for the nostalgia factory known as *Grease*) and did not embrace it again until fairly recently, in what has been termed "Jukebox Musicals." These shows draw heavily upon the catalogues of such once widely popular artists as Abba, Johnny Cash, the Four Seasons, Buddy Holly, Billy Joel, and John Lennon.

Shakespeare meets the Jukebox Musical in *Fools in Love*, first staged in 2005. This adaptation of *A Midsummer Night's Dream* – geared primarily for younger children – ranges through pop hits of the late 1950s and early 1960s to find songs appropriate to the dramatic situations in which the characters find themselves. Helena's pursuit of Demetrius into the woods (in this version, outside West Athens, California) is accompanied by a doo-wop cover of Little Peggy March's 1963 hit "I Will Follow Him"; Hermia and Lysander settle down to sleep separately to the strains of "Goodnight Sweetheart, Goodnight," which the Spaniels recorded in 1954 (and which figures memorably on the soundtrack of the 1973 film *American Graffiti*). The Millenium Talent Group's Sarah Rosenberg – who was for decades a teacher in Los Angeles schools – and Louis Reyes Cardenas were responsible for the concept; Rosenberg also directed the New York production. *Fools in Love* illustrates not only the comfortable relationship that now exists between pop music and Shakespeare in performance; it also helps to demarcate Broadway's somewhat limited comfort zone when it comes to pop Shakespeare. A few titles recur as inspiration for adaptations: *A Midsummer Night's Dream* gave rise to *Swingin' the Dream* and *The Donkey Show*, a disco-flavored version which has been running, off and on, since 1999, as well as *Fools in Love*; *The Comedy of Errors* provided source material for the rap-style *The Bombitty of Errors* (original run, 1999–2000) as well as *The Boys from Syracuse*; *Romeo and Juliet* and *West Side Story* together led to *Rome and Jewels*, a hip-hop dance piece designed by Rennie Harris and the Pure Movement Dance Theatre, and which premiered in 2000. Especially after *West Side Story* confirmed its source play's status as a "youth culture" text, *Romeo and Juliet* has also served as inspiration for innumerable pop songs in a wide range of musical idioms.

There's a place for Will

In the immediate wake of *West Side Story*, vocalist Peggy Lee invoked the names of Romeo and Juliet in her 1958 rewrite of Otis Blackwell (writing as John Davenport) and Eddie Cooley's "Fever," which had previously been a rhythm-and-blues hit for Little Willie John in 1956. Lee's expanded lyrics include a few examples of legendary lovers, including Shakespeare's most famous pair:

> Romeo loved Juliet
> Juliet she felt the same
> When he put his arms around her
> He said Julie, baby, you're my flame
> Thou givest fever . . .[10]

The synthesis of 1950s slang and Elizabethan diction heralds a new era in viewing these characters, if not necessarily Shakespeare himself, as the audience's contemporaries. This conflation of time periods may have reached its peak in the pop-chart success of the Love Theme that Nino Rota composed for Franco Zeffirelli's 1968 film version of *Romeo and Juliet*. Zeffirelli interpreted the play very much through the lens of his own time's generational conflicts; filmgoers responded enthusiastically, as did record buyers. Rota's theme forms the basis for a song heard on the film's soundtrack, "What Is a Youth?," which is sung by a troubadour-figure during the Capulets' ball, at which the lovers first meet. The song's original lyrics are borrowed from songs in other Shakespeare plays, including

Twelfth Night and *The Merchant of Venice*; a subsequent recording of the song, with new lyrics, became a modest international hit.[11] This version, entitled "A Time for Us," is clearly indebted to *West Side Story* through its song "Somewhere" (which begins "There's a place for us"); subsequent rock responses to Romeo and Juliet would be similarly indebted to the Broadway musical's integration of early modern tragedy and street-savvy youth of the twentieth century's second half.

Several prominent recording artists contributed to the musical lore of Romeo and Juliet as characters. Through much of his songwriting career, Bruce Springsteen has demonstrated a fascination with the characters as reconfigured through the romanticized view of adolescent street life that *West Side Story* overlaid onto their tale. One of Springsteen's most striking references to the characters is an extended analogy in that appears in "Incident on 57th Street," which features on his 1973 album, *The Wild, the Innocent, and the E-Street Shuffle*. The song tells the story of the ambivalent love shared by "Spanish Johnny" and "Puerto Rican Jane": Johnny is described as being "like a cool Romeo," uncertain as to whether to go beyond simply making "moves"; Jane as being "like a late Juliet," uncertain as to whether to believe any of Johnny's gestures towards devotion.[12] Other artists who have responded, in ways both affirmative and skeptical, to the *West Side Story* view of Romeo and Juliet include Tom Waits, in the noir-ish "Romeo Is Bleeding" on his 1978 *Blue Valentine* album, and Lou Reed, with his fierce "Romeo Had Juliette" on the 1989 album *New York*. Mark Knopfler wrote and performed with Dire Straits his "Romeo and Juliet," which appears on the pertinently named album *Making Movies*, released in 1980. The song deftly combines materials from Shakespeare's play, Zeffirelli's film, *West Side Story*, and youth-oriented pop. When Knopfler's "lovestruck Romeo sings a streetsuss serenade," he interrupts Juliet's own rendition of the Angels' 1963 hit "My Boyfriend's Back" – and apparently Romeo is no longer the boyfriend. Despite their present estrangement, Romeo persists. Though he claims to "forget the movie song," Romeo echoes words prompted by the Zeffirelli version of the play and by the musical: he insists "it was just that the time was wrong," suggesting that for this pair there will not be another "Time for Us"; he also asks Juliet to remember another song, one that announces "There's a place for us." Knopfler adds further complexity to the lyrics by having Romeo repeat this Juliet's words back to her: "I love you like the stars above, I'll love you till I die."[13] This sharing of verbal authority becomes even more intricate in a memorable cover version of the Dire Straits song recorded by the Indigo Girls. In this version, found on the 1992 album *Rites of Passage*, Amy Ray takes on the vocal, assuming the role of Knopfler's Romeo as she offers feminist and same-sex recodings of one of the defining narratives of heterosexual romance. Bracing appropriations of the story have also been performed by rap artist Sylk-E. Fyne (her own "Romeo and Juliet" on the 1998 album *Raw Sylk*) and Shirley Manson, vocalist for Garbage, in her rewrite of the band's "#1 Crush," among other tracks commissioned for Baz Luhrmann's 1996 film of *William Shakespeare's Romeo + Juliet*.[14]

These examples, centering on Juliet, demonstrate how the conjunction of Shakespeare and popular music over the last several decades has often reconfirmed the energies unleashed by their conjunction in Shakespeare's own time and in the plays themselves. The rest of this essay will shift attention from Juliet to Ophelia, who in many ways will allow us to explore more directly the interrelationships at work between Shakespeare's text and popular music forms. Many examples of "Musical Shakespeare," especially those involving Romeo and Juliet, often avoid demonstrating any intimate knowledge of the source text. Although these characters are often named in pop songs, as Douglas Lanier notes, "they are almost never quoted, for their youthful rebellion is directed precisely against what Shakespeare's language represents" to many young people.[15] Since pop music and rock were drawn to Romeo and Juliet for reasons connected with the rise of a separate "youth culture," songwriters faced the conundrum of wanting to invoke the tragic story while maintaining distance from the actual words by which the story is told. Similarly, when Broadway musicals and jazz have borrowed from Shakespeare in a range of legitimization strategies, they sometimes have deployed Shakespearean language at their own peril. As we will see, songs about Ophelia regularly borrow significant details and, in one instance, a lengthy passage directly from *Hamlet* itself.

Early modern pop: ballads and jigs

This is an important gesture because popular music is already a formidable presence within Shakespearean texts, not simply an overlay upon the plays, a lens through which to view them, or a bridge between them and later audiences. Ross Duffin's recent compilation of the materials that comprise *Shakespeare's Songbook* builds upon centuries of scholarship in detecting as many of the playwright's allusions to – and appropriations from – the vocal music of his time and endeavoring to connect those references to the actual music. A great many references in the plays are to ballads, the most recognizably "base, common, and popular" (to use Ancient Pistol's phrase in *Henry V*, 4.1.39) form of the early modern period, but also the form and content most widely recognizable. Ballads were so familiar to most people,

Duffin contends, "from the lowliest groundling to the highest noble," that passages which "for us may seem like obscure allusions were for them clear, obvious references to universally recognized artifacts of popular culture."[16] Present-day popular music has returned the favor, invoking Shakespeare's works as perhaps the closest thing we have to universally recognized artifacts of literary culture.

Shakespeare regularly associates balladry with the carnivalesque, as with Sir Toby Belch's riotous snatches from "Three Merry Men," "There Dwelt a Man in Babylon," and "O' the Twelfth Day of December" within just a few lines in Act 2, Scene 3 of *Twelfth Night*. Similarly, Falstaff and his companions allude to several ballads in Act 5, Scene 3 of *Henry IV Part 2*, including "Robin Hood," "Where Is the Life That Late I Led" (also recalled by Petruchio in *The Taming of the Shrew* 4.1), and "King Cophetua and the Beggar Maid." Along with a sense of festival, however, Shakespeare also conveys a sense of societal ambivalence. Both Sir Toby and Sir John are proud of their status as gentry, but open to the charge of failing to fulfill the duties of their station. In *Much Ado About Nothing*, Signor Benedick expresses disdain for balladry, as well as love, when he declares that "Prove that ever I lose more blood with love than I will get again with drinking, pick out mine eyes with a ballad-maker's pen and hang me up at the door of a brothel house for the sign of blind Cupid" (1.1.233–37). Pistol's and Falstaff's clear allusions to "King Cophetua," along with Benedick's implicit echo of the ballad, express further ambivalence through the ballad's narrative. An African monarch, disdainful of love, is compelled by Cupid to desire Penelophon, a poor beggar; despite her "degree so base" (as the maid herself says), he seeks her out and proposes marriage. Penelophon accepts and quickly adjusts to the role of Queen: on the wedding day, the ballad says, "She had forgot her gown of gray / which she did wear of late," apparently accepting the bright attire of royalty. Like the priest of the proverb who "knoweth not his estate" while saying mass, the one-time beggar maid transcends class. The King is paradoxically humbled but ennobled by his passionate devotion to the woman with whom he shares a "princely reign" so beneficent that the entire realm – "lords," "ladies," and "commons" – keenly mourns their deaths.[17]

Shakespeare recognizes that balladry, then, can either challenge degree or simply provide an imaginative respite from its claims. Both the challenge and the respite can be viewed as benign or threatening. As the story of King Cophetua and the Beggar Maid also suggests, balladry can destabilize gender roles as well. Early modern stagecraft often associated ballads with the feminine, an association complicated by the practice of having female characters performed by boys and young men. Shakespeare exploits this blurring of boundaries by giving lines from ballads and, in one memorable instance an entire ballad, to female characters who have to confront the uttermost limits of their accepted social roles. Bruce Smith has astutely observed that "what ballads offer the singer and the listener is the possibility of becoming many subjects";[18] through ballads, Shakespeare allows his characters, along with their hearers, the opportunity to assert and experience multiple identities and multiple forms of expression. In *Hamlet*, Ophelia uses ballads not only to express grief but also to assert a prophetic judgment against male authority. (Similarly, Desdemona in *Othello* gives voice to her fatal premonitions through a widely recognized ballad.) In their polyvocality, their capacity for critique, and their openness to topical or local application, ballads, in effect, provide an analogue to the theatre itself. Even so, Shakespeare's use of popular music reflects mixed feelings towards it.

There existed several tensions among the various voices at work in the theatre of Shakespeare's time, which reveal themselves at surprising points in *Hamlet*:

> *Ophelia.* You are merry, my lord.
> *Hamlet.* Who, I?
> *Ophelia.* Ay, my lord.
> *Hamlet.* O God, your only jig maker! (3.2.116–19)

The brief exchange between two of the Shakespearean characters most often mentioned – after Romeo and Juliet, of course – in pop lyrics contains much of the tension implicit in the relationship between Shakespeare and popular music. The "jig" to which Hamlet refers is not simply the lively dance or sprightly tune that bears that name; it was also a wildly popular form of theatrical entertainment. Jigs were bawdy farces featuring balladry and dance. For over a decade in the late sixteenth century, they concluded each performance at the public theatres. No matter what kind of entertainment had been presented in the course of an afternoon, the stage was given over to the clowns: even the Prince of Verona's somber observation that "For never was a story of more woe / Than this of Juliet and her Romeo" was quickly followed with riotous song and dance, featuring the talents of a comedic performer like Dick Tarlton or Will Kemp, as James Shapiro notes.[19]

The abrupt shift in tone may have been remarkable, but audiences readily accepted it. The jig was a guaranteed crowd-pleaser, combining star-power, humor, energetic dance (as the name itself suggests), and the kind of music that appealed to a wide spectrum of listeners. Shapiro's definition of the theatrical staple is worth considering in detail: "Jigs were basically semi-improvisational one-act plays, running to a few hundred lines, usually performed by four actors. They were rich in clowning, repartee, and high-spirited dancing and song, and written in traditional ballad form."[20] The ballad, the words and music shared across the social strata of early modern England, provided the formula for the jig-maker. The writer of a jig could shape words suitable for any number of ballad melodies, but which concentrated on the themes that animated the jig's wild energies – "adultery, deception, and irrepressible sexual desire."[21] Jigs were rarely published, partly due to their acknowledged libidinousness and partly due to the pale reflection offered in print of their exuberance and vitality in performance. Instead, jigs were committed to memory and shared outside the theatre. The Elizabethan satirist Edward Guilpin records his impression that sexual outlaws and moralists alike were captivated particularly by one of Kemp's jigs, so that one might hear "rotten-throated slaves ... coney-catching knaves, / Whores, Beadles, bawdes, and Sergeants filthily / Chaunt" it.[22] The ballad form is conducive to memorization – think of the long narratives that some ballads contain – and any link with a well-known tune would make the jig even more irresistible or insidious, depending on one's point of view.

In *Hamlet*, Shakespeare's ambivalence about this successful and formerly inescapable genre repeatedly emerges whenever the Players are on or near the scene. Polonius's complaint that the First Player's speech "is too long" provokes a scathing retort from the Prince of Denmark: referring to the elderly counselor, Hamlet declares that "he's for a jig or a tale of bawdry, or he sleeps" (2.2.503–04). In the passage quoted above, Hamlet himself has indulged in bawdy talk about "country matters" with Ophelia, from whom (as the entire court knows) he has been estranged. Ophelia's observation that Hamlet is "merry" carries a certain censure with it: to be thought merry, in early modern usage, was to be thought wild and wanton as well as cheerful. Hamlet wants Ophelia to repeat the accusation. She does so, albeit punningly (I, Ay). His response bitterly accepts the characterization and takes it further. The would-be playwright, who has adapted a standard of the tragic repertoire for his own investigative purposes, declares himself to be nothing more than an ink-stained wretch who supplies the minimal text upon which the performers improvise to undeserved acclaim.

Hamlet here comments on his own "antic disposition" (1.5.173), which provides comic contrast to his previously ostentatious mourning, while he draws attention to "how cheerfully [his] mother looks" (3.2.120–21) after the death of her husband, Hamlet's father. He also comments on the place of bawdy lyrics and balladry in or near the kind of theatre that *Hamlet* the play is helping to create. While Hamlet here expresses disdain toward jigs, jig-makers, and balladeers, he nevertheless supplies a jig at the abrupt conclusion of "The Mousetrap." After Claudius has called for lights and left the hall, the Prince jubilantly sings in ballad meter:

> Why, let the stricken deer go weep,
> The hart ungallèd play,
> For some must watch, while some must sleep,
> Thus runs the world away . . .
> For thou dost know, O Damon dear,
> This realm dismantled was
> Of Jove himself, and now reigns here
> A very, very – pajock. (3.2.259–62, 269–72)

As Horatio notes, the second verse does not rhyme; Hamlet has substituted a vain and vicious animal, the peacock, for the more plainly risible creature, the ass. Between verses, Hamlet declares himself a suitable candidate for a "fellowship in a cry of players" – that is, becoming a partner in a theatrical company. Horatio retorts, a bit skeptically, that the Prince has earned, at best, "Half a share," but Hamlet insists that his performances as playwright and jig-maker warrant "A whole one" (3.2.267–68). He has adapted old materials, a murder play and traditional ballads, to reflect recent events. Later in *Hamlet*, Ophelia will also adopt popular materials and infuse them with startling pertinence to her own experience. The astonishing power of her performance derives, in part, from her ability to retrieve the ballad from the conventions of the jig, working against that form's appropriations.

Ophelia takes the stage

In Act 4, Scene 5 of *Hamlet*, the distracted Ophelia offers variations on several ballads. First, she sings lines adapted from "Walsingham," briefly interrupted by the Queen and King and by Ophelia's own deft reference to "The Merry Miller's Wooing of the Baker's Daughter of Manchester."[23] Later, when she meets her brother Laertes, she sings fragments from "Bonny Robin" (as the title is given by the jailer's daughter in *Two Noble Kinsmen*, 4.1). Although all three ballads, in the forms that otherwise survive, involve "true love" (whether achieved or not), none of them depict the death of the beloved: Shakespeare shows Ophelia, even in madness, adapting familiar materials to her particular situation. Broadsides regularly addressed contemporary events, supplying commentary in verse that was meant to be sung to widely known ballad tunes; Ophelia participates in this cultural practice to devastating theatrical effect. F. W. Sternfeld, in a pioneering essay, takes seriously Ophelia's singing, but not always the words that she sings or the forms from which she borrows: Sternfeld suggests that "unrelated and incongruous burdens of popular songs" contribute to a sense of "incoherence" and a "lack of continuity" which reinforces the audience's understanding of Ophelia's insanity.[24] He nevertheless understands that in the apparent alternation of lyrical focus, Ophelia addresses the loss both of her father and of "Hamlet's affection."[25] We may go further and suggest Ophelia's songs assert profound connections between those experiences of loss: Polonius is accused as an obstacle to her true love; his and Laertes's suspicions are acknowledged as widely shared (and even celebrated) in the culture; Polonius is mourned as the beloved who abandons the singer; Hamlet is responsible for that abandonment.

Along the way, Ophelia gives voice to songs that may well be original, but that follow traditional ballad formulae, just as jigs did. In its immediate context, "Tomorrow is Saint Valentine's Day" depicts the reality of sexual mores that her father and brother invoked. But if the lines had appeared in a concluding jig, the maiden's being abandoned may not have inspired such sympathy. After all, in the world of the jig, "Young men will do't if they come to't"; the deceptive suitor's assertion that he would have married the maiden had she "not come to [his] bed" could have served as the punch line for a cruel joke, but a jest all the same. Many of the words that Shakespeare provides for Ophelia's ballads tend towards the inevitable subject matter of the jig: "adultery, deception, and irrepressible sexual desire," in Shapiro's concise summary.[26] Here, however, the raw materials for riotous farce are transformed into pathos.

Later in the scene, during her reunion with Laertes, Ophelia sings another variation on ballad materials. The song "And will 'a not come again?" proclaims, again, her grief for her father (complete with details about his white beard and hair). At the end, she provides unsettling ambiguity in

> He is gone, he is gone,
> And we cast away moan,
> God 'a' mercy on his soul.   (4.5.195–97)

Does Ophelia here counsel her listeners to "cast away moan," to leave off grief and instead trust in divine mercy? Is this the advice followed by the Gravedigger, a Clown who brings the spectre of the jig to Ophelia's grave by singing as he digs it? Or does she describe herself and her listeners as abandoned and therefore compelled to mourn – "we, cast away, moan"? To the ears of the Gentleman who pleads with Gertrude to give Ophelia hearing, the maiden speaks and sings "things in doubt / That carry but half sense" (4.5.6–7); the ears of the audience may discern an abundance, even an overload of meaning. What Ophelia expresses in madness anticipates the deepened social vision of Lear and the rejected prophecies of Cassandra in *Troilus and Cressida*.

That kind of haunting, vatic quality was not regularly associated with popular music forms over the next few centuries. When ballads did become a focus of study, emphasis was placed on purity of tradition rather than on interaction with other art forms or present-day application. When Shakespeare subsequently appeared in popular music, balladry was only occasionally the medium. Instead, as popular music increasingly became a mercantile enterprise in the nineteenth century, Shakespeare was employed in parlor music as a source of lyrics and as a legitimator of the music genre (at times, art song settings of Shakespeare's words found their way into parlors). Not surprisingly, Ophelia's songs did not often find their way into the homes of the expanding bourgeoisie – although a song with mostly original lyrics that culminated with "And will a' not come again" was written by Maude V. White and published by the Boosey company of London in 1881.[27] The developing folk movement of the twentieth century, however, led to a renewed appreciation not only of early ballads, but also of new participants in the tradition, some of whom helped to shape the emergent idioms associated with youthful consumers. Eventually, the examples of folk balladeers Woody Guthrie and Huddie "Leadbelly" Ledbetter convinced their acolyte Pete Seeger that folk idioms could once again be adapted for the purposes of immediate commentary and potentially speak yet again to a broad listening audience.[28] The most impressive successor to these three fulfilled that potential, although in ways that alarmed Seeger, among many others.[29] Bob Dylan began his musical career with traditional folk songs and with newly crafted topical ballads, after flirtations with rock and roll. He combined all these genres into an explosive hybrid, loosely called folk-rock, and made the singer-songwriter a staple figure in popular music. Early on in this period, on the album *Highway 61 Revisited* (1965), Dylan turns to a fictional predecessor – Shakespeare's Ophelia.

Ophelia as singer-songwriter

In the song "Desolation Row," Dylan reconnects Ophelia with balladry. After mastering the application of folk forms to topical commentary, Dylan changed his approach to lyric writing to something paradoxically more timely and more timeless. He increasingly borrowed from the Old and New Testaments, from classic film and literature, from fairy tales as well as folklore. In this song, Shakespeare provides two characters that resonate with Dylan's mythic imagery. "Desolation Row" is a rogues' gallery of archetypal figures who wander through a pre-apocalyptic landscape: Cinderella encounters a displaced and destructive Romeo; the Good Samaritan dresses up for a carnival; Cain and Abel join the Hunchback of

Notre Dame in keeping aloof from general love-making and anticipation of another deluge. The idea of water prompts Dylan to express fear for Ophelia, whose doom is not only palpable but desirable: "To her, death is quite romantic," which suggests both willful self-destruction and being seduced by mortality.[30] "Her death was doubtful," says Shakespeare's priest at her abridged funeral (5.1.221); "Her sin is her lifelessness," observes Dylan.[31]

Dylan has suggested that he used Ophelia, among other archetypes, as a means of identifying people he knew. In his recent autobiography, he self-deprecatingly explains that he has "a problem sometimes remembering someone, a real name," so he gives that person "another one, something that more accurately describes" the individual.[32] He specifically acknowledges the device in the later song "Dignity" (released on 1994's *Greatest Hits, Volume 3*), the verses of which originally included such figures as The Green Beret, The Sorceress, Virgin Mary, The Wrong Man, Big Ben, The Cripple and The Honkey. (Fat Man, Thin Man, Hollow Man, Blind Man, Wise Man, Mary Lou, and Prince Phillip, among others, survive on the actual record.) But more is going on than a personal mnemonic device: the names of the archetypes can only be more "accurate" if they convey a powerful (and real) identity. Many such figures he found in folk music; their presence drew him to that artistic form. Dylan asserts that for him

> Folk music was a reality of a more brilliant dimension. It exceeded all human understanding, and if it called out to you, you could disappear and be sucked into it. I felt right at home in this mythical realm made up not with individuals so much as archetypes, vividly drawn archetypes of humanity, metaphysical in shape, each rugged soul filled with natural knowing and inner wisdom. Each demanding a degree of respect. I could believe in the full spectrum of it and sing about it. It was so real, so more true to life than life itself. It was life magnified.[33]

Throughout his career, Dylan has sought to continue and help to revive this aspect of folk music by tapping into similar powers he detects in certain examples from other artistic traditions. Characters from Shakespeare regularly appear; the playwright himself is a character in "Stuck Inside of Mobile with the Memphis Blues Again" on the 1966 album *Blonde on Blonde*. The historical playwright and the contemporary character combine to figure a capacity for communication denied to the speaker:

> Well, Shakespeare, he's in the alley
> With his pointed shoes and his bells,
> Speaking to some French girl,
> Who says she knows me well.
> And I would send a message

To find out if she's talked,
But the post office has been stolen
And the mailbox is locked.[34]

Shakespeare and the "French girl" can exchange information about Dylan's narrator, while he remains unable even to ascertain how many details have been shared. There is more than a hint of Shakespeare's status as a forbidding cultural authority, one who discourages new expression.

Dylan's Ophelia is herself a frustrated songstress. She arrives on the scene in "Desolation Row" like a troubadour, ready to serenade potential listeners, but no song ensues:

Now Ophelia, she's 'neath the window
For her I feel so afraid
On her twenty-second birthday
She already is an old maid.

She is eager but unable to give voice to her desires, to reach those would-be hearers at the window. In explaining this suppression of confidence and authority, Dylan offers a striking image that recalls a film version of *Hamlet*. The song asserts that Ophelia "wears an iron vest"; Grigori Kozintsev's 1964 adaptation depicts Ophelia being helped – or forced – into a metal corset, before putting on a black dress of mourning for her murdered father. Dylan may have seen the film during its limited release in 1964 or simply a publicity still from this scene; he was keenly interested in films made outside of the United States. "There was an art movie house in the Village on 12th Street that showed foreign movies," he recalls.[35] Fellini's *La Dolce Vita*, released in the USA in 1961, was a particular favorite: it may have helped shape the nightmarish sendup of celebrity journalism in "Ballad of a Thin Man," which is part of 1965's *Highway 61 Revisited*, on which "Desolation Row" also appears. Kozintsev's Ophelia, played by Anastasiya Vertinskaya, has the life pressed out of her by the weight of societal expectations; her release comes only at her death by drowning and is visually represented by the flight of a solitary bird.[36] Dylan's Ophelia expects to be delivered from a watery fate by heavenly providence: "her eyes are fixed upon / Noah's great rainbow," the one that promised that God would never again send torrential rains to chastise humankind.

Dylan may be revising his prediction of "A Hard Rain" and may be suggesting that divine admonishment will indeed be visited upon the inhabitants of the earth by means of *The Fire Next Time* (to echo James Baldwin); nevertheless, the rainbow does not offer individual deliverance for Ophelia, who "spends her time peeking / Into Desolation Row." In Shakespeare's play, Ophelia's brother Laertes tries to refrain from weeping, since his sister has already been overwhelmed by "Too much of water" (4.7.158); his grief breaks through nevertheless. In keeping with that tone, the melody of "Desolation Row" is one of Dylan's most melancholy – when Neil Young composed his plaintive "After the Gold Rush" a few years later, he adapted the musical phrase that ends each verse for his own purposes: lines such as "As Lady and I look out tonight / From Desolation Row" confer musical, as well as lyrical resonances, as they transform to "Look at Mother Nature on the run / In the nineteen-seventies."[37]

Young's melodic borrowing parallels his assertion of identity as a singer-songwriter in the Dylan mode. The subsequent decades witnessed a long series of performers proclaimed to be "the next Dylan," including such candidates (among dozens, even in the 1970s) as Jackson Browne, John Prine, Bruce Springsteen, and Loudon Wainwright III. Relatively few women were accepted as singer-songwriters at all: Joni Mitchell's long and successful career is exceptional, while Carly Simon's limited ascendancy suggests a kind of norm and Melanie's time as a two-hit wonder offers a cautionary tale. Part of the problem faced by women in asserting themselves in this particular mode was the question of authority: at the time, any singer-songwriter had to deal with the near-mythic resonances of Woody Guthrie and Dylan himself. Eventually, what Mélisse Lafrance has termed "the interrogation of dominant normative systems" by women artists allowed them to negotiate their own version of the vatic persona.[38] The adoption of "disruptive" musical practices makes it possible "to deemphasize a patriarchal construct and substitute a feminist one," as Lori Burns observes, even if "it is never possible to eliminate the dominant references" completely.[39] The tendency within the ballad tradition to complicate established social and gender norms reanimates itself in self-conscious and self-aware feminist revisions of the singer-songwriter. The tension between disruptive and dominant discourses is palpable in women's own musical engagements with Ophelia.

Revoicing/revising Ophelia

As the role of singer-songwriter was assumed and redefined by more women, new versions of Ophelia overcame much of the reticence suffered by Dylan's rendering of the character. Nevertheless, a decidedly anxious Ophelia can be found in the song "Touch Me Fall," which Amy Ray (who had previously taken on the musical role of Mark Knopfler's Romeo) composed for the Indigo Girls's 1994 *Swamp Ophelia* and which supplies the album's title. The speaker, as sung by Ray, urges the listener, described as a "swamp Ophelia," to provide release and liberation: "Are you hiding? I am hiding / Cypress moon, bald in June / Like the granite in a stream / Swamp Ophelia, I'm torn down / Let your waters let me drown."[40] The vocal itself swims amid rich layerings of electric guitars played by Ray and bandmate Emily Saliers. Fittingly, the song recapitulates Dylan's once controversial move from acoustic guitar to electric instrumentation: many in the Indigo Girls's audiences were similarly taken aback by the unexpected shift in sound. The uncertainty and vulnerability expressed in Ray's lyrics are offset by the sonic aggression.

Rasputina, a "cello-rock" ensemble with Gothic associations, recorded "Dig Ophelia" for its 1996 debut album, *Thanks for the Ether*. Lyricist and founder Melora Creager rewrites *Hamlet*, both commenting on Ophelia and speaking for and with her. The song opens with an invitation to appreciate the character and to prepare her for burial:

> Dig Ophelia, consider it dug.
> Flowers madness and polar bear rug
> Here's the water, just ankle deep high.
> Lay back and relax and look up at the sky.[41]

The lyrics invoke such images of Ophelia as those considered at length by Elaine Showalter, in her study of the character's "role in the theoretical construction of insanity,"[42] including John Everett Millais's famous painting of the moments just before Ophelia drowns. (The members of Rasputina are admittedly obsessed with the darker aspects of Victorian culture.) Millais shows the character's face and hands still above the water's surface: her eyes are open, as is her mouth, which continues to sing. At this point in the play, however, she is reported (as the second Quarto has it) to have sung "snatches of old lauds"[43] – hymns, rather than bawdry – so Millais depicts her hands raised in prayer. Rasputina's song conflates her condition before drowning and also in death:

> Your eyes never close, your mind's not at rest,
> Lay back, get waterlogged
> Give us a kiss.

Showalter observes that Millais's composition of "Ophelia and the natural details" surrounding the figure "reduces her to one more visual object."[44] Creager's lyrics compare Ophelia to a rare flower that is reduced to the merely decorative, rather than the vital and alive: "Cut the stem and you'll see how you feel / Floating orchids just ain't no big deal." Contrast, as well as comparison, pervades the song's subtle references to Hamlet himself. The line "Never knowing's like knowing too much" suggests that Ophelia's distraction stems from being kept in the dark (by Hamlet, among others) while Hamlet's discontent follows the excess of information – and interpretive possibilities for that information – granted him. But their conditions as manipulated children, despite being of age, are similar; they share status as exceptional individuals who must be struck down. As the song's refrain warns, while "Water spreads the small seed," it is also true that "Water kills the tall weed."

Natalie Merchant provides a variation on Dylan's strategies of appropriation in her song "Ophelia," which appears on the 1998 album of the same title. Here, Ophelia is less of a single archetype and more of a common thread that ties together a range of cultural representations of the feminine. Merchant takes Hamlet's "nunnery" speeches to Ophelia as a starting point:

> Ophelia was a bride of God
> A novice Carmelite
> In sister cells
> The cloister bells
> Tolled on her wedding night.[45]

Merchant finds in Hamlet's pun on nunnery as both convent and whorehouse an enduring question of woman's place in society. Ophelia remains on the margins, whether immured within the cloister or agitating for change as "the rebel girl / A blue stocking suffragette." The spirit of the cloister persists in the song as long-sustained organ chords accompany each new incarnation of the character. The song sees Ophelia in the starlet who becomes "the sweetheart / To a nation overnight" with her "Curvaceous thighs" and "Vivacious eyes"; in a "Mafia courtesan" in Las Vegas; in a "circus queen / The female cannonball." Her power resides in her apparent unsoundness, her challenges to convention and even sanity: she is described as "a tempest cyclone / A goddamn hurricane," in the face of which "Your common sense, your best defense / Lay wasted and in vain." Her power also paradoxically resides in vulnerability to others' suffering: "For Ophelia'd know your every woe / And every pain you'd ever had." Strangely, this all-embracing empathy leaves her isolated. Eventually "Ophelia's mind went wandering" and so does she, "Through secret doors down corridors / She wanders them alone." But if one wonders, with the speaker, "where she'd gone," the song provides an answer as it fades into an auditory collage of phrases in different languages. Ophelia continues to be everywhere.

Ophelia's response to her isolation is the focal point of Toyah Willcox's "The Woman Who Had An Affair With Herself," released in 1991 on the *Ophelia's Shadow* album. Where Merchant's Ophelia endures even as she dissolves into polyglossia, Willcox's Ophelia defends herself against a single voice, in a single language, as created by a single author. The song begins with direct quotation from Shakespeare's *Hamlet*; the "nunnery" passages are again the catalyst and this time the "jig" reference is included:

> Get thee to a nunnery, go, farewell, or if thou will't needs marry, marry a fool; for wise men know well enough what monsters you make of them. God has given you one face and you make yourselves another. You jig, you amble and you lisp and nickname God's creatures and make your wantonness your ignorance. Go to: I'll no more on't: it hath made me mad. To a nunnery, go.
> (drink me)
> To which Ophelia answered
> "Oh, what a noble mind is here o'erthrown." (adapted from 3.1.139–53)[46]

The Shakespearean engagement may seem less surprising if we recall that the onetime punk songstress had appeared in Derek Jarman's gloriously transgressive film version of *The Tempest* in 1980.[47] Here, Willcox's allusion to *Alice's Adventures in Wonderland* ("drink me") conveys an appropriate sense of vertigo: Ophelia enters another world, one opened up by Hamlet's fierce dismissal. Here, the dramatic irony of Ophelia's assessment that "a noble mind" has been "o'erthrown" is underscored, as Ophelia has lost her bearings as completely as Alice. But Willcox's Ophelia finds independence in Hamlet's rejection and in the resulting isolation. She also finds a sense of identity in the water that other treatments of the character present as threatening. Becoming the "woman / From the land beyond the shore line," she "discovered part of herself she never knew of" as "The waves come." She embraces the autonomy, even though "The effect that followed / Was like being thrown into the Hawaii surf." Rather than seeking to "improve" her image, the better to attract her beloved's "attentions" (which are directed, apparently, toward metaphysical speculations "In the clouds"), she becomes "her own secret admirer." While she escapes the trap that ensnares Shakespeare's Ophelia, who is torn by conflicting personal and societal imperatives, she nevertheless verges on the narcissistic. Like Narcissus, she rebuffs the attentions of a new admirer, for "when a golden boy caught her eye / Jealousy she felt from within." Also, like Narcissus and like the play's Ophelia, she risks being consumed by water. As the song progresses, Willcox deftly shifts between third person and first person; the narrative voice ultimately becomes Ophelia herself. The combining of identities at the conclusion subsumes Lewis Carroll's Alice, as well, when the singer announces that "the waves drink me." As co-writer Tony Geballe's music fades, the song also suggests that this Ophelia goes beyond narcissism, so that she is able to nourish the waves. The album's title track overtly identifies Ophelia with Joan of Arc, a victor over the flames that consumed her; like Merchant, Willcox insists on feminist appropriations of a wide range of cultural figures.

Shakespop: authorizing Desdemona

One popular song that uses Ophelia's name can serve as a transition to the character of Desdemona. Robbie Robertson wrote "Ophelia" for his group, the Band (which helped back Dylan in his own transition from acoustic folk to electrified rock music). The song appears on the 1975 album *Northern Lights – Southern Cross*, the title of which stresses the group's curious combination of Canadian sensibilities and "American" themes: only drummer Levon Helm hailed from the southern United States. Evoking Dixieland jazz in his music (even more beautifully realized in the live version that appears on *The Last Waltz*), Robertson hints at southern fears of miscegenation in elusive lyrics about an elusive love. "Nobody knows just what became of Ophelia" perhaps because of "somethin' that somebody said" about how the speaker and his beloved "broke the rules."[48] Helm's vocal bellows out the question, "Was somebody up against the law?," and attempts to answer it with an affirmation of utter loyalty: "Honey, you know I'd die for you." Despite this, it's Ophelia who has apparently paid (or feared enough to flee from) the penalty for their transgression, leaving the speaker to plead with his absent love to "Please darken my door." Behind the clever wordplay with the melodramatic phrase, "Never darken my door again," Robertson explores feelings of deep dread over Ophelia's darkness. Near the end of the song, the southern Gothic of William Faulkner meets the spectral presence of Hamlet's father: amid "Ashes of laughter, the ghost is clear." The song's oblique concerns about interracial romance point insistently towards *Othello* and Desdemona.

Given the place of *Othello* in Western mythologies about race, it is no surprise that the play was frequently appropriated in travesties featuring minstrel songs and continues to be a site of contention about racially inflected forms of cultural expression.[49] The play has also figured in assertions of black pride, including Ellington's *Such Sweet Thunder*. But that album's title track focuses on Desdemona only as auditor, not as singer. Coming nearly full circle, Bob Dylan has recently envisioned Desdemona turning the tables on Othello, borrowing plot devices from *Hamlet*. The song "Po' Boy," on the 2001 album *Love & Theft*, includes a verse featuring these doomed lovers:

> Othello told Desdemona, "I'm cold, cover me with a blanket.
> By the way, what happened to that poison wine?"
> She says, "I gave it to you, you drank it."[50]

The lines connect with another song on the album, "Floater (Too Much to Ask)," which shows Juliet telling Romeo to get over his fixation on youth.

Here, the assertively acoustic instrumentation marks yet another return by Dylan to the traditional forms that fascinated him early in his career. Lyrically, Dylan suggests that Desdemona could have been complicit in Iago's racist verbal poisoning of Othello's trust; the verbal poisoning becomes literalized, glancing at the poisoned wine meant for Hamlet, but consumed by his mother Gertrude.

At this point, one might wonder what has happened to Shakespeare's playtexts. What results or remains when characters, devices, and themes from one play are brought into juxtaposition with their counterparts from another work – all in cultural contexts very different from Shakespeare's own? A partial answer is suggested by Andrew James Hartley in his recent study of Shakespearean dramaturgy. Aligning himself with W. B. Worthen's critiques of claims to produce Shakespeare "authentically," Hartley asserts that "theatre, like jazz, authorizes itself. It is not wholly dependent on the text, that text's author, or the period in which that text was produced . . . It is dependent on its own internal logics, its own integrity, and on the singular collaborative semiotic exchange that defines it."[51]

Hartley's felicitous comparison not only of theatre in general but of specifically Shakespearean theatre with jazz can encourage us to think of all popular music's engagements with Shakespeare as "source" in similar ways. The multiple genres of popular music (including its post-pop and mass-market manifestations) also operate within their own logics, their own integrity (or dreams of achieving it), their special collaborative exchanges with audience on a variety of semiotic levels. It is important to remember that popular music's appropriations of Shakespeare do not, as some critics declare of "inauthentic" stagings of his plays, "pander to those unworthy of the 'real thing,' trivializing it, even corrupting it."[52] Rather, they help the plays connect with one of the many sources of Shakespeare's own inspiration and dramatic impact: popular music itself.

NOTES

1. Terence Hawkes, *Shakespeare in the Present* (London: Routledge, 2002), p. 142.
2. Lawrence Levine, "William Shakespeare and the American People: A Study in Cultural Transformation," *American Historical Review* 89.1 (February 1984), 34–66; rpt. in *Rethinking Popular Culture: Contemporary Perspectives in Cultural Studies*, ed. Chandra Mukerji and Michael Schudson (Berkeley and Los Angeles: University of California Press, 1991), pp. 157–97, pp. 169–72.
3. Duke Ellington and His Orchestra, *Such Sweet Thunder* (Columbia Records, 1957); Stephen M. Buhler, "Form and Character in Duke Ellington's and Billy Strayhorn's *Such Sweet Thunder*," *Borrowers and Lenders: The Journal of Shakespeare and Appropriation* 1.1 (Spring 2005). http://atropos.english. uga.edu/cocoon/borrowers/

4. Fran Teague, "Swingin' Shakespeare from Harlem to Broadway," *Borrowers and Lenders: The Journal of Shakespeare and Appropriation* 1.1 (Spring 2005). http://atropos.english.uga.edu/cocoon/borrowers/

5. Frances Teague, "Shakespeare, Beard of Avon," in *Shakespeare After Mass Media*, ed. Richard Burt (New York: Palgrave, 2002), pp. 221–42, p. 227. See also her comprehensive account of "The Shakespearean Broadway Musical" in Frances Teague, *Shakespeare and the American Popular Stage* (Cambridge: Cambridge University Press, 2006).

6. Teague, "Shakespeare, Beard of Avon," pp. 229–30.

7. Alan Corrigan, "Jazz, Shakespeare, and Hybridity: A Script Excerpt from *Swingin' the Dream*," *Borrowers and Lenders: The Journal of Shakespeare and Appropriation* 1.1 (Spring 2005). http://atropos.english.uga.edu/cocoon/borrowers/

8. Cole Porter, "Brush Up Your Shakespeare," in *Kiss Me Kate* (New York: T. B. Harms, 1951).

9. Robert Shaughnessy, "*Romeo and Juliet*: The Rock and Roll Years," in *Remaking Shakespeare: Performance Across Media, Genres, and Cultures*, ed. Pascale Aebischer, Edward J. Esche, and Nigel Wheale (New York: Palgrave Macmillan, 2003), pp. 172–89, esp. pp. 175–80. Stephen M. Buhler, "Reviving Juliet, Repackaging Romeo: Transformations of Character in Pop and Post-Pop Music," in Burt, *Shakespeare After Mass Media*, pp. 243–64, esp. pp. 247–48. See also Kenneth Rothwell, *A History of Shakespeare on Screen* (Cambridge: Cambridge University Press, 1999), pp. 134–35.

10. Peggy Lee, Otis Blackwell (as John Davenport), and Eddie Cooley, "Fever" (Capitol Records, 1958).

11. Shaughnessy, "*Romeo and Juliet*: The Rock and Roll Years," p. 185.

12. Bruce Springsteen, "Incident on 57th Street," on *The Wild, the Innocent, and the E-Street Shuffle* (Columbia Records, 1973).

13. Mark Knopfler, "Romeo and Juliet," on the Dire Straits album *Making Movies* (Warner Brothers Records, 1980).

14. For more detailed analyses of these and other songs, see Buhler, "Reviving Juliet," pp. 248–63.

15. Douglas Lanier, *Shakespeare and Modern Popular Culture* (New York: Oxford University Press, 2002), p. 72.

16. Ross Duffin, *Shakespeare's Songbook* (New York: W. W. Norton, 2004), p. 17.

17. *Ibid.*, p. 238.

18. Bruce Smith, *The Acoustic World of Early Modern England: Attending to the O-Factor* (Chicago: University of Chicago Press, 1999), p. 201.

19. James Shapiro, *1599: A Year in the Life of William Shakespeare* (New York: Harper Collins, 2005), p. 40.

20. *Ibid.*, p. 40.

21. *Ibid.*, p. 40.

22. Edward Guilpin, *Skialetheia: or A Shadow of Truth in Certaine Epigrams and Satyres* (London, 1598), sig. D, fol. 5r–v; quoted in part by Shapiro, *1599*, p. 41.

23. Duffin, *Shakespeare's Songbook*, p. 280.

24. F. W. Sternfeld, *Music in Shakespearean Tragedy* (London: Routledge and Kegan Paul, 1963), pp. 57–58.

25. *Ibid.*, p. 59.

26. Shapiro, *1599*, p. 40.

27. Bryan N. S. Gooch and David S. Thatcher (eds.), *A Shakespeare Music Catalogue*, 5 vols. (Oxford: Clarendon Press, 1991), II: 373.

28. Benjamin Filene, *Romancing the Folk: Public Memory and American Roots Music* (Chapel Hill: University of North Carolina Press, 2000), pp. 190–93.

29. *Ibid.*, pp. 207–11.

30. Bob Dylan, "Desolation Row," on *Highway 61 Revisited* (Columbia Records, 1965).

31. *Ibid.*

32. Bob Dylan, *Chronicles, Volume One* (New York: Simon and Schuster, 2004), p. 169.

33. *Ibid.*, p. 236.

34. Bob Dylan, "Stuck Inside of Mobile with the Memphis Blues Again," on *Blonde on Blonde* (Columbia Records, 1966).

35. Dylan, *Chronicles*, p. 55.

36. Grigori Kosintsev, *Gamlet* [*Hamlet*] (USSR: Lenfilm, 1964). See also Stephen M. Buhler, *Shakespeare in the Cinema: Ocular Proof* (Albany: State University of New York Press, 2002), p. 164.

37. Neil Young, "After the Gold Rush," on *After the Gold Rush* (Warner Brothers Records, 1971).

38. Mélisse Lafrance, "A Cultural Studies Approach to Women and Popular Music," in Lori Burns and Mélisse Lafrance, *Disruptive Divas: Feminism, Identity, and Popular Music* (New York: Routledge, 2002), pp. 1–29, p. 2.

39. Lori Burns, "'Close Readings' of Popular Song: Intersections among Sociocultural, Musical, and Lyrical Meanings," in Burns and Lafrance, *Disruptive Divas*, pp. 31–61, p. 60.

40. Indigo Girls, "Touch Me Fall," on *Swamp Ophelia* (Epic Records, 1994).

41. Rasputina, "Dig Ophelia," on *Thanks for the Ether* (Columbia Records, 1996).

42. Elaine Showalter, "Representing Ophelia: Women, Madness and the Responsibilities of Feminist Criticism," in *Shakespeare and the Question of Theory*, ed. Patricia Parker and Geoffrey Hartman (New York and London: Methuen, 1985), pp. 77–94, p. 80.

43. The Oxford edition favours Q1 and F's more neutral, and secular, "tunes" (4.1.149); the Q2 reading is adopted by the New Cambridge, Riverside, and Arden 2 and 3 editions of the play.

44. Showalter, "Representing Ophelia," p. 85.

45. Natalie Merchant, "Ophelia," on *Ophelia* (Elektra Entertainment, 1998).

46. Toyah Willcox, "The Woman Who Had An Affair With Herself," on *Ophelia's Shadow* (EG Records, 1991).

47. Buhler, *Shakespeare in the Cinema*, p. 147.

48. The Band, "Ophelia," on *Northern Lights – Southern Cross* (Capitol Records, 1975).

49. Lanier, *Shakespeare and Modern Popular Culture*, pp. 73–81. See also Lanier, "Minstrelsy, Jazz, Rap: Shakespeare, African American Music, and Cultural Legitimation," *Borrowers and Lenders: The Journal of Shakespeare and Appropriation* 1.1 (Spring 2005). http://atropos.english.uga.edu/cocoon/borrowers/

50. Bob Dylan, "Po' Boy," on *Love & Theft* (Columbia Records, 2001).

51. Andrew James Hartley, *The Shakespearean Dramaturg: A Theoretical and Practical Guide* (New York: Palgrave, 2005), p. 61.

52. *Ibid.*, p. 7.

9

SUSANNE GREENHALGH

Shakespeare overheard: performances, adaptations, and citations on radio

We now come to the sensitive issue of Shakespeare on radio. And I'm afraid the less said about this topic the better in my opinion. In other words, although many have tried to make Shakespeare work on radio, it doesn't ... In short, audiences throughout the world hate Shakespeare on the radio.
And – to be honest – who's to blame them?[1]

Audio Shakespeare in its broadest sense includes all of the ways in which versions of Shakespeare's works are transmitted and disseminated in sound-only formats, whether these take the form of radio dramatizations, recordings for LPs, audio cassettes, CDs, or digital downloads for DAB radio, computers, or MP3 players. As such it is the mode of performance which is most ubiquitous and the most fully integrated into the cultures of everyday life, potentially capable of being heard anywhere, anytime. In this essay I have chosen to concentrate solely on broadcast Shakespeare; primarily the derivatives, parodies, and citations which have been part of radio from the beginning. As a radio reviewer once complained, "there are times when Shakespeare seems to get everywhere, like ants, or mice; it would be nice to be able to call in some kind of pest control service, Bardokil or Swannicide, to eliminate unwanted Shakespearean references from your life."[2] It may well be the case, though accurate statistics would be impossible to gather, that radio has originated and disseminated more allusions and references to Shakespeare than any other form of mass media. And yet historically it has also been one of the most unacknowledged and often ephemeral forms of Shakespearean remediation, and, partly for this reason, the one which has received least critical attention. In this sense Shakespeare has more frequently been "under" than "over" heard.

However, both the technologies and theories of radio have progressed significantly in the last twenty years. In Tim Crook's view, "Radio drama's ephemeral status as an art form is at an end ... Some forms of sound story telling are equal to film videos in their availability and the permanence of access for future consumption."[3] The ability to record and more recently to download radio transmissions has increased opportunity to create audio archives outside those of the broadcaster or public bodies charged with this task, such as the National Sound Archive in Britain. The last few years have seen a huge growth in the popularity of audio for personal purchase, loan, or hire, in a variety of formats. Technologies such as TiVo, which can be set to scan for and record specific types of sound broadcasts, are also coming into more frequent use. As Douglas Lanier notes "once committed to recording a performance takes on the qualities of a stable 'textual' object, allowing for much closer, analytic modes of listening made possible by repetition."[4] All these technical resources have the potential to enable and encourage criticism and theoretical consideration both of the Shakespeare broadcasts that have long been preserved and those that are only just beginning to be noticed through the opportunity for repeat listening. Nonetheless, it is only very recently that John Drakakis's fine essays on British radio drama in general and Shakespeare in particular, first published in 1981, have been augmented by valuable discussions of American radio Shakespeare and recordings of the plays, as well as by studies of the early modern "acoustic world" and sound-scapes that continue to echo in his playtexts.[5] Attention to audio Shakespeare has undoubtedly suffered from what Coleridge termed the "despotism of the eye" in Western culture, which has resulted in sound-only media being regarded as "blind" and "incomplete" modes of representation and expression compared with the audio-visual media of film and television.

The rest of this essay deals with the presence of Shakespeare on British radio, which is still, as Graham Holderness noted in 1988, "a history the tradition of which remains to be written."[6] As Drakakis has stressed, Shakespeare was a key reference in British radio's own self-exploration.

> The terms in which the debate about Shakespearean performance was conducted in the early 1920s bear a striking resemblance to those in which the early broadcasters themselves defended the new medium ... intimacy of the relationship between actor and audience, the swiftness of the transition from one scene to another made possible by the removal of naturalistic backgrounds, the primacy of poetry and spoken dialogue, all appeared as part of the justification for radio drama itself.[7]

Much Shakespearean reference and production also acknowledges the radio medium's ability not only to reflect upon itself, but to incorporate and critique the other mass media of publishing and cinema, and eventually television and the internet, as well as the technologies of recorded sound themselves. Among the hundreds of broadcasts of or about Shakespeare's works are examples of what Peter Donaldson terms "media allegory": not simply ways of embodying the metatheatricality latent in the playtext, or invoking "the special properties of the [radio] medium" but explorations of media history and transitions registered as "cross-media self-consciousness."[8]

To all intents and purposes, and certainly for the purposes of this essay, British radio Shakespeare means BBC radio Shakespeare. It is not just that more of its Shakespearean output has been noted, reviewed, and archived. It is simply that there has been more of it than on any other broadcasting network. For most of its history Shakespeare has haunted BBC radio like a ghost from one of his own plays; sometimes a reproach, sometimes a cue for action. Three of the Corporation's most popular and long-running programmes can serve as examples. The format of *Desert Island Discs* (1942–present) was devised as an escape from wartime hardship and fears of Nazi victory. Celebrities, from politicians to actors and artists, are "marooned" on an imaginary island, and invited to choose their favorite eight records, along with one luxury, to add to the Bible and Complete Works of Shakespeare already there. Although, as Drakakis notes, the programme is a "relic of English bourgeois capitalism"[9] indebted to Defoe's *Robinson Crusoe*, the very creation of an island "full of noises, / Sounds, and sweet airs" also invokes *The Tempest*. In 1942 the Complete Works and the Bible represented the values for which Britain believed it was fighting the war, not simply a conflation of Shakespeare with divine authority, as Drakakis suggests.[10] Shakespeare, like the record selection and the luxury, is there as much for personal pleasure and comfort as for the bolstering of national identity. My second example is BBC's soap opera, *The Archers* (1951–present). This everyday story of country folk is located in "Borsetshire", a cross between Worcestershire and Warwickshire, within easy reach of Stratford-upon-Avon and its theatre, to which the more affluent and "cultured" inhabitants occasionally go. However, in 1993 Shakespeare came to "Ambridge," where a whole summer was spent rehearsing and per-forming a production of *A Midsummer Night's Dream* with a cast made up of the soap's favorite characters, including the matriarch Jill Archer as Hippolyta and Joe Grundy as Bottom, and storylines that tangled up the love lives of the younger villagers with those portrayed in the play. Shakespeare's geographical and emotional place in what the Tourist Board calls the "heart of England" is endorsed, class difference is naturalized, but the "real life" conventions of soap opera narrative are also placed in a metatheatrical frame that underlines their intrinsic artificiality.

My final example is the *Today* programme, (1957–present), Radio 4's breakfast time flagship news and current affairs program, which is com-pulsory listening for the nation's opinion-formers and regularly features items on Shakespeare as newsworthy in themselves or as part of the "cul-tural" strand of the programme (the lead presenters John Humphreys and James Naughtie have each developed parallel careers as media commenta-tors on the English language and literature respectively). In a poem written for the programme's end-of-2005 poll the "radio laureate" Ian McMillan outlined the case for Shakespeare's eligibility as one of those who "ran" Britain.

> A playwright long since dead
> Who speaks to us from behind the veil,
> Whose lines invade our head
> And, more than that, dictate the way
> We see and hear the world
>
> . . .
>
> We open our mouths
> And out comes William Shakespeare's breath.
>
> . . .
>
> And on any bus, on any train
> The language of the street
> Is bolted to Shakespearean Rhythms:
> He's the man who keeps the beat.
> I celebrate the Englishes
> That permeate the air
> From Europe, Asia, Africa,
> But Shakespeare's still there[11]

Radio, Paddy Scannell argues, brings us above all "languageness . . . embodied utterance."[12] This poem, broadcast in McMillan's own Yorkshire accent, gave literal voice to a concept of Shakespeare which BBC speech radio has continually disseminated and arguably helped create; as a form of ghostly linguistic possession which comes to embody the English language itself, in all its diversities. In doing so the BBC of course continues to shore up its own national and international status as banker for a global, linguistic currency still in high demand. It is no surprise therefore that the first series of *The Routes of English* (Radio 4, 3 August 2000) discussed Shakespeare in an episode called "The Power of English." However, McMillan's poem, though it evokes the power of "Shakespeare's breath" to invade and colonize, also links it with the intimacies of ordinary speech and the "selving" that comes from that speaking.[13] Scannell proposes that when daily broadcasting began, it asserted above all "the everyday and its concerns . . . retrieved and proclaimed the social, sociable character of human life" and in so doing brought the wider world and public life close; made them "accessible and available."[14] What then is perhaps most significant about the way radio embodies Shakespearean utterance is not how it lets Shakespeare "rule" the airwaves, but how it absorbs Shakespeare into the fabric of everyday life and speech.

In the twenty-first century radio can be regarded as an "old" medium, which, though it once seemed destined for obsolescence and replacement by newer visual technologies, has proved surprisingly resilient, flexible, and mobile, at any rate in Britain. Here radio has reinvented itself over the years as warm center of the home, public voice of the nation, traveling-companion in the outside world, at work and on the move, and as a private, intimate voice to accompany mundane everyday activities, and create alternative worlds of the imagination. Within this protean medium Shakespeare has also been constantly reinvented, primarily as drama but also in all its other genres. The very processes by which different "Shakespeares" have been brought into being have themselves been the subject of scrutiny, and sometimes derision, in countless radio features, talks, and comedy shows. This vast "hinterland", requiring extensive further documentation and investigation, should be kept continually in mind as the context in which Shakespeare, in many different accents and registers, has been heard.[15]

Shakespeare and BBC sound broadcasting

English-language sound broadcasting dates from the 1920s, with the advent of commercial radio in America (1922), Britain (1922), Canada (1923), and Australia (1923). Broadcasting institutions in each national context developed distinctive ways in which Shakespeare came to occupy significantly different air space and time, and status.

> Radio is not merely a medium but a culture industry, shaped by its modes of finance, production and distribution, its systems of programming and scheduling, its matrix of genres, its rivalries and affiliations with cultural alternatives like theatre, film, popular fiction, and TV, and its star system and fan culture. And insofar as Shakespearean theatre appears on the radio, it must accommodate, or at the very least address, these institutional protocols.[16]

The distinctive cultural positioning of British radio Shakespeare comes into sharper relief when compared with the situation in America. Here commercial radio dominated from the start, producing a quantity of different stations across the nation, many, especially the larger networks, in direct competition with each other. By contrast, the private British Broadcasting Company set up in 1922 was quickly turned into a public Corporation (conveniently keeping the same initials). Its Royal Charter of 1927 granted it a monopoly and the government guaranteed funding through license fees paid by all who purchased wirelesses. In return the BBC undertook to provide a service tailored to the public good, through a judicious combination of information, education, and entertainment. The "public service" element in American radio, on the other hand, was confined to what were known as "sustaining programs," supported by the networks, rather than by commercial sponsorship, in order to meet government licensing regulations requiring a degree of "public service" content. Shakespeare adaptations most often appeared in anthology programs or series of plays, usually with set lengths. However, as Lanier has argued, in the USA the intrinsic "popularism" of a medium "characteristically inhospitable to cultural elitism" posed "a serious challenge for 'proper' Shakespeare, associated as it was with classical theatre and high culture."[17] In contrast, at the BBC, under the leadership of the first Director General, John Reith, a vision of broadcasting as a kind of public utility for the good of the nation's cultural and social health helped shape the attitudes and values that would dominate the new organization for years to come. The "popularization" of Shakespeare and other exemplars of "high art" to a wider audience was at the core of its vision; but the aim was to "raise up" the audience rather than dumb down to it, as part of what has been called a "third type of democracy" which sought to blur any boundaries that might exist between cultural and class divides.[18]

Until the postwar period this meant "mixed" programming in its national and regional services, designed so that a listener might at any point be "surprised" by a listening experience more challenging (and it was assumed therefore more rewarding) than she had consciously chosen. Shakespeare provided suitable material both in the form of play adaptations and as "a reservoir of familiar plot lines, characters, scenes and lines"[19] Moreover, Shakespeare also became a vital part of the way in which the BBC, along with other emergent components of social life, such as sport, royal ceremonial, a national education system, and even the founding of the National Trust, was synthesized into a "national culture"; experienced as a sense of collective belonging and mirrored in "real and tangible" events relayed live to audiences by the new medium.[20] Radio in Britain took on a calendrical role, creating a broadcast year based on the cyclical reproduction of "festivities, rituals and celebrations – major and minor, civil and sacred,"[21] in which commemoration of Shakespeare's supposed birth and death day on 23 April (which is also the feast day of St. George, the patron saint of England), became a regular anniversary, marked for a number of years by live broadcasts of the speeches and toasts to his memory proposed at the annual celebratory luncheon in Stratford-upon-Avon. It is possible to identify a "Shakespeare week" in the third week of April for which programmes were commissioned and to which schedulers frequently gravitated when Shakespeare-related material was on offer.

The anniversary was not only significant for Shakespeare's sake. The BBC inaugurated its radio drama programming in 1923 with scenes from Shakespeare, not just at the London station but at several of the regional ones too, and followed this up with a longer programme of extracts on the 23rd of April. A month later, one of his plays was chosen as the first full-length play to be broadcast. In the years to come the BBC would frequently choose the third week in April for other important institutional developments, such as the launch of BBC2 in 1964, also the 400th anniversary year of his birth. Even when the date itself was not selected, Shakespeare references might still be invoked, as when the Third Programme marked its transformation into Radio 3 on 3 April 1970 by transmitting a production of *All's Well That Ends Well*. The first BBC publication was a book on *Shakespeare's Heroines*, issued in association with performances by Ellen Terry, and sold in aid of funds to establish a National Theatre. When Eric Gill was commissioned to provide sculptures for the new Broadcasting House completed in 1932 a Shakespearean theme was inevitable, resulting in portrayals of Prospero and Ariel standing on a globe over the main entrance and side panels of Ariel dancing with children, Wisdom, and Gaiety. As well as Shakespeare providing a frequent reference point in writing or speaking about the radio medium – the in-house magazine took the airy spirit's name as its title – his commemoration often became an opportunity to celebrate or reflect on the progress of the BBC and its public service ideals, which its staff, many of them highly educated and with literary aspirations, saw prefigured in what they took to be the nature and achievement of Shakespeare's "national" (and popular) theatre. "When Shakespeare wrote plays, he wrote them as if he were writing for radio" summed up a prevailing attitude that Shakespeare was in some sense the BBC's "house dramatist."[22]

The role of the BBC in creating what Cardiff and Scannell call "We-feeling," built on the idea of a national culture, is vital for understanding the place and nature of Shakespeare in its output, a continuation of the processes which turned him into a "national poet" from the seventeenth century on. Equally significant, however, is the way the radio medium, so frequently a domestic experience, helped consolidate a sense of Shakespeare as a "family" event, enjoyed at the "wireless hearth" in the comfort of the home, though with awareness of the larger "national family" supposedly listening at the same time. Although it took several years for children to be given their own versions of Shakespeare separate from educational broadcasts, the scheduling of some play productions in greatly shortened and adapted forms in the early evening, just after the end of *Children's Hour*, meant that they too were included in the intended audience, as part of a "growing up" process whereby they were encouraged to become "active" critical listeners on their way to taking their places as informed and cultured participants in a democracy. The choice of the first Shakespeare scene to be broadcast on 16 February 1923 was highly appropriate as a way of inaugurating these broader processes of "domestication." The quarrel scene between Brutus and Cassius from *Julius Caesar* (4.2)[23] itself creates a domestic space on the field of war as the two leaders retreat inside a tent for an intimate exchange in which their feelings for each other and those close to them rather than the political decisions in which they are involved become the real subject matter. This mood of personal revelation is further enhanced by the everyday activities of drinking, getting ready for bed, reading, and listening to music which punctuate the scene when played in full. Consciously or not, early BBC Shakespeare implicitly privileged a "privatized" Shakespeare, received and responded to in ways that were as much personal and intimate as a poor imitation of communal theatregoing. This tendency continued in the choice of *Twelfth Night* as its first "full-length" (actually cut and adapted) play production on 28 May 1923, despite its dependence on visual comedy. The play's action, divided between the "upstairs and downstairs" worlds of two households, highlights personal dilemmas of love, loss, and self-deception. Radio's association of Shakespeare with intimacy was noted by critics, not always with approval. "Shakespeare himself falls considerably short of his stage self through the microphone. If you switch on in the middle of a speech in a Shakespeare play, you may find yourself feeling embarrassed; radio dramatic art has to be *intensely intimate*."[24] Here the misgivings seem less to do with inappropriate overacting as with the way radio production of Shakespeare abolished the "safe" distance between stage and auditorium and intensified the emotional impact to the point that it felt like eavesdropping.

In America "the overriding issue for Shakespeare on the radio ... was the mismatch between lowbrow medium and highbrow Bard."[25] In its early years the BBC saw no such "mismatch" in its ambition to ensure that the best should be popular and the popular should be the best. The view of the long-time Head of Radio Drama, Val Gielgud, reflected this: "It is the business of the BBC to make sure that broadcasting can not only do something for Shakespeare but the very best that is possible for Shakespeare."[26] The emergence of the term "middlebrow" in relation to the BBC radio audience suggests a more complex social and cultural dynamic than that encompassed in the "highbrow"/"lowbrow" binary commonly associated with Shakespeare in America, where intellectuals tended to equate radio with the threat of centralization and homogenization of culture.

> Traditionally the British middlebrow public would have read accredited literature, Shakespeare and Dickens, would have been familiar with the more popular end of the repertoire of classical music and would have learned the outlines of both classical and British history ... Through "knowingness," the middlebrow boasted the capacity to appreciate high culture and intellectual ideas and also the critical acumen to see through them, dismiss them as of marginal value in the workaday world in which sensible people lived.[27]

Although British radio Shakespeare, as in America, was associated by many with "learned, antiquated high culture,"[28] it was economically ring-fenced from commercially driven populism, and could be justified as guaranteeing the "quality" of an organization dependent ultimately on the continuing value placed on its services by its license-payers. As long as these were predominantly middle-class there was something of a consensus about the "best," but as equipment costs fell and a more socially mixed audience tuned in, demands for more "popular" material, such as music and comedy, became more insistent, especially during and after the war when "lighter" content had been a staple of both the British and American services for the armed forces. The postwar creation of the Home, Light, and Third programmes effectively reshaped radio content into a "cultural pyramid," with a mass of "popular" material accessed by the majority of listeners at the "bottom" (Light; Radios 1 and 2); survival of an element of "mixed" programming in the middle (Home; Radio 4; BBC 7); and the minority artistic and intellectual interests being served at the "top" (Third; Radio 3). The nature and genres of BBC radio's Shakespeare content would in future inevitably be shaped by these class-informed structures.

Shakespeare's breath: adapting Shakespeare for radio

Lanier has shown how, in an American radio culture dedicated to defining itself as populist, reference to Shakespeare, and especially to its theatrical performance, could be a form of "pathology," manifesting itself in depictions of Shakespearean actors as criminals and murderers, as radio drama itself fell into terminal decline.[29] In Britain the situation has been very different. Although there have been periods, for instance the mid 1960s and the 1990s, when the health of the genre of the Shakespearean appeared to falter, adaptations of the plays and new drama which quote, borrow from, parody, or otherwise appropriate Shakespeare have kept a tenacious hold on life within the BBC into the twenty-first century, the dawn of which Radio 4 *Today* program listeners marked by voting Shakespeare "Man of the Millennium." The introduction of scenes from and adaptations of the plays at the start of the BBC's existence was almost immediately accompanied by other forms of drama which dealt with various aspects of the Shakespeare myth, characters, and industry, especially the theatre. It was these kinds of plays, along with the regular Shakespeare productions, with their accompanying features, Shakespeare-related interval music, and frequent academic or more popular talks on his life, work, and significance, underwritten by Shakespeare's continuing presence in the educational and theatrical life of British society, which cemented the sense of a constant supply of "sound

Shakespeareana," which might catch a listener's attention at any point in the day.

The radio medium was thus in many ways a more hospitable and fertile environment for Shakespeare-related drama than that of film and television. One obvious reason is production costs. Radio drama requires no set or costumes, and roles can be easily doubled, often by actors from the Radio Drama Company, who specialize in such versatility. Since scripts are read rather than learned, much shorter times are required for rehearsal and production; these in turn allow a much faster turnaround than audio-visual productions, and, though far less well-paid, often fit comfortably around actors' other commitments to theatre runs or film shoots. Radio is in fact attractive to many actors, especially those who are classically trained, who enjoy the challenge to their vocal skills and its more intimate style of performance, and appreciate the opportunities it provides of playing roles that might never come their way in the theatre, film, or television, because of physical appearance, age, race, or gender. If recordings are made for sale, these offer the prospect of preserving a performance that would otherwise leave only memory traces or written reports. Since radio directors are frequently producers as well as directors, in charge of the costs and casting as well as artistic interpretation, radio Shakespeare has also been far less constrained than television and film by considerations of length and format. Historically, the BBC had a relatively flexible attitude towards running times, and later regular weekly slots for drama were created; producers were also not afraid either to cut drastically or to make use of intervals halfway through broadcast plays. All these aspects of radio production have helped encourage a regular flow of Shakespeare's plays throughout the BBC's eighty-five-year history, unlike the much more sporadic and expensive output of film and television. Moreover, this Shakespeare-friendly climate has in turn encouraged the regular commissioning of plays that cite or derive from Shakespeare and his work, since these could be easily fitted into an established schedule and attract a sufficient if not sizable audience. Such plays are far less frequent on television, where the Shakespearean "heritage," though significant, is less extensive. Furthermore, since radio drama has developed its own genres and styles, from everyday naturalism to extremes of fantasy and surrealism, and has no need to restrict its settings of time and place, much of the commissioned writing about Shakespeare or his works has been more quirky and original than its film or television equivalents. In short, while the Shakespeare trademark and the BBC brand have had a long partnership this has been particularly successful in the case of radio.

Nonetheless, despite the BBC's self-association with Shakespeare, criticism of radio drama has always been haunted by the idea that it can give only an "impoverished," "incomplete" representation, especially of artworks originally designed for audio-visual perception in the theatre. Pioneer analysts, who were often themselves producers, adapters, or writers of radio drama, frequently envisaged it as a mode of performance analogous to the Shakespearean ideal stage evoked by the opening Chorus speech of *Henry V*, in which the "imaginary forces" of the listener called up an "inner vision," variously likened to the workings of the mind in dreams, reading, "stream of consciousness," or the processes of memory.[30] Absence of visual stimuli was compensated for by an experience in which "the pictures were better," more real than the "dusty grandeur of the stage."[31] More recent theoretical discussions, however, have stressed how this "lack" of visual dimension is in fact at the core of the aesthetic of radio drama, the outcome of an intrinsically "invitational" medium that mobilizes the phenomenological, not merely mental or cerebral, experience of the listener in response to speech.[32]

> Speech . . . is the occasion when conditions which locate a person in the world, that is, their physical and cultural situation and all that they are bodily capable of in that situation, are revealed as the very same conditions that enable subjectivity to exist and act autonomously within the world. To speak, we draw on our body, our language, our social situation, but in doing so we create an utterance that is a projection of our own position in or viewpoint on the world.[33]

Far from radio listening being a state of sensory deprivation, "a series of inadequate clues from an unlit world," sound can be regarded as "a medium that opens onto and generates a world, and, as part of this world-generation, enjoys interaction and conjunction with the other senses."[34] It creates what William Stanton calls a "transitory theatre," which takes the listener "on a journey through another unconscious – not the writer's, nor the actor's, but a complex, allusive acoustic *bricolage*."[35] Radio drama thus emerges from the interaction of the personal and the social, and both de-centres and unites the author and the listening subject.

> The radio play writes us, its auditors, just as it is written – not by the invisible author, but by the interaction of the voices of actors who have already disappeared and sounds that play across and within our memories. This remains its radical power . . . a collaborative dramaturgy that, at its best, generates an extraordinarily rich intellectual, affective, sensual experience.[36]

While dramatic poetry such as Shakespeare's may be particularly powerful in this medium, requiring as it does the combination of concentrated attention to language and active imaginative construction of the *mise-en-scène*,[37] this "aural scenography" has the effect of overlaying a play with many more potential meanings and simultaneously making those meaning unstable; since place "may be real or imaginary, present or past" and atmosphere "may stimulate a different kind of affective response from what is being said."[38] The "present-tenseness" of the radio medium, the sense it gives of an experience still moving towards the future, even when its auditory codes remind us of its historicity, as in the "dated" delivery of a Shakespeare speech recorded in the 1930s, paradoxically convinces us that its utterances are living and dynamic.

Since 1923 BBC radio has mounted more than three hundred adaptations of Shakespeare's plays, and repeated many of these several times, as well as selling the broadcasting rights to other radio stations worldwide and issuing a number of them as recordings for purchase by the general public. Less frequently there have also been broadcasts of the poems, with one or more full-length dramatic readings of *Venus and Adonis, The Phoenix and the Turtle*, and *The Rape of Lucrece*, and countless versions of individual Sonnets broadcast over the years. If nothing else the statistics are a measure of the plays' popularity with the producers, if not the listeners. The two works which have received the most productions are *The Tempest* (twenty-one) and *Macbeth* (twenty), with eighteen productions of *Romeo and* Juliet, sixteen of *Twelfth Night, King Lear*, and *Antony and Cleopatra*, fifteen of *Hamlet, The Merchant of Venice*, and *A Midsummer Night's Dream*. In the second division are *Julius Caesar* and *Othello* (twelve), *Richard II, The Taming Of The Shrew*, and *Henry V*, all with eleven, followed by ten each for *As You Like It* and *The Winter's Tale*, and nine for *Henry IV* and *Much Ado About Nothing*. Two of the "problem plays" each score eight productions (*Measure For Measure* and *Troilus And Cressida*) together with a Roman and an English history, *Coriolanus* and *Richard III*. *King John* leads a group of "last plays," *Cymbeline, Pericles*, and *Henry VIII* by seven to their six, as does *All's Well That Ends Well* (five) in relation to *Timon Of Athens* and *The Merry Wives Of Windsor* (four). Bringing up the rear are *Henry VI, Love's Labour's Lost*, and *Two Gentlemen Of Verona*, all with three; and in last place the two productions each of *Titus Andronicus* and *The Comedy Of Errors*. There have also been two productions each of apocryphal Shakespeare plays, *The Book of Sir Thomas More* and *The Reign of Edward III*.[39]

A historical and analytical account of these adaptations is long overdue, but cannot be undertaken here. They appeared on the regional and national services, were maintained in truncated form during the Second World War, including broadcasts on the Armed Forces service, continued regularly on both the Light and Home service as well as in the "cultural ghetto" of the Third, with which, as Radio 3, Shakespeare is now most associated. In addition to testing out academic theories, such as an adaptation of the histories into a Tillyard-influenced "national epic" in the 1940s,[40] they experimented with the use of narrators, radical cutting, and the role of music, close miking, and "radiophonic" sound effects in clarifying, reinterpreting, and intensifying the aural experience of the plays. The current program of seventeen plays broadcast and sold by BBC World Wide as the BBC Radio Shakespeare Collection is a balance between the tradition of "all-programs," the creation of "complete edition" radio by doing all the works in a specific canon or genres,[41] however obscure, while also reflecting the view that "Radio 3 ought to be doing the major canon all the time," even if this meant repeats of old recordings.[42] Interpretations have also reflected contemporary fashions in theatre staging, progressing from relay-type evocations of large-stage, big-star performances to the intimacies of the "studio Shakespeare" that developed in the 1960s. Radio versions of modern-dress productions have been created by placing the action in a mediatized world, conveyed by the presence of radio, mobile phones, and the noise of cameras flashing. The Branagh-led wave of Shakespeare films in the 1990s influenced the development of "audio movie" versions, as when the 2001 *Much Ado About Nothing* borrowed his 1993 film's opening by having Beatrice sing "Sigh No More Ladies" to accompanying female laughter. Although mixed broadcasting has now largely been replaced by "streamed" or "strip" schedules that encourage listeners to locate their own regularly available niche products, increasingly in the form of individualized "listen again" downloads to a computer from new digital channels such as BBC7 (most of whose output is made up of "classic" stories, drama, and comedy),[43] the BBC continues to promote its Shakespearean content as an important way in which it fulfils its Charter obligations by contributing to the cultural life of Britain. Multiracial casting has become a feature, employed in both "color aware" and "color blind" ways. Where once black actors were confined to minor "voice-ons" they are now regularly found in leading roles: for instance, the casting of David Harewood as the Roman lover with Frances Barber as Cleopatra (*Antony and Cleopatra*, Radio 3, 27 October 2002) reverses conventional expectations that it is the Queen of Egypt who may appropriately be played by a black performer. Productions may also introduce "raced" voices thematically. In *Troilus and Cressida* (Radio 3, 30 October 2005) the difference between the two camps was portrayed by casting the Trojans with black actors, the Greeks by white ones; setting *Twelfth Night* on a Caribbean island created a whole musical and social environment (World Service, 31 March 1993), whilst the travels of Pericles took place in a "world" culture of different accents designed to chime with the production's "world music" score (*Pericles*, Radio 3, 27 November 2005). And in 2005 the BBC tried to safeguard its future audience by giving children the opportunity and support to make "60 Second" versions of Shakespeare in audio as well as video.

Shakespeare's lives and afterlives on radio

Right from its earliest days, under the leadership of Gielgud and others, those responsible for radio drama saw the BBC as an auteur's medium, encouraging new and experimental writing for an evolving art form in an environment graced by frequent productions of the world's classic drama. Writers who were being "nursed" into their new profession sometimes took Shakespeare as their subject matter in order to reflect on the processes of authorship itself. It was also the "private" and "intimate" aspects of the radio experience, as well as the hallowed rite of celebrating Shakespeare's "birthday," that has turned biographical drama about him into a key sub-genre within radio drama – one lampooned as "an imperishable genre known as Important Historical Figures In Their Dotage, in which the voice of The Old Master can be intercut with scenes from his early life, strong on recalled mistresses and prospective biographers."[44] Such plays often reflected the popular biographical traditions and narratives prevalent in other media and identified by Lanier in his chapter in this volume under the following headings: the "Shakespeare country" or "Stratford" motif, in which Shakespeare and his writing are shown to be shaped by a nostalgically conceived rural England of the past; the "literary legacy," in which his characters come to life; the "erotic muse" narrative, in which poetic power springs from sexual passion; and portrayals of his "life in theatre," a more varied and often less "personalized" genre, with the potential to be used for interrogation and critique of other performative modes.[45] It is significant, therefore, that it is this last biographical narrative that has been most frequently commissioned by the BBC.

Often these commissions were directed – and sometimes acted in – by those who were themselves also adapting and producing Shakespeare's plays for production, so they became both an additional form of background or applied research and a mode of self-reflection on the director's, as well as writer's, craft. In addition this stress on the Bard's personal history helped to shape the sense of the BBC radio drama world as one peopled by Shakespeare himself as well as his characters. The actors cast as Shakespeare also tended either to be already identified with Shakespearean performance on radio, or in the theatre, from where most of the early plays were borrowed. Clemence Dane's wordy blank-verse stage play *Will Shakespeare* – in which Mary Fitton, identified as the "Dark Lady" of the Sonnets, two-times Shakespeare with Marlowe, whom the Bard accidentally kills – was given a production in which Val Gielgud himself played Shakespeare (Home, 23 August 1947). Bernard Shaw's *The*

Dark Lady of the Sonnets was scheduled as a "birthday week" production on 22 April 1939, and featured the film star Robert Donat as Shakespeare and a new Prologue written and spoken by Shaw himself. Donat's casting at this time might have been especially welcomed as conveying a sense of his commitment to Britain as well as the significance of Shakespeare on the eve of war.[46] Specially commissioned radio biographies were in evidence even earlier, most of them celebrating Shakespeare as a national hero and manifestation of "Englishness," but some were also significant contributions to the developing forms of radio drama. As early as 1928 L. du Garde Peach wrote a "ballad opera," *Up the River*, which narrated a "merrie England" version of the life and times of Shakespeare, but his later plays for children, such as *Will Shakespeare of Stratford* (Home, 23 April 1939) and *St. George's Day* (Home, 23 April 1948) also about Shakespeare (and followed by a talk on the Order of the Garter), despite their conventional patriotic agendas, are credited with helping to shift speech styles in historical drama away from a "pageant style of diction ... closer to everyday contemporary speech."[47] *Shakespeare's Country* (Home Service, 27 June 1948) was another play for the Children's Hour, which linked Shakespeare and the English landscape by tracing a journey by Shakespeare's company through the shires, complete with a specially drawn map in the *Radio Times* to use while listening. The regions also laid claim to their own versions of the Bard by emphasizing the importance of accent on radio, as in P. H. Burton's *Master Shakespeare and Glendower* (Wales, 27 May 1938), described in the *Radio Times* as "part fact – part fancy," which purported to explain the strong Welsh elements in *Henry IV, Part 1*, by telling the story of the first production and introducing the Welsh mayor of Stratford.

Shakespeare was also likely to pop up as a character in plays about his rivals, such as Mary Hope Allen's production, *O Rare Ben Jonson* (12 August 1945) by L. A. Strong, himself an adaptor of the plays, which also features several of Jonson's (and Shakespeare's) fellow-playwrights. Once the Third Programme began in 1946, it tended to encourage drama or features exploring more esoteric or overtly intellectual aspects of the plays and their possible interpretations rather than "straight" (and popular) biographical drama. One exception, which, however, significantly uprooted Shakespeare from his native shore, was *The Great Desire I Had: Shakespeare and Italy* (Third Programme, 15 October 1952). The poet, critic, and translator of European drama Henry Reed presented a semi-autobiographical portrait of the artist "Guglielmo Shakespeare" as a young man journeying through Italy, who is fired by the ambition to write a great poem about the siege of Troy, but after encounters with a *commedia dell'arte* company and a local ruler, realizes that his future, as well as that of his treatment of the Troy story, lies in the theatre.[48]

By contrast, thirty years later *I, William Shakespeare* (Radio 4, 22 April 1982), by the Oxford don, John Wilders, took the form of "imagined scenes from a documentary life" which kept the Bard safely domesticated in his local habitats of Stratford and London. Shakespeare was played by Martin Jarvis, an actor who would later come to personify a mellifluous and ubiquitous "radio voice" much satirized in radio comedy impressions shows such as *Dead Ringers*. Reviewing John Powell's production, Martin Dodsworth found it an old-fashioned "Elizabethan spectacular," which avoided any kind of "materialist" reading of Shakespeare's role in the political economy of his times.

> For radio folk it is a fine radio occasion – plenty of gusts of wind, bells ringing, lads singing, men quarrelling, quills scratching – and it all rattles along at a good pace ... This is the sentimentalist's Shakespeare. The programme can't be taken seriously but, in its way, it is fun. All those quotations to place! It is a kind of game after all, a pageant in celebration. It wouldn't do to question the naïve apparent premise of this use of quotations; that there was no work, no application to his art on Shakespeare's part, but that he just took his lines from life ... It is all native woodnotes wild ...[49]

It might be assumed that the quantity of plays dramatizing various aspects of Shakespeare's personal, theatrical, or artistic life represent radio's nostalgia for the "force" of theatrical performance (especially after radio drama ceased to be a "live" production). A gentle adaptation of Susan Cooper's time-travel children's novel *King of Shadows* (Radio 4, 20 March 2003), which moves between contemporary rehearsals at the replica Globe on the South Bank and preparations for the first performance of *A Midsummer Night's Dream*, appears to fit this categorization. However, this meta-dramatic genre has also given rise to much darker and more challenging work. Don Taylor wrote and directed his own play *Merely Players* (Radio 4, 29 April 1996), which dealt with the special performance of *Richard II*, commissioned by supporters of the Earl of Essex on the eve of his rebellion, and portrayed a sexually passionate but politically cautious Shakespeare (Michael Pennington). Another theatrically focused play, concerned with sexual politics rather than conspiracies of state, was Peter Straughan's *When We Were Queens* (Radio 4, 28 April 1999), adapted by the BBC as a result of his winning the Alfred Bradley Bursary Award for radio drama. Although Shakespeare's words threaded through this harrowing portrayal of the physically and sexually abused boy players in his company who competed for the roles of Ophelia and Cordelia, this was far from a "sentimentalist's" portrayal of his theatre but a "brave and moving enterprise" which did not shirk from portraying the brutality out of which performance emerged.[50] Gary Bleasdale, the actor son of the celebrated television writer

Alan Bleasdale, also reflected bleakly on success and in-family rivalry in a play about Shakespeare's unsuccessful younger brother, also an actor, down and out on the eve of his death, in *A Song for Edmond Shakespeare* (Radio 4, 7 January 2005).

Several plays about famous forgeries and competing theories of authorship portray the Shakespearean oeuvre as unstable rather than monumentally secure. A. Gill's *The Man Who Wrote Shakespeare* (20 April 1978; rebroadcast 23 April 1981), like a number of other novels and plays set questions of authorship within the framework of police investigation, and alternated between the twentieth and sixteenth centuries. The psychoanalytic tendency evident as early as the 1930s in talks about Shakespeare and later productions of the plays has also inevitably fed into the biographical drama, which extends its interest to Shakespeare's family, especially, post feminism, to the women. His "unsatisfactory" youngest daughter was the subject of Nan Woodhouse's play *Judith Shakespeare* (Radio 4, 25 April 1996), and Robert Nye's novel *Mrs. Shakespeare* was adapted as a sex-romping Afternoon Play (Radio 4, 23 April 1998) starring Maggie Steed. Still psychologically focused but more ambitious in its portrayal of Shakespeare's relation to the ideas and politics of his time was David Pownall's *Dreams and Censorship* (Radio 3, 7 February 1993). A "think-piece about the ways that literature can answer to common dreams and fantasies, and dreams can respond to life"[51] it imagined Shakespeare (Edward Petherbridge), a year before the staging of *The Tempest*, invading the deliberations of the Oxford committee finalizing the King James Bible for publication in 1610 in order to voice on behalf of James I anxieties concerning parts of the translated Book of Revelation which depict the destruction of kings, and whose apocalyptic imagery might encourage the people to think the unthinkable and dream of revolution. The debate about censorship, and a royal performance of the play which the clerics have written about St. John on the island of Patmos composing his visionary work, move James, perhaps unwisely, to allow the apocalyptic passages to stay, whilst Shakespeare finds inspiration for *The Tempest*.

Pownall was also responsible for perhaps the most interesting example of BBC biographical drama-cum-media allegory, which also returns to the subject of censorship. *An Epiphanous Use of the Microphone* (Radio 4, 15 May 1998) was commissioned to mark the seventy-fifth anniversary of the 1923 broadcast of *Twelfth Night*.[52] Pownall's play moves between the *Twelfth Night* rehearsals at the BBC's new Savoy Hill studio, under the steely command of John Reith (Crawford Logan), and the first recorded performance of the play by the Lord Chamberlain's Men at the Middle Temple in 1602. Shakespeare (Michael Maloney) is on edge at the prospect of Queen Elizabeth (Anna Massey) joining the audience, since the play's portrayal of

Malvolio's impertinent courtship of Olivia may be taken as reference to her favorite, the Earl of Essex, who has just been executed. Whilst the BBC cast and crew struggle with the challenges of inventing appropriate acting and production styles for what Reith calls "the most difficult play of Shakespeare to make work on radio," Pownall engineers a situation which requires Shakespeare's company to perform in total darkness, a state that matches the Queen's personal mood of desolation and betrayal. Their performance in effect becomes the equivalent of the dramatic experiment in unseen Shakespeare being embarked on at the BBC in the 1920s. The play's main subject is the Reithian founding myth, which proposed the BBC not only as the inheritor and guardian of the values embodied in the Shakespearean drama, but as a kind of new media messiah, whose transforming vision will create a new kind of society. Taking a lead from the title of Shakespeare's play, Pownall plays with allusions to "epiphany," most obviously in his own title, but also in Reith's speech on the "gifts" that broadcasting represents and the "star" in the world firmament that the new BBC will become. Although it celebrates Reith's vision that "this is theatre for *all* the people, not a few," it also shows him ruthlessly cutting the play-wright's text to the needs of the medium and seeking consensus and accommodation with his political masters, in order to stage an interpretation of *Twelfth Night* as "Shakespeare's attack on the visual."[53]

Less attuned to media politics but also linked with the biographically based plays are those that deal with Shakespeare's afterlife, myth, and industry, often also used as a pretext for the exploration of characters' personal memories or self-discoveries. Helen Cross's Afternoon Play *One Day* (Radio 4, 19 April 2000; repeated 22 April 2004) explored the significance of Elizabeth Scott's architectural achievement in designing the Stratford Memorial Theatre in the lives of three women visitors, while in *Sweet William* (Radio 4, 29 November 1993) Peter Thomson made Stratford the site for a son and father to come together through their enthusiasm for the Bard. One of the scenes of seduction in Timberlake Wertenbaker's play of the same name rewrote the wooing scene between Henry and Katherine as a *coup du foudre* between a young Frenchwoman (Harriet Walter) and an English actor (Michael Maloney again) playing the lead role in *Henry V* in Paris (*Afternoon Play: Scenes of Seduction*, Radio 4, 7 March 2005). In Georgia Finch's *Romeo And Juliet in Southwark* (Radio 3, 12 September 2004) a cross-racial love affair took place against the backdrop of a performance of Shakespeare's tragedy at the new Globe.

These last two plays could also be categorized as "derivatives," plays which take up a character or aspect of a Shakespearean work and create a new play around it. Although some do little more than keep alive the nineteenth-century theatre's tradition of Shakespearean burlesques aimed at a middle-class audience, others, especially those which were broadcast on the Third Programme and Radio 3, took their fun more seriously. Here *Hamlet* emerged as something of a Coleridge-type fixation. The novelist Erik Linklater introduced the series *Imaginary Conversations*, a "fluid" and indeed novelistic radio genre with "no fixed convention," designed to "convey the thinking and emotions of their chosen subjects and to present them through their living voice."[54] In the first year of the Third's existence G. W. Stonier explored the reasons for Ophelia's madness in a special commission which was part of a "birthday week" season and towards the end of the 1940s there were several *Hamlet*-related programs, including *The Hawk and the Handsaw* (19 November 1948) by the academic and crime-writer, Michael Innes. The following year saw a version of James Joyce's *The Second-Best Bed: A Usyless Discussion on Hamlet or Hamnet* (2 January 1949), another Hamlet "conversation" by the experimental novelist, Rayner Heppenstall, and a collaboration with Innes, *The Mysterious Affair at Elsinore: A New Investigation*, (26 June 1949). *The Fool's Stage – Hamlet in Scandinavia*, also by Heppenstall, was broadcast a day later (27 June 1949). This introspective "literary" fashion appears to have run its course by the mid-fifties with a translation of Jules Laforgue's *Hamlet; or, The Consequences of Filial Piety*, by Henry Reed (20 June 1954).

By the 1960s BBC radio was feeling the effects of television's rising popularity and theft of listeners, and a consequent perception that radio was becoming the preserve of the highbrows, the traditionalists, or the older generation. Although the Drama Department continued to promote itself as the playwrights' patron it wasn't until towards the end of the next decade that Shakespeare re-emerged strongly as subject matter and citation in plays, apparently revitalized by writers aiming at, or having already achieved, careers in the theatre. The potential that Shakespearean meta-dramatic reference can have as a vehicle for authorizing political comment and self-reflection on the radio medium is most vividly illustrated by one of the BBC's most acclaimed radio plays. *Pearl* (Radio 4, 3 July 1978) by John Arden, was written and broadcast as a Monday Play for radio, following his abandonment of theatre in the wake of an unhappy experience working with the Royal Shakespeare Company. It portrays the writing and performance of a play intended to inspire the overthrow of Charles I by Parliamentarians and the end of English rule in Ireland, and opens with a performance of *Julius Caesar*. However, the radical goals of the play's authors, a playwright in the tradition of Shakespeare and a young woman of half-Irish, half-Native American descent (both roles clearly standing for Arden and his wife and collaborator Margaretta D'Arcy) are sabotaged by royalists, who introduce distracting spectacle and pornography into the production.[55] Radio, the play suggests, is now the only medium where political theatre can be authentically performed.

In the same year that *Pearl* was first put on Tom Stoppard's *Rosencrantz and Guildenstern are Dead* was given a Christmas Eve performance on Radio 3, and another Pownall play, *Richard III Part Two* (Radio 4, 2 July 1978) was broadcast. This had already been staged by the Paines Plough theatre company, established to encourage new writing, the previous year. Like Pownall's subsequent Shakespeare plays it made the most of radio drama's ability to move fluidly between past, present, and future, and implicitly explored the nature of the radio medium, by juxtaposing George Orwell's work in 1948 at the BBC (the model for his "Ministry of Truth" in *1984*), with the dystopian future ruled by Big Brother that the novel portrays, and Richard III in 1484, a year before his death at Bosworth would leave him to be demonized in future historical accounts – including of course Shakespeare's own play – by Tudor propaganda. More recently Snoo Wilson's *Hippomania* mixed a surreal brew featuring the poet John Benjamin as a spy in wartime Dublin encountering Laurence Olivier at work on his film of *Henry V* and Irish fairies who speak in blank verse (Radio 3, 26 September 2004).

Also in a lighter vein are several plays by the American Perry Pontac which have taken comic angles on Shakespeare's best-known plays in pastiche blank verse. Amusing though these modern burlesques undoubtedly are they require familiarity with the plays for the jokes fully to work. *Hamlet, Part II* (Radio 3, 27 April 1992) was a sequel to the play scheduled the day after Kenneth Branagh's much hyped performance in the Renaissance Theatre production of the play. It portrays a returning ambassador (Peter Jeffrey) arriving to discover that everyone, even those who survive in Shakespeare's play, is dead. With the help of the palace librarian (Harriet Walter) and the Fool (Simon Russell Beale) he mounts his own claim to the throne – having ruled out that of a remote Scottish cousin, Macbeth – but is murdered by the Ghost. *Prince Lear* (Radio 4, 18 November 1994) as the title suggests, tells the story of Lear when young, and answers the question of what happened to the mother of Goneril, Regan, and Cordelia by portraying him falling in love with everyone, until she commits suicide out of jealousy, whereupon he proposes to Kent, who turns out to be a girl in disguise. It was aired later in the same year as the production of *King Lear* starring John Gielgud, enabling John Moffat to mimic his fluting tones. *Fatal Loins: Romeo and Juliet Reconsidered* (Radio 4, 29 October 2001) is also a sequel, telling the story of what might have happened if the friar's letter had been delivered, and the lovers lived. Predictably – since this is a comedy – the great romance has dwindled into bickering family life, destroyed by children, Juliet's weight gain, and Romeo's infidelity. The Friar (John Moffatt, who also played Lear in 1994) and Nurse (Pam Ferris) meddle again to try and reignite the spark of passion. Other productions extracted characters from the original plays with different effects. *Shakespeare's Fools* (Radio 3, 31 December 2000) highlighted the complex nature of comic performance in a relay from Wilton's Music Hall, whilst John Morrison's Afternoon Play, *Macmorris* (Radio 4, 4 October, 2004) imagined the Irish captain who plays a minor role in *Henry V* leading an anarchic uprising of other characters demanding to be made more central to their plays.

Conclusion

This brief overview of the British radio drama "Shakespeare experience" confirms some of Lanier's findings about the mediating effects of recorded Shakespeare.[56] Here, too, "interiorization" and "privatization" are key aspects, although a medium that is still currently free at the point of use does not blatantly advertise its "commodification," other than in the sale of recordings of its productions and the occasional special publication. Whether the ability to create one's own digital archive of Shakespearean greatest hits (blank verse to jog by, perhaps) will in time generate a greater sense of radio Shakespeare as a personal possession, equivalent to a set of books or prized record collection, still remains to be seen. "Textualization" is also less in evidence, despite reviewers quite frequently judging the success or failure of a radio adaptation by whether they have had to follow it in the printed version. What is also evident is that the self-identification of BBC broadcasting with Shakespeare throughout its history has in turn generated a number of "meta-radio" plays which interrogate its nature, role, and relation with other media, whether through the figure of Shakespeare himself or his works. Parallel patterns are almost certainly to be found in radio comedy and features. What I hope also emerges is the extent to which Shakespeare has indeed been heard, if not always listened to. As soon as technology allowed, radio turned itself into a mobile medium, a ready companion whenever required. Perhaps surprisingly, and in surprising ways, it has often made a regular personal companion of Shakespeare too.

NOTES

1. Patrick Barlow, *Shakespeare: The Truth* (London: Routledge, 1993), p. 185. This parody of Shakespearean scholarship was transmitted on radio as *Desmond Olivier Dingle's Compleat Life and Works of William or, "Shakespeare, the Truth"* (dir. Hilary Norwich, Radio 4, 6 September 1995).
2. Robert Hanks, "Apocalypse Then," *Independent*, 9 February 1993, p. 14.
3. Tim Crook, *British Radio Drama – A Case Study History*, www.irdp.co.uk/britrad6.htm.

4. Douglas Lanier, "Shakespeare on the Record," in Barbara Hodgdon and William B. Worthen (eds.), *A Companion to Shakespeare and Performance* (Oxford: Blackwell, 2005), pp. 415–36, p. 418. I am grateful to Douglas Lanier for allowing me to read his essay prior to publication.

5. See John Drakakis, "Introduction," in *British Radio Drama*, ed. John Drakakis (Cambridge: Cambridge University Press, 1981), pp. 1–36, and "The Essence that is Not Seen: Radio Adaptations of Stage Plays," in *Radio Drama*, ed. Peter Lewis (London and New York: Longman, 1981), pp. 111–33; Douglas Lanier, "WSHX: Shakespeare and American Radio," in *Shakespeare After Mass Media*, ed. Richard Burt (Basingstoke: Palgrave, 2002), pp. 195–219, and "Shakespeare on the Record," pp. 415–36; Bruce, R. Smith, *The Acoustic World of Early Modern England: Attending to the O-Factor* (Chicago and London: University of Chicago Press, 1999); Wes Folkerth, *The Sound of Shakespeare* (London: Routledge, 2002). I must also acknowledge here the generous assistance of Michael P. Jensen, who shared with me his extensive research on Shakespeare-related broadcasts worldwide.

6. Graham Holderness, "Boxing the Bard: Shakespeare and Television," in *The Shakespeare Myth*, ed. Graham Holderness (Manchester: Manchester University Press, 1988), pp. 173–89, p. 178.

7. Drakakis, "Introduction," p. 2.

8. Peter Donaldson, "'In Fair Verona': Media, Spectacle, and Performance in *William Shakespeare's Romeo + Juliet*," in Burt, *Shakespeare After Mass Media*, pp. 59–81, pp. 59–61.

9. John Drakakis, "Theatre, Ideology, and Institution: Shakespeare and the Roadsweepers," in Holderness, *The Shakespeare Myth*, pp. 24–41, p. 24.

10. *Ibid.*, p. 25.

11. Ian McMillan, "Shakespeare Rules Britain" (Radio 4, *Today* Program, 15 December 2005). I am grateful to Ian McMillan for giving me permission to quote from it.

12. Paddy Scannell, *Radio, Television, and Modern Life* (Oxford, Blackwell, 1996), p. 165.

13. *Ibid.*, p. 164.

14. *Ibid.*, pp. 163, 167.

15. See the entries on "Radio" in *Shakespeares After Shakespeare: An Encyclopedia of the Bard in Mass and Popular Culture*, ed. Richard Burt (Westport, CT: Greenwood Press, 2006). The British Universities Film and Video Council will complete an online database of audio-visual Shakespeare by 2008.

16. Lanier, "WSHX," p. 198.

17. *Ibid.*, p. 199.

18. J. C. W. Reith, *Broadcast Over Britain* (London: Hodder and Stoughton, 1924), p. 168; Andrew Crissell, *An Introductory History of British Broadcasting*, 2nd edn (London: Routledge, 1997), p. 34.

19. Lanier, "WSHX," p. 198.

20. David Cardiff and Paddy Scannell, *A Social History of British Broadcasting: Volume One 1922–1939: Serving the Nation* (Oxford: Basil Blackwell, 1991), pp. 277, 278.

21. *Ibid.*

22. G. Carleton Pearl, "The Stage Still Learns from Radio," *Radio Times*, 16 September 1938, p. 17.

23. See Alan Beck, *"The Invisible Play." B.B.C. Radio Drama 1922–1928*, published by *Sound Journal*, online publication (2000) www.kent.ac.uk/sdfva/invisibleplay/index.html.

24. John S. Woods, "The Radio Highbrows," *Radio Times*, 15 January 1937, p. 10.

25. Lanier, "WSHX," p. 198.

26. Val Gielgud, *The Listener*, 10 March 1937, p. 250.

27. David Cardiff, "Mass Middlebrow Laughter: The Origins of BBC Comedy," *Media, Culture and Society* 10 (1988), 41–60, pp. 43–44.

28. Lanier, "WXHX," p. 203.

29. *Ibid.*, p. 208.

30. See Martin Esslin, "The Mind as a Stage," *Theatre Quarterly* 1:3 (1971), 5–11; Frances Gray and Janet Bray, "The Mind as Theatre: Radio Drama since 1971," *New Theatre Quarterly* 1:3 (1985), 292–300; Tim Crook, *Radio Drama: Theory and Practice* (London: Routledge, 1999).

31. Tyrone Guthrie, *The Squirrel's Cage and Two Other Microphone Plays* (London: Cobden-Sanderson, 1931), p. 9.

32. Clive Cazeaux, "Phenomonology and Radio Drama," *British Journal of Aesthetics* 45:2 (2005), 157–74, p. 158.

33. *Ibid*, p. 169.

34. *Ibid*, p. 173.

35. William Stanton, "The Invisible Theatre of Radio Drama," *Critical Quarterly* 46:4 (2004), 94–107, p. 103.

36. *Ibid*, p. 105.

37. *Ibid*, p. 104.

38. *Ibid*, p. 99.

39. This estimate was completed at the end of 2005.

40. E. M. W. Tillyard, "Shakespeare's Chronicle Plays ... Our Nearest Approach to a National Epic," *Radio Times*, 3 October 1947, p. 4.

41. Humphrey Carpenter, *The Envy of the World: Fifty Years of the Third Programme and Radio 3, 1946–1996* (London: Weidenfeld and Nicolson, 1996), p. 92.

42. John Drummond, cited in *ibid.*, p. 329.

43. BBC 7 repeated *Much Ado About Nothing* and *Macbeth* as part of the "ShakespeaRe-Told" radio and television season, November 2005.

44. Martin Cropper, "Hunger Through the Headphones," *The Times*, (15 January 1991).

45. See Lanier in this volume, pp. 93–113.

46. Donat's star status and success in American-financed films would have made it easy for him to spend the war in the USA, but he chose to stay in Britain.

47. Ian Rodger, *Radio Drama* (London and Basingstoke: Macmillan, 1982), pp. 34–35.

48. Henry Reed, *The Streets of Pompeii and Other Plays for Radio* (London: BBC Publications, 1971).

49. Martin Dodsworth, "I, William Shakespeare," *Times Literary Supplement*, 23 April 1982, p. 460.

50. Martin Hoyle, "Baptists and Thespians," *Financial Times*, 1 May 1999, p. 6.

51. Hanks, "Apocalypse Then," p. 14.

52. David Pownall, *An Epiphanous Use of The Microphone*, dir. Martin Jenkins (BBC Radio 4, 15 May 1998). Published in David Pownall, *Radio Plays – An*

Epiphanous Use of The Microphone, Beef, Ploughboy Monday, Flos, Kitty Wilkinson, Under the Table (London: Oberon Books, 1998).

53. Pownall, *An Epiphanous Use*, pp. 52, 42, 51.
54. Douglas Cleverdon, *The Art of Radio in Britain*, unpublished monograph for UNESCO, cited in Rodger, *Radio Drama*, p. 81.
55. John Arden, *The Monday Play: Pearl*, dir. Alfred Bradley (BBC Radio 3, 3 July 1978). Published in John Arden, *Pearl: A Play about a Play within a Play* (London: Eyre Methuen, 1970).
56. Lanier, "Shakespeare on the Record," p. 417.

10

NICOLA J. WATSON

Shakespeare on the tourist trail

One side-effect of the increasing veneration of Shakespeare over the course of the eighteenth century – a period that turned Shakespeare from a rough untutored playwright of incidental "beauties" into the National Poet – was the first stirrings of the Stratford tourist industry as we know and love it today. To visit Stratford-upon-Avon today is to visit Shakespeare's town, set in the heart of Shakespeare Country. Indeed, Stratford has been Shakespeare's town for the better part of two centuries, even though the euphoric road signs announcing this are of relatively recent date. The sheer extravagance of the tourist industry in Stratford would seem to a skeptical glance to have developed in defiance of likelihood; on the evidence of his plays and poems (with the exception of the history plays), Shakespeare had little interest in real locations realistically portrayed, and certainly none at all in the area around Stratford – the chief exception being Sly's offhand reference to "Marian Hacket, the fat alewife of Wincot" (Wincot being a village in the environs of Stratford) in the Induction to *The Taming of the Shrew*. Moreover, the relative scantiness of Shakespeare's biographical record prior to his London fame and fortune, and its thoroughly unromantic documentation of his thrifty prosperity thereafter, might equally and reasonably have damped the spirit of literary pilgrimage. Yet Stratford, an unremarkable and rundown little market town, came as a result of eighteenth-century bardolatry to be looked at differently, and eventually actually to look different. Shakespeare, too, has come to look different as tourism has established itself as one of the principal means by which popular culture understands and exploits him.

The obvious explanation of why it was that Stratford developed into a literary shrine is simply that it was where Shakespeare, the greatest dramatic poet of his time and since, was born and buried. (Nor, briefly to be pragmatic, did it hurt that over the course of the eighteenth century the growth of Birmingham resulted in the improvement of the road up from London.)[1] But this explanation begs as many questions as it appears to answer. Why should it be of the slightest interest where a dramatist was buried? And still less, where he was born? The conventional answer to this conundrum has been that literary pilgrimage is modeled upon religious pilgrimage, and that with the decline of religious sensibility came the secularization of pilgrimage and the replacement of the saint and his or her holy and healing places with the author's homes and haunts. It is certainly true that the literary pilgrimage takes over much of the language, protocols, and emotional structures of the religious pilgrimage, as Péter Dávidházi has shown.[2] Yet this observation does not in itself explain the desire to substitute places associated with writers' bodies for those associated with saints. This desire is typically taken for granted by modern travelers, with literary pilgrims commonly speaking of their wish to "get closer" to the writer, as though assuming that by visiting the haunts of Shakespeare they will access the "real" Shakespeare. One way of glossing this impulse is to suggest that the literary pilgrim aspires to assuage an uneasy sense of the mass-produced and secondary nature of the text through which the author is otherwise apprehended, grounding the relationship between author and reader by an unmediated one-to-one spiritual telephone call. They will found their reading experience on a more inarguably physical and personal experience. The virtuality of print culture and of the reading experience itself will be grounded in place and occasion.

Yet looked at historically the very opposite is true. Although the pilgrim's desire to bypass or supplement the author's incarnation in mass print culture necessarily denies this, Shakespeare's Stratford did not in practice precede print culture but, rather, was created by it. The growing desire to visit Stratford is virtually contemporaneous with Nicholas Rowe's great edition of the plays, which he prefaced with a groundbreaking biography, and published in 1709.[3] Rowe's edition had, in this context, two major effects. It participated in the removal of Shakespeare's plays from the stage to the page, extending the experience of "Shakespeare" from the theatrical and communal to the individual reader's silent and isolated communion with print in closet and drawing-room. And, in conforming to the biographical imperative of providing dates and places of birth and death, it located Shakespeare not primarily in the London theatre but in the provincial town of Stratford. The story of the development of "Shakespeare country" which I will trace in this essay is the story of the rise and elaboration of this biographically driven urge to imprint the virtual, readerly experience of Shakespeare onto topographical reality – most emphatically in a market town on the edge of the Cotswolds, but latterly in London and well beyond. It is the story of how the Forest of Arden slowly but surely sprouted snippets of Shakespeare tacked to trees, of how Bankside came to be sprinkled with plaques showing his head, of how a balcony in Verona came to be captioned with the Bard's lines.

Stratford now

Where his first infant lays sweet SHAKSPEARE *sung* ...[4]
*Upon entering the town of Stratford, a feeling, I trust, something more elevated
than that of mere curiosity, naturally directs the steps of every admirer of our
divine Poet towards that spot which gave birth to the most extraordinary
genius this or any other country has ever produced* ...[5]

Stratford today is the product of two centuries of development, and its emotional affect is recognizably derived from those offered to and described by the nineteenth-century visitor. "Doing" Stratford is an exercise in spatialized biography, a tour through time between the Bard's birth and death. Accordingly, the neophyte is most likely to start at the Birthplace.[6] Entry at present is through a cunningly designed portal exhibition, redesigned in April 2000, through which the visitor is acclimatized to a provincial Tudor past which supposedly infuses the plays and provides a backdrop for what biographical detail we have about Shakespeare. Seduced by a discreet and ever-changing soundscape accompanying large visual displays, we are inducted into a locality peopled by constables like the ones in *Much Ado About Nothing*, by many different tradespeople such as those featured in *A Midsummer Night's Dream*, and by traveling players who "probably" provided the young Shakespeare with his first contact with the theatrical world. It is a world enlivened by spectacular local events such as the visit of Queen Elizabeth to Kenilworth in 1575, "possibly remembered ... years later when [Shakespeare] wrote *A Midsummer Night's Dream*." The whole dramatizes Stratford as both epitomizing and embosomed in "Shakespeare's countryside," and as energizing the plays in general and in particular: "his plays and poems abound with references to rural characters, country customs, wild flowers, animals and birds."[7] In keeping with this pastoral aesthetic, the visitor enters the Birthplace proper through a garden, planted up with flowers and herbs mentioned in the works. The Birthplace itself is displayed principally as a house, rather than as a museum, conspicuously free on the whole of print information, which is instead confined to a room containing displays telling the history of the Birthplace itself. Here can be seen details of the visit of John Adams and Thomas Jefferson in 1786, the first visitors' book from 1812, the collection of *Extemporary Verses, written at the Birthplace of Shakespeare at Stratford-upon-Avon by People of Genius* ... (1818) made up by the then owner of the Birthplace, Mary Hornby, visitor statistics then and now, and the famous window from the "birthroom" (so-called from the early nineteenth century, though the term is more redolent of obstetrics than of belles-lettres), which preserves what remains of the sanctioned practice of graffiti indulged in by some of the earliest visitors, including Sir Walter Scott. Even this room is principally designed not so much as a museum as a warm-up act, demonstrating the importance past celebrities have accorded to their visits. Depictions of the birthroom emphasize this as well, though apparently in contradictory ways: a photograph taken in 1882 is included largely to illustrate previous visitors' practice of scrawling their signatures upon the whitewashed walls, whereas the painting *In Shakespeare's House, Stratford-upon-Avon* by Edwin Landseer and Henry Wallis emphasizes the romantic emptiness of the room, instinct with future genius signified by the casual litter of a shield, a skull, a spade, a rat, a glove, a dog, and a Bible. The room itself ("please turn off your mobile phones!") is consciously empty and blandly domestic, down to the cradle standing by the bed.

To visit the Birthplace nowadays is thus explicitly to recapitulate two and a half centuries of previous pilgrimage and yet to come to an empty silent space, potential, secretive, and blank, signifying the space or time before "Shakespeare," before there was anything to remember. To visit the next stop on a conventional, biographically organized pilgrimage around the Shakespeare Properties, Anne Hathaway's Cottage, out in the village of Shottery, is also to visit context prior to text, but in a yet more domestic, privatized, and feminised mode, as befits a place which has traditionally been associated with young love. Enfolded lavishly within an idea of an English cottage garden reminiscent of thirties embroidered tea-tray cloths, a garden fluffed up with hydrangea, goldenrod, marguerite, and lavatera, punctuated by thistle, box, and hollyhocks, and scented with roses, nicotiana, and verbena, Anne Hathaway's Cottage exemplifies air-brushed English rural charm, and is emphatically feminine in presentation. Guides in the first room sing paeans to its cunning domestic conveniences; it is enviably housekept down to the last sprig of rosemary laid out in blazing pewter. Shining with beeswax, the artifacts on display all speak of women's work: butter pats, pattens, milking stools, an iron, lace-making equipment, a linen-press, a nursing-chair, and samplers. The annexed exhibition also chronicles the history of delight in Shakespearean domesticity by means of a case of antique souvenirs, which include a nineteenth-century biscuit-ware model of the cottage, a cottage-shaped musical-box, a late nineteenth-century trinket chest with a painting of the Cottage on the lid, and an early twentieth-century souvenir bust of Anne. In keeping with this ethos visitors are then solicited to buy pretty views of the Cottage variously stamped on birthday cards, jig-saws, trays, mats, coasters, a tea-cosy, china boxes, and tea-towels, and, less obviously branded but part of a more general romance of housekeeping, aprons, lavender, lace, pewter plates, and most seductive and impractical of all, "beeswax furniture polish as used in the Shakespeare Houses." Although the famous settle upon which Victorians reverently supposed Shakespeare to have courted his bride-to-be is nowadays deliberately downgraded in importance by allowing tourists to sit upon it, the Cottage remains associated with courting, and this is summed up in the prevalence of depictions of the Cottage in spring and early summer. Both Cottage and Birthplace in their different ways therefore celebrate source and potential rather than achievement, fame, or status, and both see them as provincial, rural, and above all, richly fertile, or so the gardens crammed to bursting with plants manage to suggest. More than merely virtuoso exercises in herbaceous planting with a historical twist, the physicality of these gardens acts as an uncaptioned analogy linking the fecundity of generation with literary procreation. Indeed, the effort made more recently to import a more explicit sense of Shakespeare's texts into the tourist experience by peopling the orchard attached to the Cottage with awkward sculptures representing the plays, only serves to point up the greater reticence and thus greater charm and convincingness of both the Birthplace and the Cottage in this respect.

The indefatigable tourist, with or without souvenir beeswax polish purchased for future use, would now return to Stratford to see Nash's House (famous solely for being next door to the site of the now vanished New Place, Shakespeare's own house), Hall's Croft (home of the more respectable of Shakespeare's sons-in-law), and then perhaps foray out to Wilmcote to see Mary Arden's House (the former home of Shakespeare's mother, only identified as such in 2001), and perhaps also the house formerly known as Mary Arden's House, which still serves as The Shakespeare Countryside Museum. They might then take tea to recruit their strength for the evening's performance of Shakespeare at the Royal Shakespeare Theatre or its satellites (though many more tourists visit Stratford than its theatres), before perhaps paying a visit to Shakespeare's grave. But I suggest instead a pause for breath at this juncture. We have taken a look at the two properties that, with the exception of Shakespeare's tomb itself, have had the longest history as Stratford tourist sites. The history of the development of these three sites into the core of the present-day tourist experience of Stratford through their representation and reproduction is the subject of my next section.

Stratford then

The site that originally attracted visitors was Shakespeare's tomb and monument, and it is the first to be illustrated, in Sir William Dugdale's *Antiquities of Warwickshire* (1656). In 1737 the artist and antiquary George Vertue made a visit, and, in addition to sketching the monument, commissioned a local sculptor to make him a cast to display at home, the first ever souvenir reproduction.[8] He was by no means alone in his desire to appropriate the piece, for by that time the monument was in a poor state of repair, thanks to the vandalism of a growing number of relic-hunters. Monies were therefore raised to restore it in 1748, a first restoration that would be overtaken in 1793 when Edmond Malone, the age's most influential Shakespeare editor, notoriously persuaded the vicar to paint the colored bust stone-color, so as to render it, as he thought, more as it must have been originally.[9] By 1824 it was commonplace to scrawl a signature upon the bust – a practice presumably facilitated by the whitewash and which is clearly related to a desire for one-to-one emotional exchange between writer and reader.[10] If you could not take away a piece of the bust, presumably the alternative was to leave your mark – both were forms of appropriation. Later in the century, there would be many and variously priced souvenir reproductions of the monument offered for sale in Stratford to meet the demand for an artifact to certify the admirer's visit.

What evidence survives of eighteenth-century visiting practices indicates that in addition to a swift though punctilious visit to the tomb, there was, as early as the 1740s, a further informal tourist itinerary developing. Homage paid to the sacred bones was supplemented with something living and delightfully garnished with biographical anecdote; the grave was supplemented with a growing interest in where Shakespeare had lived. In 1742 the young David Garrick, accompanied by his friend the actor Macklin, came to Stratford specifically to view, indeed to sit under, the mulberry tree growing in the garden of New Place, which, according to Rowe, was supposedly planted by the hand of its previous owner, Shakespeare himself. They were taken round by the then owner Sir Hugh Clopton. Eleven years later, they would not have met with such a kind reception. By 1756, the next owner, the Rev. Francis Gastrell, was already complaining of the tiresomeness of the growing number of visiting enthusiasts to his summer home, all eager to view, touch, and take their own twigs from the mulberry tree becoming ever more famous with every reprint of Rowe's edition.[11] The infuriated Gastrell first felled the mulberry tree in 1756, and subsequently, in an effort to avoid tax, demolished the house entirely in 1759. Deprived of a prime tourist lure, Stratford's cannier residents set about promoting other locations associated with Shakespeare in its stead. In 1762, for example, the correspondent of the *British Magazine* stayed at the White Lion in Henley Street, and reported that the landlord had showed him Shakespeare's birthplace, and further, had taken him over to Bidford to show him a crab-apple tree nicknamed "Shakespeare's canopy."[12] This crab-apple tree was that under which Shakespeare was supposed by tradition to have slept off a drinking binge, and through the multiplication of accounts such as that of the *British Magazine* it became so celebrated that it was steadily destroyed by further plundering relic-hunters, finally collapsing in 1824.[13]

But it was undoubtedly the success of the leading actor of the day, David Garrick, in staging the first major public celebration of Shakespeare, the Jubilee in 1769, that put Shakespeare's Stratford on the national map for the generality of tourists, beginning the process of making it a must-see location in itself, rather than merely a coaching town in which the traveler might idle away the hours waiting for his dinner by visiting places of local interest, including Shakespeare's tomb. In August 1769, Garrick's publicity machine brought a large crowd drawn from high society out from London to Stratford, to celebrate Shakespeare's two-hundredth birthday five years and four months late with a heady cocktail of miscellaneous entertainments – a breakfast, an oratorio, a concert, a ball, a horse race, a procession of one hundred and seventy Shakespearean characters, a set of songs sung round the streets, an ambitious "Ode" celebrating Shakespeare's achievements composed and recited by Garrick himself, a masquerade, an Assembly, and fireworks. In the event, Garrick was unlucky in the weather (a persistent downpour meant that the procession had to be canceled, and the performance of the "Ode" was almost flooded by the rising Avon), and many and various acid comments were passed about the nature of the entertainments; most eye-witness accounts reported the event as an expensive fiasco. Yet, fiasco or no, Garrick's extravaganza contributed notable elements to the developing Stratford tourist industry, even though the persons who attended the Jubilee at Stratford in 1769 were not exactly tourists as we would understand the term, and nor was the Jubilee exactly a tourist event in that it was essentially occasional.

In the most general terms the Jubilee codified, expanded, and boosted a small-scale provincial industry by successfully linking different Shakespeares – the Shakespeare of the London stage, the Shakespeare of the printed page, the rural Shakespeare of Stratford, the increasingly mythic "Shakespeare" praised by critics and nationalists – within a multimedia spectacular staged in a single location.[14] Garrick's many and various entertainments did not include any performance of Shakespeare's actual works, and contemporaries were so unsurprised by this that no comment was passed at all; this suggests that both impresario and audience shared a sense that the Jubilee was not a conventional theatrical experience, but rather a theatricalization of the biographical within topography. The script of the Jubilee established Stratford, together with the surrounding countryside of Warwickshire, as a plausible, indeed a "natural," rather than an arbitrary location of a Shakespeare cult, partly by general invocation of the Bard as a local ("the Will of all Wills was a Warwickshire Will," as the hit-song of the festival chorused), and partly by theatricalizing real locations within the town. Places were effectively made into scenery for the drama of Shakespeare's birthday, and they were reciprocally dramatized, gaining added meaning and value. The prime example of this process was the treatment of the Birthplace, which was made into the center-piece of the Shakespeare tourist cult for the first time; reports of the Jubilee were illustrated by the first public print of the Birthplace in the *Gentleman's Magazine.*The rained-off procession of Shakespeare characters was planned to stop at the Birthplace, hung with an allegorical banner representing the sun bursting out from behind clouds to enlighten the world, which was to be draped from the window of the room that Garrick had decided (arbitrarily, and without any actual scholarly evidence, though the attribution has stuck) had been the birthroom. Here they were to sing:

> Here Nature nurs'd her darling boy . . .
> Now, now, we tread inchanted ground,
> Here Shakespeare walked and sung![15]

Individually dramatized locations were linked into a biographical narrative by the moving of the procession from spot to numinous spot – from the Birthplace to the monument in the church, where Shakespeare's tomb was ritually heaped with flowers. So fundamental did this narrative of location become to the cult of Shakespeare that it remains the underlying itinerary of the Shakespeare Birthday Procession to this day, a procession that takes place annually on 23 April and culminates in the ceremonial laying of flowers by dignitaries on the writer's tomb.

The Jubilee did more than invent this prototype tourist itinerary; it invented a prototype tourist sensibility and protocols to match. The lines above, for example, suggest an essentially touristic audience for the Birthplace. Rather than viewing the house as an interesting "antiquity," the audience is solicited to a theatrical experience lived in the moment and fundamentally sentimental in its effort to put the Tourist into the same place and thus, by an effort of time-defying imagination, almost into the presence of the Poet. To serve as a memento and mark of this charged moment, the Jubilee also invented the literary souvenir proper. Relics, in the shape of bits of the felled mulberry tree, had already made the fortune of a local craftsman, William Sharp, who had bought up much of the timber and proceeded to turn out an implausibly large number of expensive knick-knacks which he sold for good prices from 1756 onwards to all comers, including David Garrick himself. These objects operated within the Shakespeare cult with something of the power of the shards of the True Cross, although the wood itself, carved, polished, and often inlaid, served as its own reliquary. The Jubilee, however, introduced the first mass-produced souvenirs – manufactured objects designed to be taken away as a memento of the occasion, and as certification of having been there. In addition to the sale of "Shakespeare favors" (specially woven colored ribbons made into sashes and rosettes, attached to badges and medals with a likeness of Shakespeare on one side and an inscription on the other that devotees were to wear as a sort of uniform), cotton handkerchiefs printed in red with eight characters from the plays were on sale to the less well-heeled. The Jubilee committee also sponsored an "Official Jubilee Bookseller" who purveyed copies of Garrick's Ode, the collection of Jubilee songs entitled *Shakespeare's Garland*, and other assorted opportunistic occasional publications, from a stall set up in the birthroom.[16]

That glimpse of the bookseller, swathed in the glorious colored light falling through the birthroom window from the allegorical silk banner hung across it, epitomizes the way in which the Jubilee succeeded in securing print culture to biographicized place. Yet the need to hang an allegorical painting from the Birthplace window at all also illustrates how this particular place had yet to become recognizable, let alone iconic, and let alone a locus promising a supremely authentic tourist experience. That authenticity and uniqueness, paradoxically, was only achieved through the mass reproduction and dissemination of its likeness as part of the wide publicization of the Jubilee across Europe. In this sense the engraving in the *Gentleman's Magazine* did what ecstatically pausing the procession outside the Birthplace could not do fully; it linked the Birthplace and the Shakespeare you might read at home together within the medium of print culture, making one the recognizable origin of the other. Something similar was achieved by the smash-hit part-satirical depiction of the Jubilee's aspirations and discomforts which Garrick himself staged at Drury Lane in order to recoup his costs, his afterpiece *The Jubilee*.[17] This piece was provided with painted backdrops of Stratford in such realistic perspective that on visiting Stratford for the first time in the 1780s, John Byng recognized the White Lion hotel "because it had been so well painted at Drury Lane theatre."[18] This new recognizability was extended to other locations in Stratford as well; the scenery also included a depiction of the parish church. The Jubilee established Stratford as the privileged destination for Shakespeare pilgrims, and Stratford residents duly gave the credit to Garrick. As Mrs. Hart, lucky tenant of the Birthplace, said to Byng, while showing him "Shakespeare's old chair": "It has been carefully handed down by our family, but people never thought so much of it till after the Jubilee, and now see what pieces they have cut from it, as well as from the old flooring in the bedroom!"[19] Taking the hint, Byng seized his opportunity while he could, and acquired the bottom strut of the chair, probably at an extortionate price.

If the first stirrings of a modern tourist aesthetic are thus visible at the peripheries of Garrick's Jubilee, it does not fully model modern literary tourism. As that allegorical banner suggests, the Jubilee did not locate Shakespeare in Stratford principally according to a realist aesthetic. It would take three decades after the Jubilee to complete the transfer from the allegorical to the biographical suggested by Garrick's words for the song at the end of his performance of the Ode, in which Ben Jonson's largely figurative "sweet swan of Avon" was transformed into an unintentionally comic vignette of Shakespeare catching his death of cold from endlessly lying about on the damp banks of the river:

> Thou soft-flowing Avon, by thy silver stream,
> Of things more than mortal, sweet Shakespeare would dream,
> The fairies by moonlight dance round his green bed
> For hallow'd the turf is which pillow'd his head.[20]

Although Shakespeare's earlier biographers, notably Aubrey and Rowe, had connected the Bard with Stratford and its environs, the man who first elaborated Shakespearean biography with visually realized locations by way of illustration, and who modeled appropriate tourist sentiment in a romantically enthusiastic first-person narrative of his pilgrimage, was Samuel Ireland, now best remembered as the father of the forger of Shakespeare's letters, William Henry Ireland. *Picturesque Views on the Upper, or Warwickshire Avon* (1795) successfully joined up long-familiar Shakespearean oral traditions into an itinerary for an extended excursion into the country, which could then be readily repeated by readers fired with the sort of enthusiasm that one traveler was already expressing in 1793: "STRATFORD! *All hail to thee!* When I tread thy hallowed walks; when I pass over the same mould that has been pressed by the feet of SHAKESPEARE, I feel inclined to kiss the earth itself."[21]

Ireland's frontispiece to *Picturesque Views* in many ways typifies the late eighteenth-century emergent sense of authorial location within a landscape (Figure 11 – Ireland frontispiece), uneasily combining the neoclassical allegorical with the realistic. On the right lolls a disconcertingly not-quite-life-size Bard, festooned with harp, scrolls, and masks of comedy and tragedy, identified by a rather pointed swan, and solicited by a variety of classically undressed females including "Nature" to what, if we're to go by the strategically placed net and fishing-rod, seems to be an impromptu fishing-trip on the Avon. Though rather wooden, this Shakespeare is recognizably the one Garrick and many other poetic travelers before him had invoked, perpetually picnicking on the inspirational river-bank sward. In 1767, for example, William Dodd had visualized the scene beside the Avon, where "gentle Shakespeare's youthful feet, / Beside thee frolic rov'd."[22] On the other hand, the background to this classical montage is dominated by a

Here NATURE listning stood, whilst Shakespear play'd
And wonder'd at the Work herself had made! *Churchill.*

London Pub. for Sam.l Ireland Feb.y 1.st 1795.

11 Frontispiece to Samuel Ireland, *Picturesque Views on the Upper, or Warwickshire Avon*, London, 1795.

thoroughly realistic view of the church spire at Stratford-upon-Avon (albeit an anachronistic one – Holy Trinity's tower boasted no spire until the eighteenth century). The documentary detail of the church unavoidably suggests the chilliness of those river nymphs, and inadvertently solicits all sorts of explanatory narrative as to the nature and occasion of this ill-conceived outing.

Much of the rest of Ireland's *Picturesque Views* could be seen as dedicated to providing the explanatory narrative and the documentary detail that transforms Shakespeare's Stratford from an allegorical to a real location. The text is lavishly illustrated with detailed engravings of locales associated with Shakespeare: Charlecote House (where Shakespeare was alleged to have been caught stealing deer by Sir Thomas Lucy), Fulbrook Lodge (the alternative scene of the deer-stealing episode, according to John Jordan), "the kitchen of Shakespeare's House" (including "Shakespeare's Chair"), the monument in the church, Anne Hathaway's Cottage (the first ever representation), and an artist's impression of the temporary rotunda in which Garrick had recited his Ode at the Jubilee nearly thirty years earlier. Perhaps of especial interest is a marvelously implausible reconstruction of New Place complete with Tudor figures. It looks nothing like what we know New Place to have looked like in Tudor times, but it does look like what contemporaries felt the Tudor should have looked like. Here, Ireland previews the Victorian desire to make Stratford adequately Tudor and so Shakespearean, going to the lengths of putting Shakespeare's crest above the Adam-style neoclassical doorway.

Ireland thus models for his reader a must-do itinerary, a useful guide to appropriate sentiments, and appropriate activities, including the acquisition of relics and souvenirs. Though Ireland's publication is not what we would understand as a guidebook, being more a cross between travel narrative, coffee-table book, and antiquarian notes, it brings together for the first time biography, pictures, and a first-person account of visiting the place, describing a visit which readers are effectively urged to repeat for themselves. And it is demonstrably invested in that sense of the local, particular, and topographically accurate that is peculiar to the nineteenth century, a sense that would, for example, inform the realistic painted backdrops for Charles Kemble's 1829 production of the first English play to boast the young Shakespeare as its hero, Charles Somerset's *Shakespeare's Early Days*. This, according to the playbill, included "the outside of the HOUSE in which SHAKSPEARE WAS BORN," a "DIORAMIC VIEW of Stratford-upon-Avon, the River, Church, etc," and a "view of Charlecote Hall."[23]

If Shakespeare's monument is recognizably the product of a seventeenth-century aesthetic, and the Birthplace the product of an essentially romantic cult of the origins of genius, Anne Hathaway's Cottage as it is presented

Sam. Ireland del.

House at Shotery, in which Ann Hathaway the wife of Shakspere resided.

12 "House at Shotery, in which Ann Hathaway the wife of Shakspere resided" from Samuel Ireland, *Picturesque Views on the Upper, or Warwickshire Avon*, London, 1795.

today is clearly derived from the way in which the Victorians visualized and understood it. Shottery, it is true, had featured in the Jubilee, but only as a location for horse-races. Ireland's account of his pioneering visit in 1795 is clearly antiquarian rather than sentimental in spirit: "I shall conduct the reader to the village of Shottery ... The cottage in which [Ann Hathaway] is said to have lived with her parents is yet standing, and although I have doubts as to the truth of the relation, I have yet given a faithful representation of it in the annexed view ..."[24] (Figure 12 'House at Shottery.') Victorian interest in the Cottage grew subsequently in large part out of a desire to have a sober and domestic Bard, in the teeth of the troubling facts of Shakespeare's marriage at eighteen to a woman some eight years his senior, and already heavily pregnant, the provision in his will pointedly leaving only the "second-best bed" to his wife, and the general embarrassment of the Sonnets, which, whether addressed to man or woman, were clearly not addressed to his wife. Emma Severn's truly execrable novel *Anne Hathaway, or, Shakespeare in Love* (1845) suggests the contours of this Victorian investment in Shakespearean domesticity. Purporting to narrate the love-affair of Shakespeare and Anne, this novel expends a great deal of time and effort upon describing the Cottage's interiors – some ten pages in the first hundred.

The Cottage itself is presented as a virtuous rural retreat, not unlike the cottage bought by Celia and Rosalind in *As You Like It*, and it is surrounded by a magical and botanically simultaneous countryside infested with fairies, escapees from *Midsummer Night's Dream*, jealous of the marital happiness of the two lovers: "The sprites drooped mournfully, and wept till the hare-bells and violets of Stratford Wood and Shottery lawn were brimmed to overflowing with fairy tears of grief, envy, and despair."[25] Regrettable though Severn's prose is, her celebration of the Cottage was very much in line with mainstream sentiment. When William Howitt, author of the influential *Visits to Remarkable Places* (1840) and *Homes and Haunts of the Most Eminent British Poets* (1847), made his visit to Stratford in 1839, he consciously diverted his footsteps away from the Birthplace towards neglected Shottery, which he found authentic and unchanged, testimony to a newly domestic, marital, and retired Bard. By the 1880s the Cottage was firmly fixed as a locus for an idealized pastoral love of the sort that is conspicuously absent from the comedies but was nonetheless felt to be authentically Elizabethan (one hack-writer burbled of the stream across the lane, "no doubt many a flower has been dropped in its limpid current by the happy lovers").[26] To Americans especially it summed up all that was English: a guide of the 1890s wrote it up as a "perfectly representative and thoroughly characteristic bit of genuine English rustic scenery."[27] In 1886 William Winter, perhaps the most influential American writer on Stratford after his countrymen Washington Irving and Nathaniel Hawthorne, was much taken with this "rustic retreat" as "the shrine of Shakespeare's love."[28] Typically for his time, he traces Shakespeare's supposed love of flowers and of pastoral landscape to his happy memories of the scenes of his wooing, and reverently carries away a "farewell gift of woodbine and roses from the porch."[29] Though this portrait of the poet in love is more than faintly comic, it demonstrates the way in which by the 1880s Shottery had evolved into a satisfactory location for the heady mix of rustic chivalry, merrie Englandism, fairies, botany, and romantic domesticity that "Shakespeare's England" was supposed to have been. By 1901, courtesy of this enthusiasm, the whole set-up had become a good deal less "rustic" than advertised; Christian Tearle in his *Rambles with an American* noted rather sourly that "The meadow paths are not nearly as sylvan as the guide-books would lead one to expect. The endless stream of excursionists, which has flowed along them throughout spring, summer and autumn for so many years, has left its mark."[30]

By the middle of the nineteenth century, then, Stratford was the center of a thriving and well-codified tourist industry. The Birthplace had fallen out of the hands of its private owner, and had been rescued in 1847 for the nation from a rumored American plan to ship it to the United States, there to exhibit it at fairs around the country. The Birthplace Trust was formed to preserve the site, and subsequently the house was aggressively restored to Tudor picturesqueness for the 1864 tercentenary. The garden was planted up with "Shakespearean" plants, a museum established next door, and a set entry charge levied. The Trust subsequently acquired the Nash House and the site of New Place in 1864, Anne Hathaway's Cottage in 1892, and the house then believed to be Mary Arden's House in 1930. The town would become increasingly monumentalized with statues and plaques, including the Jubilee fountain in the marketplace (given by an American with strong temperance leanings and a desire to lay to rest the local folklore about Shakespeare's boozing), and, after many false starts such as the proposal around 1868 to put a theatre on the site of New Place, the Memorial Theatre eventually opened in 1879. Tourist numbers climbed steadily: in 1806, when records began to be kept, there were about 1,000 visitors a year; 2,200 came in 1851, but, after the opening of the railway line from Warwick in 1860, 6,000 came in 1862; in the tercentenary year of 1864 some 2,800 visitors came in the festival fortnight alone; by 1900, there were some 30,000 visitors a year; in 1937, it is thought that there were 85,222 visitors; and by the 1980s well over a million visits were being paid annually to the Trust's five properties together.[31]

As this account of the invention of Stratford as Shakespeare's town might suggest, it is as much a story about the power of print culture as it is a story about preserving the ancient fabric of the town. The dissemination of publications about Stratford, combined with the dissemination of visual representations ranging from prints to pop-up models to ceramics, meant that Stratford increasingly became familiar to many who had never, and might never, set foot there. As William Winter observed in 1886: "Every pilgrim to Stratford knows beforehand, in a general way, what he will there behold. Copious and frequent description of its Shakespearean associations have made the place familiar to all the world."[32] Yet these publications and pictures, far from satisfying curiosity, solicited individuals to visit themselves to try for the authentic experience of pilgrimage, for the sense of "surprise to the sight and a wonder to the soul."[33] To avoid creating disappointment similar to that of Nathaniel Hawthorne (who complained that the Birthplace was "a smaller and humbler house than any description can prepare the visitor to expect," that indeed, there had been too much description – the visitor had "heard, read, thought, and dreamed" too much about the place for it to live up to expectations), Stratford increasingly strove to become more like the Stratford of the imagination, stripping off its modern facades to become more "Tudor."[34] Such judicious prettification attempted to match tourist expectations produced by historical genre paintings such as the series of mid nineteenth-century watercolors by Charles Cattermole. Locating Shakespeare in Stratford and the

13 Early twentieth-century postcard reproduction of a watercolor by the Victorian artist Charles Cattermole (1832–1900), "May Day Sports at Shottery – Shakespeare the Victor."

Warwickshire countryside with scrupulous fidelity to biographical, documentary, and antiquarian detail, they show the church with the avenue of lime trees ("The Christening in Stratford-upon-Avon Church"), the Warwickshire countryside ("William Shakespeare Meets the Strolling Players"), the hall at Charlecote ("Shakespeare Before Sir Thomas Lucy"), the Cottage ("May Day Sports at Shottery – Shakespeare the Victor"), Clopton Bridge and a distant view of the church ("Shakespeare Leaving Home – The Farewell"), the Birthplace ("Shakespeare's Return to Stratford-on-Avon"), the mulberry tree ("Shakespeare With His Friends at New Place"), and the church again, seen from a window beside Shakespeare's deathbed ("Shakespeare's Last Hours at the New Place"). The flavor of these may be demonstrated by just one – "May Day Sports at Shottery." (Figure 13 – Charles Cattermole, 'May Day Sports at Shottery'). (It is only appropriate that these paintings, now part of the Royal Shakespeare Company's art collection in Stratford, should soon have been reproduced in sepia as souvenir postcards.) Taken together, these pictures not only make Stratford recognizable, but demonstrate how recognizable Stratford had become, and how a sense of this location had come to be obligatory in any conception of Shakespearean biography. At the same time the dialectic between disappointment and achieved sublime experience became ever more commonplace, if written accounts are anything to go by. Tearle's American tourist, Mr. Fairchild, complained in 1901 both that the tidied-up Birthplace was "offensively modern," and that it was still too archaic: "so mean and so dark that you can't think of any civilised person living in it, without a sort of pity." The sense of Shakespeare as "some great natural wonder" forces the discerning Mr. Fairchild out into Shakespeare's countryside to bathe "in Shakespeare's river," and, having disgustedly flung away his souvenir plaque into the Avon because it was adorned with an inaccurate transcription of Shakespeare's lines, he plucks instead a few leaves of ivy from the Birthplace.[35] In this he is entirely in the spirit of modern literary pilgrimage; though brought to Stratford by the power of print culture, he tries to discard print culture in favor of something non-commercial and natural, an immediate physical or organic experience rather than a representation or reproduction.[36]

One of the problems for the Victorian literary pilgrim, as Hawthorne acutely observed, was that Stratford delivered a "flesh-and-blood individual" rather than the National and International Poet:

> The Shakespeare whom I met there took various guises, but had not his laurel on. He was successively the roguish boy, – the youthful deer-stealer – the comrade of players ... the careful, thrifty, thriven man of property who came back from London to lend money on bond and to occupy the best house in Stratford ... the victim of convivial habits, who met his death by tumbling into a ditch on his way home from a drinking-bout.[37]

Victorian travelers would share Hawthorne's unease at this redaction of Shakespeare's career. They would continue and expand a love affair with the Shakespeare country surrounding Stratford, Washington Irving's "poetic ground."[38] They would ever more romantically and elaborately connect episodes from the biography with the countryside in paintings, novels, and criticism, rooting the Sonnets and comedies into the locality with claims for where they were written and inspired, a tradition that would find expression in Caroline Spurgeon's frontispiece illustrating Clopton Bridge in her study *Shakespeare's Imagery and What It Tells Us* (1935), which connected one of Shakespeare's similes to the characteristic movement of the water around the bridge's piers. Stratford, then, as we know it today, is very much a Victorian formulation of golden-age England: no wonder that it was recreated by the Edwardians all across the stockbroker suburbs of Surrey, where the affluent lived in recreated mock-Tudor pastoral. Stratford represented, and still largely represents, a Victorian dream of Englishness, an energetic dreaming that turned Stratford into the world's first theme-park. But the Victorians would also seek to locate Shakespeare in other, rather grander places, supplementing the national of the countryside with the national of the metropolis – London.[39] A writer among writers, a writer moving in the highest circles, this was how the later Victorians wanted to see Shakespeare in London, and this is the subject of my next section.

London

> I consider the fame and genius of Shakespeare to be the property of the whole kingdom, and I cannot consent to confine it to the town of Stratford ... I therefore hope that the statue may be placed in the metropolis.[40]

In this effort to imagine Shakespeare in Elizabethan London, the Victorians were only following up Ben Jonson's hint:

> Sweet Swan of Avon, what a sight it were
> To see thee in our waters yet appear,
> And make those flights upon the banks of Thames
> That so did take Eliza and our James![41]

The first place that the curious tourist might have started out in search of Shakespeare in London would have been Poets' Corner, with its sumptuous statue of an elaborately casual Bard by Scheemakers, installed in 1741. This Shakespeare, gesturing towards a large scroll of paper on which part of Prospero's "The cloud-capped towers, the gorgeous palaces" speech is mistranscribed, is emphatically a writer. The Scheemakers statue can be seen in part as an eighteenth-century effort to provide the provincial Shakespeare with poetic gravitas – more body, more writing, in a place that embodied the establishment.[42] But by 1820 or so, visitors were typically more taken with the peculiar and picturesque obscurity of the Stratford tomb than with the neoclassical grandeur of the Abbey. Irving, preferring Holy Trinity, dismissed Poets' Corner as a desirable resting-place: "What would a crowded corner in Westminster Abbey have been, compared with this reverend pile, which seems to stand in beautiful loneliness as his sole mausoleum!"; Benjamin Robert Haydon was not untypical when he wrote of his 1828 visit to Stratford that "The most poetical imagination could not have imagined a burial place more worthy, more suitable, more English, more native for a poet than this."[43] John R. Wise's guide of 1861 comments of Shakespeare's tomb that "this is better than being buried in Westminster Abbey or St. Paul's, to lie at peace amongst your own," while the *Shakespeare Almanac* of 1871 baldly describes the Westminster statue as "inadequate."[44] In keeping with the Romantic and Victorian desire to authenticate text by reference to the author's originary body, and by extension, by reference to originary place, such visitors found the whole idea of Poets' Corner teetering on the edge of the arbitrary, and insufficiently invested in the historical specificity and physicality of the writers it commemorated. Insufficiently native, poetical or picturesque, Poets' Corner was insufficiently biographical as well.

Far more to Victorian taste was the delightfully casual way in which Sir Walter Scott conjured up Shakespeare in his novel of Elizabethan England,

Kenilworth (1821). Scott's Shakespeare moves with graceful casualness within the London orbit of the great; his only appearance in the flesh neatly links him with Spenser, Sidney, and Leicester, and identifies him as at once poet, playwright, and theatrical entrepreneur. Leicester, about to embark on the Queen's barge on the Thames, greets Spenser, and then Shakespeare: "Ha, Will Shakespeare – wild Will! – thou hast given my nephew, Philip Sidney, love-powder – he cannot sleep without thy Venus and Adonis under his pillow! We will have thee hanged for the veriest wizard in Europe. Hark thee, mad wag, I have not forgotten thy matter of the patent, and of the bears."[45] This technique of providing a fleeting glimpse of Shakespeare within an imagined Tudor London becomes characteristic not just of historical novels and historical genre paintings after Scott, but, through them, of the beginnings of nineteenth-century Shakespeare tourism in London.

But where to look for (or put) Shakespeare in London? As Howitt put it in his groundbreaking *Homes and Haunts of the Most Eminent British Poets* (1847), by comparison to Stratford and its environs, modern Victorian London, developing explosively, was a poor hunting-ground for the romance of the past:

> where are the homes and haunts of Shakespeare in London? Like those of a thousand other remarkable men, in the accidents and the growth of this great city, they are swept away. Fires and renovation have carried everything before them. If the fame of men depended on bricks and mortar, what reputations would have been extinguished within the last two centuries in London! In no other place have the violent necessities of a rapid and immense development paid so little respect to the "local habitations" of great names.[46]

The consequence of rapid development was, as William Winter also lamented in 1886, that visitors would have "more and more difficulty both in tracing the footsteps of fame, and in finding that sympathetic, reverent spirit which hallows the relics of genius and renown."[47] Unhappily for the tourist intent upon retracing Shakespeare's footsteps, little remained of Shakespeare's London: the Mermaid Tavern, supposed to have been a favorite hang-out of the Bard, had been destroyed in the Great Fire; so too had the Boar's Head, Falstaff's local, though as early as 1760, Oliver Goldsmith was imagining himself into *Henry IV* as he sat in the (rebuilt) Boar's Head at Eastcheap, congratulating himself on sitting "by a pleasant fire, in the very room where old Sir John Falstaff cracked his jokes, in the very chair which was sometimes honoured by prince Henry, and sometimes polluted by his immoral merry companion," in a manner that previewed Washington Irving's similar reverie in the Red House in Stratford some fifty years later.[48] Irving himself went in search of the tavern, but found only a box made from the wood of the old tavern, with a lid painted with a picture of the inn and Falstaff and Hal carousing outside. And if the taverns had not survived, neither had the houses in which Shakespeare might have lived, nor the great houses of Shakespeare's patrons, nor the theatres in which Shakespeare had worked, the Blackfriars, The Theatre, the Rose, and, especially, the Globe.

There was, in short, nothing much to see, on Bankside or elsewhere. But that very difficulty seems to have inspired a particular urgency in visitors. Hampered in their efforts to trace Shakespeare's footsteps by how little was known about where Shakespeare might have lodged or lounged, the Victorians transferred onto Shakespeare a relatively new tourist practice, an imaginative practice so familiar to us nowadays that it is hard to see it as historically specific – the London literary ramble.[49]

Victorians set about reanimating the Shakespearean past by strong efforts of imagination reinforced by strong pairs of boots. First hinted at in Howitt's *Homes and Haunts*, the Bankside walk first makes an extended appearance in Christian Tearle's *Rambles with an American* (1901), in which an Englishman of an antiquarian turn takes Mr. Fairchild, the American enthusiast whom we have already met in Stratford, round London locations associated with Shakespeare. This is the earliest account that I have been able to locate of a physical pilgrimage to Bankside, via streets dating from Tudor times, to the approximate sites of the Globe, the Rose, and the Bear Garden. The visit is not initially a success because the American finds it "difficult to associate that forlorn prospect with the site of the old playhouse."[50] However, he perks up at the site of the Falcon – supposedly "the favourite haunt of Shakespeare and his friends"[51] – and eventually, with the aid of old maps, is bitten with the bug of reconstruction; pleasantly imagining Shakespeare as "slipping away from the Falcon crew some summer evening, and strolling along that lane as it was in his time, with the wild roses in blossom."[52] The friends conjure up in place of the squalid actuality of Bankside warehouses, docks and alleys "a vague picture of flat, green water-meadows, from which one saw across the river the London of Elizabeth, all shadowy in a June twilight."[53] Superimposing the pastoral upon the urban, the sights and sounds of a lost Thames upon the modern commercial river, they make a virtue of the need for strong imagination to cope with the inadequacy of the present:

> We have here in these alleys and passages the very paths by which Shakespeare made his way to and fro, and I'm not at all sure they don't bring one as near to him in imagination as if we still had the very buildings associated with him – his house, or his theatre, or the tavern where he met his friends.[54]

This habit of trying to reanimate and even briefly to inhabit the Shakespearean past finds elaborate expression in, say, Alfred Noyes's collection of poems, *Tales from the Mermaid Tavern* (1913), in which the poet magically enters the Elizabethan inn, bringing to life a selection of celebrities. Noyes's volume is exactly contemporaneous with the development of the Bankside Shakespeare walk, firmly established with a standard itinerary by the 1920s, and the aesthetic of both clearly informs later works of the period such as Virginia Woolf's *Orlando* (1928).[55]

Though Tearle's travelers, visiting Bankside by the light of the moon, fall successfully into "grave pleasantry" – "Surely we ought not to pass the Falcon without crushing a cup?," etc., – other visitors seem to have needed more help.[56] The early twentieth century accordingly slapped helpful plaques on buildings in all directions. By 1909 there were rival plaques marking the site of the Globe, one on a teahouse, and the other, more visible (and still in place), located close to Southwark Bridge; by 1912 a large effigy had been installed in Southwark Cathedral; by 1923 there was a memorial window in Curtain Road church, site of The Theatre which, once moved to Southwark, became the Globe, commemorating Shakespeare's arrival in London; 1923 saw the installation of a plaque in Silver Street commemorating Shakespeare's residence on the site. The 1909 Southwark plaque, showing Shakespeare in front of a pastoral Southwark very like that imagined by Tearle, was for years the site of an annual performance of Shakespeare scenes to mark the Birthday, a performance that followed a set Shakespeare "ramble."[57] These plaques could be said to be first cousins to the replica of the Globe theatre that now stands near-ish to the site of the original theatre, and which has substantially taken over the present-day business of the Shakespeare Walk. Their shared intention is to stamp Southwark as Shakespeare's London, and to offer imaginative access to Shakespeare's London, too. They are related to a remarkable number of efforts to build a theatre in London that would commemorate Shakespeare, including a late nineteenth-century proposal by William Poel to construct a replica of the Globe in Battersea Park.

The modern replica of the Globe constructed under the auspices of Sam Wanamaker has been the subject of much academic commentary since it officially opened in 1997. At stake in much of the commentary have been the claims to "authenticity" of the theatre; rather less has been said of the relation of tourism to the theatrical experience provided by the Globe.[58] What is certainly true is that the Globe offers the experience that Tearle's characters yearned for – a chance to occupy the imaginary space and consciousness of the past, bolstered by antiquarian accuracy, and the chance to go for a guided Shakespeare walk that wanders in the footsteps of the Bard through a secret, indeed, an invisible Bankside. Whereas Stratford may be said to have been invented and inflected by text, Bankside is instead all textualized place.

Elsewhere

Although the vast bulk of tourism inspired by Shakespeare has been associated with Stratford and London, there has also been a more slender tradition of touristic interest in the locations of his plays, which first developed in the late eighteenth century. We have already glanced at the importance of Falstaff in this respect. Goldsmith was by no means the only tourist to imagine himself into Falstaff's milieu; sometime after 1733 two figures of Falstaff and Prince Hal were carved on the Boar's Head's inn-posts, and they were extant until 1834, more than forty years after the inn itself had ceased trading.[59] James Boswell flirted with the idea of joining a Shakespeare Club that met at the Boar's Head. Under the influence of Scott's bestselling *Kenilworth*, which did more than anything else to reanimate the Tudor past within the present for Victorian culture, it became possible to visit the ruins of Kenilworth, as Hawthorne did, as a generally "Shakespearean" site. In a similarly sentimental and quasi-biographical fashion, Victorian tourists from the 1820s would also visit "Shakespearean" sites in Italy. These developed under the influence of a Victorian belief that Shakespeare must have traveled to Italy, which both produced and was bolstered by nineteenth-century editorial and stage practice which provided highly specific locations for individual scenes coupled with elaborately painted realistic backdrops. Nineteenth-century guidebooks identified a palazzo in Venice as the house of Desdemona, and the palace of the Moro family was similarly identified as Othello's house.[60] Though these last are no longer part of the tourist trail, Juliet is still a major draw to Verona as she was when Heinrich Heine visited in 1828 and Dickens paid tribute in 1844.[61] (Stratford fought back fiercely: the official guidebook for the Tercentenary insisted that Shakespeare had wooed his future wife in the very words of Romeo, and that "This once admitted as an article of our literary creed, Verona pales in comparison with Shottery." Indeed.)[62] Juliet's supposed tomb in the cloister of the Capuchins was comprehensively plundered by Napoleon's second wife, Maria Luigia, Duchess of Parma, who had necklace, bracelet, and earrings made of its stone, but the house and marble balcony are still shown, the balcony now helpfully garnished with Romeo's speech to Juliet. Less popular, but still extant, is "Desdemona's garden" at the fortress of Famagusta, Cyprus, labeled as such. It is today possible to take "a Grand Tour of Shakespeare's Italy, Venice, Verona, and Rome" in the company of an actor specializing in "bringing to life characters from Shakespeare's plays right in the streets where they lived." (The website adds, at once cautiously and comfortingly, that "absolutely no knowledge of Shakespeare is necessary.")[63] Meanwhile, in Denmark, Kronborg castle, aka Elsinore, is nowadays habitually shown with reference to its status as the setting for *Hamlet*.

However oddly beside the point these sites seem, their invention was driven by the same nineteenth-century desire for a physical origin and equivalent to the printed text that produced Shakespeare's Stratford. There are, however, signs that the desire for this physical authenticity is selectively breaking down with reference to Shakespeare tourism. At least, the contrast between the history of late nineteenth-century and early twentieth-century replicas of the Globe and late twentieth-century replicas of the Globe and other Shakespeare properties suggests as much. In 1933 a replica of the Globe theatre served as the centerpiece of a mock "English village" constructed for the World's Fair in Chicago. Subsequently, it was acquired for the Great Texas Fair in Dallas in 1936. Presumably fearful that it would not root properly, the organizers applied to the directors of the Stratford-upon-Avon festival company for a small supply of earth from Shakespeare's garden, and water from the Avon, with which to consecrate the building. The intention was manifestly to breed authenticity by energizing American soil with a magically fertile and fertilizing bit of the real thing, old England.[64] Since then, there have been many replicas of the Globe built, latterly in Rome, Berlin, Tokyo, and Sweden (this last a temporary ice structure) but chiefly in North America. Although they all look roughly the same, their claims to authenticity are founded in widely differing fashions: some, like the Folger Shakespeare Library's, have been designed to antiquarian specifications (in this instance, now touchingly obsolete); others, often associated with Shakespeare Festivals, offer an authentically Shakespearean theatrical experience; some have been designed much more nebulously to offer an authentically "English" experience.[65] Although all these types of replica have their genesis in the original "English village" at the Chicago World's Fair, their sense of the necessity of authenticity in terms of connection to an origin in the authentic location seems to have waned markedly.

Closely associated with these replica Globes are replicas of other Shakespeare properties. Epitomizing English pastoral, Anne Hathaway's Cottage has proved easier to translocate than the Birthplace, since it is general rather than particular in meaning. One of the earliest examples of the replication of the Cottage appears courtesy of the devoted efforts of Mrs. Emma Shay, an English teacher in South Dakota, and her husband Professor Clark Shay, who in 1932, enthused by having already developed a Shakespeare Garden, built a replica of Anne Hathaway's Cottage, drawing the plans from a picture postcard of the original brought back from Stratford itself. The result was a fairly good likeness of the left-hand side of the Cottage. The house has recently been restored and improved, and continues to provide a site for "teas, tours, Maypole Dances, and even weddings" and the epicenter for a Christmas "tour of homes" in the locality.[66] The combination is vividly reminiscent of Cattermole's picture of respectably sexy festivities with an appendix of good housekeeping very much in the vein of the beeswax polish that, as I've already remarked, you can still buy at the Cottage today. The later replica in Victoria, British Columbia, offering as it does "The Enhanced Cottage Tour Experience . . . which incorporates . . . live theatrical vignettes," also suggests that Victorian ideas about the Cottage have survived transplantation virtually intact: "Envision a *Midsummer Night's Dream* coming alive as you enter the cottage, the kitchen becomes a stage for *The Taming of the Shrew*, and who could forget Juliet's heart aching for her dear Romeo . . ." Disneyworld's replica of "Anne Hathaway's Cottage" complete with garden "in which you may have a chance encounter with Pooh, Alice, or the Queen of Hearts" must be the most blithely inauthentic of all replicas, a free-floating sign of regressive rurality.[67] However, on the whole, the world has been more reticent about replicating the Birthplace. Despite American investment in the portability of European culture – it's worth remembering that it was an American, P. T. Barnum, who proposed to buy the Birthplace, ship it over, and display it as a traveling show round the States – America does not boast a Birthplace, though Japan (in the Shakespeare Country Park), does. It is probably Perth, Australia that has given birth to the ultimate commentary on Shakespeare tourism; there you can for a small price enjoy bed and breakfast in a faithful copy of the Birthplace. The Stratford B& B, titivated up with Shakespearean kitsch in between the cornflakes and packeted butter, the chintz and the sachets of shampoo, is in Perth taken to its logical extreme and quite outshone.

All these sites, whatever their stated pretensions to offering access to a buried Englishness, are tourist sites, requiring tourist mobility or pilgrimage, and function under the brand "Shakespeare." Most work on Shakespeare tourism has focused on what is supposed to be the inevitably failed project of the tourist – to reach through to a sense of Shakespearean presence in order to mitigate the alienation and fragmentation of postmodern life. Academic accounts are inclined to relish the whole thing as a con-trick played on the naive tourist, pointing out how Shakespeare is de-sacralized by the very tourism that seeks out his sacred places: "his image and work are drawn into the very processes of reproduction, mediatization, and commodification from which Shakespeare seems to promise escape," to quote Douglas Lanier's version of this charge.[68] But, despite its investment in unique, sacred places, as my brief history has pointed out, literary tourism is actually produced by print culture, not by the places themselves. It is actually an *effect* of reproduction, mediatization, and commodification. These are the causes of tourism, not its accidental and regrettable side-effects.

Moreover, the tourist's experience is not generated by the sacred unique place (although he or she typically imagines this is the case), but by the tourist's negotiation between text and place. In visiting the real place, the tourist seeks to verify what he or she has learned from prior representation. The reality of the experience, however, is generated by the tourist, not the place, and so is not dissimilar to the experience of reading. This is the sophisticated point of one of the immortal William stories, "William and the Lost Tourist," in which William, smitten by a beautiful young American woman, lost deep in the English countryside in search of Stratford, simply produces his own home town as a convenient simulacrum to assuage her impending disappointment, starring himself as lineal descendant of Shakespeare and one of his bosom enemies as Anne Hathaway, complete with satisfyingly squalid cottage. The American tourist leaves perfectly enchanted, and perfectly content, and, after all, since she was in search of the archetypal Englishness of Anne Hathaway's Cottage, well she might. The laugh is at her expense, maybe, but she has her "authentic" experience all the same, and, back home, gives a series of entirely successful lectures on it.[69]

NOTES

1. See *The Traveller's Pocket-Book: or Ogilby and Morgan's Book of the Roads Improved and Amended* ... (London, 1758), Preface. Though this road-book notes the growing popularity of the London–Birmingham route via Stratford and remarks on gentlemen's seats and other sights of interest, it maintains a most perfect silence on the subject of Shakespeare.
2. See Péter Dávidházi, *The Romantic Cult of Shakespeare: Literary Reception in Anthropological Perspective* (Basingstoke: Macmillan, 1998), pp. 63–88.
3. Rowe's biography gathered up extant biographical material, both oral tradition and print, including that already published in Aubrey's *Brief Lives*, so to that extent it was not new material; what was new was its exhaustive form and privileged position fronting a collected and much re-published edition of the complete works.
4. Robert Bell Wheler, *History and Antiquities of Stratford-upon-Avon* (Stratford-upon-Avon, 1806), p. ii. Possibly a quotation from the Reverend Joseph Greene's party-piece at an evening designed to raise money for the whitewashing of Shakespeare's bust in 1793.
5. Samuel Henry Ireland, *Picturesque Views on the Upper or Warwickshire Avon* (London: for R. Faulder and T. Egerton, 1795), pp. 186–87.
6. For a detailed reading of Stratford as a present-day tourist site, concentrating on "tours, individual site displays, artefacts, descriptive materials and catalogues, souvenirs and trinkets" in a way which space here prohibits, see Barbara Hodgdon, *The Shakespeare Trade: Performances and Appropriations* (Philadelphia: University of Pennsylvania Press, 1998), pp. 191–240. The displays have changed in one crucial way, however, since Hodgdon published her study, in that they now extensively

gesture towards the specific histories of each property, and indeed towards the history of Shakespeare tourism.

7. Display board in anteroom to the Birthplace.
8. Christian Deelman, *The Great Shakespeare Jubilee* (London: Michael Joseph, 1964), p. 35.
9. *Ibid.*, p. 35.
10. *An Excursion to Stratford-upon-Avon* (Leamington: W. T. Moncrieff, 1824), n.p.
11. Deelman, *Jubilee*, pp. 35, 46.
12. Nicholas Fogg, *Stratford-upon-Avon, Portrait of a Town* (Chichester, Sussex: Phillimore, 1986), p. 86.
13. Samuel Schoenbaum, *Shakespeare's Lives* (Oxford: Clarendon Press, 1970), p. 114.
14. Douglas Lanier, *Shakespeare and Modern Popular Culture* (Oxford: Oxford University Press, 2002), p. 146.
15. Quoted in Ivor Brown and George Fearon, *Amazing Monument: A Short History of the Shakespeare Industry* (London: William Heinemann, 1939), p. 81.
16. Deelman, *Jubilee*, p. 259.
17. See Michael Dobson, *The Making of the National Poet: Shakespeare, Adaptation and Authorship, 1660–1769* (Oxford: Oxford University Press, 1992), pp. 214–27.
18. Deelman, *Jubilee*, p. 282.
19. Fogg, *Stratford-upon-Avon*, 104.
20. Deelman, *Jubilee*, p. 220.
21. Edward Daniel Clarke, *A Tour through the South of England, Wales and Part of Ireland, made during the summer of 1791* (London, 1793), p. 379.
22. William Dodd, *Poems* (London: Dryden Leach, 1767), "On Seeing a Single Swan on the Banks of the Avon," lines 5–6. See also John Huckell, *Avon: A Poem in Three Parts* (Birmingham, 1758) and Thomas Warton, "Monody, written near Stratford upon Avon" (1777), in *The Poetical Works of the late Thomas Warton . . .* (Oxford: Oxford University Press, 1802). Ireland quotes from Warton elsewhere in the text.
23. Playbill in writer's own collection. On the changed sense of location in the nineteenth century see Roger Sale, *Closer to Home: Writers and Places in England, 1780–1830* (Cambridge MA: Harvard University Press, 1986), p. 2. On Kemble's production, see Jane Martineau *et al.*, *Shakespeare in Art* (London: Merrell, 2003), p. 152.
24. Ireland, *Picturesque Views*, p. 206.
25. Emma Severn, *Anne Hathaway, or, Shakespeare in Love*, 3 vols. (London: Richard Bentley, 1845), III. 81.
26. *Shakespeare's Country: A Short Description of the Route of the East and West Junction Railway*, 2 vols. (London, 1886), I. 17.
27. *A Guide to Stratford-upon-Avon . . . with a description of the historic memorials and relics of Shakspeare* (Manchester: Abel Heywood, *c.* 1890s), p. 22.
28. William Winter, *Shakespeare's England* (Edinburgh: David Douglas, 1886), p. 83.
29. *Ibid.*, p. 84.
30. Christian Tearle, *Rambles with an American* (London: Mills and Boon, 1910), p. 81.
31. Fogg, *Stratford-upon-Avon*, p. 147; Brown and Fearon, *Amazing Monument*, p. 60; Ivor Brown and George Fearon, *The Shakespeares and the Birthplace*

(Stratford-upon-Avon: E. Fox and Son, 1939), p. 6; Ian Ousby, *The Englishman's England: Taste, Travel, and the Rise of Tourism* (Cambridge: Cambridge University Press, 1990), pp. 51–52. For numbers of American visitors, see C. Roach Smith, *Remarks on Shakespeare, His Birthplace etc. suggested by a visit to Stratford-upon-Avon, in the autumn of 1868* (London: privately printed, 1868–69), p. 1. Figures quoted by authorities vary widely, possibly because of variation in the use of sources: early figures are based on records kept by the Birthplace and visitors' books at the inns.

32. Winter, *Shakespeare's England*, p. 79.

33. *Ibid.*, p. 80.

34. Nathaniel Hawthorne, *Our Old Home: A Series of English Sketches* (Boston: Ticknor and Fields, 1863), pp. 112, 115.

35. Tearle, *Rambles*, pp. 77, 78, 80, 94.

36. For a more extended reading of Shakespeare's Birthplace and its construction as the place of origin of a national Bard, see Nicola J. Watson, *The Literary Tourist: Readers and Places in Romantic and Victorian Britain* (New York and Basingstoke: Palgrave, 2006).

37. Hawthorne, *Our Old Home*, pp. 116, 117.

38. Washington Irving, *The Sketchbook of Geoffrey Crayon* (Leipzig: Tauchnitz, 1843), p. 314.

39. For more on the Victorian sense of the relationship between the Queen and Shakespeare, see Michael Dobson and Nicola Watson, *England's Elizabeth: An Afterlife in Fame and Fantasy* (Oxford: Oxford University Press, 2002), 128–46; on Elizabethan nostalgia and tourism, see esp. pp. 138–46.

40. Lord Egremont on the question of the location of a commemorative statue for the tercentenary of Shakespeare's birth in 1864, quoted in Richard Foulkes, *The Shakespeare Tercentenary of 1864* (London: The Society for Theatre Research, 1984), p. 2. A statue was eventually erected in Leicester Square.

41. Ben Jonson, "To the memory of my beloved, the author Mr. William Shakespeare, and what he hath left us," in the prefatory materials to the First Folio.

42. See Dobson, *Making of the National Poet*, pp. 135–46.

43. Irving, *Sketchbook*, p. 309; Benjamin Robert Haydon, *Diary*, cited in Martineau, *Shakespeare in Art*, p. 204.

44. John. R. Wise, *Shakspere: his Birthplace and its Neighbourhood* (London: Smith, Elder & Co., 1861), p. 22.

45. Walter Scott, *Kenilworth* (London: Henry Froude, Oxford University Press, 1910), p. 231. I cite this edition because this episode was felt to merit an illustration too, "Laneham preferring his request to the Earl of Leicester: Spenser and Shakespeare in attendance."

46. William Howitt, *Homes and Haunts of the Most Eminent British Poets*, 2 vols. (London: Richard Bentley, 1847), I. 41.

47. Winter, *Shakespeare's England*, p. 183.

48. Oliver Goldsmith, "A Reverie at the Boar's Head Tavern in Eastcheap" (1760), in *The Collected Works of Oliver Goldsmith*, ed. Arthur Friedman, 5 vols. (Oxford: Clarendon Press, 1966), III. 98.

49. The development of the London literary walk is too large a subject to tackle here; suffice it to say that the Shakespeare walks were modeled in their sensibility upon the literary walks that rapidly developed around the life and works of Charles

Dickens from the 1880s onwards. Indeed, Shakespeare was obliged to share Southwark with the ghosts of Dickens and his characters. See Christian Tearle's *Rambles with an American* in which the enthusiast Mr. Fairchild divides his attention between the two in exploring Southwark.

50. Tearle, *Rambles*, p. 41.
51. *Ibid.*, p. 45.
52. *Ibid.*, p. 52.
53. *Ibid.*, p. 52.
54. *Ibid.*, p. 62.
55. See, for example, William Martin, *Lunchtime Rambles in Old London: No 7 In the Steps of Shakespeare Along the Bankside* (London: The Homeland Association, [1924]), which provides a map detailing the main sites of interest; William Kent, *London for Shakespeare Lovers* (London: Methuen, 1934), which provides a final chapter devoted to two Shakespeare Rambles, one along Bankside, and the other on the north side of the river locating Shakespeare's house, and the Boar's Head.
56. Tearle, *Rambles*, p. 56.
57. See Kent, *London*, pp. 146, 169, 174; William Bailey Kempling, *Shakespeare Memorials of London* (London: T. Werner Laurie Ltd, 1923) for photographs of assorted monuments.
58. For a notable exception see Dennis Kennedy, "Shakespeare and Cultural Tourism," *Theatre Journal* 50 (May 1998), 175–88, p. 186. For a discussion of the Globe experience as a tourist experience hybridized with pure theatrical experience, see William Worthen, *Shakespeare and the Force of Modern Performance* (Cambridge: Cambridge University Press, 2003), chapter 2.
59. See Kent, *London*, pp. 146ff.
60. Martineau, *Shakespeare in Art*, p. 205.
61. Charles Dickens, *American Notes for General Circulation and Pictures from Italy*, ed. F. S. Schwarzbach and Leonée Ormond (London: J. M. Dent, 1997), pp. 369–73.
62. *The Official Programme of the Tercentenary Festival of the Birth of Shakespeare, to be held at Stratford-upon-Avon* (London: Cassell, Petter, and Galpin, 1864), p. 29.
63. www.shakespearesitaly.com
64. For a lively account of this affair, see Graham Holderness, "Bardolatry: or, the Cultural Materialist's Guide to Stratford-upon-Avon," in *The Shakespeare Myth*, ed. Graham Holderness (Manchester: Manchester University Press, 1988), pp. 2–15, pp. 2–3. I am indebted to this essay for my information.
65. On the replica of the Globe in Virginia, and its meanings and uses as compared with the Globe on the South Bank, see Diana E. Henderson, "Shakespeare: The Theme Park," in *Shakespeare after Mass Media*, ed. Richard Burt (New York: Palgrave, 2002), pp. 107–26.
66. See the official website http://www.shakespearegarden.org/History.htm
67. See the official website for the Cottage in Victoria, British Columbia: www.victorialodging.com/annehathawayscottage; see also "Deb's Unofficial Walt Disney World Information Guide" posted on www.allearsnet.com
68. Lanier, *Shakespeare and Modern Popular Culture*, p. 145.
69. 'William and the Lost Tourist' was published in the collection of stories by Richmal Crompton entitled *William the Conqueror* (London: George Newnes, 1926), republished by Macmillan (Basingstoke, 1984), pp. 75–95.

II

W. B. WORTHEN

Performing Shakespeare in digital culture

I began thinking about this essay in the central library of the Czech Academy in Prague, as good a platform as any to stage an inquiry into the ways Shakespearean drama engages with digital culture. It's a large nineteenth-century room, two stories, with a mezzanine of book stacks around the upper level, a large ironwork skylight, and modern furniture. Although the shared computers for internet use are old and slow, the worktables each have several high-speed ports, so that you can connect your own laptop and work at your usual speed; there is high-speed wireless as well. As the day waxes, a number of writers, scholars, and students arrive to check mail, do research, and watch movies online. Cellphones are strictly prohibited, according to the signs at least: we are warned that even one ring will be cause for immediate ejection and loss of privileges. But phones ring, and to judge by the number of people grabbing for their pockets, many people simply have the ringer set to vibrate: there's little apparent concern about having a yellular conversation – at that somewhat irritating, loudish cellphone volume – though most other conversations are ritually hushed. This is not really a problem, though. No one complains, there are even relatively few nasty glances. Some people wear headphones; the woman opposite me seems to be transcribing or perhaps translating a long document, occasionally speaking into a webcam; and between bouts of actual writing, email, and internet searching, I'm playing and replaying the Almereyda *Hamlet*. Others are watching movies, too, and not always with headphones: a group of college-age men are gathered around a laptop which issues, with increasing frequency, the sounds of screeching tires and muffled explosions.

The elegant Národní Divadlo, the Czech National Theatre building, is almost directly across the street, spatializing a familiar image of the conflicted identity of Shakespearean drama, and of our understanding of Western drama more generally: to move between the institutions of drama – the page and the stage – you have to cross the street. At least, you did until very recently, until digital technologies brought performance to the digital screen, the same screen that most of us use for reading and writing. Shakespearean drama has, for a century now, had several sites of performance. Shakespeare speaks to us from the pages of a stunning variety of printed materials; from the radio; from phonograph records, reel-to-reel and cassette tapes, compact audio disks; from the big screen in the movie theatre and (now, with much greater frequency) from videotape and digital video disk recordings on the television screen. While live theatrical performance remains for many people the privileged site of performance, having – like writing (though perhaps not like print) – an ontological connection to the media in which Shakespeare composed his plays, the identity of Shakespearean drama no longer seems to shuttle solely between the page and the stage. Not only is our access to Shakespearean drama mediated by digital technology (even in live performance, where computers operate most theatre systems), our imagination of Shakespearean drama is shaped by the forms and moods of digital culture: the "penny dreadfuls" of Julie Taymor's *Titus*, Ethan Hawke's editing and re-editing of his pixellated experience in Michael Almereyda's *Hamlet*, the animated clouds in the storm scene of Baz Luhrmann's *William Shakespeare's Romeo + Juliet*, to say nothing of the thoroughgoing impact of digital editing in all three films.[1]

This observation should cause neither elation nor undue alarm: while some students enter the library only when they cannot find appropriate research material online, I'm able to sit in Prague and consult digitized facsimiles from archives thousands of miles away, and check out the photo gallery and auditorium technical specs of the Národní Divadlo across the street, to say nothing of watching Ethan Hawke and Julia Stiles pout at one other.[2] At the same time, it's also clear that our understanding of Shakespearean drama no longer oscillates dualistically between page and stage, page and screen, screen and stage. Insofar as the digital screen represents text and image through the same means, it tends to blur the distinction between the drama's traditional delivery systems. The digital screen represents text *as image*, and increasingly as an animated image, making no distinction between writing and performance as dataforms. Moreover, when the screen on which we read Shakespeare's plays – in a wide range of formats, from texts stored in a wide range of locations – and see Shakespearean performances is *connected*, Shakespearean drama is itself part of a worldwide simultaneous interactive archive. The Czech Academy may be across the street from the Národní Divadlo, but in digital culture the page and the stage are, potentially, both part of the same network, dissolved into the same medium, realizable wherever I can get a connection on my laptop.

Like many claims made for the wonders of the digital world, this one is more exuberant than exact: in point of fact, while there's an abundance of Shakespeare imagery and textuality online, there's little Shakespeare performance there. At the same time, the transformation of the forms of human communication – writing and acting, in this case – into digitized information and the ability to transmit that information to a variety of devices and so to realize that information in an ever-expanding array of personal and social contexts are changing the ways we live. To judge by the reading room of the Czech Academy, "connexity" seems an indispensable, even inalienable accessory of human being, changing the practice of being in this most "human" of spaces, the library.[3] For many, perhaps most, people in the West, the virtual connective tissue of digital culture is a sometimes threatening (is my bank account being hacked?), often irritating (turn off your cellphone!), mainly mysterious (why won't this thing work?), and increasingly unremarkable aspect of daily life (for much of the world population – which has yet to use the telephone – digital culture is simply absent from daily life, however much it may operate in the institutions that govern it). It's unthinkable that the practices of digital culture could so transform everyday life – the apparent necessity of ubiquitous communicative potential, the predication of "meaning" on "information" – without transforming our sense of performance in general, and dramatic performance more specifically, that genre (to paraphrase both Aristotle and Clifford Geertz) in which we conceive ourselves by telling stories to ourselves about ourselves in the mode of human enactment. We are not to the point of beaming bodies, *Star Trek* fashion, around the globe, but even the contours of liveness and locality witness the pressure of this transformation, as our means of being present to one another, and the technologies of representation we use to articulate that presence, evolve.

To the extent that new technologies both embody and reshape changing social relations, the emerging digital culture will not leave the practice of drama and the understanding of Shakespeare untouched. As Jon McKenzie notes, the computer has become a kind of "metatechnology," incorporating "a wide range of information technologies including the book itself, as well as the post, photography, telephony, film, television, typewriter, radio, video, compact disc, copy machine, fax, and an astonishing array of artistic media and scientific instruments."[4] While the principal medium disseminating Shakespearean drama surely continues to be the book, the availability of texts, films, images, and research materials through electronic means is expanding and altering the practice of research and our understanding of Shakespearean drama itself.[5] Since the rise of print, Western culture has framed "the drama" across two different platforms, two incommensurable modes of materialization – the page and the stage – and has traced the conflicted identity of Shakespeare's plays through a familiar dualism. Is Shakespeare's "work" bound to its writing, the performance a secondary, derivative, edition-like iteration? Or is the text merely a sketch or ground-plan or score or map or blueprint (to evoke a few of the common metaphors)

for a work that takes its real existence onstage, typically in forms of performance (Method acting, epic theatre, kabuki) or spaces of performance (the
high-tech modern proscenium theatre, the reconstructed fire-proof Globe),
that Shakespeare could hardly have imagined? With the onset of recording
technologies, we have practiced Shakespearean drama across three platforms –
the page, the stage, and recorded performance. Many of the innovations
associated with film have their visible counterparts in stage production; so,
too, much critique of film Shakespeare replicates the text-oriented structure
of stage-oriented criticism. And since watching film in a movie house tends to
replicate the ideology of "private" consumption that sustains the dominant
form of theatrical modernism, stage realism, the increasingly "private" consumption offered by home viewing on television or video might be understood as part of a longer trajectory of the commodification of performance
tracing its origins to the late nineteenth-century stage. Film has transformed
the pace, visual field, and psychological dynamics of modern Shakespeare,
and has greatly expanded both the field of Shakespeare's adaptation to
modern life and the global dissemination of Shakespeare performance.
Recorded performance has decisively altered our access to Shakespearean
drama in other ways, too: film and video recordings can be viewed again and
again; they preserve performances for a much longer duration than a stage
production does (though it has always been possible to see a long-running
production many times, and there is perhaps even a corollary between the
small changes that develop in a long-running live performance and the
inevitable degradation and demagnetization of film and video stock).
Nonetheless, recorded performances maintain the dynamic fissuring of
the identity of drama characteristic of the age of print, the tension between
the drama's identity as a form of writing and its identity as a form of
performance.

I don't mean to undersell the extraordinary impact of film and video on
our understanding of Shakespearean drama. But to engage the impact of
digital technologies on the drama, we must attend to the distinctive ways in
which digital technologies operate, their ways of inhabiting and representing
the temporality and spatiality they share with us, their distinctive ways of
encoding and processing representation, and their distinctive articulation as
cultural practice. Given the prominence of Shakespearean drama in book,
stage, sound, film, and video formats, and the widespread dissemination of
Shakespearean writing and performance in digitized forms, Shakespeare
provides a revealing site for the question of the impact of digital culture on
our sense of the drama. At the same time, it's important to recognize that this
transformation – if that's what it is – is barely underway. For this reason,
then, I'd like to narrow our discussion quite severely here, to the performance

of Shakespeare on DVD. What are the implications of watching DVDs of Shakespearean drama on the computer screen? What might the practice of watching Shakespeare on the active, connected, digital screen tell us about the identity of drama, and how that identity relates to the shifting technologies of performance? And how might the structure of digitized performance relate to the dominant paradigm sustaining the identities of Shakespearean drama both in Western culture generally, and in the narrower spheres of academic critique and disciplinary demarcation: "text vs. performance?"

DVD: text or performance?

Although a vigorous critique of this dichotomy has emerged both in Shakespeare studies and more widely in drama studies, it continues to shape the contemporary understanding of the work of drama. This dichotomy is, perhaps, more familiar in Shakespeare studies than in other areas of literary or performance studies, largely through the massive cultural investment in the textual identity of Shakespearean drama and the foundational role of Shakespeare in literary studies and pedagogy. In related fields, however, this dichotomy looks somewhat different: contemporary theatre and performance studies, for example, tends to regard discussion of the drama, and often of dramatic performance, as "merely literary." From this perspective, the presumed "authority" of the text over certain forms of performance witnesses the cultural and conceptual exhaustion of dramatic performance.[6] Yet in the tech-forward world of digital performance, DVD Shakespeare takes a surprisingly atavistic stance, invoking the book rather than the performance as the site of play. As Richard Burt and others have noted, the DVD surrounds the performance of Shakespearean drama with a range of ancillary materials – theatrical trailers, deleted scenes, a version of the film with simultaneous commentary by the director/designers/performers, interviews, documentaries about making the film, music videos, video games, elements of the marketing plan and print advertising, teaching materials and/or the ability to link to internet teaching materials if the DVD is loaded onto a computer – and organizes these materials according to a familiar strategy, one that recalls the otherwise transcended interface between print and theatre: the book-like menu "chapters."[7] While some videos have also provided "extras" placed before or after the film, the structure of digital technology not only enables these materials to be organized chapter-wise (for reference, cross-checking), but enables the performance to be both represented and engaged chapter-wise, or (following the conventions somewhat haphazardly originating in the early quartos and the Folio), by flipping to the appropriate act and scene. Both film and video are fundamentally bound to the temporality of live performance. Rewinding is not only cumbersome and inexact, but constantly enacts the fact that moments in a given performance are distinct, separated by duration, caught in a temporality that can be mechanically accelerated or reversed, but that cannot be undone. Like books, digitized performance permits the precise random access of information files, and so paradoxically offers a considerably more bookish engagement with Shakespearean drama than earlier recording technologies. It's much easier to jump back and forth between scenes, to bookmark units of the performance, and to synchronize the film in one window with your reading, researching, and writing in other windows on the digital desktop. Finally, digitized performance can represent performance as a form of the book because it shares its constitutive logic with the printed book: it is composed within a single encoding structure. Books use paper, ink, and type to represent the data – the play – in a single medium: the signs and signals of written language. Computers use a network of transistorized switches to represent the data – the film performance – in a single medium: the electronic signals of binary code, susceptible to being interpreted (provided you have the proper hardware and software) as text, speech, still and moving image. In this sense, the "chaptering" of the DVD performance points to a more fundamental textualization, in which the digital code not only represents performance in ways hitherto associated with print, but realizes both writing and action as the same thing, in the same code.

While Burt argues that the consequence of digitization is "that film reception has become posthistorical," in that audiences are no longer bound to the ritual occasion of the film's showing in a movie theatre (in the here and now, in other words, that filmgoing shares with theatregoing), in another sense, Shakespearean performance on DVD has simply migrated to another form of historicization, as the material DVD now provides the moment of the performance's entry into the discourses of history and critique.[8] Far from being posthistorical, digital Shakespeare shares with print the fact of its encoding in a cultural as well as an electronic sense. In its packaging and marketing, in the "features" it provides, as well as in the details of the performance itself, the DVD bookishly instantiates and preserves a moment in the historical emergence of the performance work. As in many other respects, Baz Luhrmann seems to have been among the first to realize the impact of digital technology on Shakespearean performance. Not only are the practices of digital editing central to his vision of *Romeo and Juliet*, and not only does the presence of "text" onscreen signal the impact of digital code (rendering text and performance as the same thing, merely different ways of refreshing the pixellated screen), but Luhrmann understands the capital to be gained from releasing a second, "special edition" of *William Shakespeare's Romeo + Juliet*, packed with features that seem designed to address both a general and a more pedagogically invested (teachers, students, scholars) audience.[9] Although the material form of the DVD – the plastic slipcase with the printed paper insert, the plastic disk itself – is perhaps unremarkable, the "features" function as additional "chapters." As a "special edition" the DVD at once invokes and subverts the iterative ideology of print, the sense that mechanical reproducibility guarantees the work's enduring identity across a range of different printed versions. Surrounding the performance with commentary, outtakes, designs, and so on, the DVD testifies to the labile distinctiveness of performance, the delicate dependence of *this* performance on a series of choices, its specific non-identity with other versions of "the play," including all merely textual incarnations. At the same time, the DVD polytext also asserts itself as an edition, and a special edition at that, of the film and of *William Shakespeare's* play, incorporating *Romeo + Juliet* within the external, cultural framework of print, and simultaneously incorporating those values internally, in the chapter-wise design of our engagement with the performance itself.

Enabling its audiences to *read* performance, the DVD replicates the film product but situates it within a new network of cultural and technological relations, relations perhaps more evocative of print culture than of its raffish cousin, the stage.[10] Print is a familiar technology, but it has taken the rise of digital means for reproducing and analyzing print to alert us fully to the consequences of the rhetoric of print technology *as* rhetoric: the fact that print's evident emphasis on the consistency implied by mechanical reproduction masks the extraordinary, even incoherent variety of its products (how many *Hamlet*s are on your shelf? And in how many of them does Hamlet actually speak the same words?). In part, of course, the power of this rhetoric depends on the iterative "logic" of print: print could assert the irrelevance of paper stock, trim size, design, in view of the overwhelming suggestiveness of the fact that the words themselves could be so readily duplicated and disseminated.[11] Mechanical reproducibility asserts the sameness of its representations in the face of their evident material difference (difference which frequently extends to the words on the page). Transforming its "data" into code, digital technologies suggest not merely a difference in degree but a difference in kind: the same data can now be realized on a dazzling – and growing – range of devices, instantiated in different material forms and so performed in a wider range of environments. The "data" are realized in such different ways that we might well ask whether the performance is still the thing itself. Is the Folio *Hamlet* the same thing as a modern edition of the Folio *Hamlet*? As a modern photo-facsimile of the Folio *Hamlet*? Even though the encoded data are – far more than printed words – transmitted through the identical code to all devices, is Almereyda's *Hamlet* the same thing on the big screen, the DVD player, the computer screen, the airline seatback screen, the cellphone? Beyond that, because the encoded data can be processed through various applications (not just as ink and paper), it is readily susceptible to being exchanged, combined, remixed, edited by the user. While mechanical reproducibility underwrites the illusion of sameness, digital reproduction seems to guarantee the stability of the data in order to underwrite its manifestation as difference – on different devices, in different places, transformed to different uses.[12]

Whether we narrowly regard digital technology as a successor to print, or more broadly as a "metatechnology" that "overcodes and inscribes almost all others," digital technologies and the ways we use and understand them are, at least for now, often locked in a dialectical embrace with earlier forms of production, an embrace fully enacted on the screen of our own writing, where print is represented without the defining characteristic of print, a stable materiality.[13] While DVD performance has been rapidly naturalized to the culture of recorded performance, it's important to recognize that like all new technologies – and particularly like those rapidly instrumentalized by the commodification of information, such as print – the DVD exemplifies the ways in which the interests and investments of technical design ultimately undergo what Andrew Feenberg calls "closure."

> The process of "closure" ultimately adapts a produce to a socially recognized demand and thereby fixes its definition. Closure produces a "black box," an artifact that is no longer called into question but is taken for granted. Before closure is achieved, it is obvious that social interests are at stake in the design process. But once the black box is closed, its social origins are quickly forgotten. Looking back from that later standpoint, the artifact appears purely technical, even inevitable.[14]

For Feenberg, "closure" lends credibility to the "deterministic illusion" that technology governs the practices of its use, rather than arising in a dynamic and reciprocal interplay between technological invention and social imperatives. Feenberg's comments here evoke the recent history of the history and sociology of the book, in which scholars from a variety of fields (D. F. McKenzie, Jerome McGann) have worked to exhume the "social origins" of the practices of print, as a way both to make its products appear less inevitable and to alienate in a strictly Brechtian sense our attitudes and beliefs about how print works, and what it works to do.[15]

Slipping the DVD into your computer drive is hardly a neutral activity: like all engagements with technology, it slips you into a complex network of agency. First of all, the technology itself is difficult to alienate, make visible, let alone comprehensible to most users. Compared even to the principle of film – light projected through a series of still photographic frames, set in motion at a standard speed to produce the illusion of movement – the principle of the DVD is opaque.[16] The unimaginable speeds (which *are* imaginable and quantifiable to the engineers and designers of the computer systems) at which these data are read, transmitted, and at which the screen's display of information is updated is one measure of the "closure" of this technology from most users; needless to say, the mathematical principles on which computer science is founded will remain opaque to all but the most highly trained. More to the point, though, the pedestrian engagement with digital Shakespeare is part of a larger debate on the theory of technology itself, whether we regard technologies like the DVD, the computer, the cellphone, as primarily "instrumental" in character, or as bearing the "substantive" values of the culture, society, and economy that created them. As Feenberg has argued in a series of books, the instrumental theory "offers the most widely accepted view of technology. It is based on the common sense idea that technologies are 'tools' standing ready to serve the purposes of their users. Technology is deemed 'neutral,' without valuative content of its own." This is not to say, however, that instrumental views of technology are not without their ideological and social freight. Conceived as "pure instrumentality," technology sustains an ideologically loaded set of cultural attitudes. Instrumentalized technology is regarded as "indifferent to the variety of ends it can be employed to achieve," so that technologies are understood as "only contingently related to the substantive values they serve"; technology "appears to be indifferent with respect to politics"; the "socio-political neutrality of technology is usually attributed to its 'rational' character and the universality of the truth it embodies," so that, like "scientific ideas," technology can be expected to maintain its "cognitive status in every conceivable social context. Hence, what works in one society can be expected to work just as well in another"; and, finally, the "universality of technology also means that the same standards of measurement can be applied in different settings," in "different countries, different eras, and different situations." At the same time, the instrumental theory has been countered by a "substantive theory, best known through the writings of Jacques Ellul and Martin Heidegger," that sees technology to constitute "a new type of cultural system that restructures the entire social world as an object of control," in a sense offering a radically deterministic understanding of the relationship between technology and social life.[17]

Working to mediate these positions, Feenberg understands technology not as "destiny but a scene of struggle. It is a social battlefield, or perhaps a better metaphor would be a *parliament of things* in which civilizational alternatives are debated and decided."[18] To grasp this distinction, though, requires us to grasp a distinction we typically overlook in daily life, the distinction between tools and technologies. We tend to regard computers, their peripherals, and the software they run as tools, as instruments like a hammer or an ax, a hawk or a handsaw, that let us accomplish a specific local task. Computers and their software do function as tools: today I want to accomplish the task of writing, and I've chosen my laptop – rather than the pen and paper I often use in the early stages of writing – to make something, the first draft of this paragraph. And, like other tools I have, I can eventually decide whether this one performs the task in a way adequate to my purposes: when my saw gets dull, I can get it sharpened or buy a new one; when, in comparison with my newer computer at work, my laptop seems too slow, I will have to get a new one. Yet insofar as the computer and its software participate in technology, they also have a larger public, social character, in that technologies "are not limited objects present for control by individual wills. Instead they consist of patterns of conduct through which particular desires are literally incorporated and made manifest. In this sense, a technology is a set of dynamic orientations, a way of biasing the movement of natural resources, labor, capital, and so on."[19] As Peter Hershock argues, technologies are "value-driven and value-producing patterns of conduct" that create, depend on, and encode cultural relationships: "every new technology amounts to a novel biasing or conditioning of the quality of our interdependence."[20] Much as "knives, forks, and spoons are not just strips of metal, but imply a whole system of eating behavior with respect to which each actual meal is a performance,"[21] so too computers and the digital technologies that drive them are always used simultaneously as tools to accomplish a local purpose, and as technologies that value and conceive that purpose within a wider network of social, cultural, economic, and even political conduct, as performance so to speak.

The critical theory of technology enables us to put a somewhat different pressure on the question of digital Shakespeare, alerting us to the fact that while we often use the DVD as a tool, it is better understood (as the interface designer Brenda Laurel urged some time ago) as a "medium."[22] Insofar as the DVD at once represents text/performance, even represents performance-as-text (and our evanescent texts as momentary virtual performances), echoing the dynamics of print even as a means of engaging performance, we might ask how the technological relations of conduct alter the perception of the identity of drama, bear on the ways drama is changed when it occupies a digital medium. If the DVD is a tool, what is it used for? And as technology, what networks of conduct and relationship does it support and engage?

Performing the DVD

As a technology of dramatic performance, Shakespeare's theatre required a complex and emerging network of social relations, involving the evolving profession of playwright, the functioning of a professional company of performers, the construction, maintenance, and occasional moving of a theatre building, as well as a dense network of legal relations to local and national government officials. There is a striking asymmetry, however, between any theatrical performance and Shakespeare performance in the age of DVD: performance in the theatre tends to dramatize the social complicity and ideological determinacy of the technologies of the stage. Even in the modern era, in which the aesthetic priority of individual subjection is manifest in the darkened house, individual seating, and a massive technological infrastructure designed to integrate the spectacle before the viewer (and, in this sense, to integrate the viewer, too), across the invisible screen of the proscenium, theatregoing demands the negotiation of the social/technological interface: the transport, the box office, the crowded lobby and toilets, the rituals of seat-taking, the latecomers, the applause, the curtain calls dramatize the sense in which the technology of theatre is still relatively "open," visible.

The DVD, on the other hand, seems to articulate one understanding of the printed play as a technology of drama: the DVD provides a material means to revisit the drama, stored in a format that enables its retemporalization (emerging again in human time) and respatialization (it can be accessed nearly anywhere). Dramatic performance is at once public and local; even when the show is a touring production, it's mediated by the evident – sometimes too evident – materiality of the local theatre. Although DVD performance is manifestly framed by the corporate structure of both film-making and digital hardware and software technologies, its performance tends to background this corporate interface. While the technology of computer-mediated communications (CMC) surely connects the individual user within a network of potentially active social relations, the relations remain virtual until engaged by the user, and to a large extent seem to be controlled by the user.[23] In this sense, DVD performance resembles other activities undertaken onscreen, like writing, email, internet searching: it is a private viewing, in which the apparatus and function of the performance itself is relatively unavailable (I can see how my pen leaves an ink trace, but have no direct contact with the means by which a keystroke creates a letter on my screen), and in which the viewer's insertion in a dense network of social mediation appears to be optional. As in the theatre, the corporate-technological apparatus that structures this kind of use, this engagement of performance (despite the incessant pop-ups and advertising, to say nothing of the business-friendly format of most operating system interfaces) asserts its transparency.

Feenberg's "black box" is suggestive of that other black box, the modern stage: both provide the illusory experience of subjective agency and experience in a structure of performance that is highly overdetermined, one in which the narcotic, culinary pleasure of the individual subject is constructed, as Brecht recognized, on the occluded power relations engrained in the means of representation itself. DVD Shakespeare fully participates in the instrumentalizing rhetoric of digital technologies, both in the claim to facilitate globalized communications and cultural transfer and in the claim that the technological realization of performance as information is value-neutral to the data it represents. DVD Shakespeare dramatizes the role of English, and of Western culture, in a pervasive "global monoculture," one long recognized in terms of the dissemination of art forms (music, film, television), political institutions, and commodities (McDonald's, Mercedes, Nokia, Nestlé), but in which "the dominance of English in computation is part of this broader picture."[24] But while the globalization of technology facilitates travel, enables us to summon distant libraries to the screen, connect with media, and contact individuals world wide, in a sense the "axiological commerce – the exchange of basic human values" encoded in this technology remains, at the present time, largely a one-way trade.[25] While the percentage of internet traffic conducted in languages other than English has risen substantially in the past decade – from 10 percent in 1996, to 46 percent in 2001, to an estimated 67 percent in 2005 – both the commercial and non-commercial content of the internet "is permeated by Western values of individual freedom (including freedom of expression), religious agnosticism, open sexuality, and free-market capitalism." Not only are these values, or their specific configuration, often the sign of "foreign ideology" online, but even "the technology itself – its codes, software, protocols, and interface designs – incorporates an English-language/Western cultural bias"[26] (as anyone using these functions well knows, Microsoft Word is very poorly designed for multilingual writing: it is difficult to impossible to spellcheck several languages in the same document, and indeed many of the language options listed under the Tools menu are not necessarily functional).

While we might think that one of the dominant trends in Shakespeare performance has to do with the "intercultural" reach and reconfiguration of Shakespearean drama, the globalization of performance on DVD is dependent on a coherent structure of technology, technology which is instrumentalized within an embattled sphere of value. Although intercultural performance, at its best, promotes critical conflict and indeterminacy across the contested frontiers of cultural communication, the globalization of technological performance often appears to depend on the repression of that interface, the none-too-subtle lamination of Western cultural products and values to the instrumental "neutrality" of the digital code. Many of the DVD performances we might choose to watch strike a decidedly "globalist" or

"intercultural" perspective. I'm thinking here both of Luhrmann's *Romeo +
Juliet* and of the recent, densely historical *Merchant of Venice*, directed by
Michael Radford and featuring an international and multiethnic cast, which
stages both Venice and Belmont as densely transnational spaces, and crucially foregrounds the ways the liberal, capitalist, legal structure of Venice is
challenged by the incorporation of marked religious outsiders, potentially an
allegory of the contemporary response to Islam in Europe.[27] Yet despite their
"global" thematics, these DVDs are clearly marked for a less-than-global
audience: *Romeo + Juliet* has subtitles in both English and Spanish; *The
Merchant of Venice* in English and French. While the fact that the United
States and North America (Region 1) DVD has only two language options is
lamentable – surely Italian, or perhaps Hebrew for *Merchant*? – it also
witnesses the fiction of the "global" performance product, too. Despite
digitization and the worldwide dissemination of playback software, the
film and distribution industries have an interest in maintaining regionalized
distribution. The DVD maintains another odd symmetry with print, here,
especially given the historical relationship between print and the emergence
of national languages. The texts of Shakespeare's plays had to be translated
into, say, Czech before they could be performed for vernacular audiences;
today, if I am lecturing in Prague on the Almereyda *Hamlet*, my Region 1
DVD is useless, unless I pack my own translator/performer and project the
film from my own laptop.[28]

Despite the proximity of print and digital technologies as technologies of
dramatic storage, Shakespeare's participation in a digital global monoculture is not participation in a culture of signification, a culture of performance, but in a culture of information. "Information" is not identifiable with
"meaning" in a technological sense: it is dissociated from the contextual field
of meaning, abstracted from a material conveyance, and then selected from a
field of transmission. Information arises from the statistical probability that
this message is capable of being differentiated meaningfully, not that it bears
meaning in itself. Digital technologies depend on this statistical conception
of "information," the probability that a given set of signals can be isolated
from the field of static: too much redundancy or too much variety tend to
drive the system towards communicative entropy.[29] As Mark C. Taylor puts
it, "On the one hand, information *is* a difference, and, therefore, in the
absence of difference, there is no information. On the other hand, information is a difference that *makes a difference*. Not all differences make a
difference because some differences are indifferent and hence inconsequen-
tial. Both too little and too much difference creates chaos."[30] Both writing
and print are also information systems in this sense. It is through the
repetition-with-variation of a limited set of standard elements – letters,

punctuation, spacing – that we are able to isolate potentially significant signals and construe them according to hierarchically nested protocols, as words, sentences, and paragraphs, which are themselves understood within larger generic structures (essay, novel, poem, play) which are not, however, part of the communicative message itself. WexxAReyyyablezzzzzin fact to xxxxxdealxxwithxzzxzx Axcxcxconsiderablebbbbbamount of STATIC, though clearly unduebbbbbbvariation burnthispageburnthispageburnthhispagexxxxor undue ccccreduncancy redundancyredundancyredundancyredundancy cccchindersxxxxthe efficiency and effectiveness of the communication.

Information theory, then, necessarily defines information as distinct from both the vehicle of transmission and from the context of materialization, what we usually understand as meaning. Divorcing the notion of information from meaning and context has the effect of allowing "information to have a stable value as it [is] moved from one context to another," a decisive recognition enabling the entire digital revolution; yet as N. Kathleen Hayles argues, this understanding of information has cultural consequences as well, to the extent that information has come to be "conceptualized as if it were an entity that can flow unchanged between different material substrates." It is precisely this ability to abstract "information from context and thus from meaning" that drives the reification of "information into a free-floating, decontextualized, quantifiable entity."[31]

To the extent that it clarifies the deep contextuality and contingency of performance meanings, drama seems not readily assimilable to "information," much as it may be possible to describe aspects of performance in "information" terms. Different costumes may be worn by the Montagues and Capulets, but if we isolate the field of costume from the plot, without an understanding of the relationship between those groups, this difference is insignificant, mere static, meaningless differentiae. In Norbert Wiener's terms, it's the possibility that this difference might register more than one contingency, that it might register more than just difference, but a second contingency, that lends it potential as "information." Yet while such metaphorical applications of "information" to our understanding of performance may be trivial, the pervasive grip of "information" on the cultural imagination of "meaning" surely has important implications for our understanding of what drama and performance are and what they do, particularly when they are themselves conveyed as digitized information, as people come to associate "information" with value apart from the context of delivery in ways that run counter to a materialist sense of cultural production: the sense that a photo carries the same "information" whether it is displayed on my cellphone, laptop screen, in the newspaper, or in a gallery exhibition. Although the language and structure of computer culture has deeply colored our metaphors of human subjection (how many people now "access" their memories rather than remember them? when did the expression "TMI" for "too much information" come into use?), the transformation of signification to information has been at once profound and difficult to grasp.

How does the digitizing process – the encoding of a performance as binary signals susceptible to a potentially infinite variety of decoded representations – transform our understanding of the character of performance itself? The answers to this kind of question lie in the future, but the drama's unstable place in print culture again provides a surprising and perhaps cautionary example. The notion that "drama" retains its identity across platforms is one of the urgent consequences of the rise of print, a precursor in a sense to the notion of "information" dislocated from the context of its realization. The widespread assumption that Shakespeare's plays can mean the same thing as texts and as performances, or that a performance is even capable of reiterating textual meanings is, in a sense, an "information theory" understanding of text-and-performance arising from the iterative character of print: in this view, dramatic writing functions like encoded data, which can be properly (and identically) downloaded with the proper theatrical software. And yet the history of theatre witnesses the fallacy of this understanding, while its widespread currency also witnesses the ongoing ideological sway of print rhetoric, another precursor to the ideological sway of "information." For the drama seems less to resemble the data than a self-evolving software, enabling us to frame conventions of contemporary human behavior (including contemporary theatrical behavior) in specific, meaningful, and changing ways.

The disjunction between information and knowledge has important implications, both for our understanding of cultural phenomena, and for our own habits as readers and writers, and presumably as audiences as well. Jon McKenzie notes that the "networked computer culminates a process that has been underway since the invention of photography and phonography: *the radical transformation of the citational network of discourses and practices*," a transformation not only enacted in the ways in which university teaching now presents material, instruction, and the research process to students, but that is practiced every time we engage in writing.[32] In his effort to chart the transformation of the disciplinary structure of knowledge of the eighteenth and nineteenth centuries to the performative structure of contemporary culture, McKenzie is rightly more preoccupied with a deeper, tectonic movement than with shifting fenceposts on the surface. And yet our engagement with the regime of performance happens through performance, notably through the differential ways we perform – conduct ourselves, Hershock might say – through emerging technologies. Attending to differences between manual and digital writing, for instance, Phil Mullins contrasts the practices of knowing of print culture and those of information media: whereas to be "a knower is a social endeavor that involves contextualizing such that one becomes an effective agent," in electronic information culture, it is an "'appetite for correlations' that aptly characterizes a writer's or a reader's habits of thought about communication in an environment in which the computer is the primary tool."[33] Facilitating the task of writing as a kind of bricolage, the computer transforms literacy, too: "It seems likely that electronic culture's emerging notion of literacy will focus on skills for manipulating electronic resources necessary to make such correlations. The late print-culture notion of literacy as individual expression and critical thinking, the ability to articulate informed judgments based on a global, internalized, coherent framework of knowledge, is being subtly reshaped."[34] More to the point, insofar as the text itself is not only not a thing, an object, but an image, and is networked on the screen with other texts and images, both the electronic medium and the culture of information "is slowly shifting our tacit notion of text from a stable, discrete body to a fluid network format. There are no permanent borders or boundaries for electronic materials ... In the same way, there are no final distinctions between reading and writing in the electronic world."[35]

The Shakespeare DVD inserts performance into this multiplex legibility. Although we have yet fully to inhabit the interface (or, more to the point, to imagine and demand that we *should* inhabit the interface) in the way Brenda Laurel imagines – as a field in which we "act within a representation" – the DVD enables us to follow the performance, to interrupt and reread the performance, to cut away from the linearity of the performance to other information (for example, to check out the costume designs), and to supplement the performance by going online while it is running.[36] In this sense, DVD Shakespeare oddly asserts the performance not as the completion, fulfillment, alternative to or realization of the text, but as a lack, as requiring the supplementarity of commentary, explanation, other forms of engagement in order to be entertaining, to hold us apart as Victor Turner might have put it, *in* the performance.[37] Live performance is local and synchronous; delocalized and desynchronized, recorded performance resembles writing. Digitized performance is not only delocalized, it's portable, and personalized, too, and always potentially connected to cyberspace's ineluctable blurring of "the notions of unity, identity, and location."[38] Much as Shakespeare-on-television must be understood within the technological, economic, and social uses and constraints of the medium, so too the DVD's potential articulation with cyberspace articulates a changing valuation of Shakespeare performance.[39] Rather than a closed, distinctive structure of enactment, DVD drama provides an opportunity like other online activities, to "entertain" ourselves in an alternate performance, in which the process of the drama articulates with other activities.

To reduce the drama merely to yet another site of multitasking is, perhaps, not a terribly attractive proposition. What is perhaps more disappointing, though, is the fact that despite the much-touted interactivity of online experience, this genre of performance still provides so few opportunities to act as agents within the representational field. Karaoke Shakespeare DVD would, in a sense, merely demonstrate the fact that digital Shakespeare tends to imagine the spectator (or "user") as an absence, to enable only a centripetal agency, one directed outside dramatic performance. Even in the most conventional, fourth-wall theatrical performance, the spectator has a degree of agency within the performance: not only can we applaud, laugh, shout, sigh, or weep, but these acts have a marked effect on the process of the performance itself, on what happens on stage (the actors pause for the laugh, and pause longer for a long laugh) and on the quality and character of the theatrical event as a whole. In this sense, digital interactivity, while perhaps equally conventionalized, models a different sense of the spectator's activity and agency around the drama. As Peter Hershock remarks, in contemporary online culture, "we are trained to maintain an essentially 'iconic' pattern of awareness in which we passively select what we want or do not want from a menu of possible experiences."[40]

While to some critics the simultaneity promised by the internet makes certain kinds of digital interaction "live," like performance, most of the recorded performances we now see contain this level of interactivity only in potential.[41] Given the pervasive impact of "hypermediating media," the Shakespeare DVD is admittedly a rather residual corner of the digiverse, evidently constrained to forms of representation arising in a culture of presence, a culture in which the consequences of print dissemination on personal and cultural identity were still being explored.[42] At the same time, though, it's precisely this interface with the past that dramatic performance has historically provided, an interface we have nonetheless tended to misconceive when we have grasped performance merely as an act of literary recovery or reiteration. Dramatic performance involves the engagement of the otherness of writing – in the case of Shakespeare, now, the otherness of densely historicized writing – by technologies of production decisively marked by their presentness: this was as true of Burbage's performances as it was of Garrick's, or Olivier's, or of Ethan Hawke's today. Rather than understanding DVD Shakespeare merely as a means of decanting "closed" performances, we should be aware of the ways in which they structure our own performance, articulating our engagement with Shakespeare according to the forms and moods of digital practices. Mark C. Taylor describes an emerging sense of networked identity in which

> Bits of information become pixels, which, like a Chuck Close painting, organize themselves into the patterns of 'my' life. In the midst of these webs, networks, and screens, I can no more be certain where I am than I can know when or where the I begins and ends. I am plugged into other objects and subjects in such a way that I become myself in and through them, even as they become themselves in and through me.[43]

Regarding the Shakespeare DVD merely as a tool for storing and recovering complete performances, we run the risk of ignoring its more profound implication in the contemporary practice of digital representation. Transforming both "Shakespeare" and "drama," digital performance represents "the Shakespeare play" and "the Shakespeare performance" as a distinctive site of activity – still, perhaps, more potential than actual – in which our subjection in and by the play is enacted not through the visibly textual character of print, nor through the spectatorial relations of the theatre, nor through the consumer relations of the movie house, or the TV set, but through the diffuse connectivity of digital communications. We have only begun to chart the cultural and social consequences of this, our new Cleopatra, in which all things – including the familiar habits of reading and seeing Shakespearean drama and the acts of identification they imply – will henceforth become themselves.

NOTES

1. I have discussed the Almereyda *Hamlet* and the impact of digital editing more generally in "Fond Records: Remembering Theatre in the Digital Age," in *Shakespeare, Memory and Performance*, ed. Peter Holland (Cambridge: Cambridge University Press, 2006), pp. 281–304.
2. My information on undergraduate research practices is hardly scientific, deriving from an informal email survey I've conducted of my classes. Although the students I've taught tend overwhelmingly to prefer online research ("in a world that moves as fast as it does, i believe most students would agree with me that they find it more convenient to work from home and thus, over a computer"), the library has yet to become fully virtual for them: "I most often use online resources, rather than the hard copy. But sometimes both" is a typical comment. As one student reported, "I'd say there's a 3:1 ratio of online versus library research. I usually do both, but the bother of having to physically walk to the library is what discourages me from hardcopy research." On the Národní Divadlo, see www.narodni-divadlo.cz, 2 September 2005.
3. Geoff Mulgan, *Connexity: How to Live in a Connected World* (Boston: Harvard Business School Press, 1997).
4. Jon McKenzie, *Perform or Else: From Discipline to Performance* (London: Routledge, 2001), p. 186.
5. Again, my unscientific study of undergraduates suggests that most prefer to read Shakespeare's plays from published print materials, from books. The most common view is that "i like to use my book because i can take notes in it, but the online resources are nice because they often give summaries at the end of each scene in

modern English"; however, several remark that they do use online Shakespeare texts: "i believe i read all the plays online and then right before class i would rent the hard copy from the library" (interesting use of the language of video rental for free access to the library!); "If I don't have a hardcopy of shax, I'll read it online, but I prefer a book in my hand to looking at a screen." Indeed, the eyestrain caused by the screen is one of the most-reported reasons for preferring to read from print sources.

6. For a more extended discussion of these perspectives, see W. B. Worthen, "Disciplines of the Text/Sites of Performance," *TDR: The Drama Review – The Journal of Performance Studies* 39:1/T145 (Spring 1995), 13–28, the gathering of "Responses to W. B. Worthen's 'Disciplines of the Text/Sites of Performance'," by Jill Dolan, Joseph Roach, Richard Schechner, Phillip Zarrilli, pp. 28–41, and "Worthen Replies," pp. 41–44 in the same issue. See also W. B. Worthen, "Drama, Performativity, and Performance," *PMLA* 113 (1998), 1093–107.

7. Richard Burt, "Introduction," *Shakespeare the Movie, II: Popularizing the Plays on Film, TV, Video, and DVD*, ed. Richard Burt and Lynda E. Boose (London: Routledge, 2003), pp. 1–4.

8. *Ibid.*, p. 4.

9. Baz Luhrmann, dir., *William Shakespeare's Romeo + Juliet*, "Special Edition" (DVD: Fox Home Entertainment, 2002). In this regard, Julie Taymor's *Titus* DVD more clearly resembles the first Folio, a lavish first-edition DVD that substitutes a host of "Bonus Features" for commendatory verses; see *Titus* (DVD: Fox Home Entertainment, 2000).

10. Diana Henderson asks, "How different *is* our moment from those when film, and then television, became widely accessible? . . . Has the DVD blurred the big/small screen distinction, or does Shakespeare's verbal scale still 'fit' the large screen more successfully"; see Diana Henderson, "Introduction: Through a Camera, Darkly," in *A Concise Companion to Shakespeare on Screen*, ed. Diana Henderson (Oxford: Blackwell, 2006), pp. 1–7, p. 6.

11. On "print logic," see Alvin B. Kernan, *Printing Technology, Letters, and Samuel Johnson* (Princeton, NJ: Princeton University Press, 1987), pp. 48–55.

12. It's worth remembering, too, that printing is now a digitally driven process, as books are set in type from code; and, of course, we are now able to reuse books that once existed only in printed form – the Shakespeare first Folio – as digital texts, downloading and copying digital photo-facsimile into texts of our own composition.

13. McKenzie, *Perform or Else*, p. 113.

14. Andrew Feenberg, *Questioning Technology* (London: Routledge, 1999), 11. On the "notion of *information-as-commodity*" see William J. Martin, *The Global Information Society* (Aldershot: Aslib Gower, 1995), pp. 20–26.

15. I have in mind D. F. McKenzie, *Bibliography and the Sociology of Texts* (Cambridge: Cambridge University Press, 1999), and, of the several books by Jerome McGann, especially *The Textual Condition* (Princeton, NJ: Princeton University Press, 1991) and *Radiant Textuality: Literature after the World Wide Web* (Basingstoke: Palgrave, 2001).

16. You insert the DVD into the drive, which is capable of varying the rate of spin of the DVD (since the data will be read on a spiraling track from the rim to the center,

the drive has constantly to vary the rate at which the disk is spinning so that the laser-beam reading the data maintains a constant linear velocity over the data); a laser beam penetrates the protective plastic layer to read the first transparent data layer of the DVD, which consists of tiny "pits" and the flat "lands" between them; when the laser strikes a pit, the light is scattered, but when it strikes "land" it is reflected back, creating a signal to the read head; these pit nonsignals (= o) and land signals (= 1) of light energy are converted into bursts of electricity that can be interpreted as binary code; data on the DVD is recorded in spiral tracks, so that when the laser has read all the data on the transparent layer from the rim to the center of the DVD, it then refocuses on a second, reflective layer of plastic which is similarly pitted; it reads this second layer from the center out to the rim. The signals are fed through data lines that organize the pulses into groups of eight (bytes), and then feed this through the DVD software that interprets the data and tells the machine how to configure and reconfigure the pixels on the computer screen. I take this summary from Ron White, *How Computers Work*, 7th edn (Indianapolis: Que, 2004).

17. Andrew Feenberg, *Critical Theory of Technology* (New York: Oxford University Press, 1991), pp. 5–7. A revised edition of this book has been published under the title *Transforming Technology: A Critical Theory Revisited* (Oxford: Oxford University Press, 2002).

18. Feenberg, *Critical Theory of Technology*, p. 14.

19. Peter D. Hershock, *Reinventing the Wheel: A Buddhist Response to the Information Age* (Albany: State University of New York Press, 1999), p. 21.

20. *Ibid.*, p. 22.

21. Feenberg, *Critical Theory of Technology*, p. 85.

22. Brenda Laurel, *Computers as Theatre* (1991; rev. edn Boston: Addison-Wesley, 1993), p. 126. Laurel's impact on interface design is traced in Allucquère Rosanne Stone's fascinating book, *The War of Desire and Technology at the Close of the Mechanical Age* (Cambridge, MA: MIT Press, 1996).

23. Online sociability has, however, a sometimes-overlooked surveillance aspect, as the traces of internet contacts are generally stored both on the agent's computer system and as a record on the contacted site.

24. Kenneth Keniston, "Language, Power, and Software," in *Culture, Technology, Communication: Towards an Intercultural Global Village*, ed. Charles Ess with Fay Sudweeks (Albany: State University of New York Press, 2001), pp. 283–306, p. 295. Keniston's searching article outlines several reasons why there is relatively little vernacular software, even in some of the emerging centers of technological production, such as India.

25. Hershock, *Reinventing the Wheel*, p. 87.

26. Susan C. Herring, "Foreword," in Ess and Sudweeks, *Culture, Technology, Communication*, pp. vii–ix, p. viii.

27. Michael Radford, dir., *The Merchant of Venice* (DVD: Sony Pictures Classics, 2005).

28. Insofar as films are not released simultaneously worldwide, the film industry has an interest in preventing a movie that is already on DVD in, say, the USA from being sold in London or Paris or Tokyo, where the theatrical film may still be running, or have yet to be released. It is possible to purchase a region-free DVD player and even to alter some conventional players to play DVDs from other regions, but the film industry is vigilant on this front, and inserts various codes

into the disk to prevent play on machines of this kind. See Robert Silva, "Region Codes – DVD's Dirty Secret," http://hometheater.about.com/cs/dvdlaserdisc/a/aaregioncodesa/htm, 26 August 2005.

29. On entropy, see Norbert Wiener, *Cybernetics or Control and Communication in the Animal and the Machine*, 2nd edn (Cambridge, MA: MIT Press, 1962), p. 10. The first edition was in 1948.

30. Mark C. Taylor, *The Moment of Complexity: Emerging Network Culture* (Chicago: University of Chicago Press, 2001), p. 110.

31. N. Katherine Hayles, *How We Became Posthuman: Virtual Bodies in Cybernetics, Literature, and Informatics* (Chicago: University of Chicago Press, 1999), pp. 53–54, p. 19. The classic text here is Claude Shannon and Warren Weaver, *The Mathematical Theory of Communication* (Urbana: University of Illinois Press, 1949).

32. McKenzie, *Perform or Else*, p. 186.

33. Phil Mullins, "Sacred Texts in the Sea of Texts: The Bible in North American Electronic Culture," in *Philosophical Perspectives on Computer-Mediated Communication*, ed. Charles Ess (New York: State University of New York Press, 1996), pp. 271–302, p. 284, p. 286.

34. *Ibid.*, pp. 286–87.

35. *Ibid.*, p. 290.

36. Laurel, *Computers as Theatre*, p. 21.

37. Victor Turner, *From Ritual to Theatre: The Human Seriousness of Play* (New York: Performing Arts Journal Publications, 1982), p. 41.

38. Pierre Lévy, *Becoming Virtual: Reality in the Digital Age*, trans. Robert Bononno (New York: Plenum, 1998), p. 62.

39. On the social context of television viewing and its impact on the structure of performance, see W. B. Worthen, "The Player's Eye: Shakespeare on Television," *Comparative Drama* 18 (1984), 193–202.

40. Peter Hershock, "Turning Away from Technotopia: Critical Precedents for Refusing the Colonization of Consciousness," in *Technology and Cultural Values: On the Edge of the Third Millennium*, ed. Peter D. Hershock, Marietta Stepaniants, and Roger T. Ames (Honolulu: University of Hawai'i Press, 2003), pp. 587–600, pp. 597–98.

41. H. Jiuan Heng discusses playing personae in textually mediated Multi-User Domains, arguing that it resembles the "unique feature of theater," that it "brings audience and artist together in the same time/space to collaborate in cocreating character and scene"; in virtual performance, "the entire performance is extemporized." See "The Emergence of Pure Consciousness: The Theater of Virtual Selves in the Age of the Internet," in Hershock, Stepaniants, and Ames, *Technology and Cultural Values*, pp. 559–73, p. 571.

42. The phrase is Jon McKenzie's, *Perform or Else*, p. 22.

43. Taylor, *Moment of Complexity*, 231.

CAROL CHILLINGTON RUTTER

Shakespeare's popular face: from the playbill to the poster

For the past few years, as "prep" for their first Shakespeare seminar, I've set my undergraduates the opening two pages of a play I'm pretty certain they won't know, *Henry VI Part I*, reproduced from Hinman's facsimile of the First Folio. Their assignment: to answer what sounds like a simple enough question, "Where does a play begin?" Showing up for class a couple of days later, however, they know they've been stung. "*Which* play?" they now ask. "The play read? Or the play performed? And who are 'we' – early moderns or postmoderns?" There's a different beginning to a play, they observe, if "we" are picking up a book or taking a seat in the stalls – or, neo-Elizabethans, standing in the yard of the London Globe. One brave student offers Bedford's opening speech as the beginning – perhaps the standard place to start as a reader. But another student points out that Bedford has to get on stage before he starts talking. So the play has to begin with an entrance – like the stage direction says: "*Enter the Funerall of King Henry the Fift.*" But before that, someone else observes, "There's a music cue: '*Dead march.*' The play begins with sound." Then even that beginning recedes under pressure from another student's rhetorical musing, "Wouldn't you *know* what play you were going to? Wouldn't the play begin when you went to *The Comedy of Errors*, not *King Lear*?" (Or *Henry VI* not *Henry V*: what a world of narrative difference stands in that single digit.) Of course: spectators anticipate a different experience when they – notional Elizabethans – pay their penny for "*The Tragedie of Othello the Moore of Venice*" as against "*The Famous History of the Life of Henry the Eight.*" We do too, Shakespeare's latest spectators, for whom, besides, the play undoubtedly (also) begins with the great heap of what we already know (from school, adaptations and remakes, advertising, greeting cards, tabloid newspaper headlines, pop songs, the very air we breathe) about, say, a play called *Romeo and Juliet* before we see it, even for the first time. Can we offload our cultural baggage, think our way back to the Shakespeare play as premiere? Where does the *new* Shakespeare play begin? How did Shakespeare's first audiences get news of the new play? And how, today, do new spectators, people new to Shakespeare (whose plays will be new to them) get drawn into the theatre? Is there a place where "popular culture" meets a "streetwise Shakespeare," where "the people" meet "the Bard" and decide to risk a blind date?[1] If so, who's the fixer, the go-between?

Proclaim'd on every post

These are questions that also tease the "documentary" opening sequences of two great films that work to situate the Elizabethan theatre in a richly imagined (and "authentic") populism. Given that the later film quotes (and parodies) the earlier classic, it's no surprise that both travel across similar space, settle on the same go-between: Bill! Or rather, a (play)bill. Laurence Olivier's *Henry V* (1944) opens with a shot of empty sky, a sheet of paper dancing into view on the wind. Making a final somersault, it pastes itself (evidently) onto the camera lens. So now we can see what it is: a playbill torn loose from somewhere, announcing a title (billing that doubles for the film). The typography and lay-out establish this playbill as "the real thing" (except that it behaves also like a movie: giving us half the news then scrolling up to deliver the rest, managing always to keep Will's name in view):

THE
Chronicle History
OF
KING HENRY THE FIFT
with his battell fought
at Agincourt
in France
BY
Will Shakespeare
will be played by
The Lord Chamberlain's Men
AT THE
GLOBE PLAYHOUSE
THIS DAY
The FIRST of MAY
1600

Some of this advertisement is authentic, lifted straight from the title page of Thomas Creede's 1600 quarto (the title, the trailer, the company); some, a supplement (the playwright's name, not mentioned on the quarto title page); more, shrewd invention, what (I guess) Olivier's screenwriter guesses early modern advertising would *have* to tell prospective playgoers. This "facsimile" playbill does two jobs at once. A prologue to the play's opening prologue that delivers the film's credits, it works also (fixing itself onto the camera lens) to fix the film's viewing conceit: it makes us filmgoers Elizabethan *playgoers* and sets us up to watch the play from a particular cultural point of view, aligned to a particular historical authority. As it dissolves, we discover we're looking at the Tower of London. Now the camera tracks back to begin a slow pan across Visscher's 1616 "view," westward, skirting London Bridge and St. Saviour's, then along Bankside, taking in two circular structures, obviously playhouses. Pausing, the camera seems to consider zeroing in on its target. It starts in to close up on one of the playhouses, but then checks itself – an "oops" moment – swings a couple degrees eastward, locates the *other* playhouse.[2] That is: not the Rose (Shakespeare's *last* theatre). The Globe. His latest. On stage, a billboard facing the audience opposite the prompter (a balding man, looking suspiciously like the "Bill Bard") reproduces the playbill's advertisement – the punters filling the playhouse are getting what they've paid for.

Fifty-four years on, the opening sequence of John Madden's *Shakespeare in Love* (1998) remembers and reworks Olivier's tropes. Expository titles announce a date and a venue, and trail a narrative – "London. 1593"; "two playhouses ... fighting it out" – before cutting to blue sky, overwritten with more titles – "the Curtain." Already, the camera is tracking across a thatched roof, down into the wooden-O, panning across vacancy: hollow galleries, stray props abandoned on the empty stage, bits of straw drifting down desultorily into the yard – of "The Rose." Obviously closed. Zooming right down into the pit the camera focuses on a torn piece of waste paper. A playbill. We read:

September at noon,
MR EDWARD ALLEYN and the LORD ADMIRALL'S MEN
At the Rose Theatre. Bankside
The Lamentable Tragedie of the
MONEYLENDER
REVENG'D

Cuing who, what, when, where, the trashed playbill puts us (filmgoers) in the know while simultaneously marking us (Elizabethan playgoers) absent, the Rose, shut, any performance a forlorn memory. But even as it's simulating authenticity – the font is worn, the lines of type, wonky; the space after "September" is filled in by hand with dates; the blank centre of the bill is illustrated with a woodcut of two men in doublet and hose going fisticuffs – this playbill is passing off an elaborate joke, for as we're reading it, we're hearing noises off: the advertised performance that we're *not* seeing on stage is playing itself out at this very moment in the tiring house, where the

"Moneylender" is being "Reveng'd" on Henslowe, hapless owner of the Rose, who's feeling the heat. Fennyman's thugs are toasting Henslowe's boots (his feet still in them) over hot coals. "Lamentable Tragedie?" Actually, farce. And part of the joke is what the playbill withholds, the role Will Shakespeare will play in saving Henslowe's soles: here at the Rose in 1593 Shakespeare is not yet *Shakespeare*.

It's impossible to say how close these film openings come to reproducing anything like "real" performance practice respecting playbills in the Elizabethan theatre.[3] As imaginative riffs, however, they interest me for the way they fill up the liminal space between the (fictionally constituted, historicized) playgoer and the play, on the threshold of choice, where the punter, presented a bill of fare, decides, today, to consume this rather than that, *Henry V* versus *The Moneylender Reveng'd*, theatre versus other billed entertainments (sermons, executions, public trials, like Hermione's, "on every post/ proclaim'd" [*The Winter's Tale*, 3.2.100–01]). In these representations, the playbill is both a text ("words, words, words" [*Hamlet*, 2.2.195]) and a performance (cutting capers in the sky, abashed in the dirt); both of the theatre and of the marketplace; both "pre" and "post." These playbills anticipate performance, then remember it: left behind in the yard when the spectators go, performance's trace, its leftover. Teaser, trailer, bait: they take us *in*, an apt proxy for what they're selling, composed of words, of pictures, action, a paper interface between two worlds. They address *us*. Seek *us* out. (Even as we, in Madden, are drawn ineluctably to them.) They fix our meeting with the play – and so make something of us, punter turned playgoer. (Again, Madden savors the running joke: near the end of the film, when everything has gone disastrously wrong – Viola's little cross-dressed adventure, found out; the Rose, closed; *Romeo and Juliet*, on ice; Will plunged into despair, she into matrimony – it's a playbill that fixes the happy ending, that transforms her from newlywed to runaway to playgoer to player; from fake Kent rehearsing Romeo to real Viola playing Juliet.) But if they're passports, are playbills also safe conducts? And what kind of performance record to they constitute?

Devised ... to take spectators

Caught up in these fictional histories set in Shakespeare's "original" playhouses, I consider why I find the fantasy life of the Elizabethan playbill – so sturdily plebeian, so alarmingly ephemeral: one category of playhouse document of which not a single example survives – so absorbing. It's this: the playbill is the one early modern playhouse document that explicitly imagines *me*, that, "devised ... to take spectators" [*The Winter's Tale*, 3.2.35–36] speaks to *my* part in the theatre. Of course, how to "take spectators" is not just a heated question for Madden's Henslowe. It's a perennial concern to theatre managers and administrators at all times. So what, I want to ask, shifting from older histories to more recent ones, has been "devis'd" by latter-day Henslowes "to take spectators" at the theatre today's world recognizes as Shakespeare's "home address": the most globally renowned popular Shakespeare theatre in the world, the one built not in the bustling, affluent capital where he worked but, three hundred years after his birth, in the provincial market town where he died, a theatre whose failure was predicted before it even opened by sniffy London critics who, looking down their metropolitan noses at provincial folly in Stratford-upon-Avon, wondered "[W]ho will the spectators be?"[4] That is, I want to look at the Royal Shakespeare Company's playbills – and how those playbills look at their spectators. Rifling through the portfolio of early playbills preserved in the Royal Shakespeare Company's archive at the Shakespeare Birthplace Trust (eighty years'-worth of street advertising before the RSC *was* the RSC) to reach 1965, the year the image changed beyond recognition, I want to study Shakespeare's popular face, the one the RSC displays on theatre posters in Stratford-upon-Avon today.[5]

The playbill that announced the "Inaugural Festival" to open the "Shakespeare Memorial Theatre" on "Shakespeare's Birthday, Wednesday April 23, 1879" was something of a graphic double of the building it was also, that day, inaugurating. The one, "frankly fantastical,"[6] married mock-Tudor to Gothic revival, Elizabethan half-timbering to Victorian red brick, Warwickshire gables to oriental turrets and minarets; the other, equally "fantastical," set out in a dozen typefaces and sizes from gothic to italic to poplar the eleven performances that constituted the entire festival – and the building's entire *raison d'être*. Decorative initial flourishes, a bold geometric border, eye-catching colors (red for titles; black for actors and Shakespeare – who, topping the bill, presided over this graphic performance): this handsome playbill looked impressive. It advertised wealth, the rich cultural legacy of the "master mind" to whom the new theatre paid memorial tribute; the rich commercial success of the Stratford brewer, Charles Flower, on whose near single-handed endowment the whole visionary (or crackpot) venture depended. And it offered the typographic equivalent of the First Folio's invitation "To the great Variety of Readers": something, by the look of it, for everyone. (But is there a visual bluster in the graphics that works also to overwhelm us, to distract us – notional Stratfordians, 1879 – from asking hard-headed questions? About the sanity of building a theatre – in Purbeck marble and York stone – to open ten days *a year*?)

Eye-baffling typography aside, this playbill does the business of advertising the season: four performances of *Hamlet*, three of *Much Ado*, two of *As You*

Like It, a concert, and a dramatized reading of *The Tempest*. Enough? Not for the metropolitan critics – who sneered, and decamped after *Hamlet* on 24 April. But perhaps for the locals – wooed, after the opening, with handsomely adjusted ticket prices. Offering them comedy, tragedy, music, recitation, evening entertainment, and twice-weekly matinees, the playbill set out not just the fare; it listed the principal players and their parts, Barry Sullivan's company (Sullivan himself playing Hamlet, Benedick, and Jacques) having been engaged and brought up from London complete with costumes, props, sets, and pre-fab productions. But it promised provincial spectators more: a "Birthday Play" (a tradition still observed) featuring "Mrs. Theodore Martin," aka "Miss Helen Faucit," as Beatrice, "for ONE NIGHT only." The playbill didn't need to say Faucit was the greatest actress of her generation – everybody knew that. But equally, it didn't make hay of the fact that she was emerging from retirement to make this appearance – for good reason? Faucit was sixty-two. (Never mind; her Benedick was fifty-eight.) For spectators, the glittering lure lay in that phrase: "for ONE NIGHT only."

Usefully, the playbill told them how much they'd have to pay to be entertained (thereby inscribing differentials registered in the layout of the 700-seat theatre itself): on the gala opening night, 20 shillings for the best seats, 5/- for the cheapest, reduced to 10/- and 2/6 from 28 April onward. (Another hastily got-up bill, posted on the Saturday, adjusted these prices even further – and aimed at passing traffic: half a crown on the "Floor," and, in the upper circle, only 1/- for "UNRESERVED" seating, "payment at the Door"). Usefully, too, the playbill told them how they could get home: late trains laid on by Great Western. (Already, it was recognized that Flower's theatre would snarl up Stratford traffic. A separate bill, posted by the Lord Mayor's office, set out "Police Regulations" – whose enforcement clearly counted on local knowledge: "All Carriages and Motors to set down and take up at entrances to Theatre facing towards the Church."[7])

It's worth observing that this first playbill was produced in three versions: the "gala" poster, measuring $24'' \times 18''$; a down-market copy, printed on cheaper paper; and a "commercial" blow-up, $48'' \times 24''$, clearly meant for pasting up on walls. Much simpler, it elbows fussiness, printing HAMLET and MUCH ADO ABOUT NOTHING in lettering you could read from across the street. It's also worth observing that this playbill's inventiveness is entirely typographic: "performance" here is a readerly experience. Stratfordians would see something very different when Augustin Daly's Company of Comedians hit town in August 1888 "from NEW YORK CITY, USA" with "Mr Daly's Restored Version of Shakespeare's TAMING THE SHREW."[8] Printing his playbills in stars-and-stripes colors, red, white, and blue, Daly additionally issued full-color posters ("LITHO PRINTED IN NEW YORK") featuring cameos of the players (as themselves) framed in laurel wreaths, mapped onto a half-length portrait of the star attraction, Miss Ada Rehan, who, posed halfway between herself and Kate, displays naked arms and plenty of décolletage. This sort of graphic design ("from a photo by. . . .") wouldn't appear on SMT playbills for another seventy-five years. In Stratford, visual interest was entirely in the playbill's lettering, the design and layout set perhaps by F. R. Benson, who arrived in 1886 (and conducted all but five of the festival seasons until 1919), but certainly by the time Osmond Tearle "And his Specially Engaged and Selected Company" played *Henry VI Part I* in 1889. The standard Stratford playbill was a long narrow strip, 30″ × 10″, printed in royal blue ink on a buff background.

By 1886 Flower's festival, billed under Benson as "THE ANNUAL SERIES OF DRAMATIC PERFORMANCES," was running to a fortnight. Benson's playbills listed dates, ticket prices, railway arrangements; but not the players (perhaps because he didn't know when the bill went to print what team he'd be able to field), and regularly, some "hook." In 1891, "New and Special Scenery" was advertised, and "Costumes by M. V. Barthe"; in 1893, concessions: "Children under twelve years of age half-price to the Afternoon Performance only"; in 1892, a chance to purchase "The Memorial Edition of Shakespeare's Plays . . . Cloth 1s; Paper covers 6d. each post free." The 1902 playbill announced *Henry VIII*, "performed for The First Time at the Memorial Theatre," with "MISS ELLEN TERRY," who "has kindly consented to take the part of 'Queen Katherine'". In 1899 the hook was *Hamlet*, but not just any *Hamlet*. The "ENTIRE PLAY OF HAMLET" – as the playbill rather oddly put it, squashing the title under the season opener, "HENRY VI. (PART 2)," in smaller type that somehow fails to register the significant event. For what spectators in Stratford were offered was a chance to see the first full-text *Hamlet* ever staged. (The point the compositor didn't get was made elsewhere: top whack seats that season were 5/-, but for *Hamlet*, 9/-. Moreover, the playbill's fine print noted that a "Ballot for reserved seats" for *Hamlet* would be "drawn on 21 March at 10 a.m.")

Ironically, what strikes the modern reader of these playbills as utterly mind-boggling was the very thing contemporaries took for granted: the repertoire. In the 1899 fortnight, Benson's company performed *Henry V, Henry VI Part 2, Richard II and III, Twelfth Night, As You Like It, The Merry Wives of Windsor, The Merchant of Venice, Macbeth, Hamlet* ("ENTIRE") and Sheridan's *The Rivals*, with Benson playing Hamlet, Macbeth, both Richards (but only one Henry), Cardinal Beaufort, Orlando, Malvolio, Shylock, Dr. Caius, and Capitan Absolute. On successive nights, paying 2/- in the pit (or half that in the gallery), the whole season for just over a guinea, a spectator could see a major chunk of the *Complete Works*.[9] And if he missed anything, he could count on seeing it

14 Shakespeare Memorial Theatre playbill for the 1899 season.

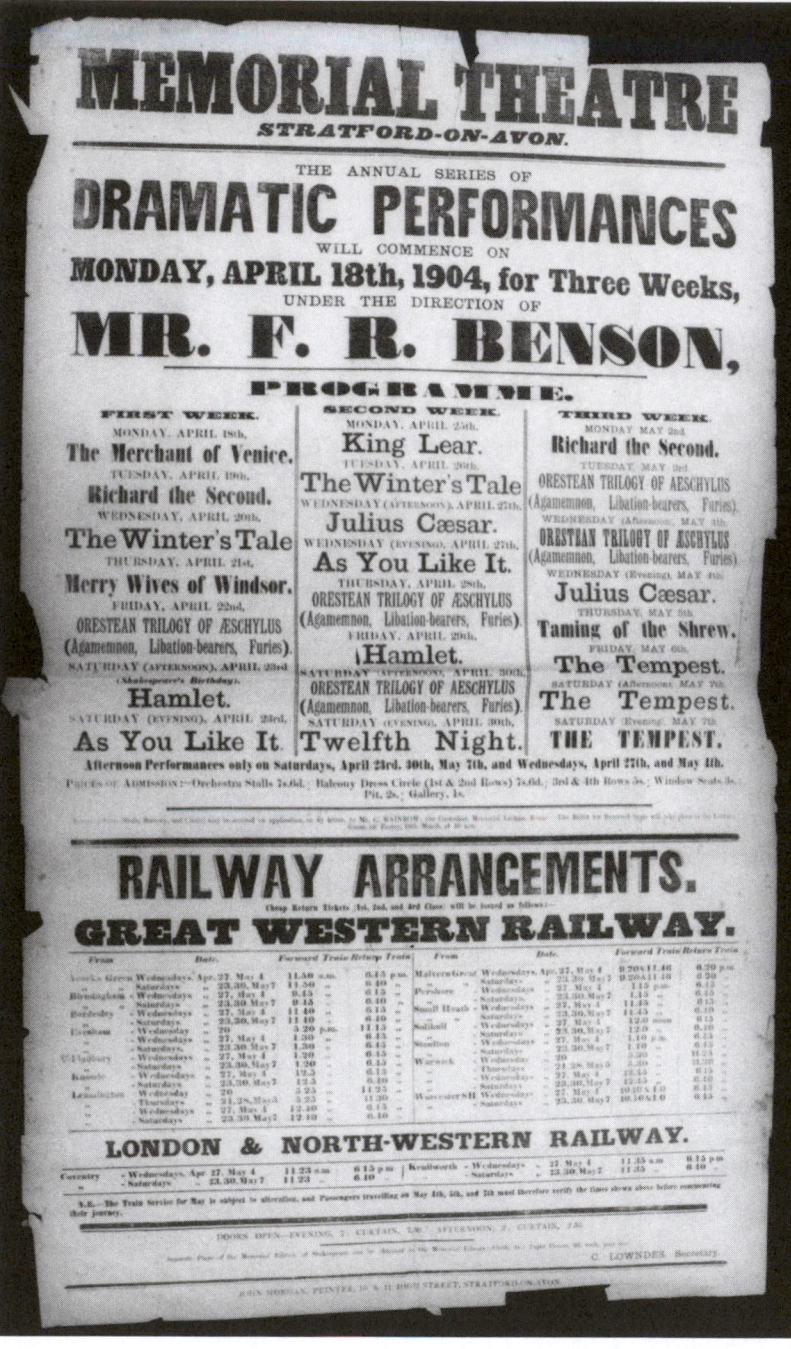

15 Shakespeare Memorial Theatre playbill for the 1904 season.

next season – or indeed, his son seeing it five years hence. For season on season, some of these plays returned with deadening frequency – or was it popular demand? *Henry V*, seen first in 1897, appeared every year between 1905 and 1916; *The Merry Wives* had only two years off between 1897 and 1916; *Hamlet*'s annual return was only cut short by the Great War. Equally, however, this repertoire had ambitions beyond Shakespeare: in these years, Benson's company also played *Paolo and Francesca*, *Every Man in His Humour*, *She Stoops to Conquer*, *Virginius*, *The Rivals*, *The School for Scandal*, *You Never Can Tell*, *If I Were King*, *The Devil's Disciple*, and in 1904, *The Orestean* [*sic*] *Trilogy of Aeschylus*, Benson as Clytemnestra.

That year the festival season grew to three weeks – and the playbill to three columns, still royal blue on buff, but in a larger format. Benson's name was big and bold; Shakespeare's had dropped off the billing; ticket prices were slightly up (7/6 for best seats in the stalls but still 1/- in the gallery); eleven Shakespeares were on offer, plus Aeschylus; railway arrangements were fuller than ever. But after twenty-five annual festivals, seeing the "usual suspects" filling the bill yet again (a repertoire Benson himself took to calling *The Merry Shrews of Venice*[10]) Stratfordians might well have started scanning Benson's playbills more critically. What did they say about production values? Variety was a mirage – unless you were attending the festival for the first time. The *Merchant* you saw Benson play in 1898 was the same you'd see in 1916. This was a theatre of repetition, not exploration; of fixing a play, not investigating it; of giving the audience what they expected, what they *knew* of "Shakespeare's fancy."[11] In short, this was a theatre without rehearsal – notionally or practically. What was there to rehearse? Textual cuts, stage business, moves, props, costumes were standard. So Cleopatra could go on in 1911 with one hour's instruction.[12]

At the tercentenary of Shakespeare's death in 1916, the only changes to the festival visible in the playbill were superficial: red and black ink, not blue; Shakespeare's name writ large; Benson's "Shakespearean Company," principal players only, listed alphabetically, and below them, a list of theatrical "toffs" specially appearing (Oscar Asche, Ben Greet, Ellen Terry). The "Tercentenary Commemoration Performance" was a gallimaufry of recitations and soliloquies from assorted actors, "Under the Patronage of Their Majesties the King and Queen" (who didn't attend, but whose names bumped up top ticket prices from 7/6 to £1/1). And on the festival bill: *Henry V*, *The Merchant of Venice*, *The Merry Wives*...

Bring up the brown bills – or yellow

After 1916, a gap opens in the RSC archives, no playbill surviving between the tercentenary and 1925. But turning from one to the other, it's obvious that the world has changed. The 1925 playbill is traditional in format – the same size as Benson's in the 1890s. But it's smarter, sharper, modern: gone, the welter of typographical confusion. Printed in Shakespeare's heraldic colours, yellow and black on white, it's aware of PR. And it advertises a festival under new management, an artistic director, William Bridges-Adams (significantly *not* an actor manager like Benson) heading a company whose principals are listed A–Z: new faces in Stratford, or if not new, like Randle Ayrton, then promoted to lead roles too-long Benson's personal property. This is a playbill for the automotive age: designed to be read at speed – no longer printing train times. Punters could see titles in one column of uniform bold print; in another column, performance dates and times: a playbill designed to throw attention onto the plays in the season rather than the calendar. Fine print at the bottom documented other modernizations: a "BOX OFFICE OPEN DAILY 10 am to 4 pm"; a number – "Stratford on Avon 45" – for telephone bookings. A management structure was in place: director, stage manager, general manager, and secretary (these last two positions had been filled for donkey's years by old Flower family retainers; only now did the jobs get titles and public recognition, a preliminary to Bridges-Adams quietly retiring them).

The biggest change was the one those new graphics put squarely in view, the fact that the season was longer (including, now, a Birthday Festival in April–May, a summer season from July, and a short regional tour connecting the two), but the repertoire, shorter, "only" seven Shakespeares plus Sheridan's *The Critic*. An impoverishment? Paradoxically, the reverse. For this change signals the massive fight Bridges-Adams had on his hands, to modernize, to re-imagine, the artistic values of the company, to stop producing "hasty revivals, using shabby stock costumes and improvised sets;"[13] to stop rehearsing six or seven plays in five weeks; to stop, as Bridges-Adams wrote, putting "Othello on stage in three rehearsals;" to stop that "insult to the memory of Shakespeare, to any actor worthy of the part, and to the people who pay to see it."[14] And to start paying actors more. Electricity had been introduced in the SMT in 1907 – but actors were still on gaslight wages (leading men, £20 a week; beginners, £3).

1925 was the last season at the SMT: the theatre burned to the ground the following March. For the next six years, the festival played in what the playbills called a "TEMPORARY THEATRE," formerly the town's cinema. But from the evidence they offer, it was business as usual, and when the new theatre, a building as resolutely modernist as Flower's original had been fantastic (and soon to be dubbed "the jam factory" by locals), opened in 1932, alongside the gala playbill (printed in red, black, and white, announcing eight Shakespeares and an "OPENING CEREMONY" performed by

"H.R.H. THE PRINCE OF WALES") appeared the familiar strip playbill. The company list showed Bridges-Adams achieving one of his goals: an ensemble, its core, regulars like Randle Ayrton, Kenneth Wicksteed, Dorothy Massingham, and Eric Maxon; and newcomers: excitingly, in 1933, the radiant Rachel Kempson. But the 1932 playbill also showed him failing: he wasn't able to reduce the repertoire or to stagger opening nights to allow a run-in before the next play opened. His administration was growing – nine assorted managers – and the telephone exchange getting busier. No doubt they needed the two phone numbers: in 1933, they launched a full season in Stratford from April to September. But Bridges-Adams couldn't get more rehearsal time.

Over the next twenty years the changes registered on SMT playbills look merely cosmetic – but signal major institutional shifts. The 1936 playbill, the first one surviving to name Ben Iden Payne director (he took over from Bridges-Adams in 1935), looked like every playbill since Benson – with one significant addition, in very small print. For the first time, productions were identified by directors, Theodore Komisarjevsky, for one, billed against *King Lear*. "Komis" had been brought to Stratford by Bridges-Adams in 1932, part of his revolutionary project to re-think Shakespeare play by play, to invite guests directors to *interpret* Shakespeare, to stamp their authority on productions so boldly that their artistic signature would be recognized, would, indeed, be what spectators went to the theatre *to see*. That idea – that nobody who saw a Komisarjevsky production could fail to notice it was *his* – was one the 1936 playbill discovered was worth selling.

In 1943, during Milton Rosmer's one-season stint as festival director, the sales pitch seems to have focused not on dazzling reputation but sacred location. Listing neither actors nor directors, this playbill featured an iconic photograph of the theatre, floating, it seemed, like Avalon, an image of "this England" that remembered, in bricks, mortar, and playthings, the national values Britain was fighting to defend. As *Henry V* opened, the battle in the North Atlantic was climaxing, and the Warsaw ghetto was being liquidated. This playbill established a new advertising "look," the season neatly boxed up on the page into weekly parcels, like rations, for tourist consumption, showing visitors how much they could pack into their stay – and how economically. Best seats cost exactly what they had in 1916 – 7/6.

By the time Antony Quayle took over the directorship in 1948, the SMT playbill had settled into the format it would keep for the next fifteen years: black print on stiff yellow card, a photograph of the theatre (from one angle or another) in one corner, the week-by-week season schedule printed below the season's plays, their directors, and, for the first time, designers: in 1949, "CYMBELINE Production Michael Benthall Scenery and Costumes LESLIE

HURRY." And by far the most significant change: topping the bill, not a list of principals, but *stars* – "DIANA WYNYARD, LEON QUARTERMAINE, HARRY ANDREWS." (Walk-ons certainly *didn't* get billed: among them, Michael Bates, Jill Bennett, Robert Hardy.) What this star billing showed was that Quayle, in a still-grey postwar world where Britons hungered for glamor, was bringing West End attitudes to Stratford, making the SMT *fashionable*, a stage where Peggy Ashcroft and Laurence Olivier, Paul Robeson, Michael Redgrave, Sam Wanamaker would play, where Peter Brook and John Gielgud would direct, where Paul Scofield and Claire Bloom would be discovered and nurtured, a theatre *Vogue* magazine would feature and Angus McBean would photograph, and hordes would visit. A theatre that could say "Damn London: let them come to us."[15] And it did – as the names on the playbills that survive for the next fifteen years document.

Even so, the only new visual interest on the theatre's playbills was the swan that began appearing on some of them. Only the odd London transfer – the Ashcroft/Redgrave *Antony and Cleopatra*, the Gielgud *Tempest* – merited up-scaled publicity that tied words to production photographs and pictured the stars on the hoardings. But as 1960 arrived, theatre playbills, like most things in Britain, were about to change.

Posters over sea and land

That year – his first as artistic director – twenty-nine-year-old Peter Hall revolutionized theatre in Stratford, and blazoned the revolution on his playbills. He redesigned the stage and restructured the company: out went the old star system; in came the idea of a permanent ensemble (for the first time, the playbill listed the *entire* company, and in alphabetical order). He brought in new directors and designers: William Gaskill, Clifford Williams, John Bury. He found the company a London base. And rebranded it with a new logo. And a new name: the Royal Shakespeare Company. All of this "news" appeared on the bill.

Rethinking the company's image, Hall was responding to the times: to postwar democratization, anti-authoritarianism, the end of class deference; to the Jimmy Porter phenomenon, the explosion of youth culture, popular culture, working-class culture; to student activism, protest, unrest. England was set to swing – but also to get seriously political. And in Hall's view, so was Shakespeare. On stage, Hall defined the company's new-model image in *The Wars of the Roses* (1963). And on the street? To develop Shakespeare's popular image he enlisted John Goodwin, the RSC's first Head of Publicity.[16] First, Goodwin and his graphic designer, George Mayhew, invented a completely new kind of theatre program. Packed with challenging stuff (directors' notes, critical "sightlines," archive material), it married words to pictures and was stunningly illustrated with rehearsal photographs and production images. Two seasons later, Goodwin did the same for the playbill. Indeed, he produced what, aligning Shakespeare to pop-art (Warhol, Glaser, Hockney) and to youth culture's mass art forms (album covers, psychedelic collages, pin-ups of the Beatles and Rolling Stones) would make the playbill obsolete: the RSC's first theatre poster.[17]

Remembering that poster, Goodwin points out that its publicity aim was not commercial but aesthetic, not to sell the show but to decorate the RST's blank façade, to give some idea, on the outside of the building, of what was happening *inside*. And to give spectators a material memory of performance, a paper mnemonic: something to take home to remember *that* Shakespeare. As luck would have it, 1965 was the perfect moment to launch the theatre poster as icon: that summer, hordes of teenagers descended on Stratford, queuing for tickets to a *Hamlet* that was light years from Benson's (or even Scofield's): a lanky, surly, adolescent Prince, trailing a grubby college scarf, badge of every university student in the country, a Hamlet *like them*, who gazed *at them*, as they queued, from the theatre's hoardings. Printing "**hamlet**" in white on a red background, this original poster used two photographic shots of David Warner – in profile, head-on; shadowed, bleached out – Mayhew joining and manipulating them, bleeding them in to each other, "theatricalizing" them, to produce the visual, slightly surreal, correlative of Warner's performance – and Peter Hall's direction: *Hamlet*, Hall told his actors as rehearsals started, "is one of mankind's great images. It turns a new face to each ... decade ... is a mirror which gives back the reflection of the age that is contemplating it."[18] Two faces, two minds, to-be-or-not-to-be: Mayhew's graphics gave 1960s youth culture a Hamlet who stared them down – and looked away.

But inventing the RSC poster, Goodwin and Mayhew also gave spectators a new way of engaging with Shakespeare: a new performance space, art form, site of critical discourse; the image as icon as interpretation, constantly renegotiated.[19] That original view from 1965 of Hamlet as his own double has been rethought in RSC posters ever since: in 1975, Ben Kingsley's Hamlet, dressed like one of Beckett's tramps, stares down into the grave (that is also *his*) at his unseen "other."[20] In 1980 Michael Pennington, in near dark, stares out from the half-length photographic portrait, his face a mask; at his waist, the tools of an Elizabethan scholar's trade, an inkhorn; across his chest, an arm, holding, shoulder high, an actor's prop, a white mask: two faces, cheek-by-jowl. In 1984 the poster features a painting, not a photograph; by Philip Core, in red, black, and pink, anxious colors; showing Hamlet cradling the skull, leaning fleshed head against bone, cheek-to-cheek,

16 Royal Shakespeare Company publicity poster for *Hamlet*, 1965.

17 Royal Shakespeare Company publicity poster for *Hamlet*, 2001.

eye-to-eye, a stylized angst-ridden nightmare image that is also somehow romantically Byronic. In 1997, the double that haunts Alex Jennings's Hamlet is Bogart: shot from below, his face distorted by the perspective, Jennings is a gangster prince trapped in a B-grade movie – "Hamlet" spelled in letters copied from cinema posters – an out-of-focus blur – a ghost? his bad dreams? – shadowing him. In 2001, Sam West is Pennington's double, though closer up, eyes fixed on our eyes looking back. But he's also his own double: holding a dagger that splits his face, a schizophrenic Hamlet.

After Warner, the actor's face, photographed in role, in *performance*, absorbs the viewer's interest in poster after poster, becomes a trope for seeing into the concerns of the play, a visual proxy for star billing. Looking through a smoke-screen of flecked gold into near-blackness, we observe Sinead Cusack as Portia (1981) alone, hunched up in mid-shot, pensively hugging herself, her stare fixed on three caskets, their dull metals just distinguishable. (A play about wealth and mourning; a trapped daughter; absolute discrimi- nation – but clouded choices?) Against a bruised-purple background, we see Sam West as Richard II (2000) sitting cross-legged on the ground in a heavy grey-mauve gown that looks too big for him; toying with the crown he's removed, funnelling sand through its vacant centre. (A play about a self- absorbed, self-infantilizing king; about the crown as hourglass; time's waste, wasting him?) A silver-haired Judi Dench (who first appeared in Stratford in 1961, but hadn't been back since 1979), in high ruff and Jacobean farthin- gale as the Countess Rosillion in *All's Well That Ends Well* (2003), magni- ficent in three-quarter length portrait, holds our gaze, backed by a gold sun rising through a silvered winter tree; around this central image, head-shots of Helena, Parolles, LaVatch, all positioned to gaze on her. (A play about youth surviving itself, aspiring to the graciousness of old age? A play about "a bright particular star" – and our idolatry?[21])

As Shakespeare's theatre probes illusion and representation, "true things" and "their mockeries," standing "airy nothings" on solid stages and staging the fake lives of real things (or the real lives of fake things), so graphic artists, commissioned somehow to "capture" a play in a single frame, play with notions of place and space, settings (as in the plays) actual and metaphorical. Posters say: "inside this building" is an "other where," "other when." Padua, perhaps. (In 1987 the poster for Jonathan Miller's *Shrew* was an architec- tural drawing by a Renaissance Escher of a Tuscan townscape in sun-gold, and burnt tangerine; hot; a place of uncertain perspective, where stairs, windows, balconies, overlook the one, vertiginous road into town.) Or Venice. (Bill Alexander's 1987 *Merchant* poster produced Venice in shades of grey, in the far distance, across the wide expanse of empty, misted lagoon against a steel-dark sky, Saluté just visible; we see it, looking past a hooded figure, standing on the edge of a derelict wooden pier – a monk, perhaps, or plague doctor or reveler dressed for carnival. By contrast, Venice in the 1993 poster (for David Thacker's production) was a postmodern cartoon by Ralph Steadman-after-Magrittte-after-Bosch: in one corner, glass and steel buildings by Norman Foster; in the centre, a bird's-eye-view of the (historic) City square mile – London's banking district doubling the Rialto; for the rest, a collage, crowding space with business commuters: bodies in Armani suits and pinstripes, hands gesticulating, counting, pointing, fisted, folded; their heads lopped off over sharp ties, the necks spurting blood – or ink blots; the background, graph paper, the lines plotted/blotted on them zig-zagging crazily up then down. The only "whole" person in this surreal cityscape appears in miniature, a 1950s-looking, old-school bank manager wearing horn-rim spectacles.)

Performances in their own right, posters re-perform some Shakespeare moments so frequently, imagine and place them in what Barbara Hodgdon calls the "sociocultural imagination"[22] so coercively, that their images begin to operate like textual knowledge. Take, for instance, the Macbeths caught red-handed. In the black and grey poster from Trevor Nunn's 1977 production, the Macbeths – Ian McKellen, Judi Dench, black on black – weirdly embrace, their bodies knotting without touching, twisted around their "enterprise": he, clutching two daggers, she reaching for them; his hands, a splodge of red thrown on to the paper surface, having "done the deed"; hers, not yet marked. In 1989, again, in black and grey except for a gold initial "M," Miles Anderson and Amanda Root are both bloody-handed (there's no color in the image, but you can see the "coagulate gore"). They are complicit, yet, although locked together, unconnected: she strains to embrace him, stiff-armed, hands splayed away from his white shirt; he ignores her, studies his hands' "filthy witness." In 1999 Harriet Walter and Antony Sher are pictured in head shot, an informal "take" on a contemporary couple, in black and sepia on white. But while Sher stares out, his forehead bunched, a mind full of scorpions, Walter's eyes are closed, her senses shut. Brains, not hands, are polluted here: above the couple's heads, swirls like smoke rise, dissipate, vanish; except they're red: bloody thoughts, diluting as they swill down a psychic drain.

But against such "knowledge," other *Macbeth* posters imagine what disturbs it, giving other insights on the play. The almost-empty black-and-grey poster from 1996 shows, crouched in one corner, a toddler, naked, clutching in baby hands leafless branches (a dead forest, a witch's broom?). But (a visual pre-view of moves the play will make between "fair" and "fear") the face we expect – of innocence – is not there; a skeleton mask covers it, and the eyes peering out are infinitely old. In 1986, Ian Pollock's cartoon poster is a

Spitting Image portrait in sick colors (vomit green, pus yellow) of the Macbeths – recognizably Sinead Cusack and Jonathan Pryce – as the (Un) Holy Family: his face, grotesquely elongated, hers, lantern-jawed, both red-eyed, staring; in her arms, a baby built by Frankenstein; armless, neckless, its legs mismatched, and below its blobby jowls, a line of sutures where the head's been sewn on. In 1982, another cartoon poster, this one by Ralph Steadman, his signature ink blots daubing the page under his unmistakable scrawled lettering, puts the drunken Porter downstage center. Somewhere between hunchback and gorilla, coat flapping, trousers anchored by a half set of braces, eyeballs veined red with alcohol, in one hand a tin mug, in the other, an over-sized key, his slob's mouth gaping "duh": this *Macbeth* advertises a tale told by an idiot.

In these examples, poster art essentializes Shakespeare, finds "the" image to express the play; but uses popular media – the photograph, the cartoon – to demystify the playwright, offering via such familiarizing strategies a sophisti-cated commentary, a counter-text to the play; its discourse, visual; its method, deconstructive, disorienting. Alienation is its come-on. "Make something of this!" it says. And: "What dost thou think?" Working like verbal wit in the plays, poster art invites the spectators' collusion, invites them "to play."

Moreover, because they're topical, production-specific, RSC posters con-stitute primary materials for reading theatre history. Put four *Othello* posters side by side. We see, even as they anticipate it, a record of our cultural negotiations with issues the play presents: what *Othello* "means" *right now*. Under a title written in pseudo-arabic lettering, working in shades of grey, the 1985 poster presents two faces; men's; photographed in such tight close-up the whole head isn't taken; cut up and re-assembled in photomon-tage – a technique owed to Hockney. Disturbed images. Disconcerting joins. But which one is Othello, which, Iago? This production, says the poster, is about Otherness, cultural constructions, what men make of men – but not about blackness. In 1989, in head-shot, Willard White's "coal-black Moor" holds Imogen Stubbs's "fair warrior" Desdemona tight, one huge hand around her delicate neck tilting her head back, lips close. A study of desire. Suspended. And the next frame? A kiss? Or possibly strangulation. This production, says the poster, is about marriage, a wrecked love affair, power, passion, abuse, "the pity of it." And, sensationally, race. In 1999, it's about three people, trapped in the letters spelling the title across the poster's width. Stretched almost to an "l," the initial "O" contains a slice of black Othello's (Ray Fearon) face; "l," a piece of Desdemona; the final "O," half an eye, nose, mouth of Iago. In black, blue, and grey, the only white light falling on Iago, this poster tells of distorted optics, partial viewing, of a woman caught between ways of looking, black and white. The 2004 poster offers a realist domestic scene, a slice of life, arrested just before it trips into marital violence: Desdemona in a satin slip, awakened, sitting up, wide-eyed, seen through the mosquito net draping the bed like a voluminous wedding veil – or web; in the near foreground, a black shape. Looking in. The outsider. This production, says the poster, is about a world we know; of intimacies – and of what makes men and women perpetual strangers.

Across forty years of RSC posters we see the popular image of male heroism asserted, interrogated, dismantled: in a stylized silk-screen print, Alan Howard's post-Vietnam Henry V (for the 1977 revival), in Erpingham's cloak the night before Agincourt, is caught open-mouthed, mid-speech, cutting a deal with God (behind him, like heraldic wallpaper, three warriors in medieval armour pattern the background). In a realistic black and grey photographic composition, Kenneth Branagh's post-Falklands Henry (1984) stands immobilized – no action-man, he – staring (at the future?), behind him a torch, an empty camp, a nothingness. In full color, Iain Glen's crop-haired post-Gulf War Henry (1994), in three-quarter portrait turned to the spectator, smolders in burnished armor that looks hot to the touch; behind him, the arms of England quartering France unfurl in a heraldic flag. In 1997, post-Bosnia, post-Iran/Iraq, Michael Sheen is a punk bovver-boy Henry in commando gear and mud-caked boots, bullet belt strapped across his chest, lips sneering, England's heraldic flag clenched in one fist, dragged on the ground. In 2000, anticipating Desert Storm, William Houston is combat-hardened: one of today's paras; the half of his face on show in close-up is streaked with blood, sweat, filth.

We see politics, "this England," "that England," contested. John Goodwin's award-winning design for the 1966 *Henry V* poster – splendid, self-confident, nationalistic, displaying the royal coat of arms – gives way, in 1977, to a much more troubled political consciousness: the poster for Terry Hands's *Henry VI* trilogy, in red, white, and black, its surface splattered with a rough-edged blot that looks like a blood stain. Only, dissected three ways, it becomes a CND badge, miniature medieval faces crowded into one section, another, teeming with microbes, germ warfare. That same year, Hands's *Coriolanus* poster splays a cadaver across the frame, the corpse (the body politic?) fully anatomized, chest opened, muscles dissected, skeleton revealed. More recently, Michael Boyd's English history cycle (*Henry VI* to *Richard III*, 2000) re-sites Shakespeare's politics in medieval nightmare, the poster superimposing portraits of Margaret, Henry, Cade, Richard, framed in roundels as if intended for stained-glass windows, upon Hieronymus Bosch's festering "Garden of Earthly Delights."

Across forty years we see images of "heritage Shakespeare" alternating with "new age Shakespeare": in 1969, Nicholas Hilliard's (Elizabethan) "Portrait of a Young Man" illustrates *Twelfth Night* (with Judi Dench); the following year, eight hippy Titanias, hair by Janis Joplin, silk-screened in psychedelic colours, compose a Tibetan Mandala, the poster for Peter Brook's *A Midsummer Night's Dream*. Hilliard's conservative youth returns in head shot on the 1970 *Two Gentlemen of Verona* poster – but he's acquired a conjoined twin: he's attached to someone who looks like John Lennon in smoke-tinted granny glasses. In 1969, a heavyweight Henry VIII by Holbein stands four-square at the centre of his poster, framed by quotations ("Peace, plenty, love, truth") under typeface borrowed from the First Folio. In 1983, Henry VIII is Holbein again, but drawn with exaggerated satirical verve as a royal fatso by the cartoonist, Ralph Steadman. In 1996, the head-and-shoulder "Portrait of Henry VIII 1520" by an "Unknown Artist," "Courtesy of the National Portrait Gallery," gives another Tudor image, this one of the young, lean king – but subjected (like the play?) to "new age" scrutiny: what we see on the poster is an X-ray of the painting.

Across forty years, typography – the only staple of the traditional playbill – competes with graphic art, troping, perhaps, other contestations, other (academic?) arguments happening elsewhere: Shakespeare read versus Shakespeare performed; the poet versus the playwright; the text versus the script. In 1965 Goodwin and Mayhew quite deliberately camouflaged their radical graphics project with "traditional" inscriptions, captioning contemporary visuals with lettering simulating the Folio – legerdemain still practiced: today's RSC posters put modern images under titles composed of traditional woodblock typeface. Some of Goodwin's posters appear to revert to Benson standard. The four posters in the 1972 Romans season, for example, have a single "look," completely typographic: all-white backgrounds; the play title in Folio lettering in colored ink; the cast and credits in a narrow band of small print; nothing else. Elsewhere, the competition between text and graphics is deliberately teasing: Trevor Nunn's 1967 *Shrew* poster looks like the work of a graffiti artist, daubing the title on a wall, trying out alternate versions that play upon the textual complexities of this play, crossing them out, trying again, arriving "definitively" at:

RSC IN
THE TAMING
OF ~~the~~ a
THE SHREW

Or it's profoundly evocative: the poster for the Nicholas Hytner *Tempest* (1989) is composed of six photographs of Shakespeare's Folio lying open at *The Tempest*, arranged in two columns. As, image by image, the pages turn, Shakespeare's text is gradually covered with sand drifting across it, the last pages, completely illegible, Shakespeare's words erased.

At their best, RSC posters achieve what Goodwin aimed at forty years ago. They arrest the passer-by in the street. They are theatrical. They manipulate the everyday, distort photographic realism, are never merely literal. They're graphic stand-ins for what performance does. They make us curious about the thing itself, the poster in its own right. But they're also provocative go-betweens, arranging our deeper conversation with a play, a production, a way of seeing Shakespeare. They tease us into thought, act like commentary. Take, as a final example, the poster for the 1998 *Winter's Tale*. Blue, black, grey – nightmare colors – this poster shows Antony Sher's Leontes in profile, the photograph enlarged and cropped to give just a section of face, from eyebrow to lower lip. He's staring. And as we, looking, begin to make sense of the graphic, anamorphic puzzle in front of us, we see what he's staring at. His horrible imaginings are written on his flesh. Leontes's face is composed of naked bodies embracing: a woman's bent arm constructs his nose, her nipple, a mole on his face, her reclining torso, the curve of his cheek; a youth's head dissolves into his eyeball, his neck sculpting a cheekbone. He's seeing a monster – that monsters him. This optical play captures what's at stake in *The Winter's Tale*, puts on the poster an image of the insane, ludicrous, fantastic – and, equally, self-destroying – mis-taking that consumes lifetimes in this play.[23]

The way this poster looks takes me back to the question I began with, a question about beginnings. Sometimes, I want to say now, a play begins not with a first line or first entrance or a music cue or even a title. Sometimes it begins with just looking. Sometimes, as *Shakespeare in Love*'s new-married Viola De Lesseps discovers, peeling away the pesky piece of stray print that, wind-borne, has plastered itself to her husband, pausing to read, then turning to run to the playhouse, the Shakespeare play begins on the street, when the bill – or poster – smacks you right in the face.

NOTES

1. A growing body of literature is considering popular Shakespeare and Shakespeare and tourism, or what Barbara Hodgdon, in a seminal book, calls *The Shakespeare Trade* (Philadelphia: University of Pennsylvania Press, 1998). See, too, Susan Bennett, "Shakespeare on Vacation," in *A Companion to Shakespeare and Performance*, eds. Barbara Hodgdon and W. B. Worthen (Oxford: Blackwell, 2005), pp. 494–508; Diana Henderson, "Shakespeare: The Theme Park," in *Shakespeare After Mass Media* ed. Richard Burt (Basingstoke: Palgrave, 2002), pp. 107–26; Graham Holderness, "Bardolatry: or, The Cultural Materialist's Guide to Stratford-upon-Avon," in *The Shakespeare Myth*, ed. Graham Holderness (Manchester: Manchester University Press, 1988), 2–15; Dennis Kennedy, "Shakespeare and Cultural Tourism," *Theatre Journal* 50: 2 (1998), 175–88; and Douglas Lanier, *Shakespeare and Modern Popular Culture* (Oxford:

Oxford University Press, 2002). While these writers think about everything from audiences to tea-towels, Wedgwood Shakespeares to Shakespeare bath toys, and while a number of them stroll the streets of Stratford-upon-Avon, looking like tourists, so far, the theatre poster has escaped critical attention.

2. Given the film's date and its dedication to the RAF, it is almost impossible not to think of this sequence in terms of aerial bombardment – and the playbill as perhaps escaped from a "drop" of propaganda leaflets.

3. In " 'On each Wall / And Corner Poast': Playbills, Title-pages, and Advertising in Early Modern London," *English Literary Renaissance*, 36, 1 (2006), 57–89, Tiffany Stern collects a fascinating assortment of early modern references to the necessary business of "billing" plays in advance of performance. While I'm skeptical of some of the interpretations she places on this material, I'm grateful to her for sharing her work with me.

4. Quoted in Sally Beauman, *The Royal Shakespeare Company: A History of Ten Decades* (Oxford: Oxford University Press, 1982), p. 18, on whose facts I am largely depending to help me interpret the playbills.

5. Shakespeare Memorial Theatre playbills are preserved in portfolios and catalogued by date in the Royal Shakespeare Company archive at the Shakespeare Birthplace Trust, Stratford-upon-Avon. The run of playbills is by no means complete, even for the postwar years: for example, no playbill survives for Peter Brook's first season or for the Scofield/Helpmann *Hamlet*.

6. Beauman, *The Royal Shakespeare Company*, p. 12.

7. This notice is archived among SMT playbills at the Shakespeare Birthplace Trust.

8. These posters are archived among SMT playbills at the Shakespeare Birthplace Trust.

9. Before decimalization in 1972 reorganized the old £sd English monetary system, a pound (£ = *liber*) was worth twenty shillings, and a shilling, twelve pence (d = *denarius*). A guinea was worth 21s; a crown, 5s.

10. Beauman, *The Royal Shakespeare Company*, p. 33.

11. *Ibid.*, p. 66, quoting Constance Benson's observations on Nigel Playfair's *As You Like It*.

12. Beauman, *The Royal Shakespeare Company*, p. 57.

13. *Ibid.*, p. 84.

14. Quoted in *ibid.*, p. 85.

15. Antony Quayle quoted in *ibid.*, p. 199.

16. Recruited by Hall to the RSC in 1960, Goodwin moved on with him – again, to head publicity – when Hall took over the directorship of the new National Theatre in 1968. Goodwin, then, can truly be seen as the genius behind UK theatre poster design: the man who put Shakespeare on the street. I'm grateful to him for his conversation, which I'm relying on throughout this essay – and for the brilliant poster art he and Mayhew created. I also thank Roger Howells of the Shakespeare Birthplace Trust for fixing my appointment with John.

17. I want to hedge that statement: Goodwin thinks there may have been a *Wars of the Roses* poster; if so, it hasn't survived. The earliest RSC poster in the archive is *Hamlet*, which is fitting, considering *Hamlet*'s history of innovation in Stratford.

18. Quoted from the souvenir programme, 1965.

19. Surveying forty years of RSC posters, I am aware that I am only scratching the surface of this rich material, a vast resource for future interpretation. I'm thinking

almost entirely about content, not technical production. And I am neglecting the whole issue of "authorship": posters are acts of collaboration that may involve half a dozen contributors – graphic designers, graphic artists, photographers, painters, digital technicians. As shorthand, I refer to RSC posters by date – which is how they are catalogued in the RSC archive at the Shakespeare Birthplace Trust. My thanks to Chris Hill and Andy Williams for talking to me about current RSC policy; and to Sylvia Morris, Madeleine Cox, and Sarah Cronin of the Shakespeare Birthplace Trust.

20. Originally, this *Hamlet*, like all productions at The Other Place, was billed with flyers. The poster was issued a decade later, a homage to Buzz Goodbody, the director, who committed suicide after the opening night.

21. On the Dench effect in this production, see Michael Dobson, "Writing About [Shakespearian] Performance," *Shakespeare Survey 58* (Cambridge: Cambridge University Press, 2005), 160–68.

22. Barbara Hodgdon, " 'Here Apparent': Photography, History, and the Theatrical Unconscious," in *Textual and Theatrical Shakespeare: Questions of Evidence*, ed. Edward Pechter (Iowa City: University of Iowa Press), pp. 181–209, p. 186. Hodgdon's work on theatre photography provides a theoretical model for future work on poster art.

23. On the opposite end of the spectrum I'd put the poster for Kenneth Branagh's 1992 *Hamlet*. In grainy grey, like a still captured from poor film footage, it shows a single figure, marooned in the near distance, barefoot, in a gym singlet and trousers, eyes closed, head thrown back, arms out from his sides. The hands are bandaged, the wrappings unraveling, trailing on the ground. Pretentious, solipsistic, empty of content, this poster is just "image": "Photograph of Kenneth Branagh by the Douglas Brothers." It said nothing about *Hamlet* – or about the production, which was dismally conventional in Edwardian dress.

FURTHER READING

Shakespeare and cultural history

Aers, Lesley and Nigel Wheale (eds.), *Shakespeare in the Changing Curriculum.* London: Routledge, 1991.

Alexander, Catharine M. S. and Stanley Wells (eds.), *Shakespeare and Race.* Cambridge: Cambridge University Press, 2000.

Bate, Jonathan, *Shakespearean Constitutions: Politics, Theatre, Criticism, 1730–1830.* Oxford: Clarendon Press, 1989.

The Genius of Shakespeare. London: Picador, 1997.

Bristol, Michael, *Shakespeare's America/America's Shakespeare.* New York: Routledge, 1990.

Big-Time Shakespeare. London and New York: Routledge, 1996.

Dávidházi, Péter, *The Romantic Cult of Shakespeare: Literary Reception in Anthropological Perspective.* Basingstoke: Macmillan, 1998.

Gillespie, Stuart and Neil Rhodes, *Shakespeare and Elizabethan Popular Culture,* London: Arden, 2006.

Halpern, Richard, *Shakespeare Among the Moderns.* Ithaca, NY: Cornell University Press, 1997.

Hawkes, Terence, *That Shakespeherian Rag: Essays on a Critical Process.* London: Methuen, 1986.

Meaning by Shakespeare. London: Routledge, 1992.

Shakespeare in the Present. London: Routledge, 2002.

Holderness, Graham, *Cultural Shakespeare: Essays in the Shakespeare Myth.* Hatfield: University of Hertfordshire Press, 2001.

Holderness, Graham (ed.), *The Shakespeare Myth.* Manchester: Manchester University Press, 1988.

Howard, Jean E. and Marion O'Connor (eds.), *Shakespeare Reproduced: The Text in History and Ideology.* London: Methuen, 1987.

Joughin, John J. (ed.), *Shakespeare and National Culture.* Manchester: Manchester University Press, 1997.

Lanier, Douglas, *Shakespeare and Modern Popular Culture.* Oxford: Oxford University Press, 2002.

O'Dair, Sharon, *Class, Critics and Shakespeare: Bottom Lines on the Culture Wars.* Ann Arbor: University of Michigan Press, 2000.

Schoenbaum, Samuel, *Shakespeare's Lives.* Oxford: Oxford University Press, 1991.

Taylor, Gary, *Reinventing Shakespeare: A Cultural History from the Restoration to the Present*. London: Hogarth Press, 1990.

Thompson Ann and Sasha Roberts (eds.), *Women Reading Shakespeare, 1660–1900: An Anthology of Criticism*, Manchester: Manchester University Press, 1997.

Wells, Stanley, *Shakespeare for all Time*. Basingstoke: Macmillan, 2002.

Appropriations and adaptations

Aebischer, Pascale, Edward J. Esche, and Nigel Wheale (eds.), *Remaking Shakespeare: Performance Across Media, Genres, and Cultures*. Basingstoke: Palgrave, 2003.

Burt, Richard (ed.), *Shakespeares After Shakespeare: An Encyclopedia of the Bard in Mass and Popular Culture*. Westport, CT: Greenwood Press, 2006.

Cartelli, Thomas, *Repositioning Shakespeare: National Formations, Postcolonial Appropriations*. London: Routledge, 1999.

Chedgzoy, Kate, *Shakespeare's Queer Children: Sexual Politics and Contemporary Culture*. Manchester: Manchester University Press, 1995.

Desmet, Christy and Robert Sawyer (eds.), *Shakespeare and Appropriation*. London: Routledge, 1999.

Dobson, Michael, *The Making of the National Poet: Shakespeare, Adaptation and Authorship, 1660–1759*. Oxford: Clarendon Press, 1992.

Dollimore, Jonathan and Alan Sinfield (eds.), *Political Shakespeare: Essays in Cultural Materialism*, 2nd edn. Manchester: Manchester University Press, 1994.

Fischlin, Daniel and Mark Fortier (eds.), *Appropriations of Shakespeare: A Critical Anthology of Plays from the Seventeenth Century to the Present*. London: Routledge, 2000.

Hedrick, Donald and Bryan Reynolds (eds.), *Shakespeare Without Class: Misappropriations of Cultural Capital*. New York: Palgrave, 2000.

Honslaars, Ton (ed.), *Reclamations of Shakespeare*. Amsterdam: Rodopi, 1994.

Isaaac, Megan Lynn, *Heirs to Shakespeare: Reinventing the Bard in Young Adult Literature*. Portsmouth, NH: Boynton/Cook, 2000.

Marsden, Jean E. (ed.), *The Appropriation of Shakespeare: Post-Renaissance Reconstructions of the Works and the Myth*. New York: St. Martin's Press, 1991.

Novy, Marianne, *Engaging with Shakespeare: Responses of George Eliot, and Other Women Novelists*. Athens: University of Georgia Press, 1994.

Novy, Marianne (ed.), *Transforming Shakespeare: Women's Re-Visions in Literature and Performance*. New York: St. Martin's Press, 1993.

O'Sullivan, Maurice J., *Shakespeare's Other Lives: Fictional Depictions of the Bard*. Jefferson, NC: McFarland, 1997.

Reynolds, Bryan, *Performing Transversally: Reimagining Shakespeare and the Critical Future*. New York: Palgrave Macmillan, 2003.

Sanders, Julie, *Novel Shakespeares: Twentieth-Century Women Novelists and Appropriation*. Manchester: Manchester University Press, 2001.

Theatre and performance

Bate, Jonathan and Russell Jackson (eds.), *Shakespeare: An Illustrated Stage History*. Oxford: Oxford University Press, 1996.

Berkowitz, Joel, *Shakespeare on the American Yiddish Stage*. Iowa City: University of Iowa Press, 2002.

Bristol, Michael, *Carnival and Theater: Plebeian Culture and the Structure of Authority in Renaissance England*. London: Methuen, 1985.

Brown, John Russell, *New Sites for Shakespeare: Theatre, the Audience and Asia*. London and New York: Routledge, 1999.

Cohen, Walter, *Drama of a Nation: Public Theater in Renaissance England and Spain*. Ithaca, NY: Cornell University Press, 1985.

Conkie, Rob, *The Globe Theatre Project: Shakespeare and Authenticity*. New York: Edwin Mellen Press, 2006.

Escolme, Bridget, *Talking to the Audience: Shakespeare, Performance, Self*. London: Routledge, 2005.

Gurr, Andrew, *Playgoing in Shakespeare's England*. Cambridge: Cambridge University Press, 2004.

Hattaway, Michael, *Elizabethan Popular Theatre: Plays in Performance*. London: Routledge & Kegan Paul, 1982.

Hodgdon, Barbara, *The Shakespeare Trade: Performances and Appropriations*. Philadelphia: University of Pennsylvania Press, 1998.

Hodgdon, Barbara and W. B. Worthen (eds.), *A Companion to Shakespeare and Performance*. Oxford: Blackwell, 2005.

Holland, Peter, *English Shakespeares: Shakespeare on the English Stage in the 1990s*. Cambridge: Cambridge University Press, 1997.

Holland, Peter and Stephen Orgel (eds.), *From Script to Stage in Early Modern England*. Basingstoke: Palgrave, 2004.

Kennedy, Dennis, *Looking at Shakespeare: A Visual History of Twentieth-Century Performance*, 2nd edn. Cambridge: Cambridge University Press, 2001.

Luckhurst, Mary and Jane Moody (eds.), *Theatre and Celebrity in Britain 1660–2000*. Basingstoke: Palgrave, 2005.

Massai, Sonia (ed.), *World-Wide Shakspeares: Local Appropriations in Film and Performance*. London: Routledge, 2005.

Milling, Jane and Martin Banham (eds.), *Extraordinary Actors: Essays on Popular Performers*. Exeter: Exeter University Press, 2004.

Moody, Jane, *The Illegitimate Theatre in London, 1770–1840*. Cambridge: Cambridge University Press, 2000.

Patterson, Annabel, *Shakespeare and the Popular Voice*. Oxford: Blackwell, 1989.

Roach, Joseph, *Cities of the Dead: Circum-Atlantic Performance*. New York: Columbia University Press, 1996.

Rutter, Carol Chillington, *Enter the Body: Women and Representation on Shakespeare's Stage*. London: Routledge, 2001.

Schechter, Joel (ed.), *Popular Theatre: A Sourcebook*. London: Routledge, 2003.

Schoch, Richard, *Shakespeare's Victorian Stage: Performing History in the Theatre of Charles Kean*. Cambridge: Cambridge University Press, 1998.

  Not Shakespeare: Bardolatry and Burlesque in the Nineteenth Century. Cambridge: Cambridge University Press, 2002.

Shaughnessy, Robert, *The Shakespeare Effect: A History of Twentieth-Century Performance*. Basingstoke: Palgrave, 2002.

Shaughnessy, Robert (ed.), *Shakespeare in Performance: Contemporary Critical Essays*. Basingstoke: Macmillan, 2000.

Stern, Tiffany, *Making Shakespeare: From Page to Stage*. London: Routledge, 2004.

Teague, Frances, *Shakespeare and the American Popular Stage*. Cambridge: Cambridge University Press, 2006.

Thomson, Peter, *On Actors and Acting*. Exeter: University of Exeter Press, 2000.

Weimann, Robert, *Shakespeare and the Popular Tradition in the Theater: Studies in the Social Dimension of Dramatic Form and Function*, ed. Robert Schwartz. Baltimore: Johns Hopkins University Press, 1978.

  Author's Pen and Actor's Voice: Playing and Writing in Shakespeare's Theatre, Cambridge: Cambridge University Press, 2000.

Wells, Stanley (ed.), *Shakespeare in the Theatre: An Anthology of Criticism*. Oxford: Oxford University Press, 1997.

Wells, Stanley and Sarah Stanton (eds.), *The Cambridge Companion to Shakespeare on Stage*. Cambridge: Cambridge University Press, 2002.

Wiles, David, *Shakespeare's Clown: Actor and Text in the Elizabethan Playhouse*. Cambridge: Cambridge University Press, 1987.

Worthen, W. B., *Shakespeare and the Authority of Performance*. Cambridge: Cambridge University Press, 1997.

  Shakespeare and the Force of Modern Performance. Cambridge: Cambridge University Press, 2003.

Film, television, and radio

Anderegg, Michael, *Orson Welles, Shakespeare and Popular Culture*. New York: Columbia University Press, 1999.

Buchanan, Judith, *Shakespeare on Film*. Harlow: Pearson Longman, 2005.

Buhler, Stephen M., *Shakespeare in the Cinema: Ocular Proof*. Albany: State University of New York Press, 2002.

Bulman, James C. and H. R. Coursen (eds.), *Shakespeare on Television: An Anthology of Essays and Reviews*. Hanover, NH and London: University Press of New England, 1988.

Burnett, Mark Thornton and Ramona Wray (eds.), *Shakespeare, Film, Fin de Siècle*. Basingstoke: Macmillan, 2000.

  Screening Shakespeare in the Twenty-First Century. Edinburgh: Edinburgh University Press, 2006.

Burt, Richard, *Unspeakable Shaxxxspeares: Queer Theory and American Kiddie Culture*. Basingstoke: Macmillan, 1998.

Burt, Richard (ed.), *Shakespeare after Mass Media*. Basingstoke: Palgrave, 2002.

Burt, Richard and Lynda Boose (eds.), *Shakespeare, The Movie, II*. London: Routledge, 2003.

Collick, John, *Shakespeare, Cinema and Society*, Manchester: Manchester University Press, 1989.

Crowl, Samuel, *Shakespeare at the Cineplex: The Kenneth Branagh Era*. Athens: Ohio University Press, 2003.

Hatchuel, Sarah, *Shakespeare, from Stage to Screen*. Cambridge: Cambridge University Press, 2005.

Henderson, Diana E. (ed.), *A Concise Companion to Shakespeare on Screen*. Oxford: Blackwell, 2006.

Hindle, Maurice, *Studying Shakespeare on Film*. Basingstoke: Palgrave, 2006.

Jackson, Russell (ed.), *The Cambridge Companion to Shakespeare on Film*. Cambridge: Cambridge University Press, 2000.

Lehmann, Courtney, *Shakespeare Remains: Theater to Film, Early Modern to Postmodern*. Ithaca, NY, and London: Cornell University Press, 2002.

Rothwell, Kenneth, *A History of Shakespeare on Screen: A Century of Film and Television*, 2nd edn. Cambridge: Cambridge University Press, 2004.

Shaughnessy, Robert (ed.), *Shakespeare on Film: Contemporary Critical Essays*. Basingstoke: Macmillan, 1998.

Simkin, Stevie, *Early Modern Tragedy and the Cinema of Violence*. Basingstoke: Palgrave, 2006.

Starks, Lisa L. and Courtney Lehmann (eds.), *Spectacular Shakespeare: Critical Theory and Popular Cinema*. Madison, WI: Fairleigh Dickinson University Press, 2002.

Uricchio, William and Roberta E. Pearson, *Reframing Culture: The Case of the Vitagraph Quality Films*. Princeton, NJ: Princeton University Press, 1993.

Music and the visual arts

Conrad, Peter, *To Be Continued: Four Stories and their Survival*. Oxford: Clarendon Press, 1995.

Duffin, Ross, *Shakespeare's Songbook*. New York: W. W. Norton, 2004.

Gooch, Bryan N. S. and David Thatcher (eds.), *A Shakespeare Music Catalogue*, 5 vols. Oxford: Clarendon Press, 1991.

Hartnoll, Phyllis (ed.), *Shakespeare in Music*. London: Macmillan, 1964.

Klein, Holger and James L. Harner (eds.), *Shakespeare and the Visual Arts, Shakespeare Yearbook*, vol. 11. New York: Edwin Mellen Press, 2000.

Lindley, David, *Shakespeare and Music*. London: Arden, 2005.

Lord, Suzanne, *Music from the Age of Shakespeare: A Cultural History*. New York: Greenwood Press, 2003.

Martineau, Jane (ed.), *Shakespeare in Art*. London: Merrell, 2003.

Merchant, W. Moelwyn, *Shakespeare and the Artist*. London: Oxford University Press, 1959.

Orgel, Stephen, *Imagining Shakespeare: A History of Texts and Visions*. Basingstoke: Palgrave Macmillan, 2003.

Orgel, Stephen and Sean Keilan (eds.), *Shakespeare and the Arts*. New York: Garland, 1999.

Schmidgall, Gary, *Shakespeare and Opera*. Oxford: Oxford University Press, 1990.

Sillars, Stuart, *Painting Shakespeare: The Artist as Critic, 1720–1820*. Cambridge: Cambridge University Press, 2005.

Smith, Bruce R., *The Acoustic World of Early Modern England: Attending to the O-Factor*. Chicago and London: University of Chicago Press, 1999.

Sternfield, F. W., *Music in Shakespearean Tragedy*. London: Routledge and Kegan Paul, 1963.

INDEX

Cambridge Companions to ...

AUTHORS

Edward Albee edited by Stephen J. Bottoms

Margaret Atwood edited by Coral Ann Howells

W. H. Auden edited by Stan Smith

Jane Austen edited by Edward Copeland and Juliet McMaster

Beckett edited by John Pilling

Aphra Behn edited by Derek Hughes and Janet Todd

Walter Benjamin edited by David S. Ferris

William Blake edited by Morris Eaves

Brecht edited by Peter Thomson and Glendyr Sacks (second editon)

The Brontës edited by Heather Glen

Frances Burney edited by Peter Sabor

Byron edited by Drummond Bone

Albert Camus edited by Edward J. Hughes

Willa Cather edited by Marilee Lindemann

Cervantes edited by Anthony J. Cascardi

Chaucer edited by Piero Boitani and Jill Mann (second edition)

Checkhov edited by Vera Gottlieb and Paul Allain

Coleridge edited by Lucy Newlyn

Wilkie Collins edited by Jenny Bourne Taylor

Joseph Conrad edited by J. H. Stape

Dante edited by Rachel Jacoff (second edition)

Charles Dickens edited by John O. Jordan

Emily Dickinson edited by Wendy Martin

John Donne edited by Achsah Guibbory

Dostoevskii edited by W. J. Leatherbarrow

Theodore Dreiser edited by Leonard Cassuto and Claire Virginia Eby

John Dryden edited by Steven N. Zwicker

George Eliot edited by George Levine

T. S. Eliot edited by A. David Moody

Ralph Ellison edited by Ross Posnock

Ralph Waldo Emerson edited by Joel Porte and Saundra Morris

William Faulkner edited by Philip M. Weinstein

Henry Fielding edited by Claude Rawson

F. Scott Fitzgerald edited by Ruth Prigozy

Flaubert edited by Timothy Unwin

E. M. Forster edited by David Bradshaw

Brian Friel edited by Anthony Roche

Robert Frost edited by Robert Faggen

Elizabeth Gaskell edited by Jill L. Matus

Goethe edited by Lesley Sharpe

Thomas Hardy edited by Dale Kramer

Nathaniel Hawthorne edited by Richard Millington

Ernest Hemingway edited by Scott Donaldson

Homer edited by Robert Fowler

Ibsen edited by James McFarlane

Henry James edited by Jonathan Freedman

Samuel Johnson edited by Greg Clingham

Ben Jonson edited by Richard Harp and Stanley Stewart

James Joyce edited by Derek Attridge (second edition)

Kafka edited by Julian Preece

Keats edited by Susan J. Wolfson

Lacan edited by Jean-Michel Rabaté

D. H. Lawrence edited by Anne Fernihough

Primo Levi edited by Robert Gordon

David Mamet edited by Christopher Bigsby

Thomas Mann edited by Ritchie Roberston

Christopher Marlowe edited by Patrick Cheney

Herman Melville edited by Robert S. Levine

Arthur Miller edited by Christopher Bigsby

Milton edited by Dennis Danielson (second edition)

Molière edited by David Bradby and Andrew Calder

Nabokov edited by Julian W. Connolly

Eugene O'Neill edited by Michael Manheim

George Orwell edited by John Rodden

Ovid edited by Philip Hardie

Harold Pinter edited by Peter Raby

Sylvia Plath edited by Jo Gill

Edgar Allan Poe edited by Kevin J. Hayes

Ezra Pound edited by Ira B. Nadel

Proust edited by Richard Bales

Pushkin edited by Andrew Kahn

Philip Roth edited by Timothy Parrish

Shakespeare edited by Margareta de Grazia and Stanley Wells

TOPICS